Marmalade Boy

Vol. 8

By

Wataru Yoshizumi

TOKYOPOP®

Los Angeles • Tokyo • London

Story and Art – Wataru Yoshizumi

Translator - Takae Brewer
English Adaptation - Deb Baer
Contributing Editors - Jodi Bryson and Amy Court Kaemon
Retouch and Lettering - Ron Webb and Monalisa de Asis
Cover Layout and Graphic Design - Anna Kernbaum

Editor - Julie Taylor
Managing Editor - Jill Freshney
Production Coordinator - Antonio DePietro
Production Manager - Jennifer Miller
Art Director - Matthew Alford
Director of Editorial - Jeremy Ross
VP of Production & Manufacturing - Ron Klamert
President & C.O.O. - John Parker
Publisher - Stuart Levy

Email: editor@TOKYOPOP.com
Come visit us online at www.TOKYOPOP.com

A  Manga

TOKYOPOP® is an imprint of Mixx Entertainment, Inc.
5900 Wilshire Blvd. Suite 2000, Los Angeles, CA 90036

ISBN: 1-59182-192-4

First TOKYOPOP® printing: August 2003

10 9 8 7 6 5 4 3 2 1
Printed in the USA

Main Characters

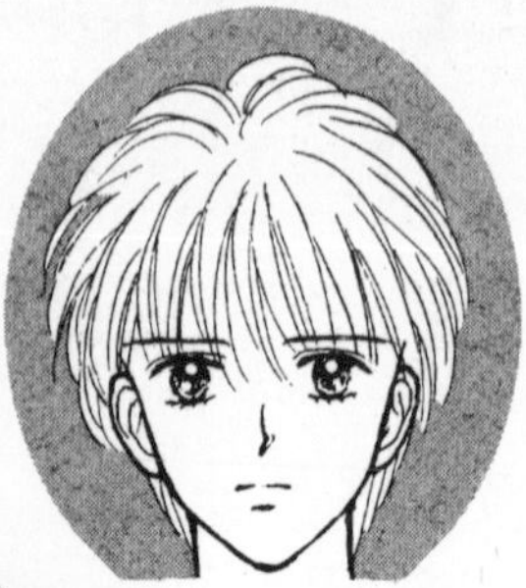

HE LEAVES FOR COLLEGE IN KYOTO. IS HE MIKI'S HALF-BROTHER?

YUU MATSUURA

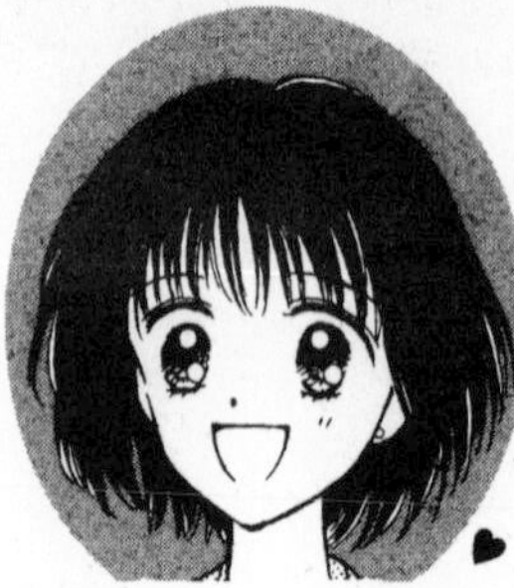

A COLLEGE FRESHMAN WHO LOVES YUU TRULY, MADLY, AND DEEPLY.

MIKI KOISHIKAWA

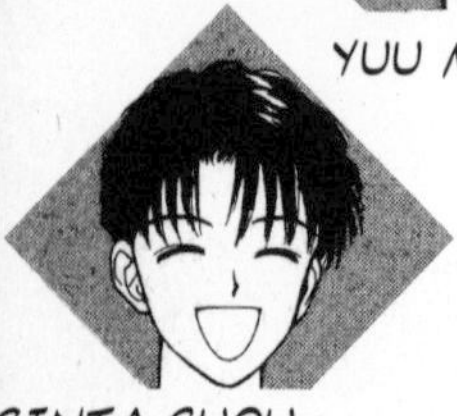

GINTA SUOU
MIKI'S CLASSMATE, WHO'S ALWAYS THERE FOR HER.

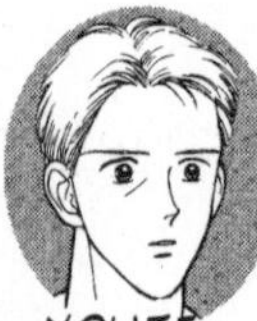

YOUJI

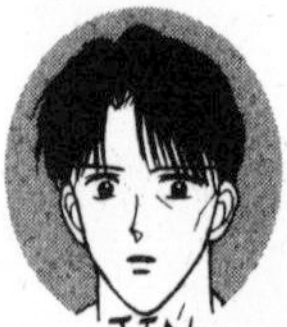

JIN

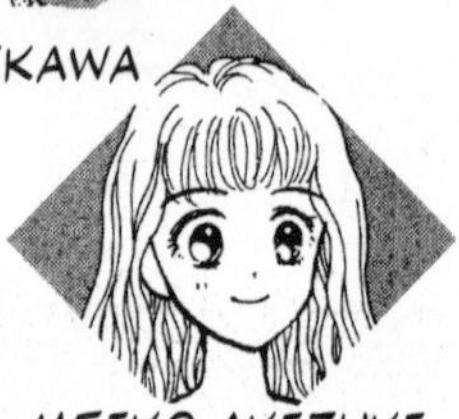

MEIKO AKIZUKI
MIKI'S BEST FRIEND, WHO MARRIED HER TEACHER.

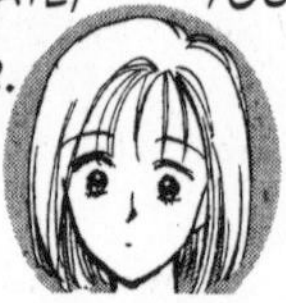

CHIYAKO

MIKI AND YUU'S PARENTS

THEY SWAPPED PARTNERS AND REMARRIED.

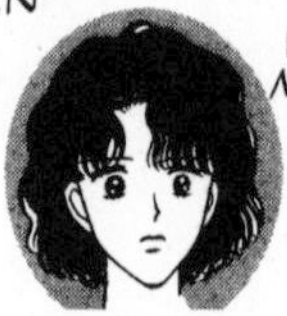

RUMI

THE STORY SO FAR...

MIKI AND YUU'S PARENTS SWAPPED PARTNERS AND REMARRIED EACH OTHER. THEIR FAMILY MOVES INTO THE SAME HOUSE AND START LIVING TOGETHER. YUU, MIKI'S STEP-BROTHER, ALWAYS TEASES MIKI BUT OFTEN SHOWS TENDERNESS TOWARDS HER. MIKI STARTS HAVING THE HOTS FOR YUU. YUU DOESN'T KNOW WHO HIS REAL FATHER IS—EVERYTHING ABOUT HIS FATHER IS A MYSTERY. YUU IS VERY UPSET ABOUT THIS. MIKI FINALLY TELLS YUU THAT SHE LOVES HIM AND YUU FEELS THE SAME WAY. ONE DAY, YUU HAPPENS TO FIND HIS PARENTS' OLD PICTURES INSIDE THEIR COLLEGE YEARBOOK. HE FINDS OUT HIS PARENTS USED TO GO STEADY WITH HER PARENTS—JUST THE SAME AS NOW. HE STARTS TO SUSPECT THAT MIKI IS HIS HALF-SISTER. THINKING MIKI IS RELATED BY BLOOD, HE TELLS MIKI THAT HE DOESN'T LOVE HER ANYMORE AND MOVES TO KYOTO TO GO TO COLLEGE. MIKI, WHO DOES NOT KNOW THE REAL REASON FOR THE BREAKUP, GETS A HAIRCUT* AND TRIES TO BEGIN A NEW LIFE WITHOUT YUU.

* EDITOR'S NOTE: WHEN JAPANESE GIRLS ARE BROKEN-HEARTED, THEY OFTEN GET A HAIRCUT TO FORGET ABOUT THEIR LOVED ONES. IT'S THEIR WAY OF CONVINCING THEMSELVES THAT THEY ARE READY FOR A NEW LIFE AND MAYBE EVEN A NEW RELATIONSHIP.

Marmalade Boy

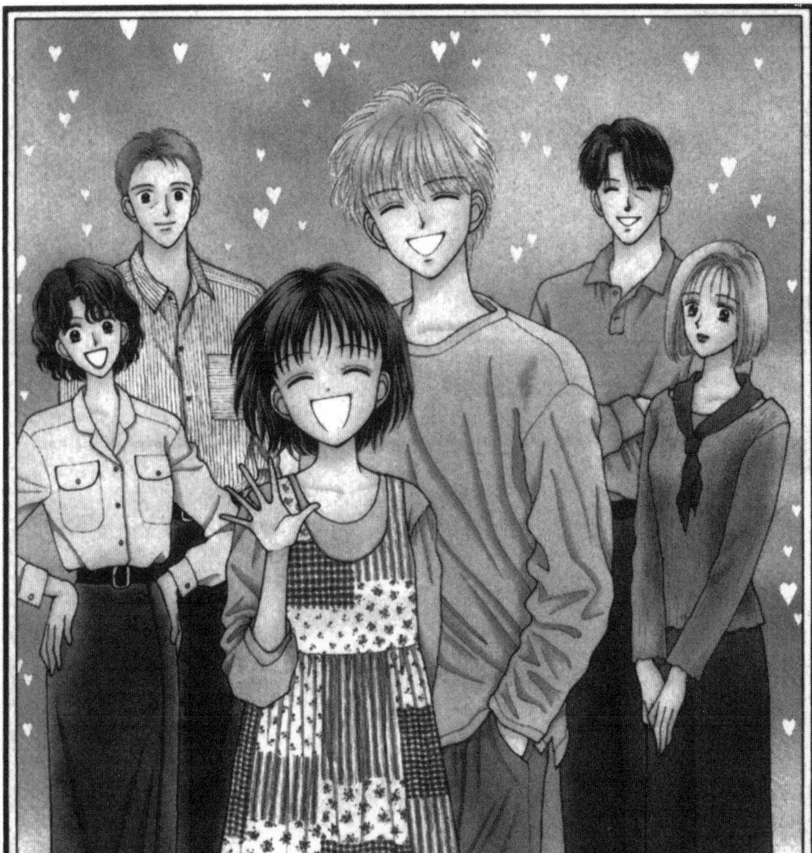

ALSO AVAILABLE FROM 🔫TOKYOPOP®

MANGA

.HACK//LEGEND OF THE TWILIGHT (September 2003)
@LARGE (COMING SOON)
ANGELIC LAYER*
BABY BIRTH* (September 2003)
BATTLE ROYALE*
BRAIN POWERED*
BRIGADOON* (August 2003)
CARDCAPTOR SAKURA
CARDCAPTOR SAKURA: MASTER OF THE CLOW*
CHOBITS*
CHRONICLES OF THE CURSED SWORD
CLAMP SCHOOL DETECTIVES*
CLOVER
CONFIDENTIAL CONFESSIONS*
CORRECTOR YUI
COWBOY BEBOP*
COWBOY BEBOP: SHOOTING STAR*
DEMON DIARY
DIGIMON*
DRAGON HUNTER
DRAGON KNIGHTS*
DUKLYON: CLAMP SCHOOL DEFENDERS*
ERICA SAKURAZAWA*
FAKE*
FLCL* (September 2003)
FORBIDDEN DANCE* (August 2003)
GATE KEEPERS*
G GUNDAM*
GRAVITATION*
GTO*
GUNDAM WING
GUNDAM WING: BATTLEFIELD OF PACIFISTS
GUNDAM WING: ENDLESS WALTZ*
GUNDAM WING: THE LAST OUTPOST*
HAPPY MANIA*
HARLEM BEAT
I.N.V.U.
INITIAL D*
ISLAND
JING: KING OF BANDITS*
JULINE
KARE KANO*
KINDAICHI CASE FILES, THE*
KING OF HELL
KODOCHA: SANA'S STAGE*
LOVE HINA*
LUPIN III*
MAGIC KNIGHT RAYEARTH* (August 2003)
MAGIC KNIGHT RAYEARTH II* (COMING SOON)

MAN OF MANY FACES*
MARMALADE BOY*
MARS*
MIRACLE GIRLS
MIYUKI-CHAN IN WONDERLAND* (October 2003)
MONSTERS, INC.
PARADISE KISS*
PARASYTE
PEACH GIRL
PEACH GIRL: CHANGE OF HEART*
PET SHOP OF HORRORS*
PLANET LADDER*
PLANETES* (October 2003)
PRIEST
RAGNAROK
RAVE MASTER*
REALITY CHECK
REBIRTH
REBOUND*
RISING STARS OF MANGA
SABER MARIONETTE J*
SAILOR MOON
SAINT TAIL
SAMURAI DEEPER KYO*
SAMURAI GIRL: REAL BOUT HIGH SCHOOL*
SCRYED*
SHAOLIN SISTERS*
SHIRAHIME-SYO: SNOW GODDESS TALES* (Dec. 2003)
SHUTTERBOX (November 2003)
SORCERER HUNTERS
THE SKULL MAN*
THE VISION OF ESCAFLOWNE
TOKYO MEW MEW*
UNDER THE GLASS MOON
VAMPIRE GAME*
WILD ACT*
WISH*
WORLD OF HARTZ (COMING SOON)
X-DAY* (August 2003)
ZODIAC P.I. *

For more information visit www.TOKYOPOP.com

*INDICATES 100% AUTHENTIC MANGA (RIGHT-TO-LEFT FORMAT)

CINE-MANGA™

CARDCAPTORS
JACKIE CHAN ADVENTURES (COMING SOON)
JIMMY NEUTRON (September 2003)
KIM POSSIBLE
LIZZIE MCGUIRE
POWER RANGERS: NINJA STORM (August 2003)
SPONGEBOB SQUAREPANTS (September 2003)
SPY KIDS 2

NOVELS

KARMA CLUB (April 2004)
SAILOR MOON

TOKYOPOP KIDS

STRAY SHEEP (September 2003)

ART BOOKS

CARDCAPTOR SAKURA*
MAGIC KNIGHT RAYEARTH*

ANIME GUIDES

COWBOY BEBOP ANIME GUIDES
GUNDAM TECHNICAL MANUALS
SAILOR MOON SCOUT GUIDES

6-5-03

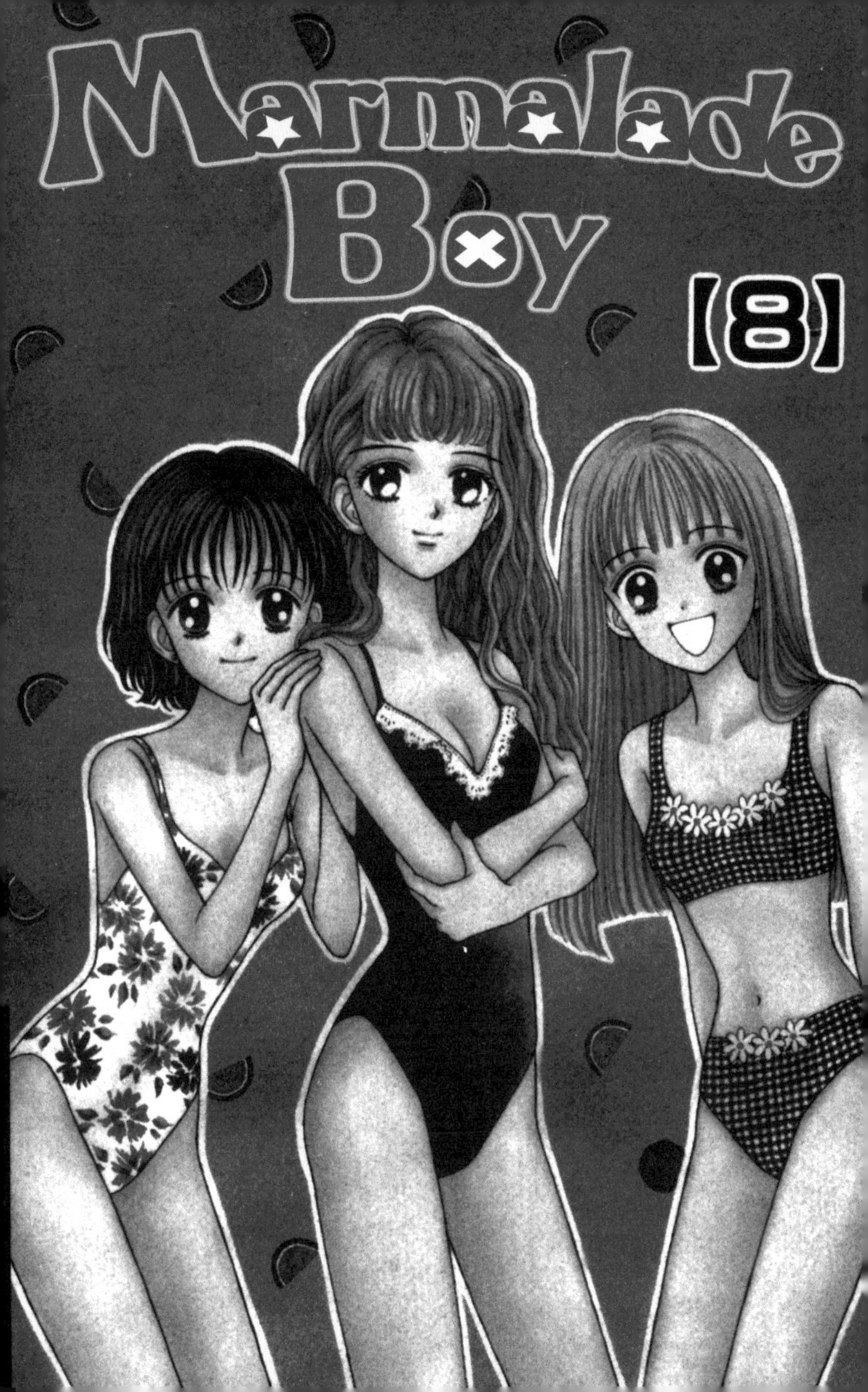
Marmalade Boy
8

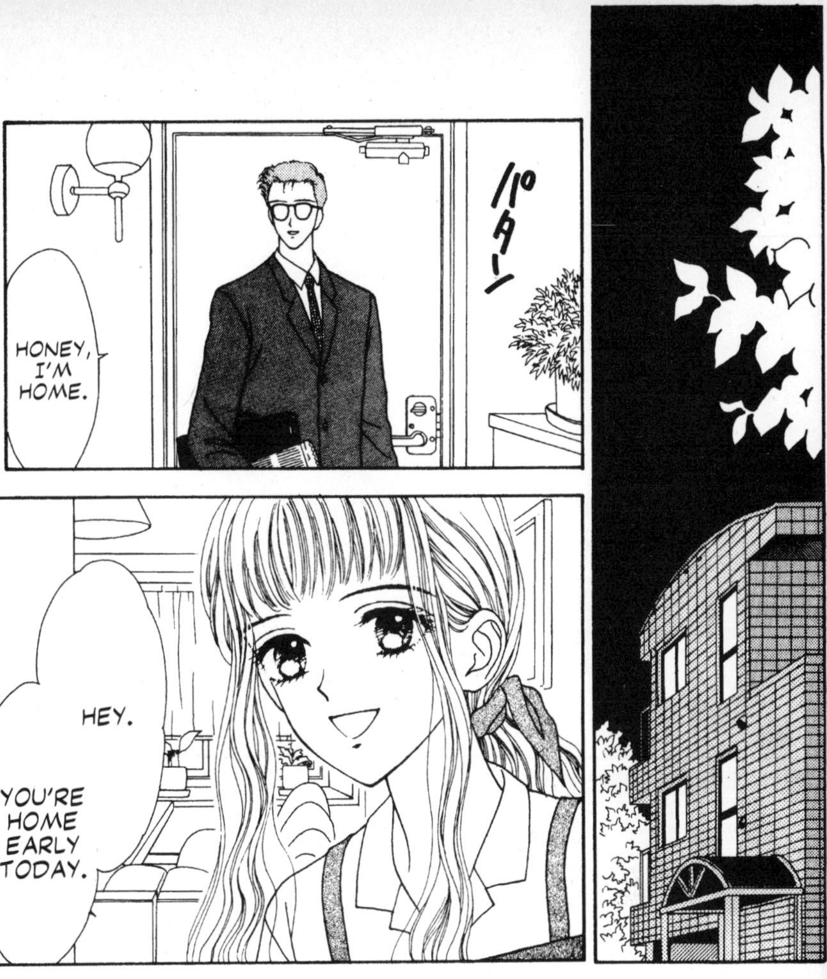
パタン
HONEY, I'M HOME.
HEY.
YOU'RE HOME EARLY TODAY.

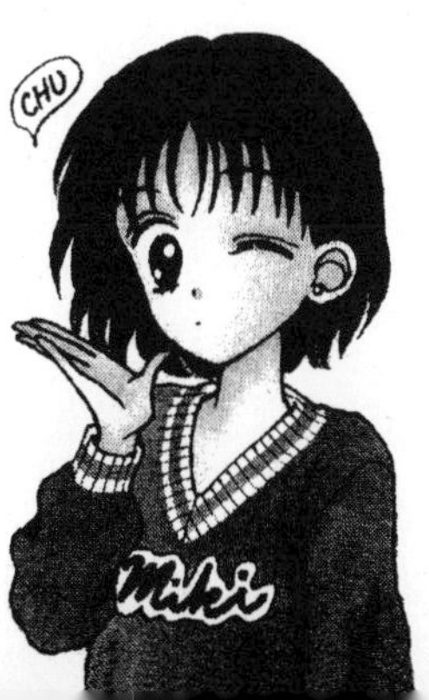
CHU
Miki

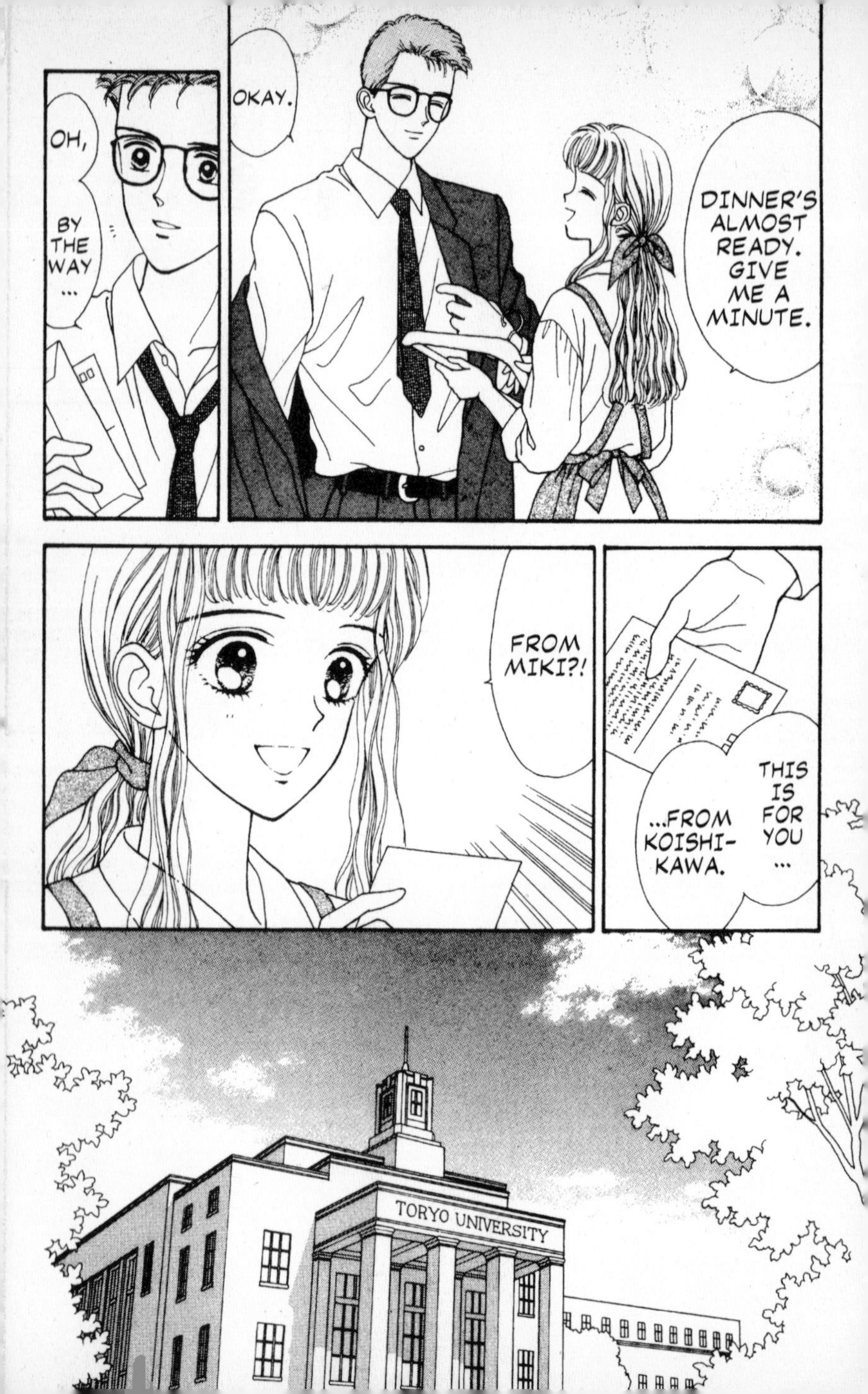
DINNER'S ALMOST READY. GIVE ME A MINUTE.
OKAY.
OH,
BY THE WAY ...
THIS IS FOR YOU ...
...FROM KOISHI-KAWA.
FROM MIKI?!
TORYO UNIVERSITY

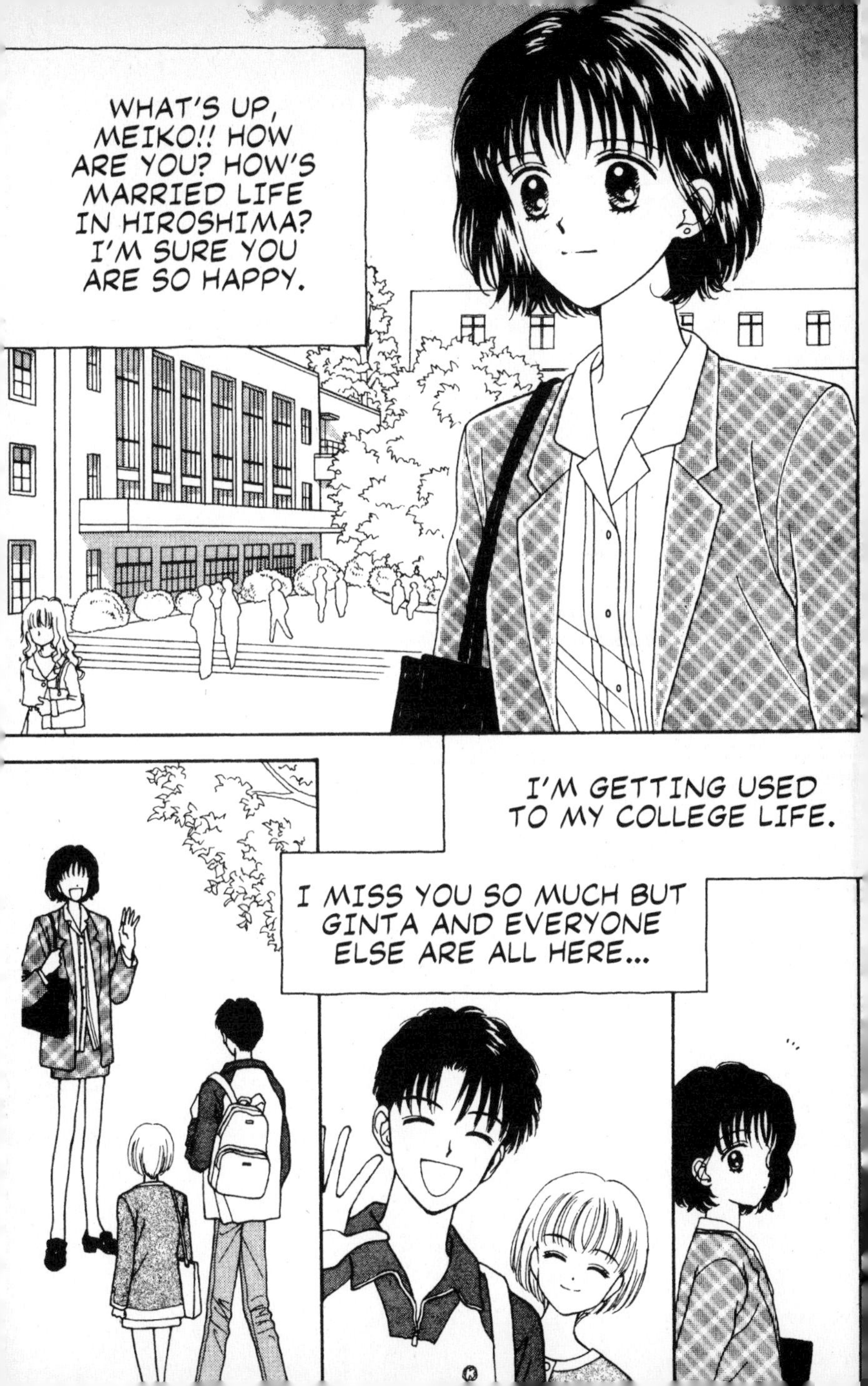
WHAT'S UP, MEIKO!! HOW ARE YOU? HOW'S MARRIED LIFE IN HIROSHIMA? I'M SURE YOU ARE SO HAPPY.
I'M GETTING USED TO MY COLLEGE LIFE.
I MISS YOU SO MUCH BUT GINTA AND EVERYONE ELSE ARE ALL HERE...

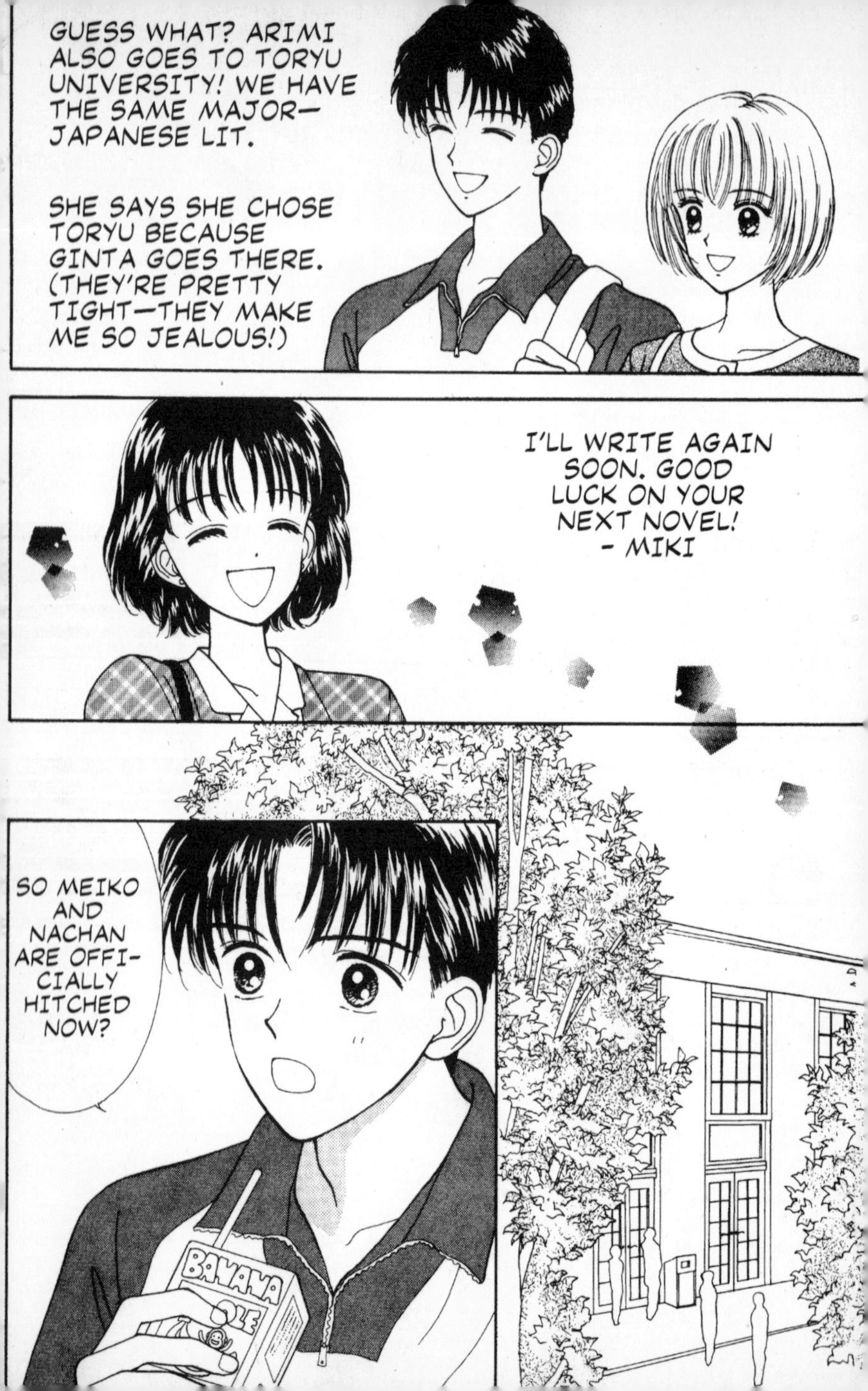
GUESS WHAT? ARIMI ALSO GOES TO TORYU UNIVERSITY! WE HAVE THE SAME MAJOR—JAPANESE LIT.
SHE SAYS SHE CHOSE TORYU BECAUSE GINTA GOES THERE. (THEY'RE PRETTY TIGHT—THEY MAKE ME SO JEALOUS!)
I'LL WRITE AGAIN SOON. GOOD LUCK ON YOUR NEXT NOVEL! - MIKI
SO MEIKO AND NACHAN ARE OFFICIALLY HITCHED NOW?
BANANA OLE

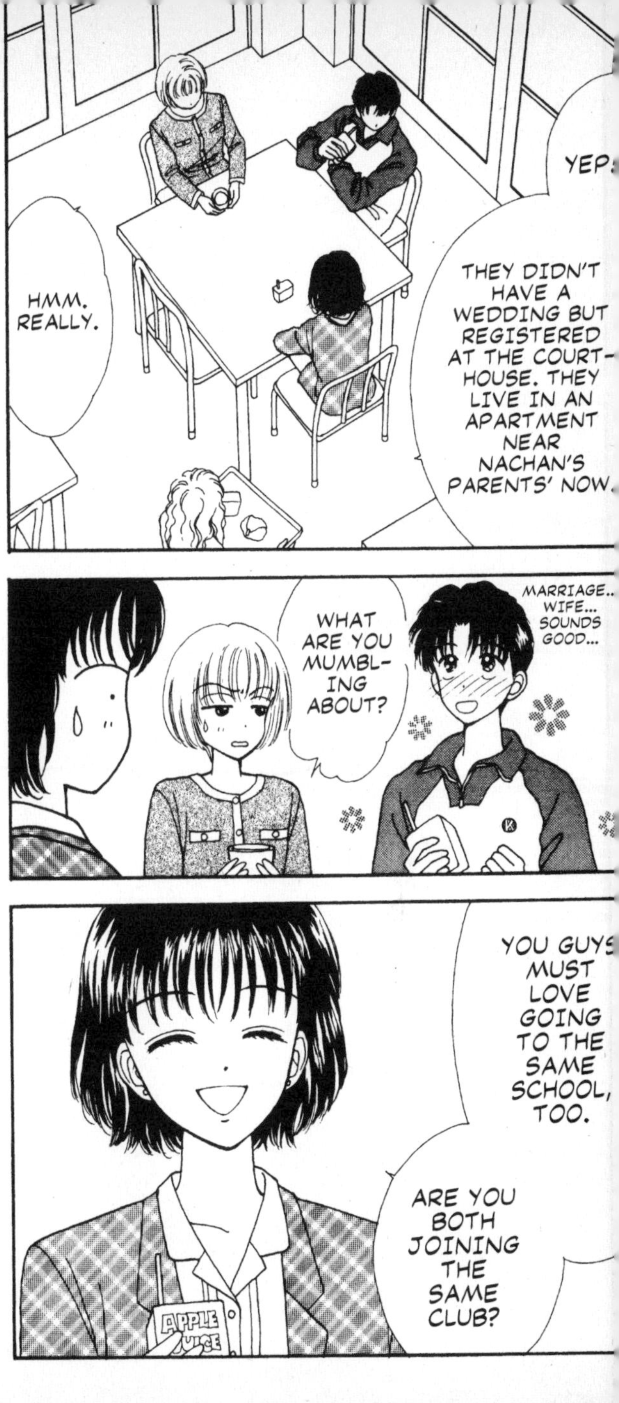
YEP
THEY DIDN'T HAVE A WEDDING BUT REGISTERED AT THE COURT-HOUSE. THEY LIVE IN AN APARTMENT NEAR NACHAN'S PARENTS' NOW.
HMM. REALLY.
MARRIAGE... WIFE... SOUNDS GOOD...
WHAT ARE YOU MUMBL-ING ABOUT?
YOU GUYS MUST LOVE GOING TO THE SAME SCHOOL, TOO.
ARE YOU BOTH JOINING THE SAME CLUB?
APPLE

FREE TALK ①

This is the very last volume of Marmalade Boy. I have already started to write the next story and Marmalade Boy is somewhat a thing of the past to me. I only have imperfect memories about what went through my mind while writing Marmalade Boy. Here I will try to remember how I felt about the work and the anime and share it with you. It was so much fun to see Marmalade Boy transformed into an anime. Character merchandise also came out. (They sold quite well, I heard. Thanks to everyone who bought those items!) I met a lot of new people. I got to see how voice actors work in the dubbing studio, and so forth. My family was also excited to see the anime version. Most of all, I was so pleased with the fact that they decided to transform my story into an anime.

(To be continued in Free Talk 2)

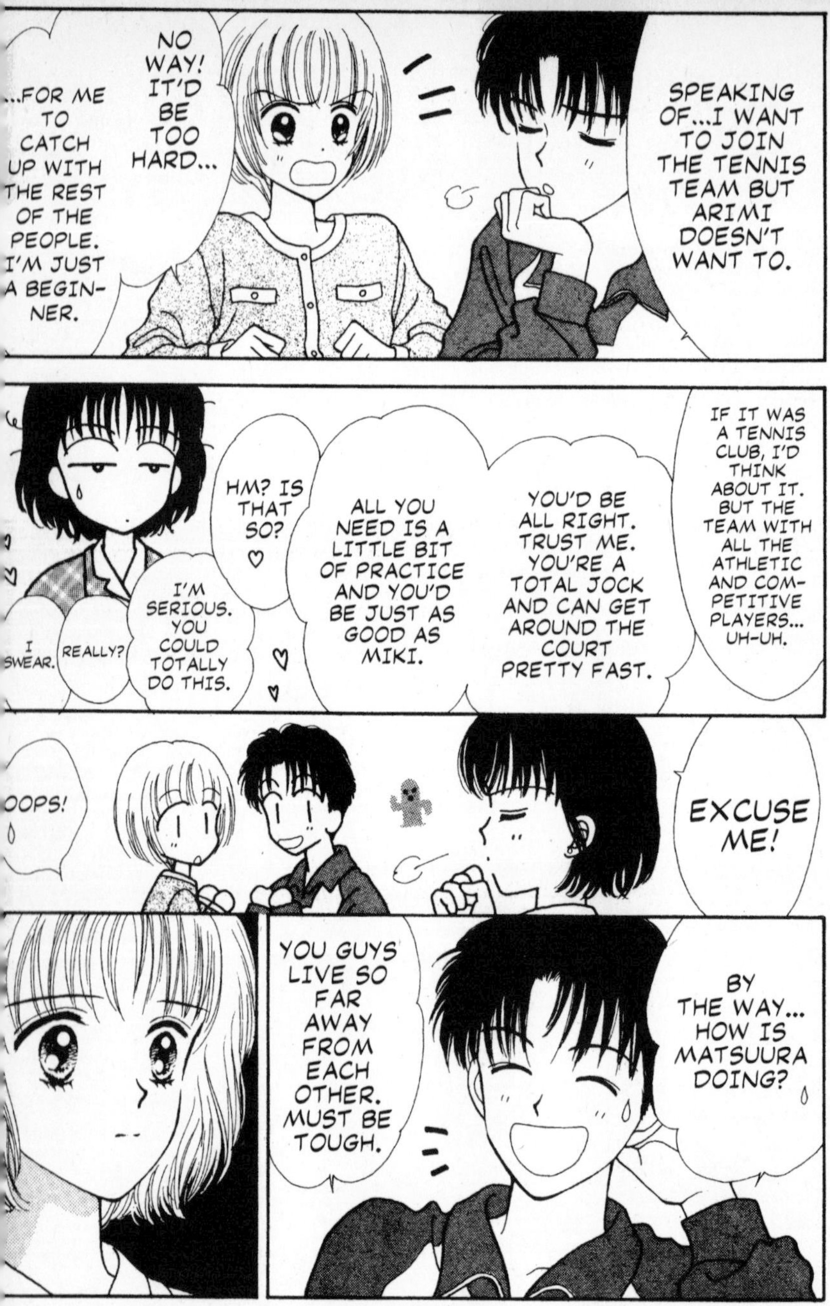
SPEAKING OF...I WANT TO JOIN THE TENNIS TEAM BUT ARIMI DOESN'T WANT TO.
NO WAY! IT'D BE TOO HARD...
...FOR ME TO CATCH UP WITH THE REST OF THE PEOPLE. I'M JUST A BEGINNER.
IF IT WAS A TENNIS CLUB, I'D THINK ABOUT IT. BUT THE TEAM WITH ALL THE ATHLETIC AND COMPETITIVE PLAYERS... UH-UH.
YOU'D BE ALL RIGHT. TRUST ME. YOU'RE A TOTAL JOCK AND CAN GET AROUND THE COURT PRETTY FAST.
ALL YOU NEED IS A LITTLE BIT OF PRACTICE AND YOU'D BE JUST AS GOOD AS MIKI.
HM? IS THAT SO? ♡
I'M SERIOUS. YOU COULD TOTALLY DO THIS.
REALLY?
I SWEAR.
EXCUSE ME!
OOPS!
BY THE WAY... HOW IS MATSUURA DOING?
YOU GUYS LIVE SO FAR AWAY FROM EACH OTHER. MUST BE TOUGH.

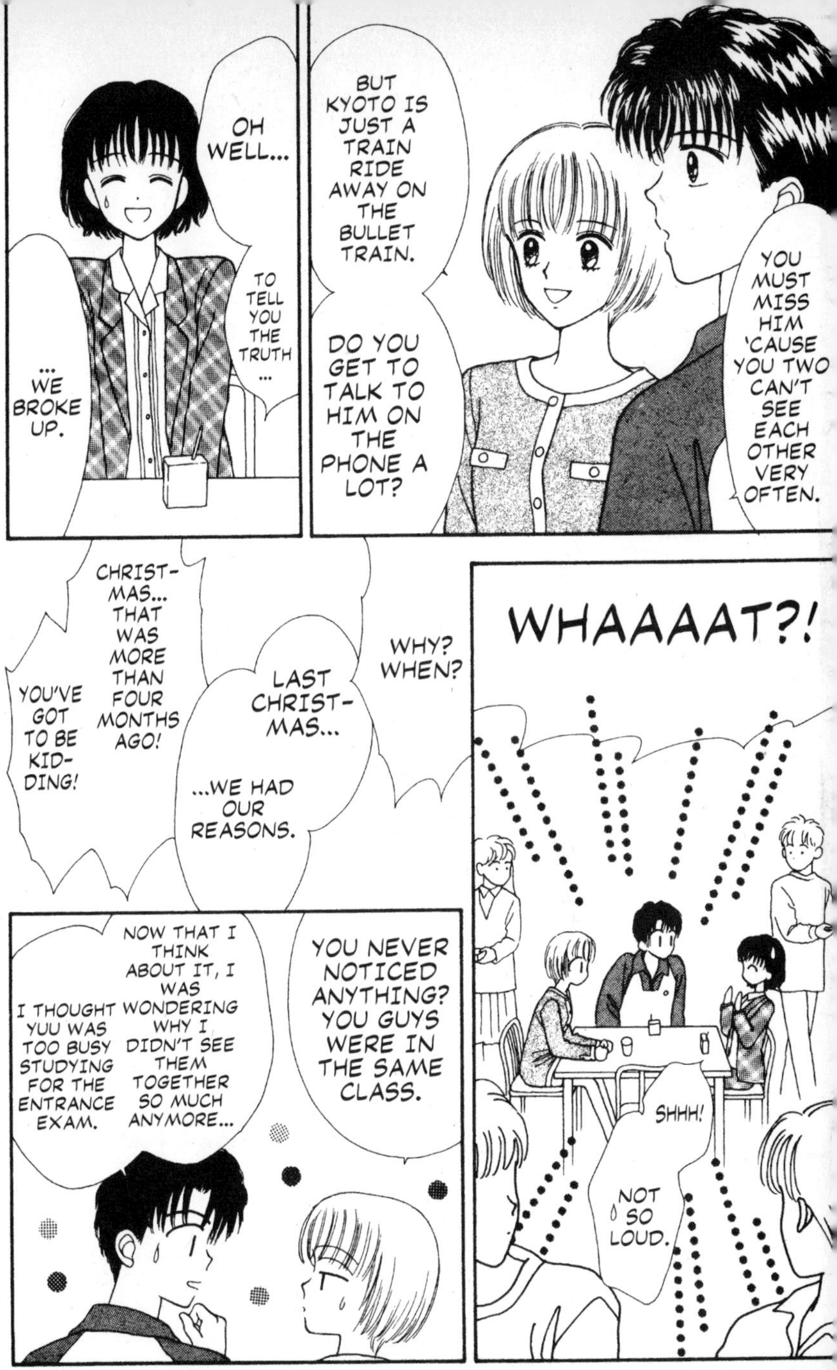
YOU MUST MISS HIM 'CAUSE YOU TWO CAN'T SEE EACH OTHER VERY OFTEN.
BUT KYOTO IS JUST A TRAIN RIDE AWAY ON THE BULLET TRAIN.
DO YOU GET TO TALK TO HIM ON THE PHONE A LOT?
OH WELL...
TO TELL YOU THE TRUTH...
...WE BROKE UP.
WHAAAAT?!
SHHH!
NOT SO LOUD.
WHY? WHEN?
LAST CHRISTMAS...
...WE HAD OUR REASONS.
CHRISTMAS... THAT WAS MORE THAN FOUR MONTHS AGO!
YOU'VE GOT TO BE KIDDING!
YOU NEVER NOTICED ANYTHING? YOU GUYS WERE IN THE SAME CLASS.
NOW THAT I THINK ABOUT IT, I WAS WONDERING WHY I DIDN'T SEE THEM TOGETHER SO MUCH ANYMORE...
I THOUGHT YUU WAS TOO BUSY STUDYING FOR THE ENTRANCE EXAM.

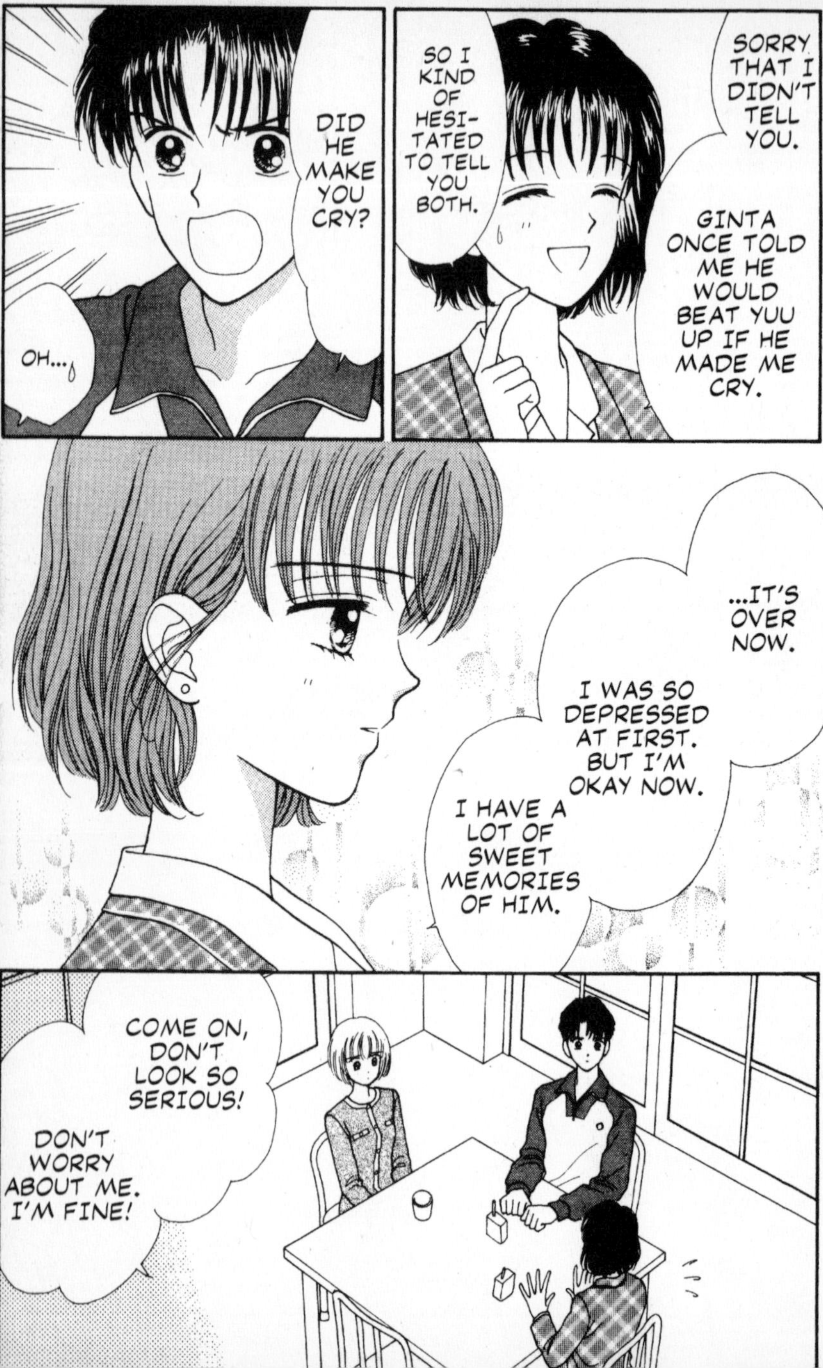
SORRY THAT I DIDN'T TELL YOU.
GINTA ONCE TOLD ME HE WOULD BEAT YUU UP IF HE MADE ME CRY.
SO I KIND OF HESI-TATED TO TELL YOU BOTH.
DID HE MAKE YOU CRY?
OH...
...IT'S OVER NOW.
I WAS SO DEPRESSED AT FIRST. BUT I'M OKAY NOW.
I HAVE A LOT OF SWEET MEMORIES OF HIM.
COME ON, DON'T LOOK SO SERIOUS!
DON'T WORRY ABOUT ME. I'M FINE!

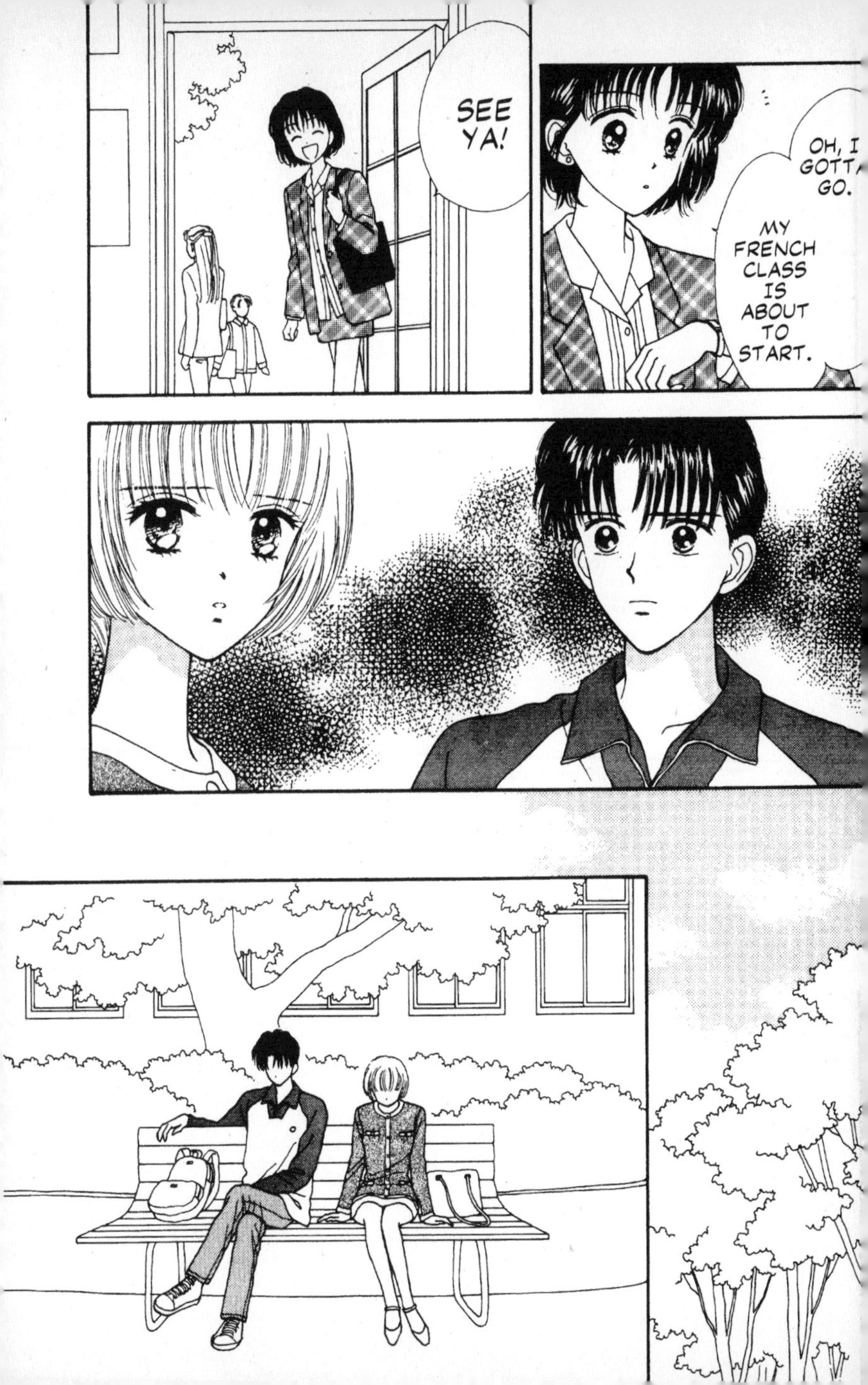
OH, I GOTTA GO.
MY FRENCH CLASS IS ABOUT TO START.
SEE YA!

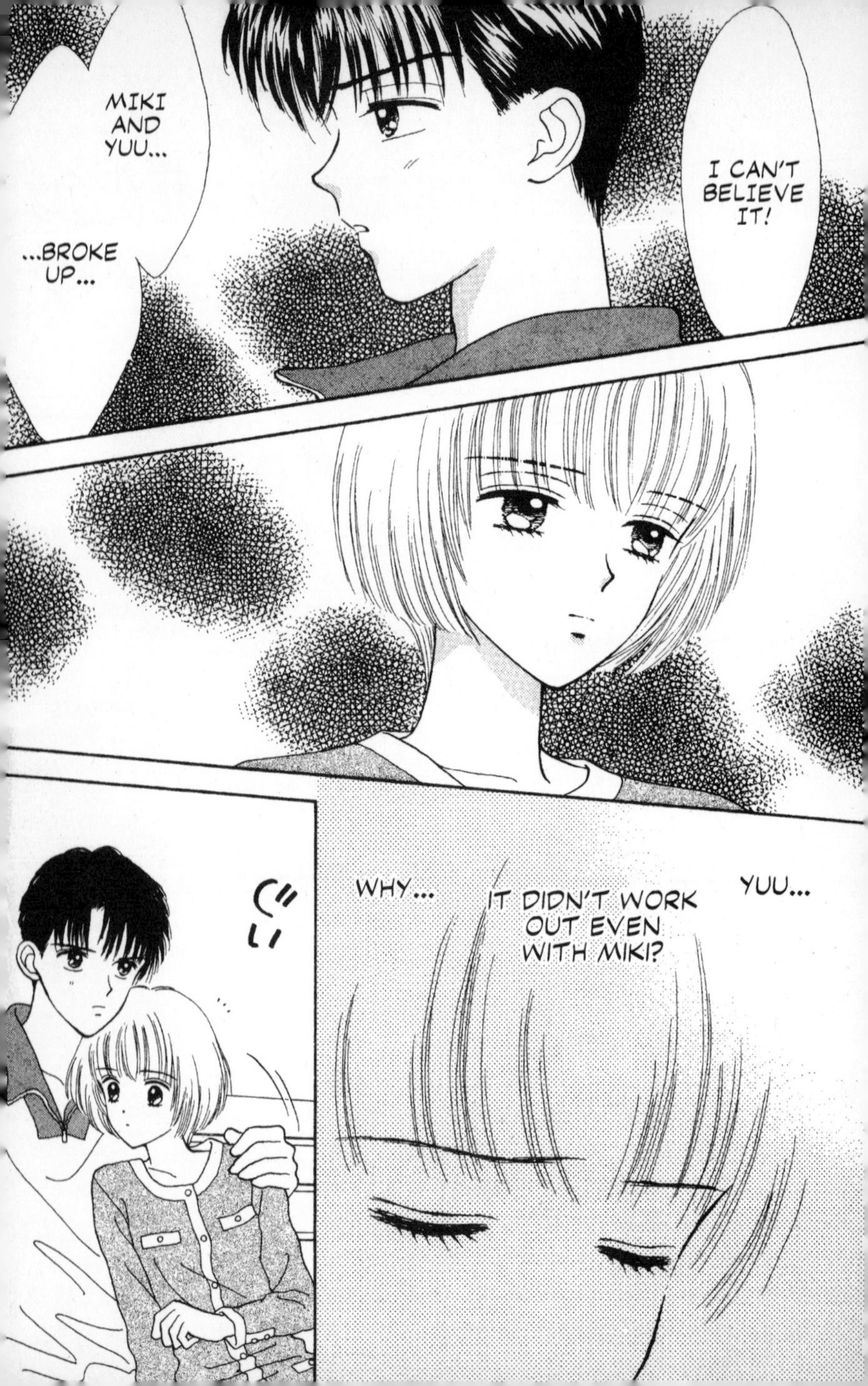
I CAN'T BELIEVE IT!
MIKI AND YUU...
...BROKE UP...
YUU...
IT DIDN'T WORK OUT EVEN WITH MIKI?
WHY...
ぐい
...

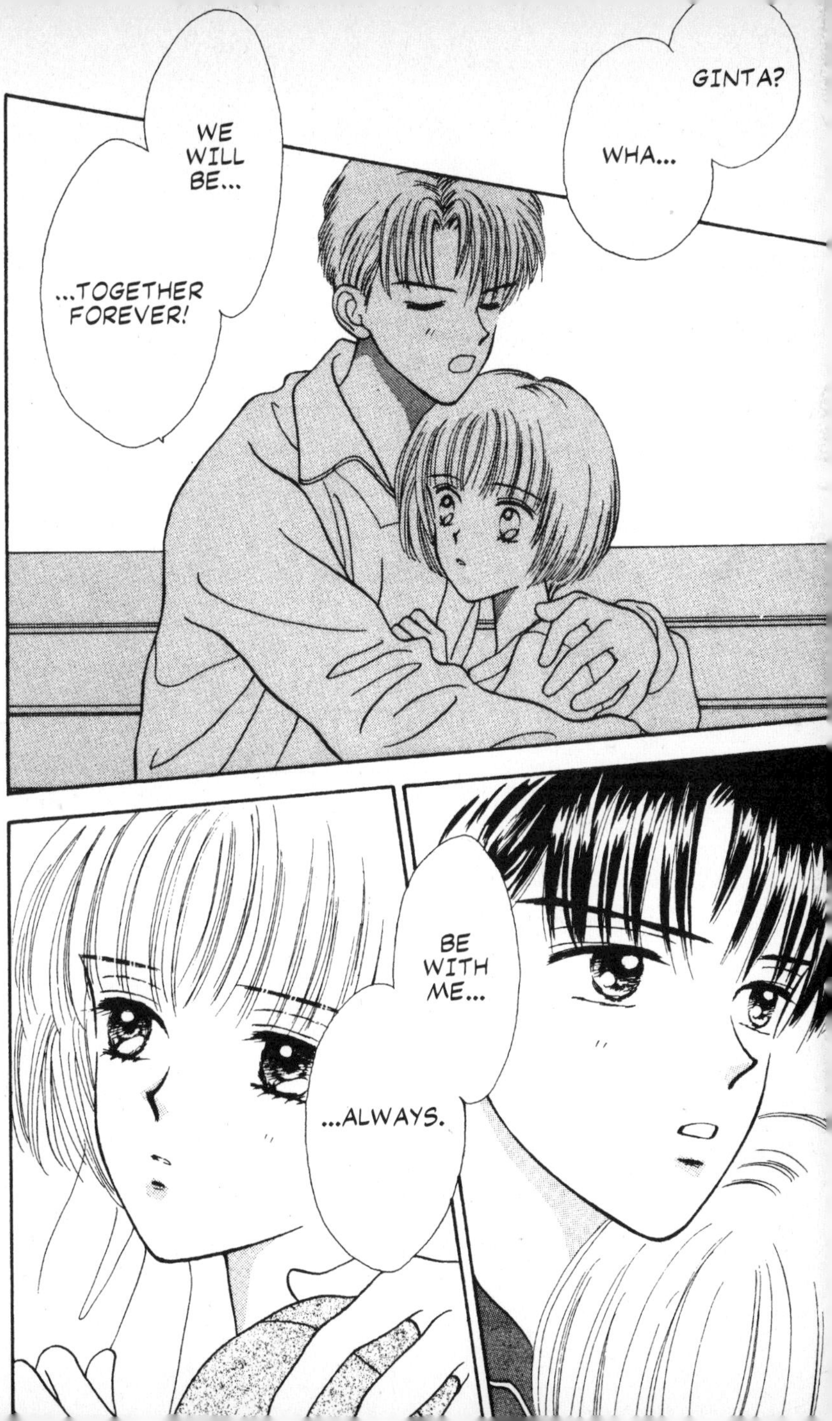
GINTA?
WHA...
WE WILL BE...
...TOGETHER FOREVER!
BE WITH ME...
...ALWAYS.

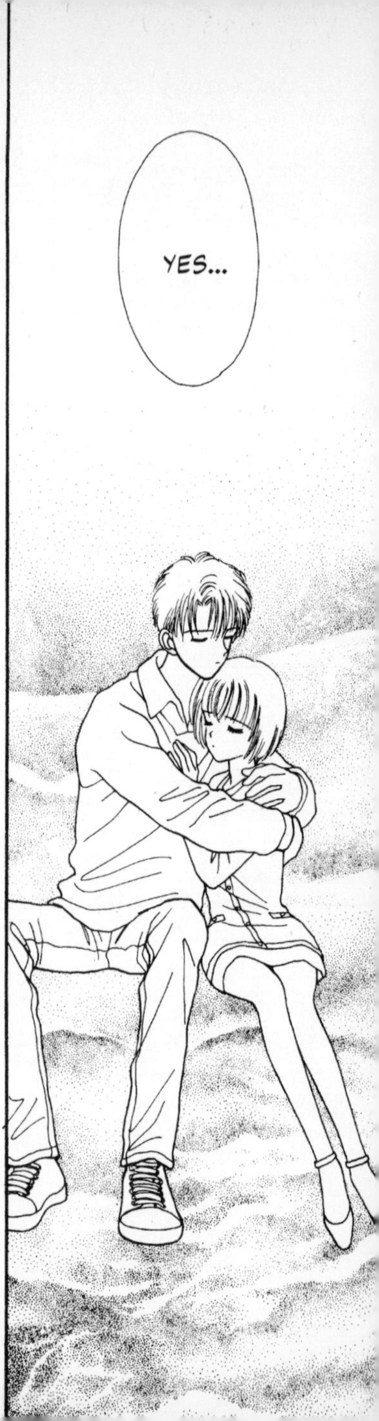
YES...

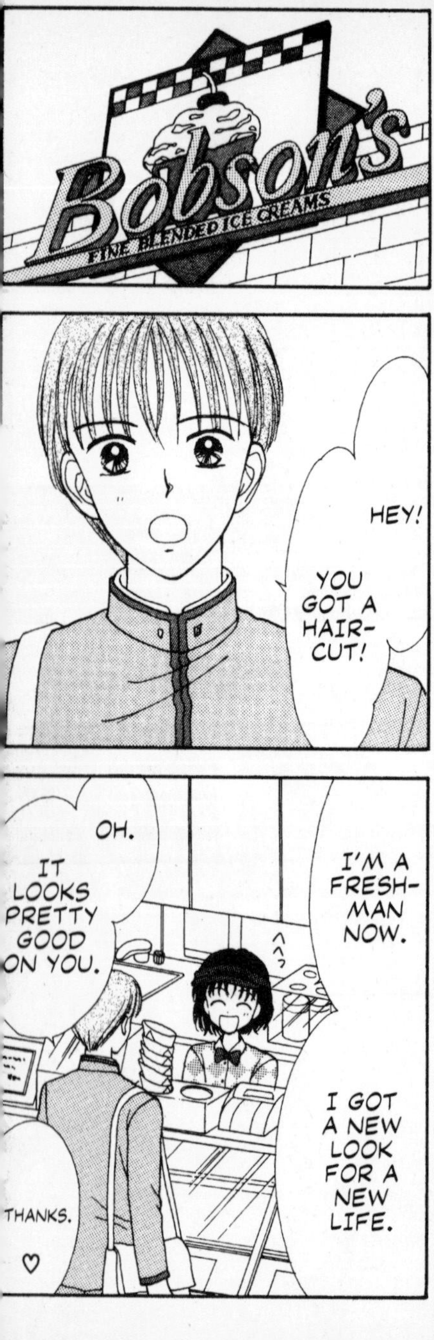
Bobson's
FINE BLENDED ICE CREAMS
HEY!
YOU GOT A HAIR-CUT!
I'M A FRESH-MAN NOW.
OH.
IT LOOKS PRETTY GOOD ON YOU.
I GOT A NEW LOOK FOR A NEW LIFE.
THANKS. ♥

FREE TALK ②

I had a lot of fun having the anime version of Marmalade Boy. But as the old saying goes, "Pleasure is the source of pain; pain is the source of pleasure." I went through some hard times too. As I wrote before, I tried to keep my nose out of the anime production business and let the anime staff work on it on their own. I wanted to keep the original story and the anime version separate. By doing that, I could keep other people's opinions off my original work. But things didn't always work the way I wanted. One thing is that they asked me to expand the story a little bit and delay the finale to go with their schedule. Making an anime is easier on a short story series such as "Akazukin Cha Cha". Even after the anime series is over, I can keep writing more short stories without any problem. On the other hand, Marmalade Boy is a serial story and I had to wait to give away the truth regarding Yuu's father until the very end.

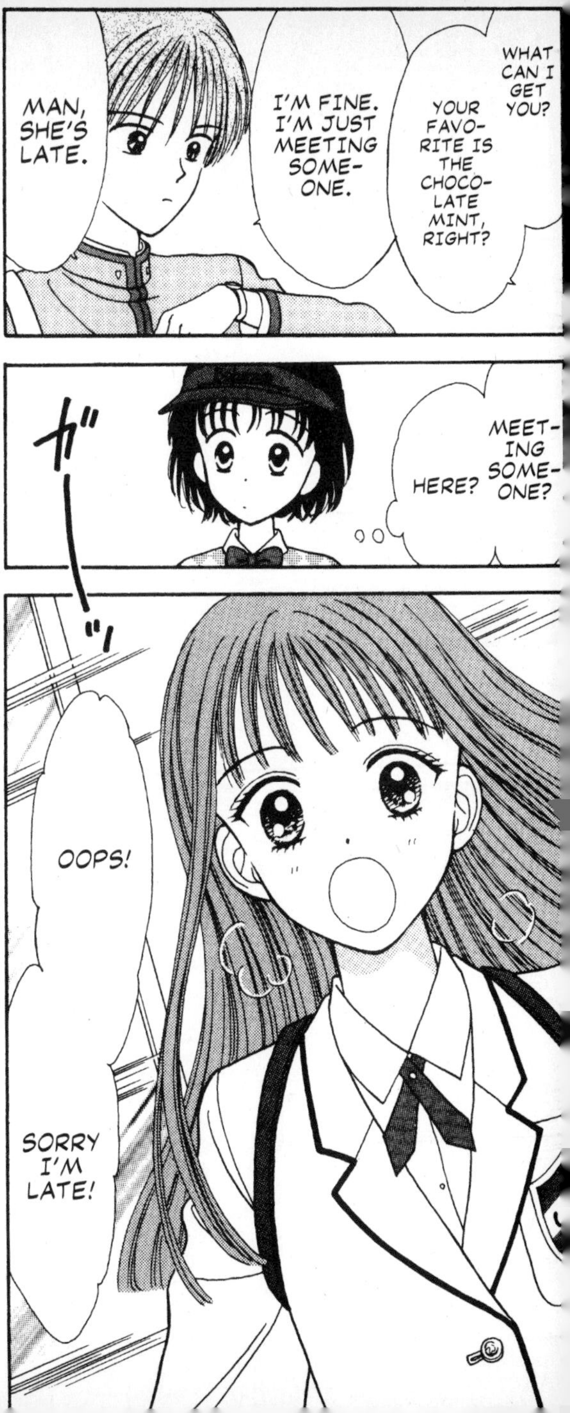
WHAT CAN I GET YOU?
YOUR FAVORITE IS THE CHOCOLATE MINT, RIGHT?
I'M FINE. I'M JUST MEETING SOMEONE.
MAN, SHE'S LATE.
MEETING SOMEONE?
HERE?
OOPS!
SORRY I'M LATE!

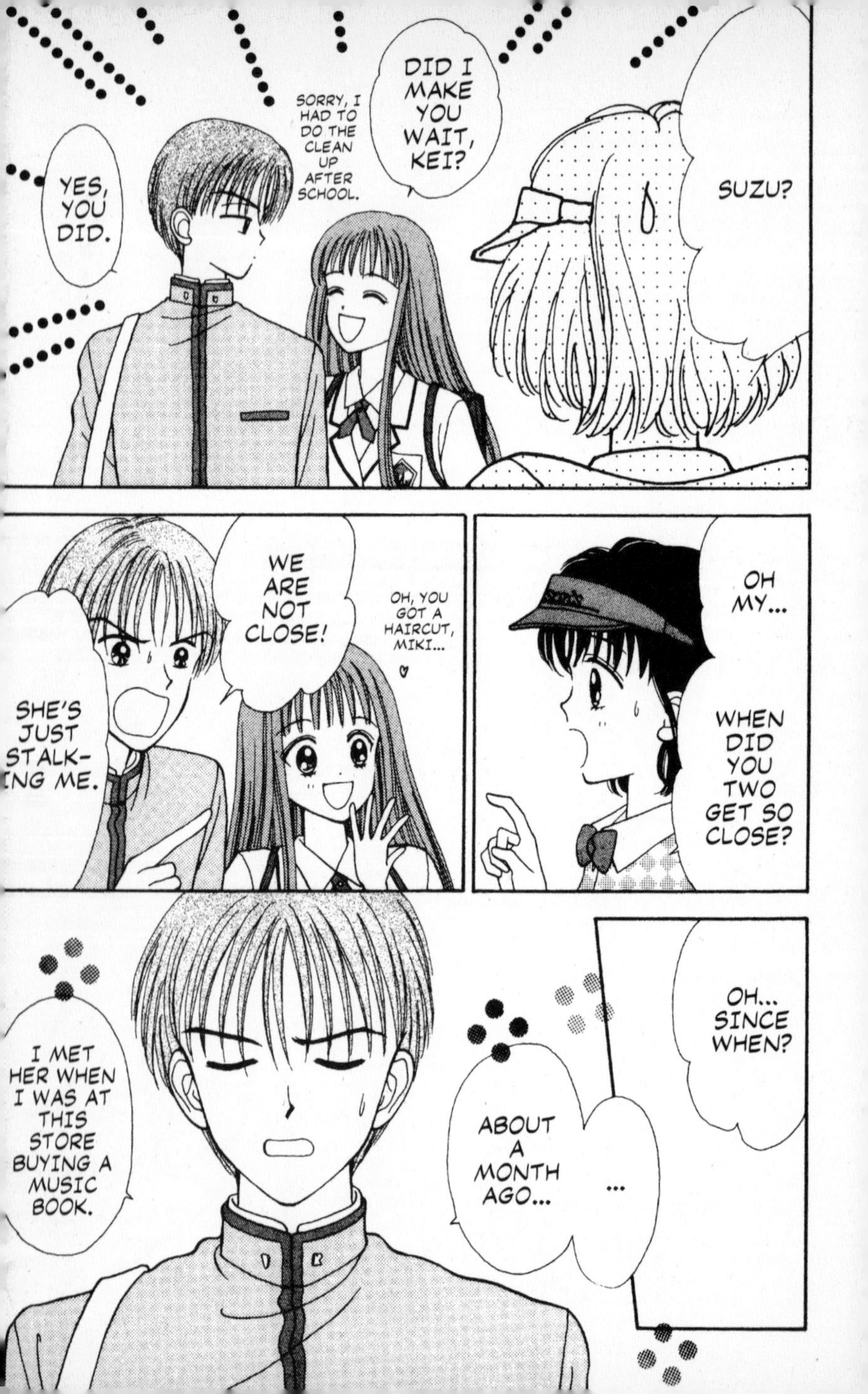
SUZU?
DID I MAKE YOU WAIT, KEI?
SORRY, I HAD TO DO THE CLEAN UP AFTER SCHOOL.
YES, YOU DID.
OH MY...
WHEN DID YOU TWO GET SO CLOSE?
WE ARE NOT CLOSE!
SHE'S JUST STALKING ME.
OH, YOU GOT A HAIRCUT, MIKI... ♡
OH... SINCE WHEN?
...
ABOUT A MONTH AGO...
I MET HER WHEN I WAS AT THIS STORE BUYING A MUSIC BOOK.

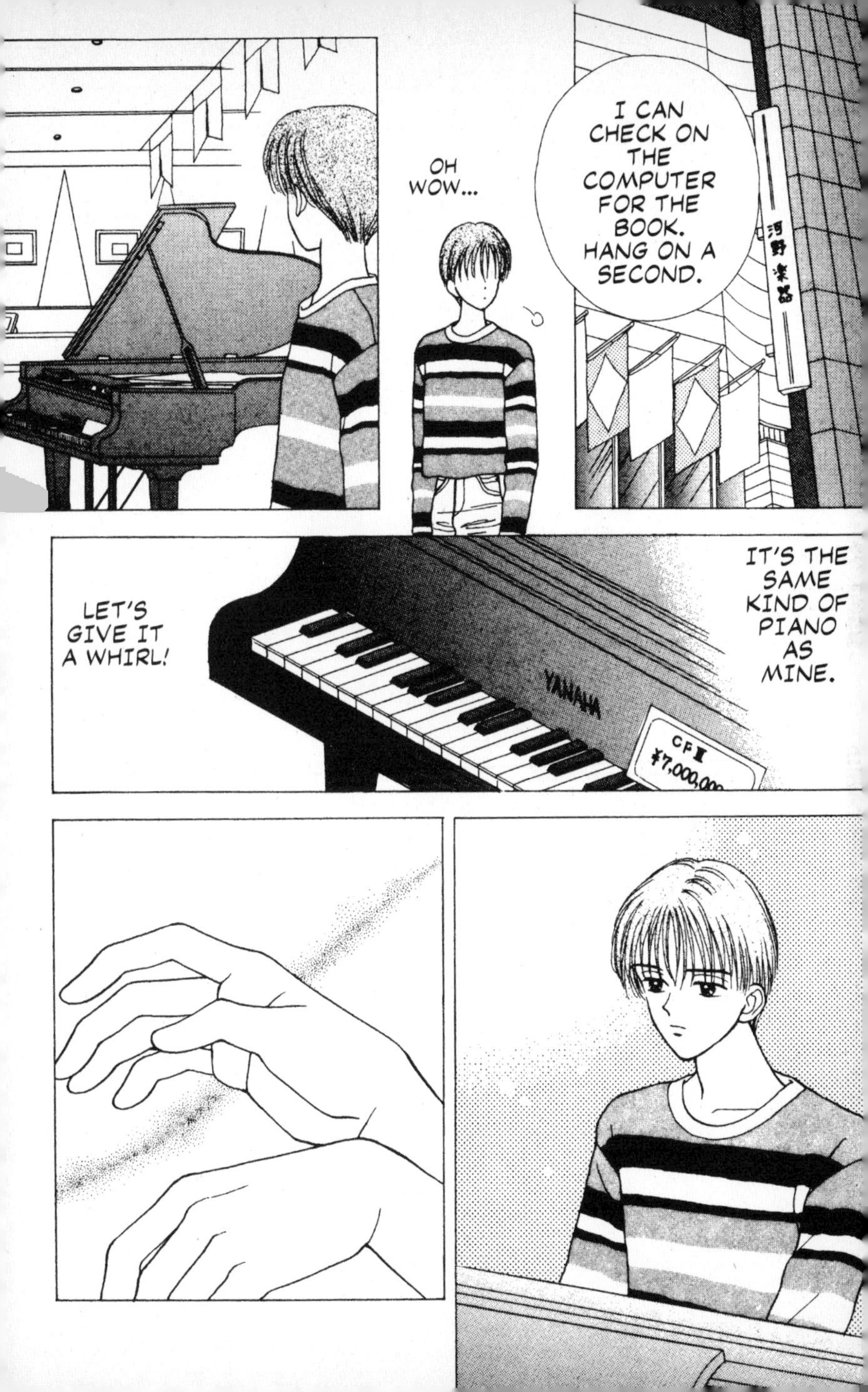
I CAN CHECK ON THE COMPUTER FOR THE BOOK. HANG ON A SECOND.
河野楽器
OH WOW...
IT'S THE SAME KIND OF PIANO AS MINE.
LET'S GIVE IT A WHIRL!

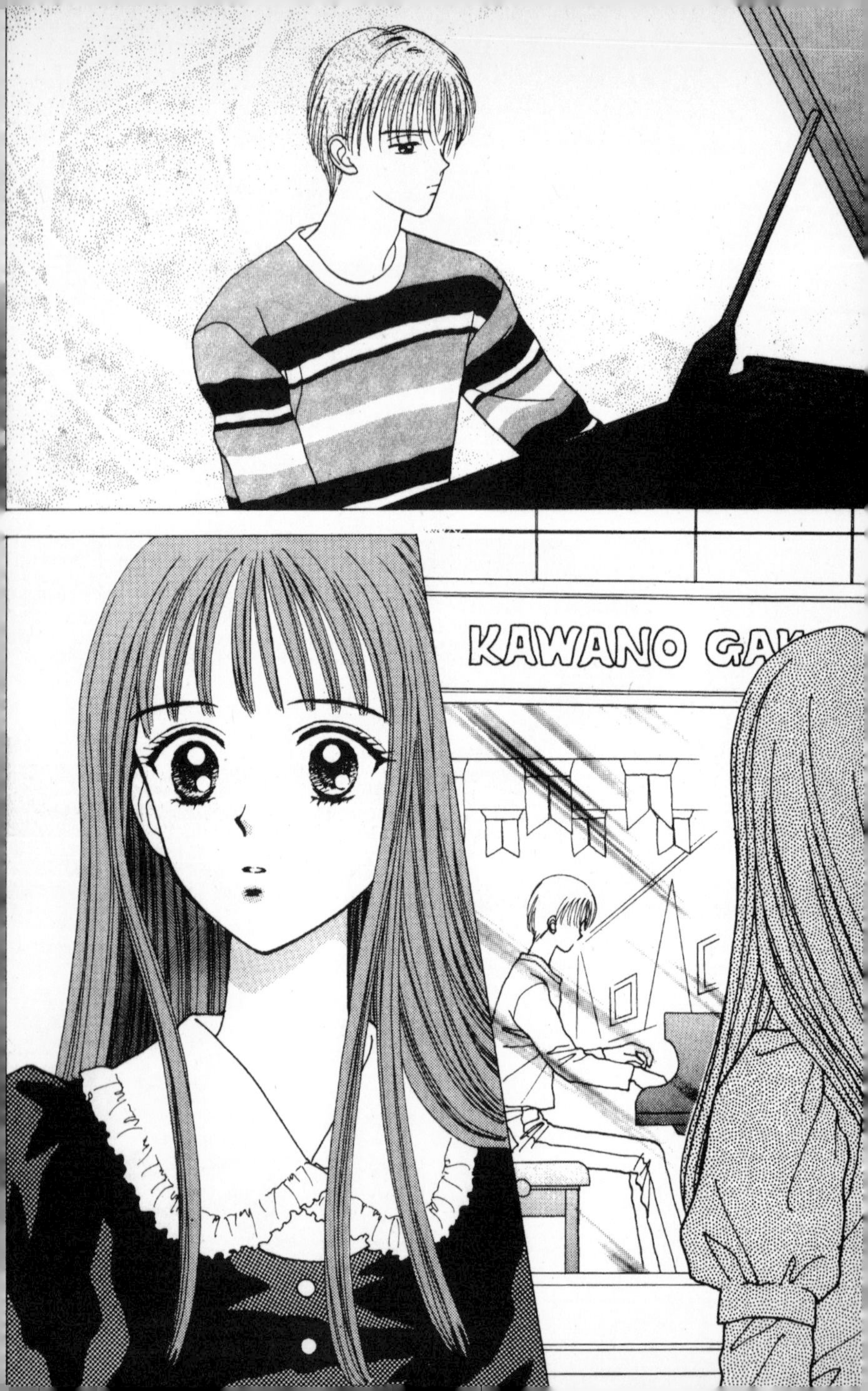
KAWANO GA

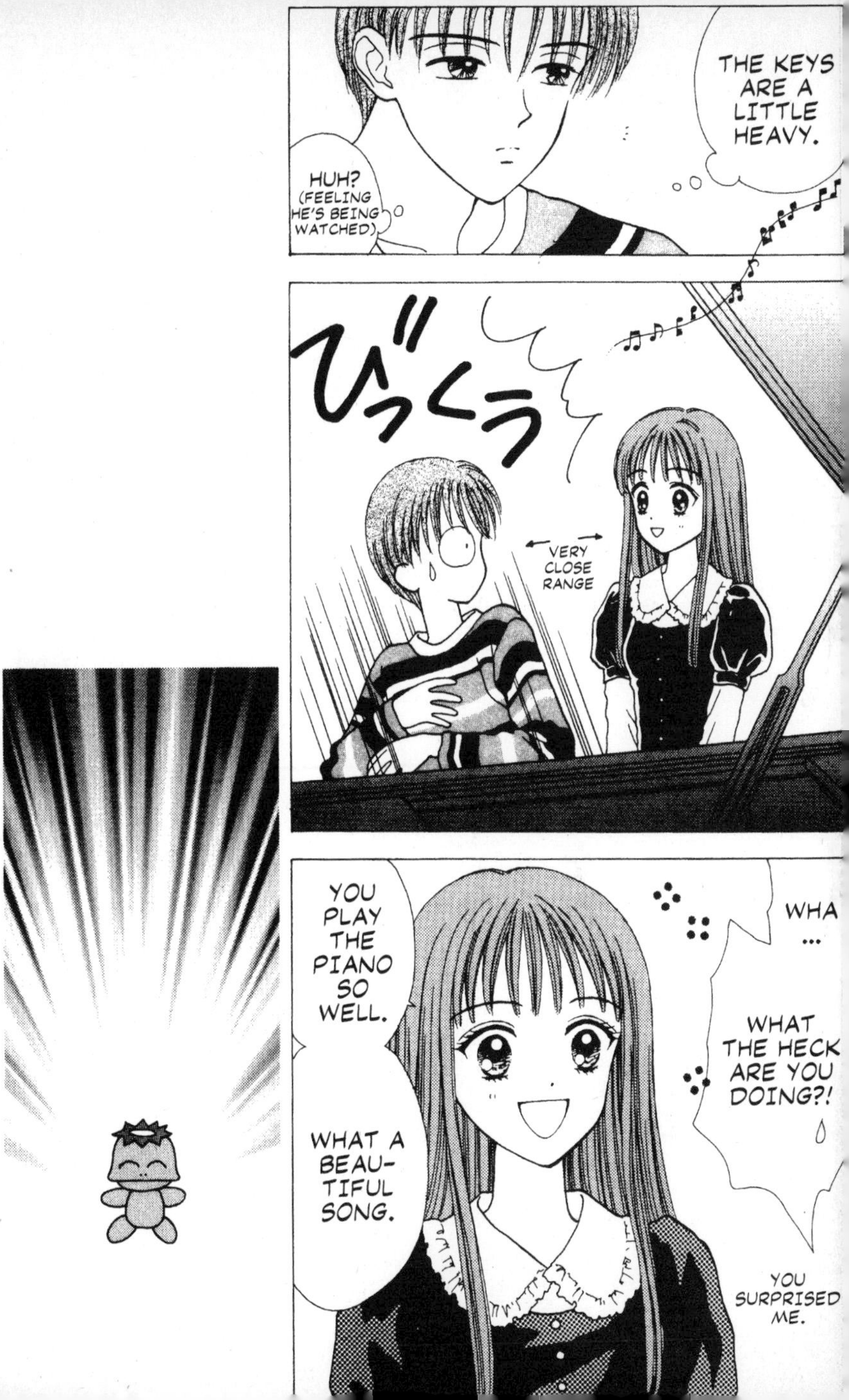

THE KEYS ARE A LITTLE HEAVY.
HUH? (FEELING HE'S BEING WATCHED)
びっくう
VERY CLOSE RANGE
WHA ...
WHAT THE HECK ARE YOU DOING?!
YOU SURPRISED ME.
YOU PLAY THE PIANO SO WELL.
WHAT A BEAU-TIFUL SONG.

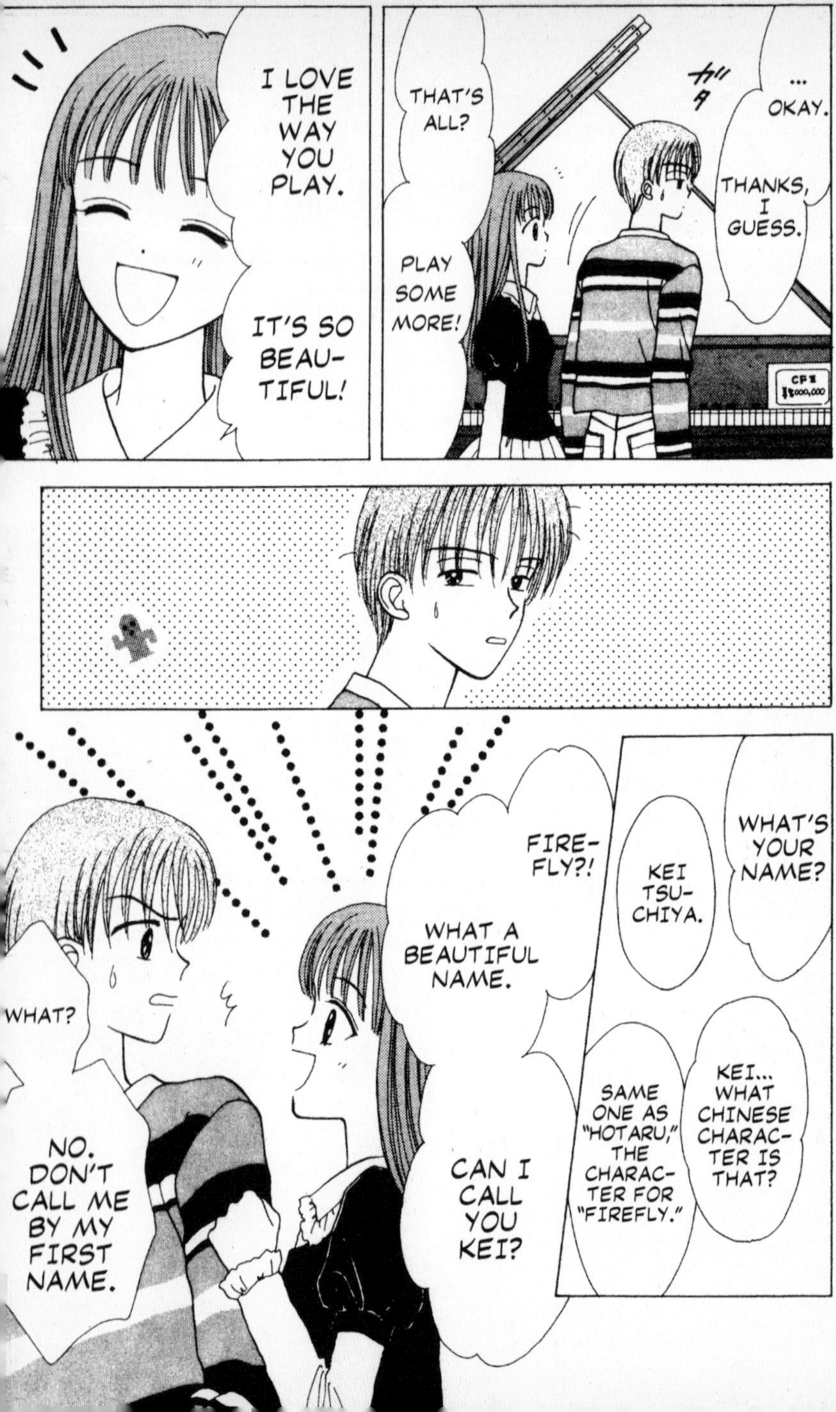

...OKAY.
ガタ
THANKS, I GUESS.
THAT'S ALL?
PLAY SOME MORE!
I LOVE THE WAY YOU PLAY.
IT'S SO BEAU-TIFUL!
WHAT'S YOUR NAME?
KEI TSU-CHIYA.
KEI... WHAT CHINESE CHARAC-TER IS THAT?
SAME ONE AS "HOTARU," THE CHARAC-TER FOR "FIREFLY."
FIRE-FLY?!
WHAT A BEAUTIFUL NAME.
CAN I CALL YOU KEI?
WHAT?
NO. DON'T CALL ME BY MY FIRST NAME.

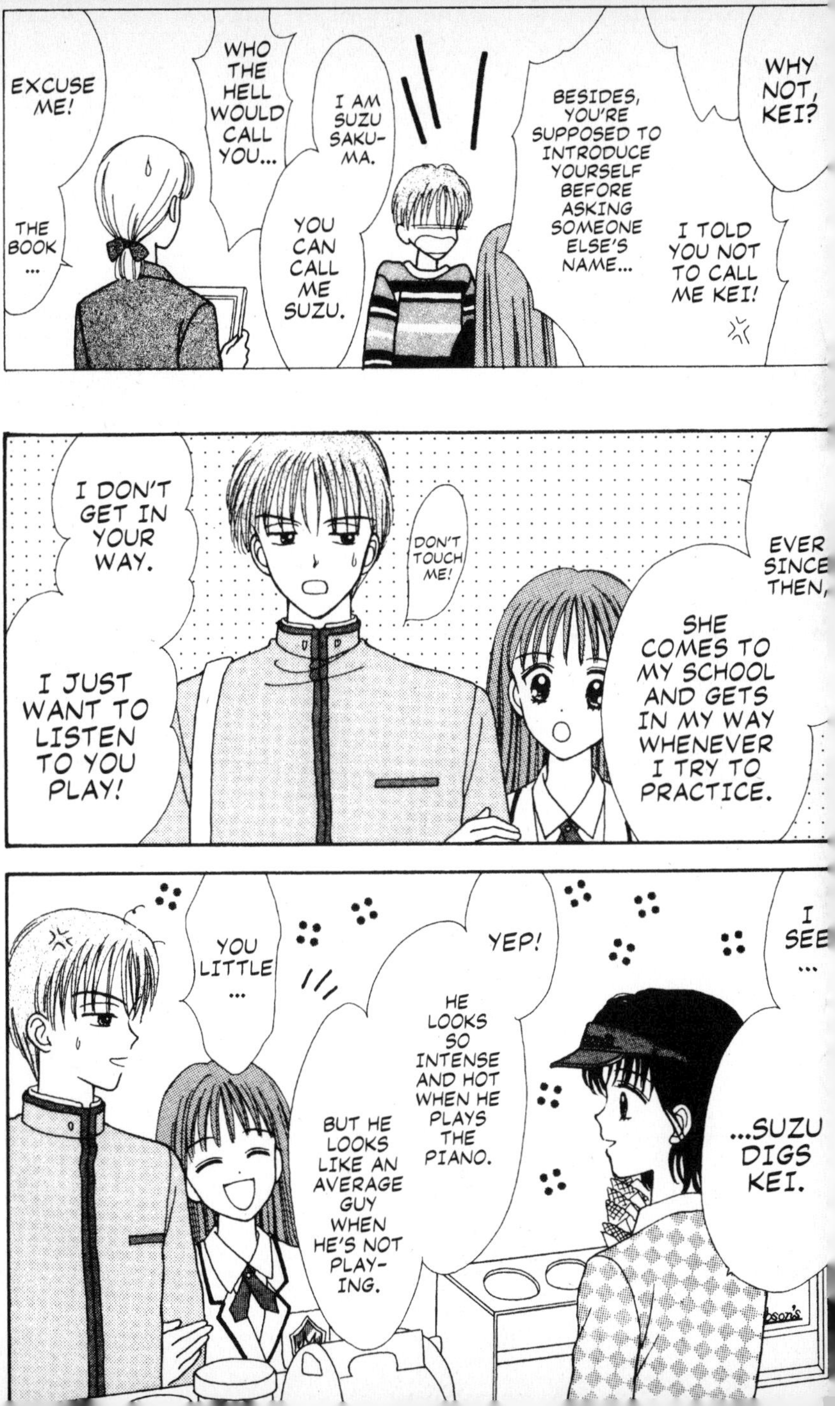
WHY NOT, KEI?
I TOLD YOU NOT TO CALL ME KEI!
BESIDES, YOU'RE SUPPOSED TO INTRODUCE YOURSELF BEFORE ASKING SOMEONE ELSE'S NAME...
I AM SUZU SAKU-MA.
YOU CAN CALL ME SUZU.
WHO THE HELL WOULD CALL YOU...
EXCUSE ME!
THE BOOK ...
EVER SINCE THEN,
SHE COMES TO MY SCHOOL AND GETS IN MY WAY WHENEVER I TRY TO PRACTICE.
DON'T TOUCH ME!
I DON'T GET IN YOUR WAY.
I JUST WANT TO LISTEN TO YOU PLAY!
I SEE ...
...SUZU DIGS KEI.
YEP!
HE LOOKS SO INTENSE AND HOT WHEN HE PLAYS THE PIANO.
BUT HE LOOKS LIKE AN AVERAGE GUY WHEN HE'S NOT PLAY-ING.
YOU LITTLE ...

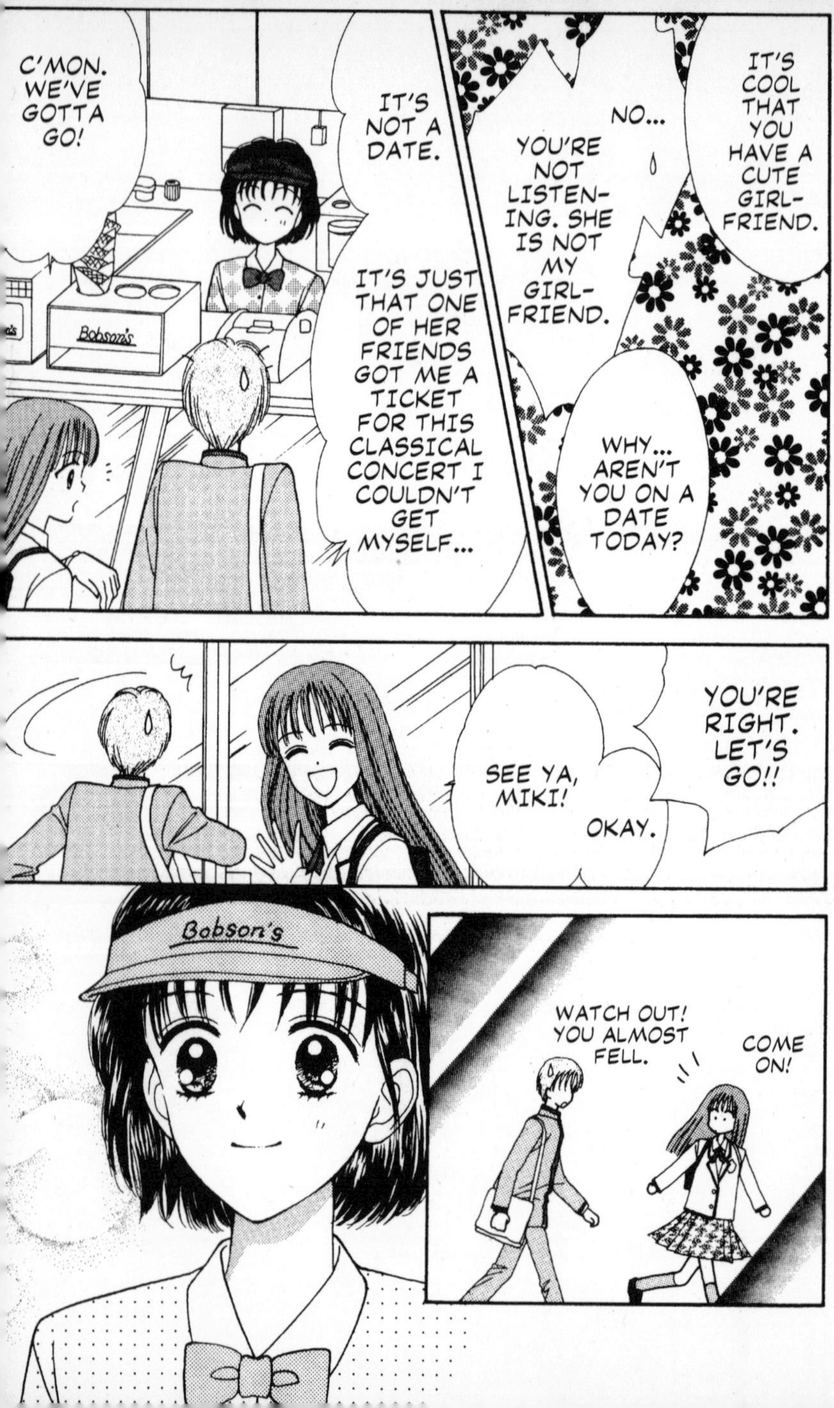

IT'S COOL THAT YOU HAVE A CUTE GIRLFRIEND.
NO... YOU'RE NOT LISTENING. SHE IS NOT MY GIRLFRIEND.
WHY... AREN'T YOU ON A DATE TODAY?
IT'S NOT A DATE.
IT'S JUST THAT ONE OF HER FRIENDS GOT ME A TICKET FOR THIS CLASSICAL CONCERT I COULDN'T GET MYSELF...
C'MON. WE'VE GOTTA GO!
Bobson's
YOU'RE RIGHT. LET'S GO!!
SEE YA, MIKI!
OKAY.
COME ON!
WATCH OUT! YOU ALMOST FELL.
Bobson's

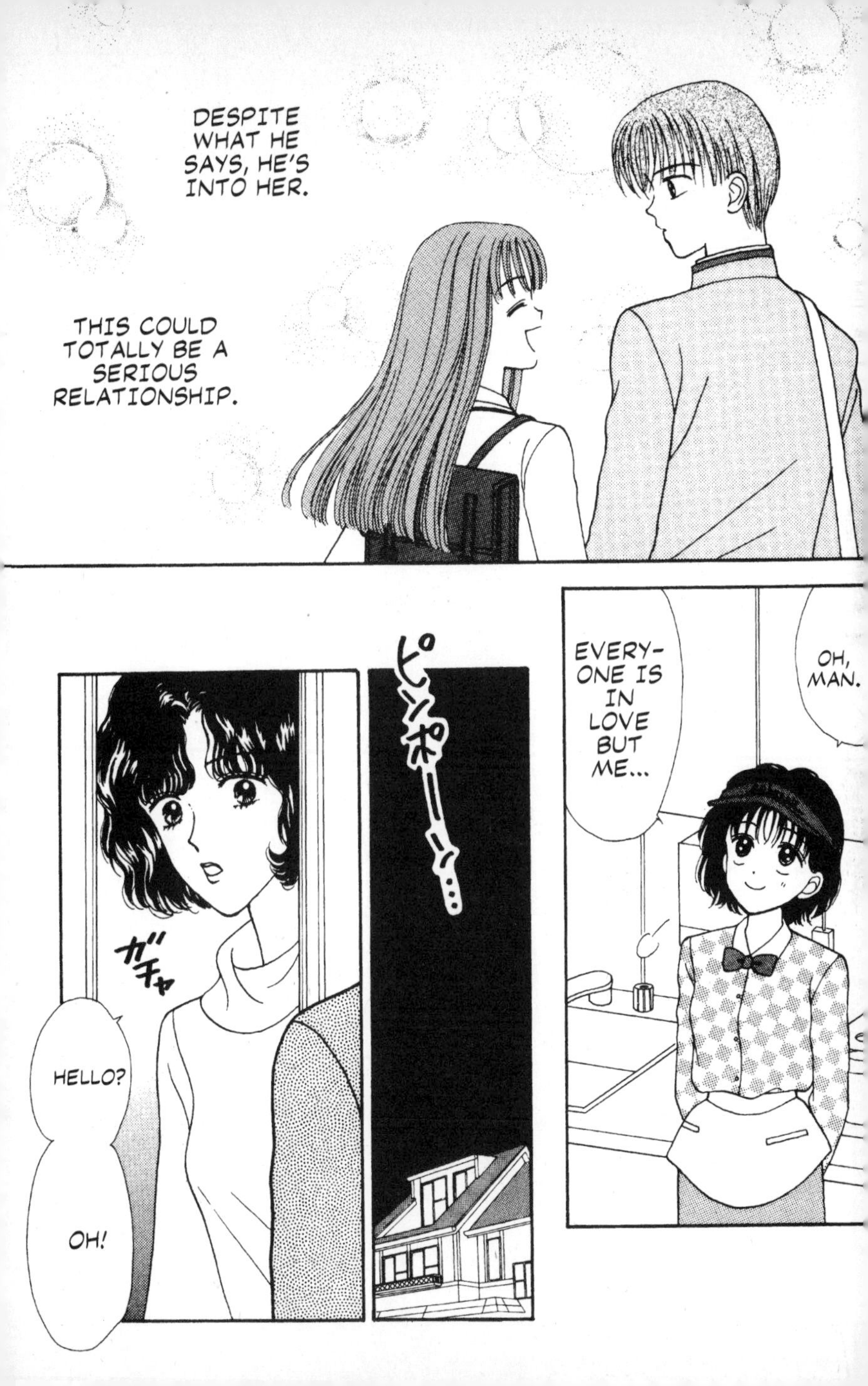
DESPITE WHAT HE SAYS, HE'S INTO HER.
THIS COULD TOTALLY BE A SERIOUS RELATIONSHIP.
OH, MAN.
EVERY-ONE IS IN LOVE BUT ME...
ピンポーーン…
ガチャ
HELLO?
OH!

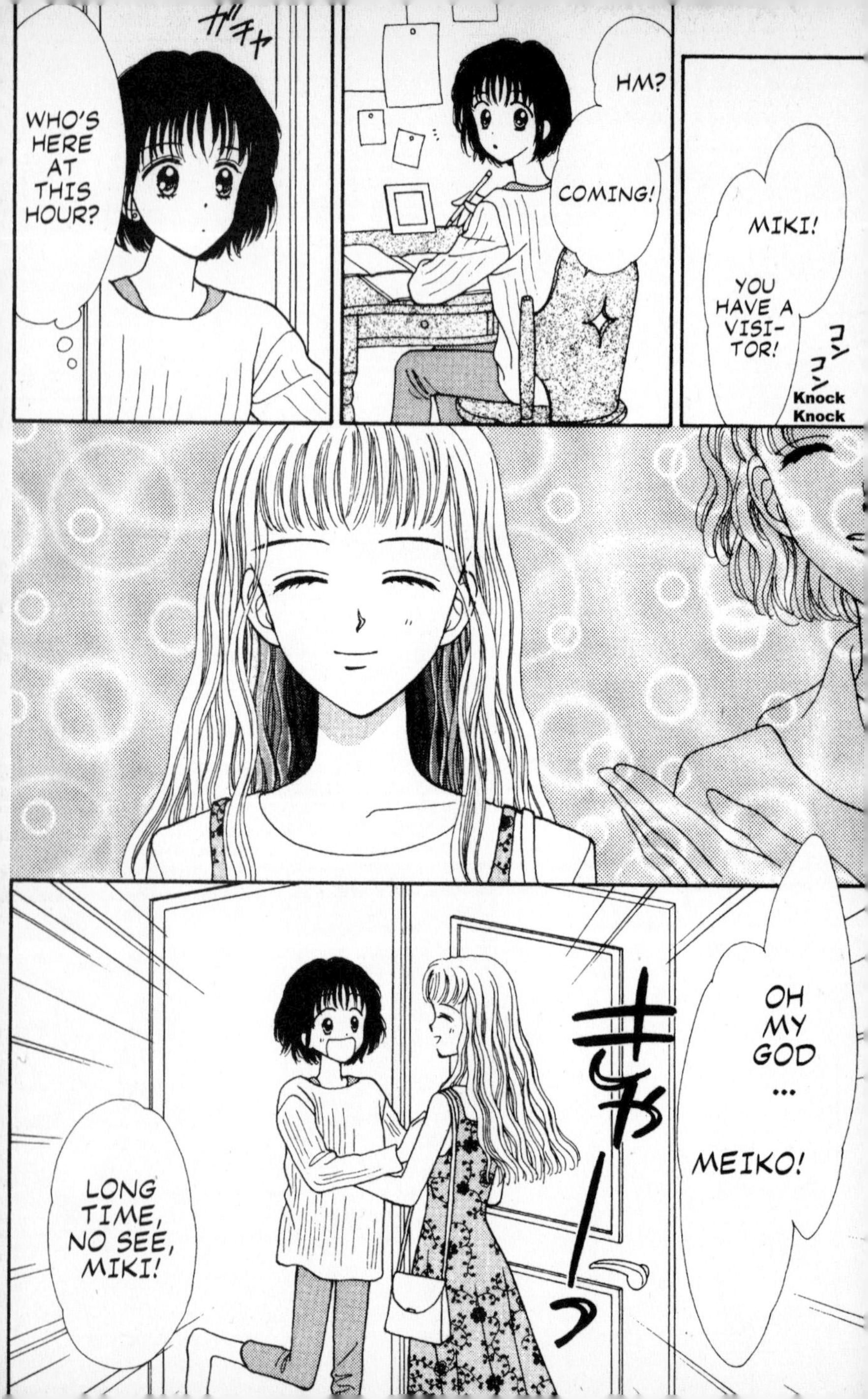
MIKI! YOU HAVE A VISITOR!
コンコン
Knock Knock
HM?
COMING!
ガチャ
WHO'S HERE AT THIS HOUR?
OH MY GOD ... MEIKO!
きゃーっ
LONG TIME, NO SEE, MIKI!

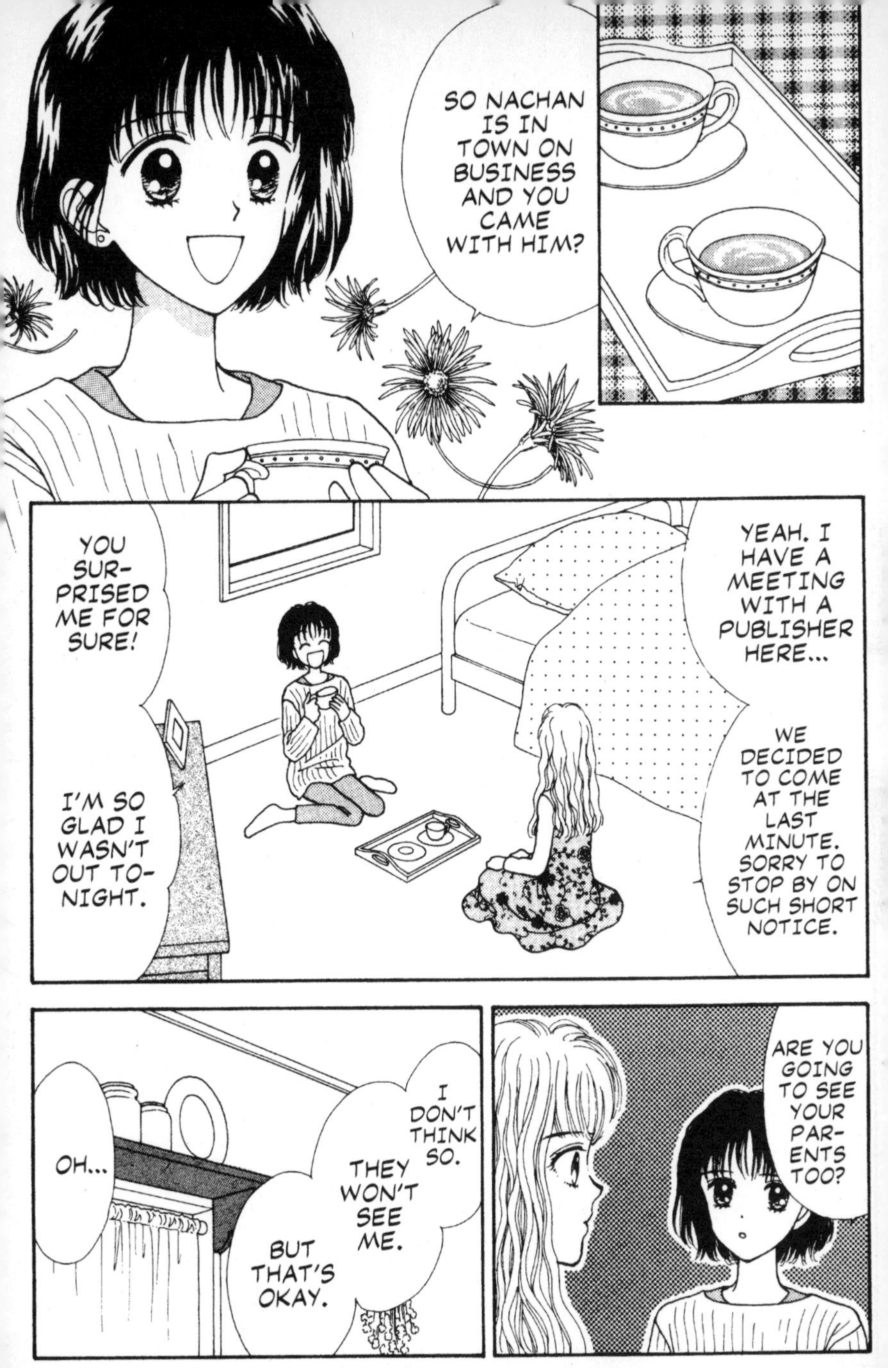
SO NACHAN IS IN TOWN ON BUSINESS AND YOU CAME WITH HIM?
YEAH. I HAVE A MEETING WITH A PUBLISHER HERE...
WE DECIDED TO COME AT THE LAST MINUTE. SORRY TO STOP BY ON SUCH SHORT NOTICE.
YOU SURPRISED ME FOR SURE!
I'M SO GLAD I WASN'T OUT TONIGHT.
ARE YOU GOING TO SEE YOUR PARENTS TOO?
I DON'T THINK SO.
THEY WON'T SEE ME.
BUT THAT'S OKAY.
OH...

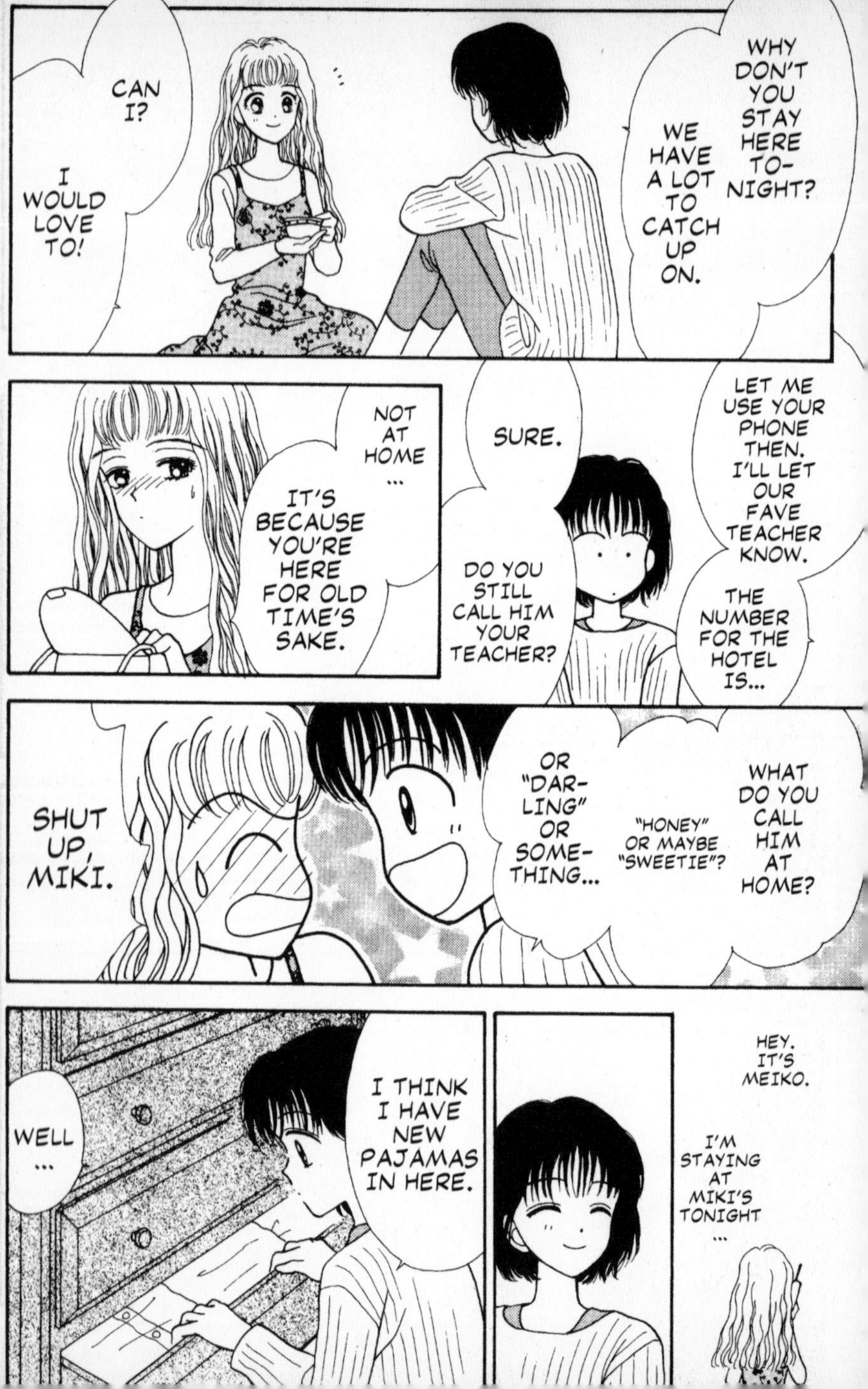
WHY DON'T YOU STAY HERE TO-NIGHT?
WE HAVE A LOT TO CATCH UP ON.
CAN I?
I WOULD LOVE TO!
LET ME USE YOUR PHONE THEN. I'LL LET OUR FAVE TEACHER KNOW.
THE NUMBER FOR THE HOTEL IS...
SURE.
DO YOU STILL CALL HIM YOUR TEACHER?
NOT AT HOME ...
IT'S BECAUSE YOU'RE HERE FOR OLD TIME'S SAKE.
WHAT DO YOU CALL HIM AT HOME?
"HONEY" OR MAYBE "SWEETIE"?
OR "DAR-LING" OR SOME-THING...
SHUT UP, MIKI.
HEY. IT'S MEIKO.
I'M STAYING AT MIKI'S TONIGHT ...
I THINK I HAVE NEW PAJAMAS IN HERE.
WELL ...

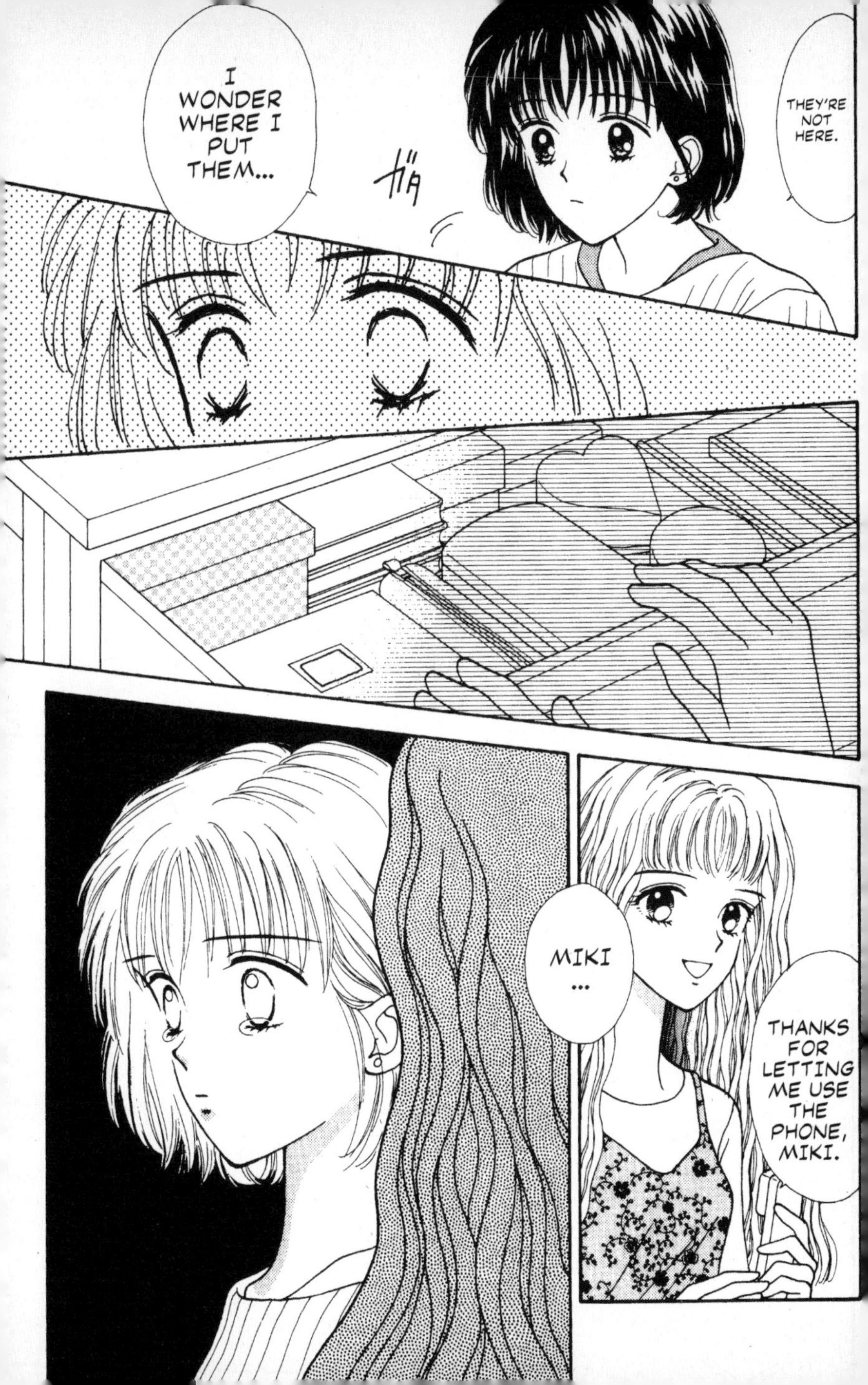
THEY'RE NOT HERE.
I WONDER WHERE I PUT THEM...
THANKS FOR LETTING ME USE THE PHONE, MIKI.
MIKI ...

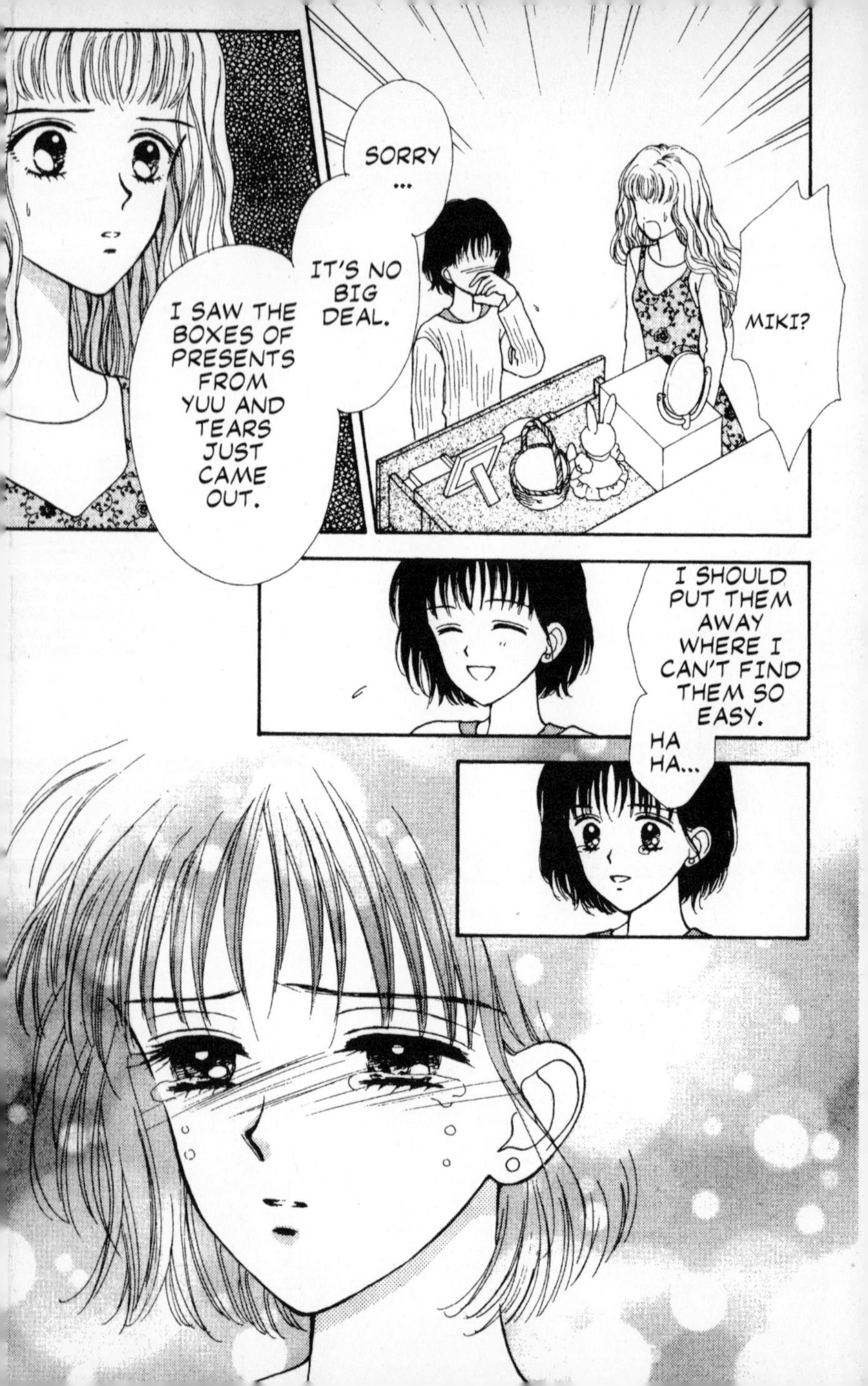
MIKI?
SORRY ...
IT'S NO BIG DEAL.
I SAW THE BOXES OF PRESENTS FROM YUU AND TEARS JUST CAME OUT.
I SHOULD PUT THEM AWAY WHERE I CAN'T FIND THEM SO EASY.
HA HA...

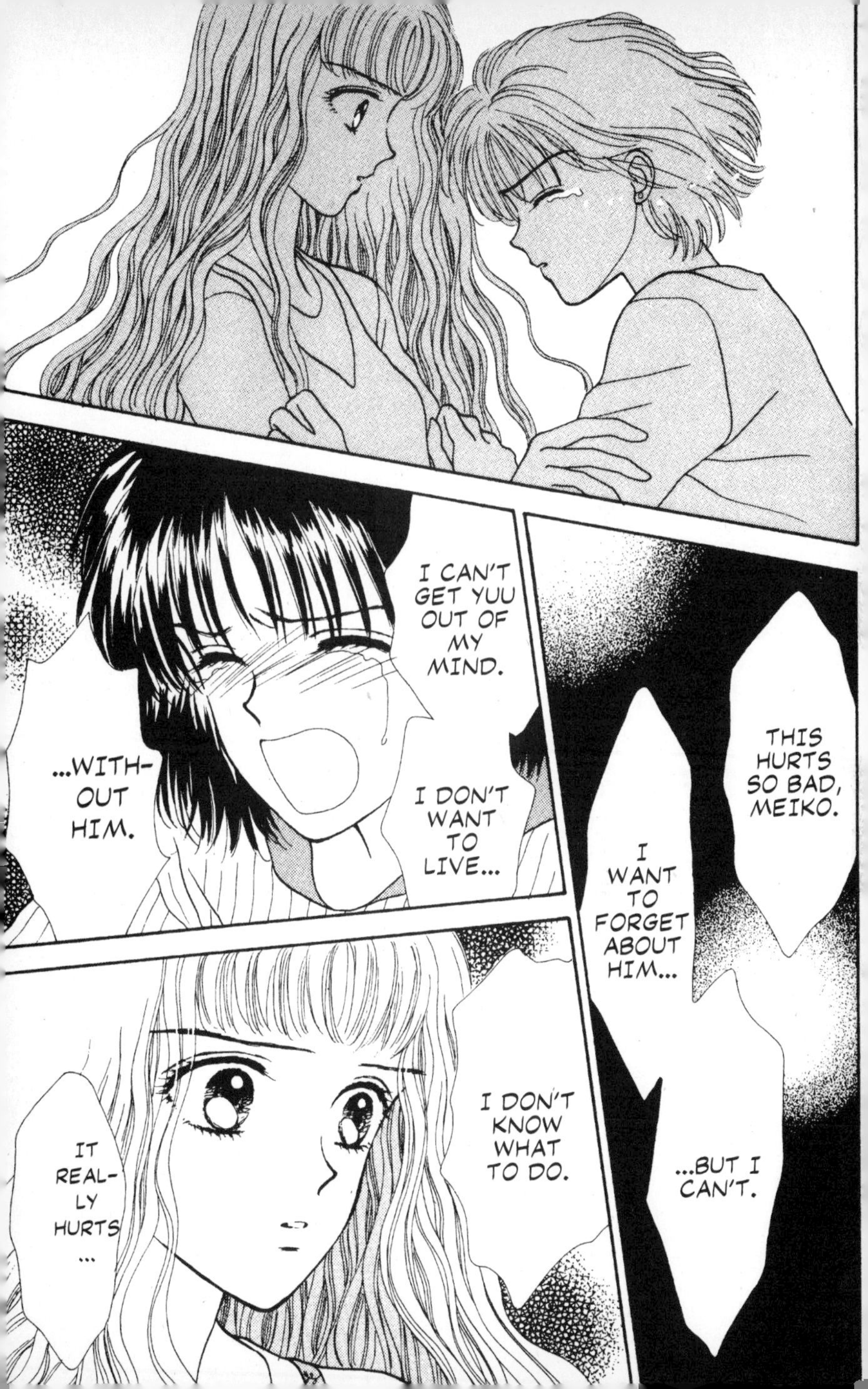
THIS HURTS SO BAD, MEIKO.
I WANT TO FORGET ABOUT HIM...
...BUT I CAN'T.
I CAN'T GET YUU OUT OF MY MIND.
I DON'T WANT TO LIVE...
...WITH-OUT HIM.
I DON'T KNOW WHAT TO DO.
IT REAL-LY HURTS...

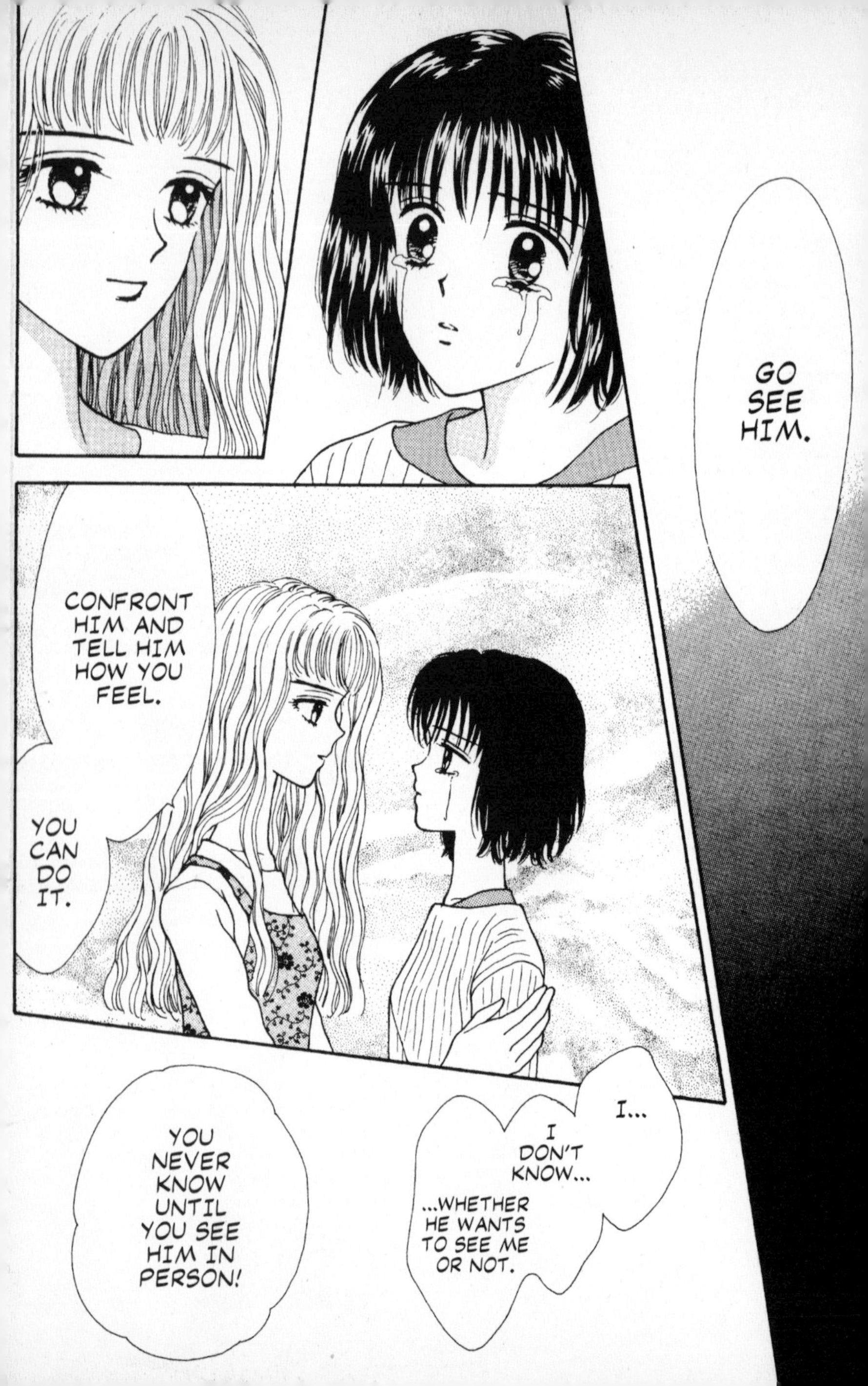
GO SEE HIM.
CONFRONT HIM AND TELL HIM HOW YOU FEEL.
YOU CAN DO IT.
I...
I DON'T KNOW...
...WHETHER HE WANTS TO SEE ME OR NOT.
YOU NEVER KNOW UNTIL YOU SEE HIM IN PERSON!

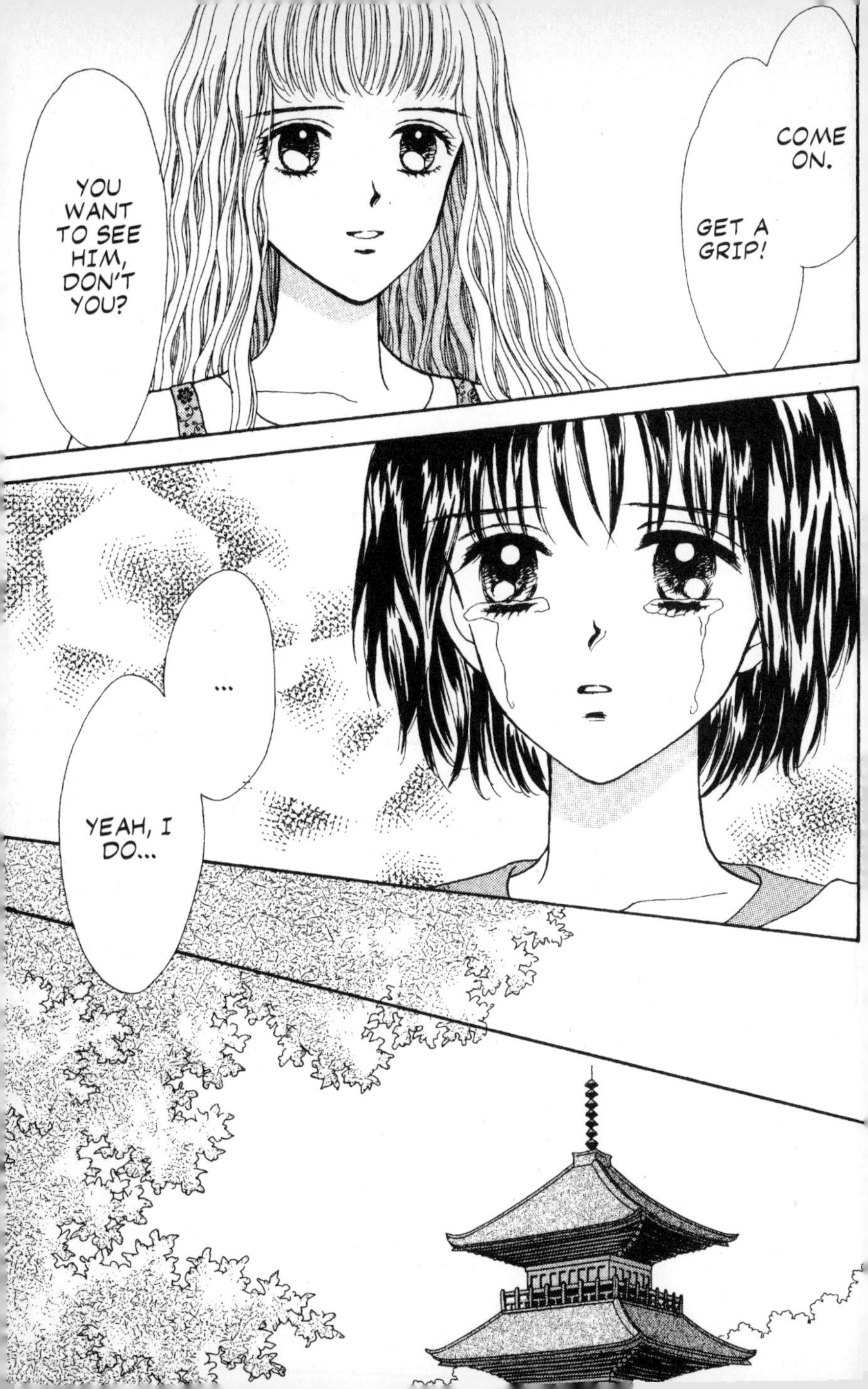
COME ON.
GET A GRIP!
YOU WANT TO SEE HIM, DON'T YOU?
...
YEAH, I DO...

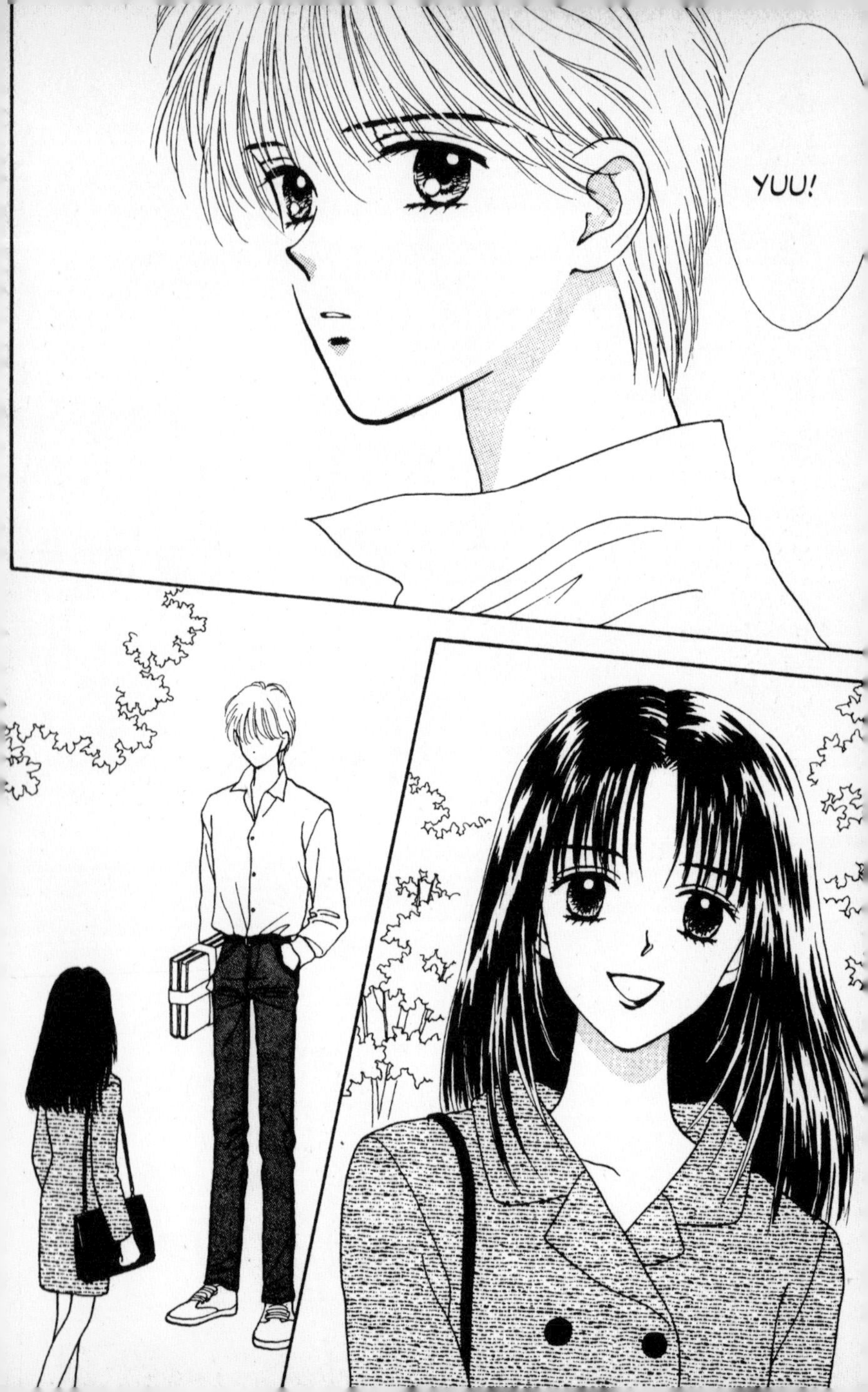
YUU!

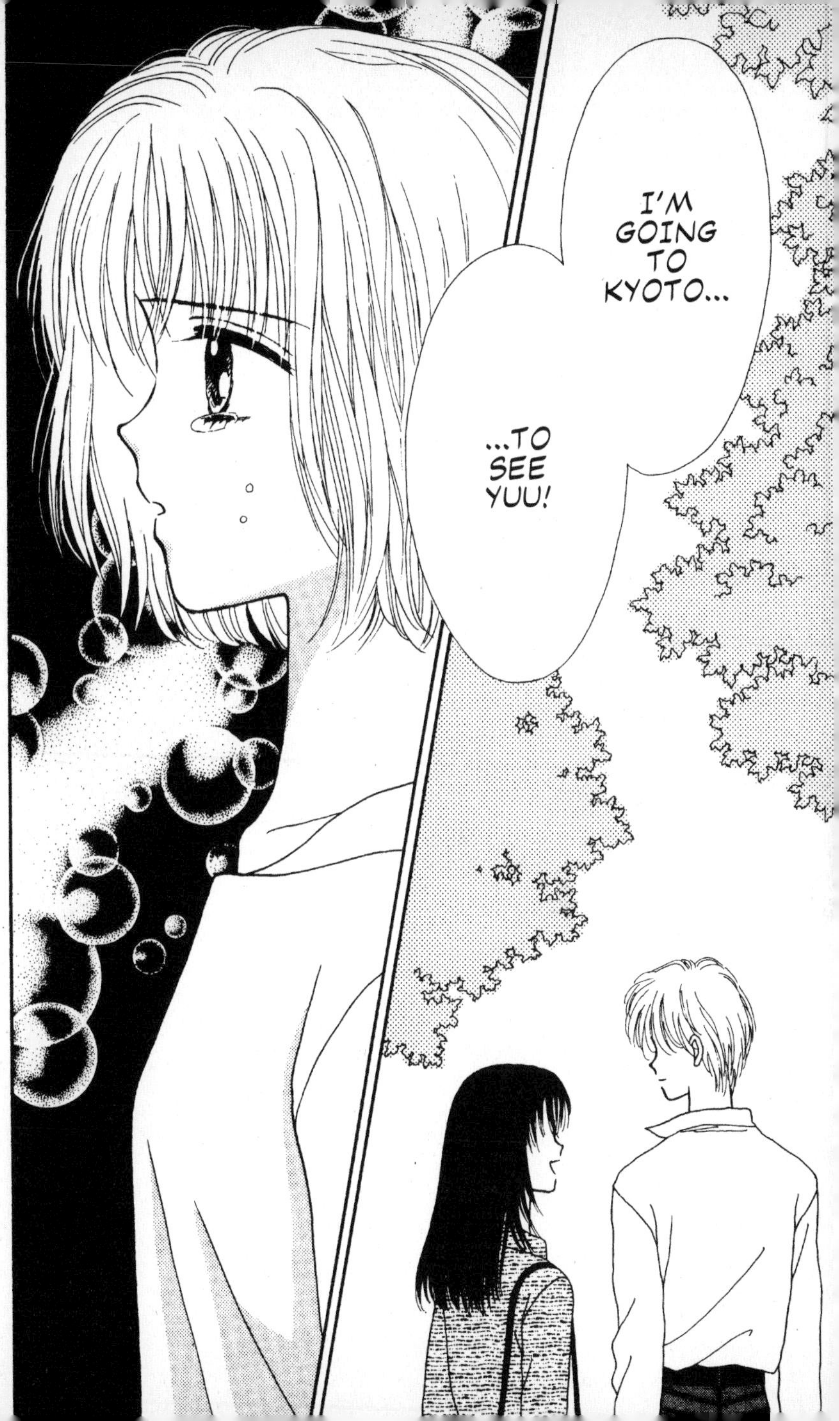
I'M GOING TO KYOTO...
...TO SEE YUU!

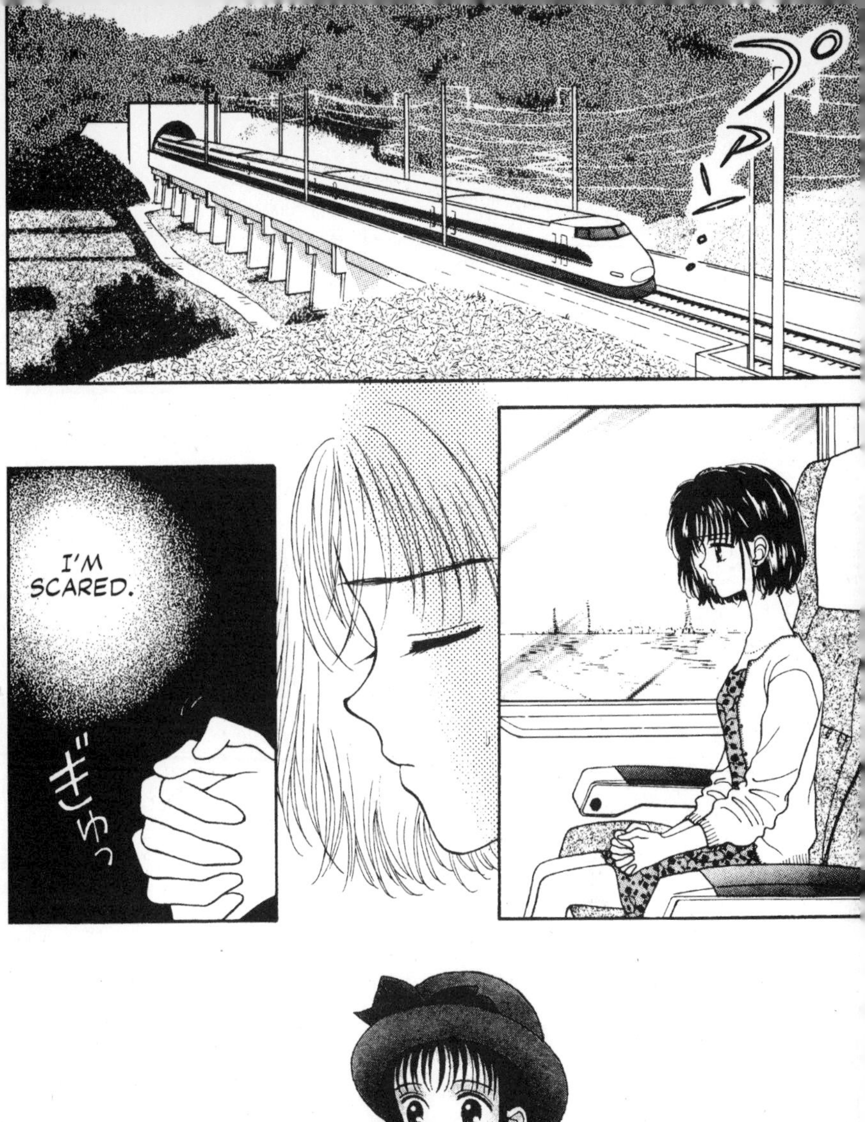
I'M SCARED.
ぎゅっ

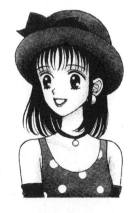

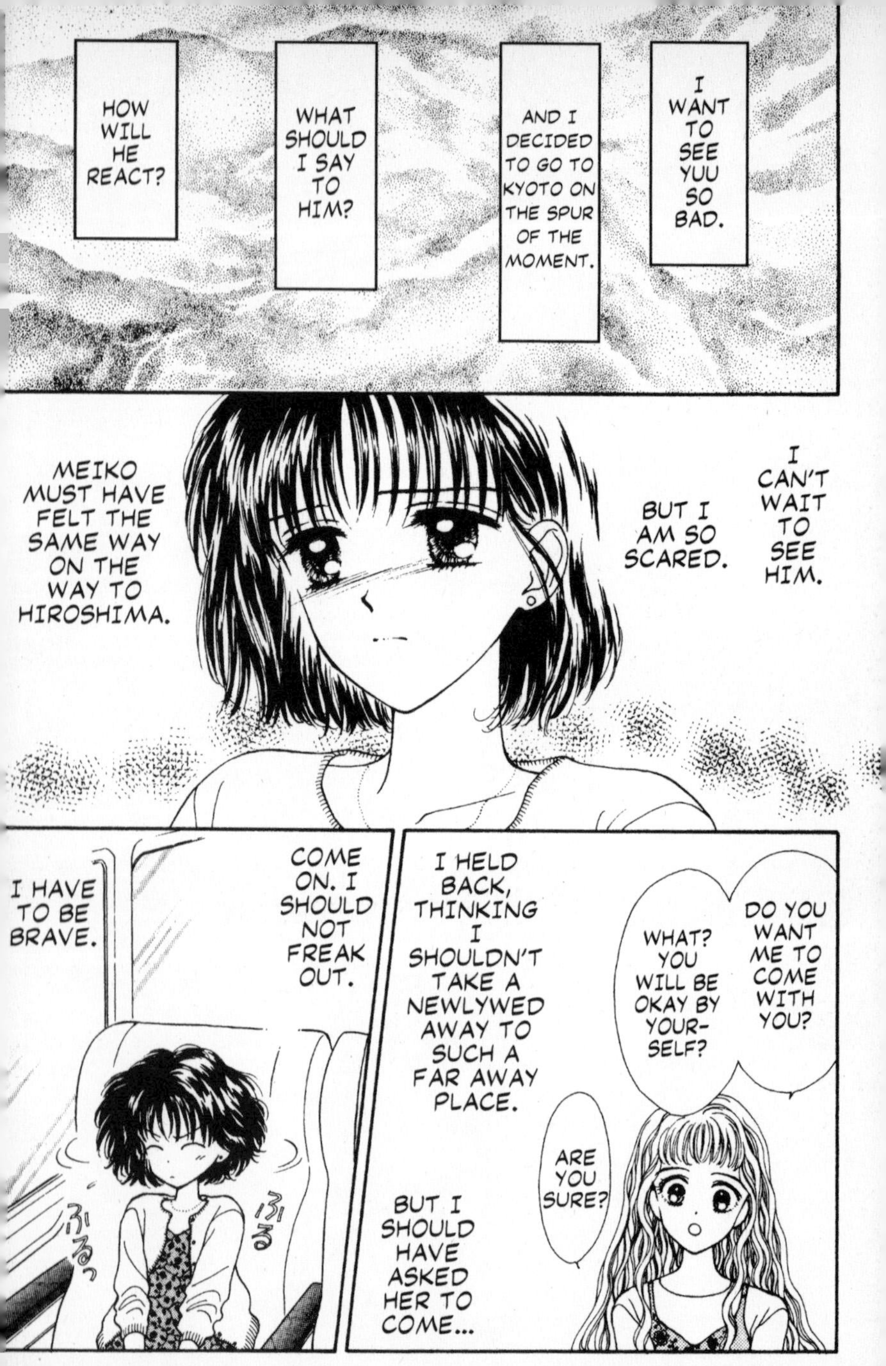
I WANT TO SEE YUU SO BAD.
AND I DECIDED TO GO TO KYOTO ON THE SPUR OF THE MOMENT.
WHAT SHOULD I SAY TO HIM?
HOW WILL HE REACT?
I CAN'T WAIT TO SEE HIM.
BUT I AM SO SCARED.
MEIKO MUST HAVE FELT THE SAME WAY ON THE WAY TO HIROSHIMA.
DO YOU WANT ME TO COME WITH YOU?
WHAT? YOU WILL BE OKAY BY YOUR-SELF?
I HELD BACK, THINKING I SHOULDN'T TAKE A NEWLYWED AWAY TO SUCH A FAR AWAY PLACE.
ARE YOU SURE?
BUT I SHOULD HAVE ASKED HER TO COME...
COME ON. I SHOULD NOT FREAK OUT.
I HAVE TO BE BRAVE.
ふる
ふるっ

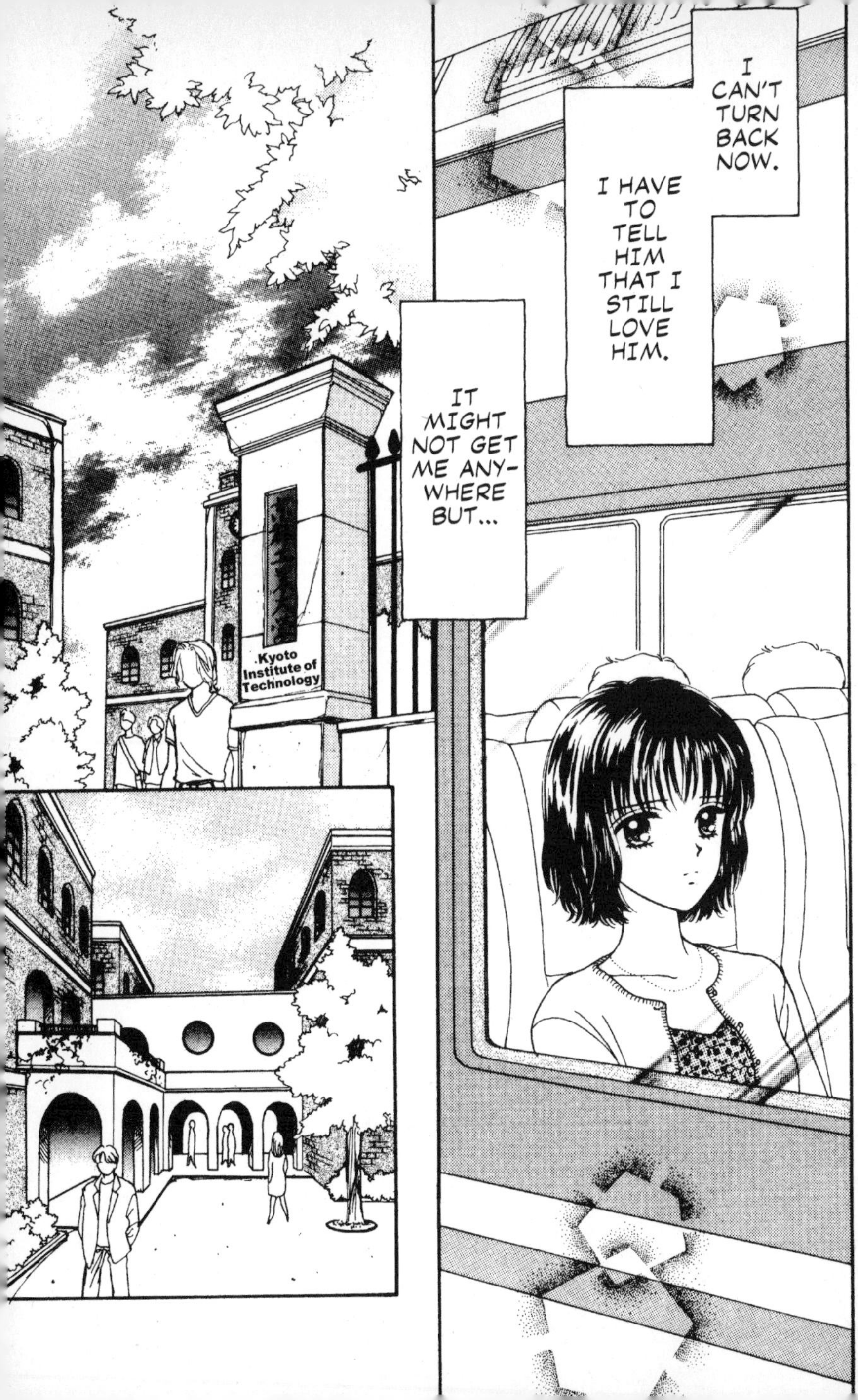
I CAN'T TURN BACK NOW.
I HAVE TO TELL HIM THAT I STILL LOVE HIM.
IT MIGHT NOT GET ME ANY-WHERE BUT...
Kyoto Institute of Technology

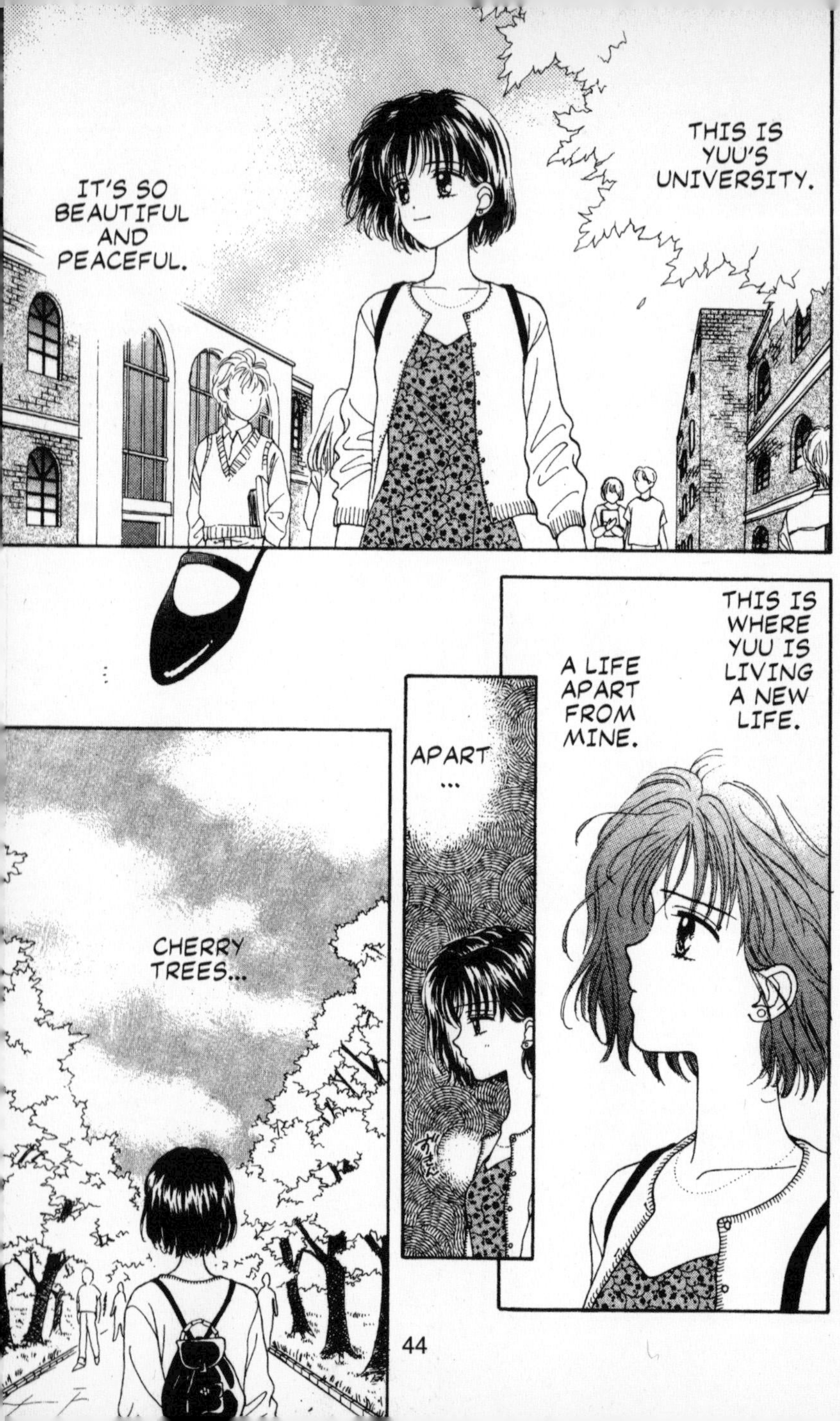
THIS IS YUU'S UNIVERSITY.
IT'S SO BEAUTIFUL AND PEACEFUL.
...
THIS IS WHERE YUU IS LIVING A NEW LIFE.
A LIFE APART FROM MINE.
APART ...
CHERRY TREES...

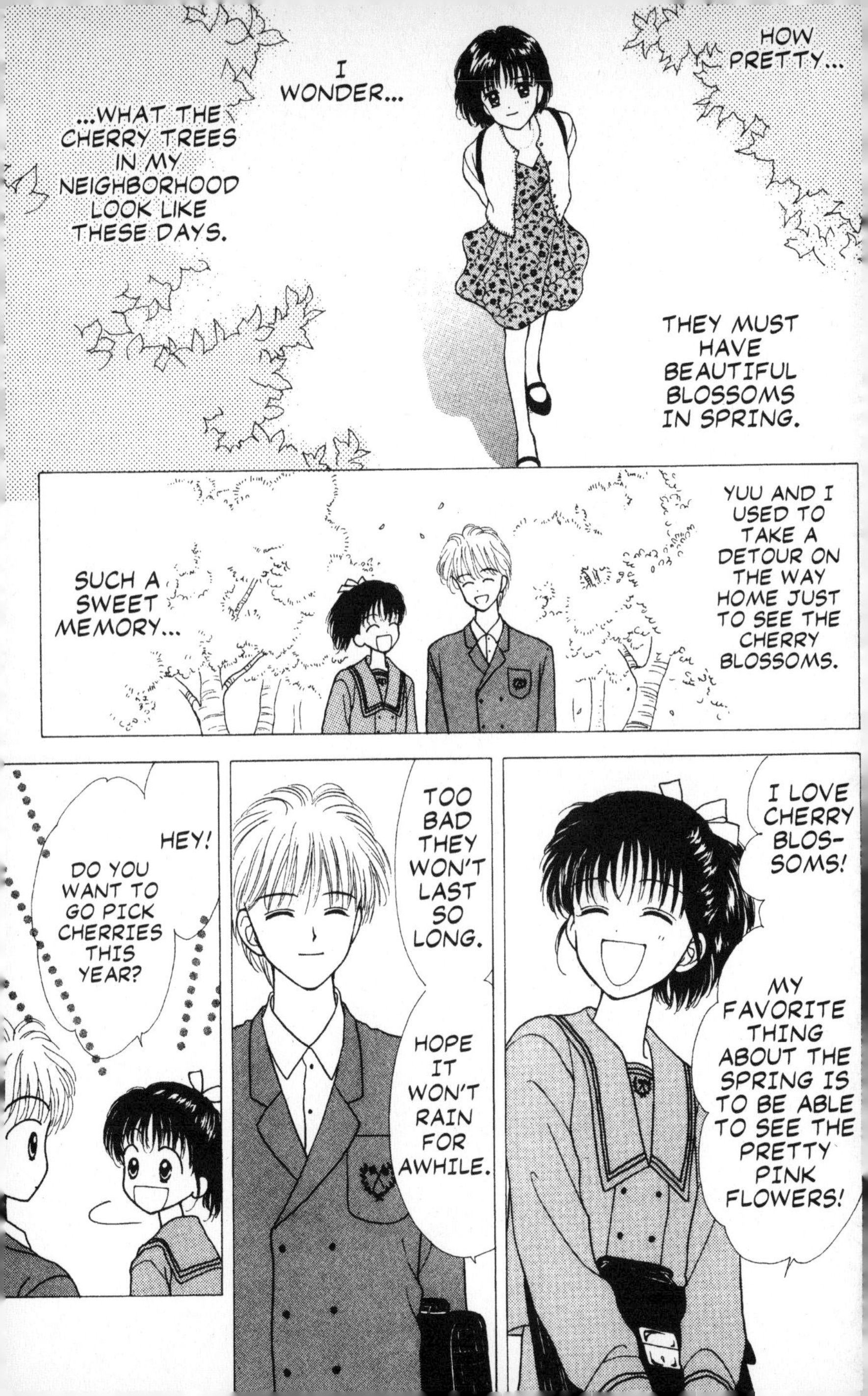
HOW PRETTY...
I WONDER...
...WHAT THE CHERRY TREES IN MY NEIGHBORHOOD LOOK LIKE THESE DAYS.
THEY MUST HAVE BEAUTIFUL BLOSSOMS IN SPRING.
YUU AND I USED TO TAKE A DETOUR ON THE WAY HOME JUST TO SEE THE CHERRY BLOSSOMS.
SUCH A SWEET MEMORY...
I LOVE CHERRY BLOS-SOMS!
MY FAVORITE THING ABOUT THE SPRING IS TO BE ABLE TO SEE THE PRETTY PINK FLOWERS!
TOO BAD THEY WON'T LAST SO LONG.
HOPE IT WON'T RAIN FOR AWHILE.
HEY!
DO YOU WANT TO GO PICK CHERRIES THIS YEAR?

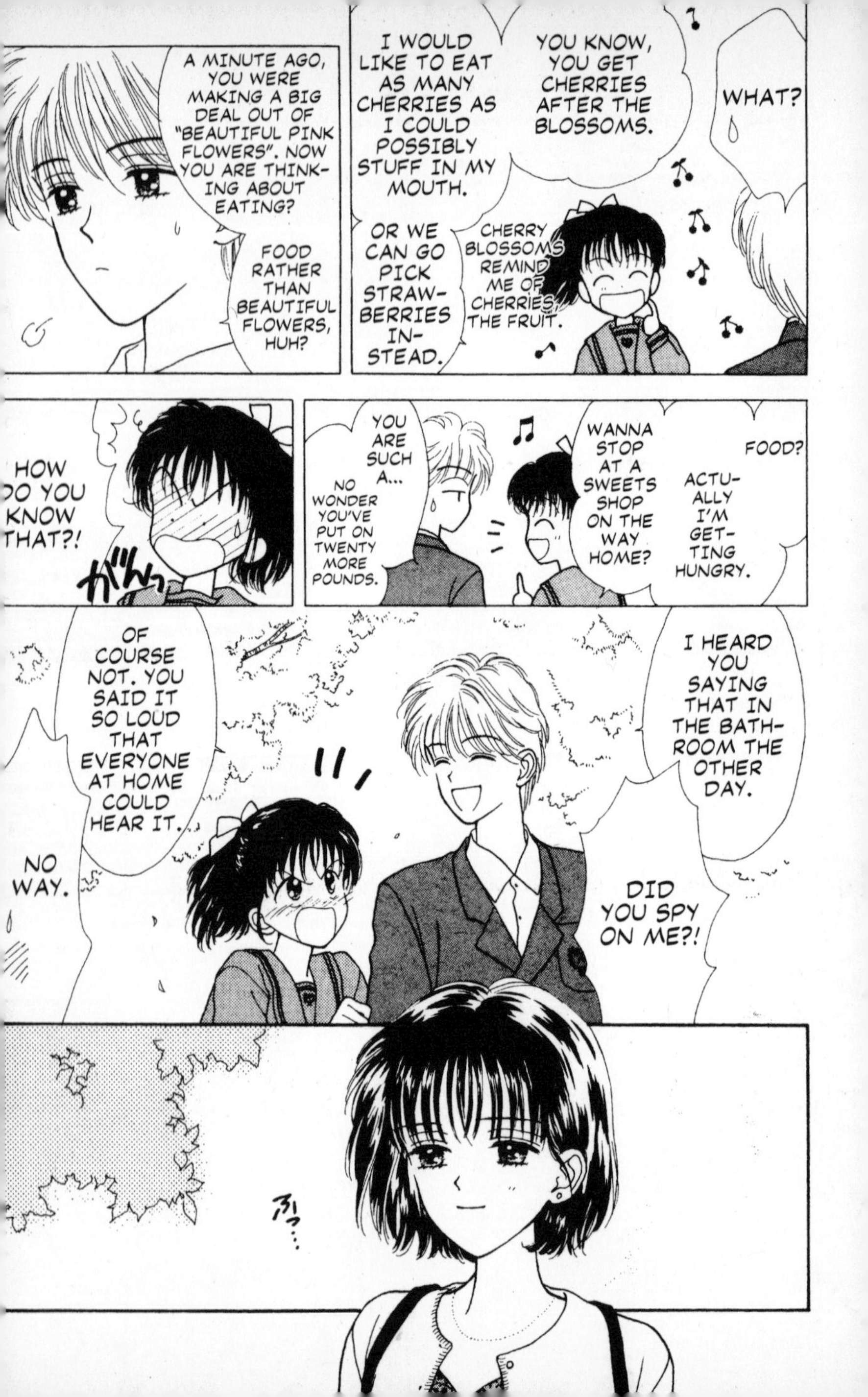
WHAT?
YOU KNOW, YOU GET CHERRIES AFTER THE BLOSSOMS.
I WOULD LIKE TO EAT AS MANY CHERRIES AS I COULD POSSIBLY STUFF IN MY MOUTH.
CHERRY BLOSSOMS REMIND ME OF CHERRIES, THE FRUIT.
OR WE CAN GO PICK STRAWBERRIES INSTEAD.
A MINUTE AGO, YOU WERE MAKING A BIG DEAL OUT OF "BEAUTIFUL PINK FLOWERS". NOW YOU ARE THINKING ABOUT EATING?
FOOD RATHER THAN BEAUTIFUL FLOWERS, HUH?
FOOD?
ACTUALLY I'M GETTING HUNGRY.
WANNA STOP AT A SWEETS SHOP ON THE WAY HOME?
YOU ARE SUCH A...
NO WONDER YOU'VE PUT ON TWENTY MORE POUNDS.
HOW DO YOU KNOW THAT?!
がんっ
I HEARD YOU SAYING THAT IN THE BATHROOM THE OTHER DAY.
DID YOU SPY ON ME?!
OF COURSE NOT. YOU SAID IT SO LOUD THAT EVERYONE AT HOME COULD HEAR IT.
NO WAY.
ぷっ…

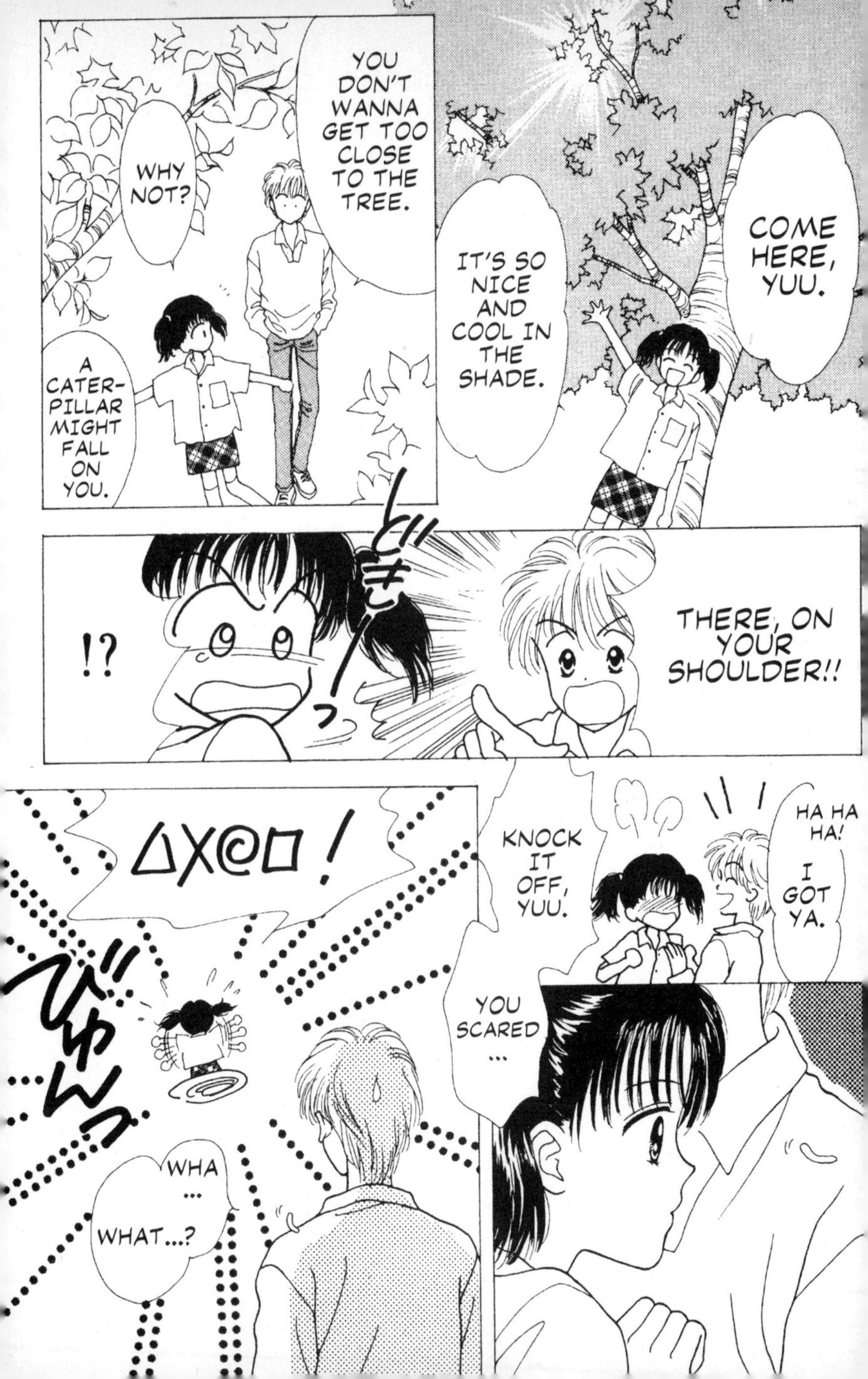
COME HERE, YUU.
IT'S SO NICE AND COOL IN THE SHADE.
YOU DON'T WANNA GET TOO CLOSE TO THE TREE.
WHY NOT?
A CATER-PILLAR MIGHT FALL ON YOU.
THERE, ON YOUR SHOULDER!!
どきっ
!?
HA HA HA! I GOT YA.
KNOCK IT OFF, YUU.
YOU SCARED ...
△X@□!
びゅんっ
WHA ... WHAT...?

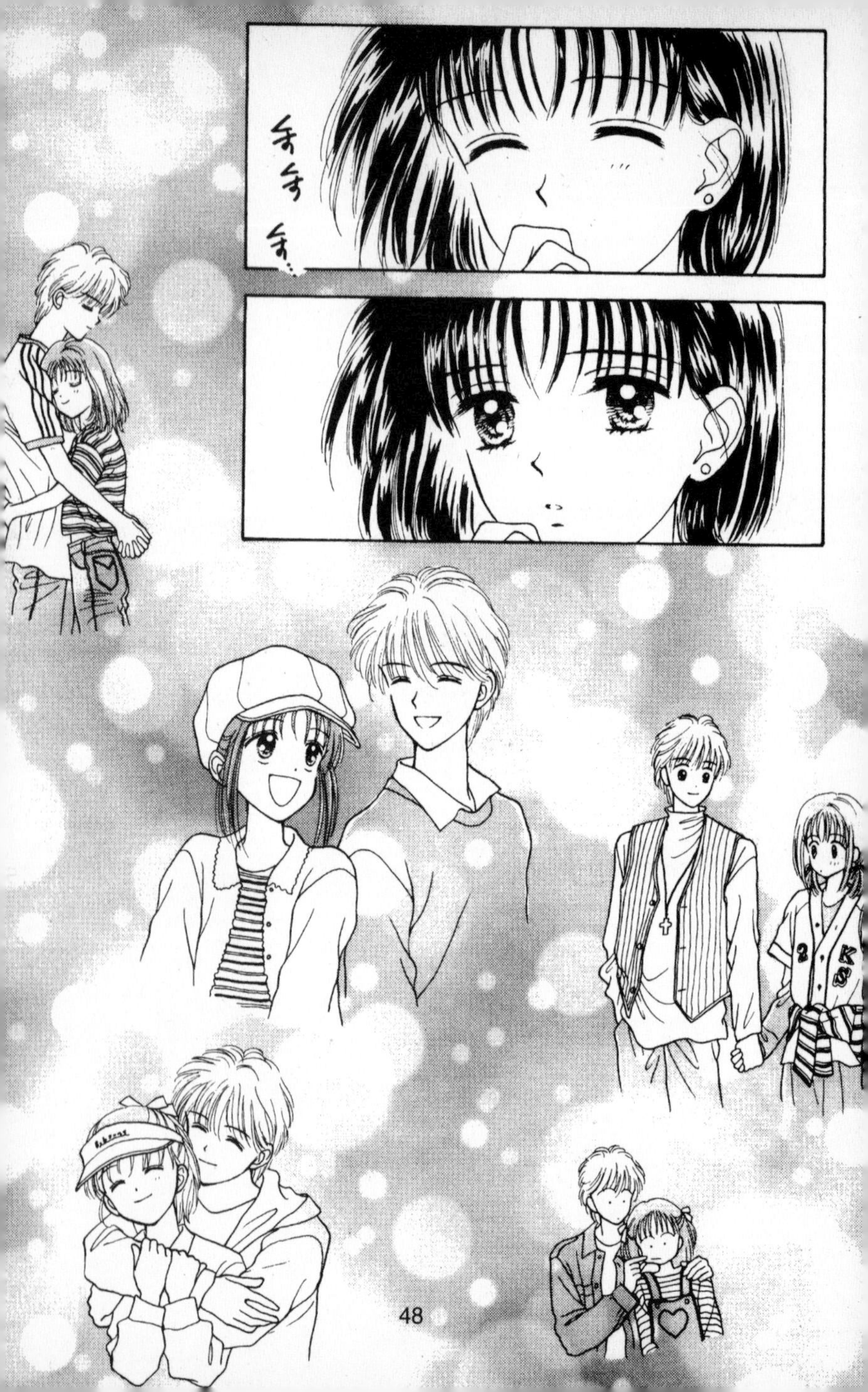

FREE TALK ③

Continuing the original story after the truth about Yuu's father has come out would be a bad idea. I had to bring the original story to an end before the last episode on TV. But as long as the anime is on TV, the story in the magazine had to continue. It needs both the anime and the original together to create the "media mix" effect, they say. The only choice was to bring both the anime and the manga versions to an end in the same month. I got a lot of letters saying, "It's quite disappointing that both the anime and the manga will be over at the same time." Now you all know that I didn't have much of a choice. Do you wonder why it was so hard to delay the finale for the convenience of the anime schedule? Because the anime staff was not sure exactly when the last episode of the anime should be. The anime was supposed to last only a year, but ended up being extended for a longer period. They were not sure how much longer it would run, though they were talking maybe three or six months.

(To be continued in Free Talk 4)

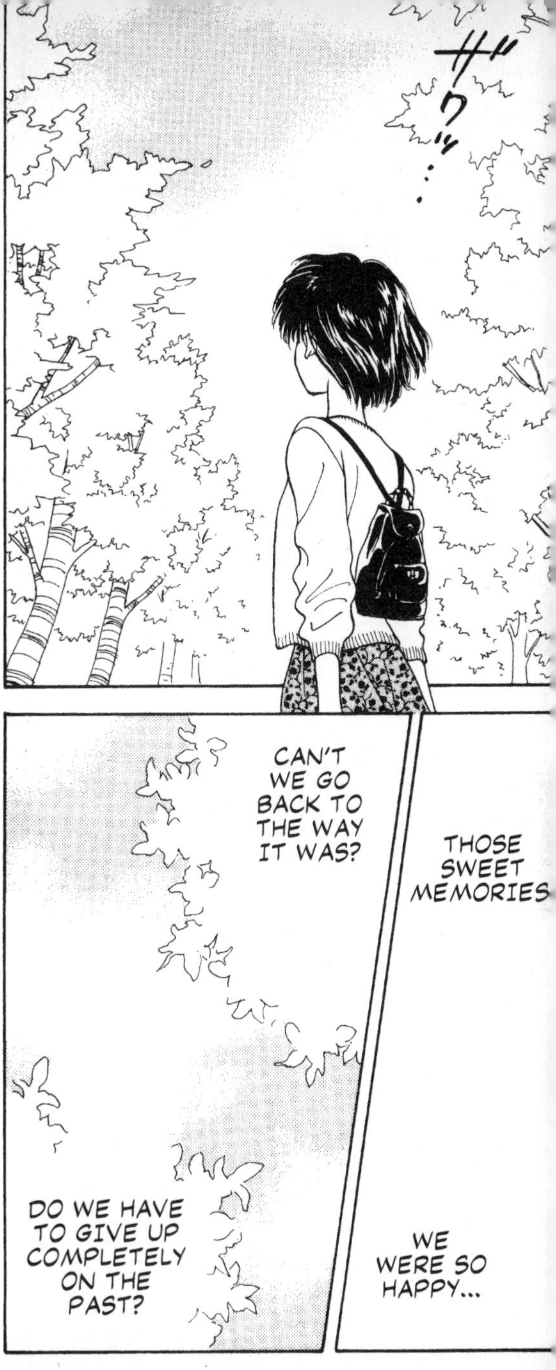
ザワッ…
THOSE SWEET MEMORIES
WE WERE SO HAPPY...
CAN'T WE GO BACK TO THE WAY IT WAS?
DO WE HAVE TO GIVE UP COMPLETELY ON THE PAST?

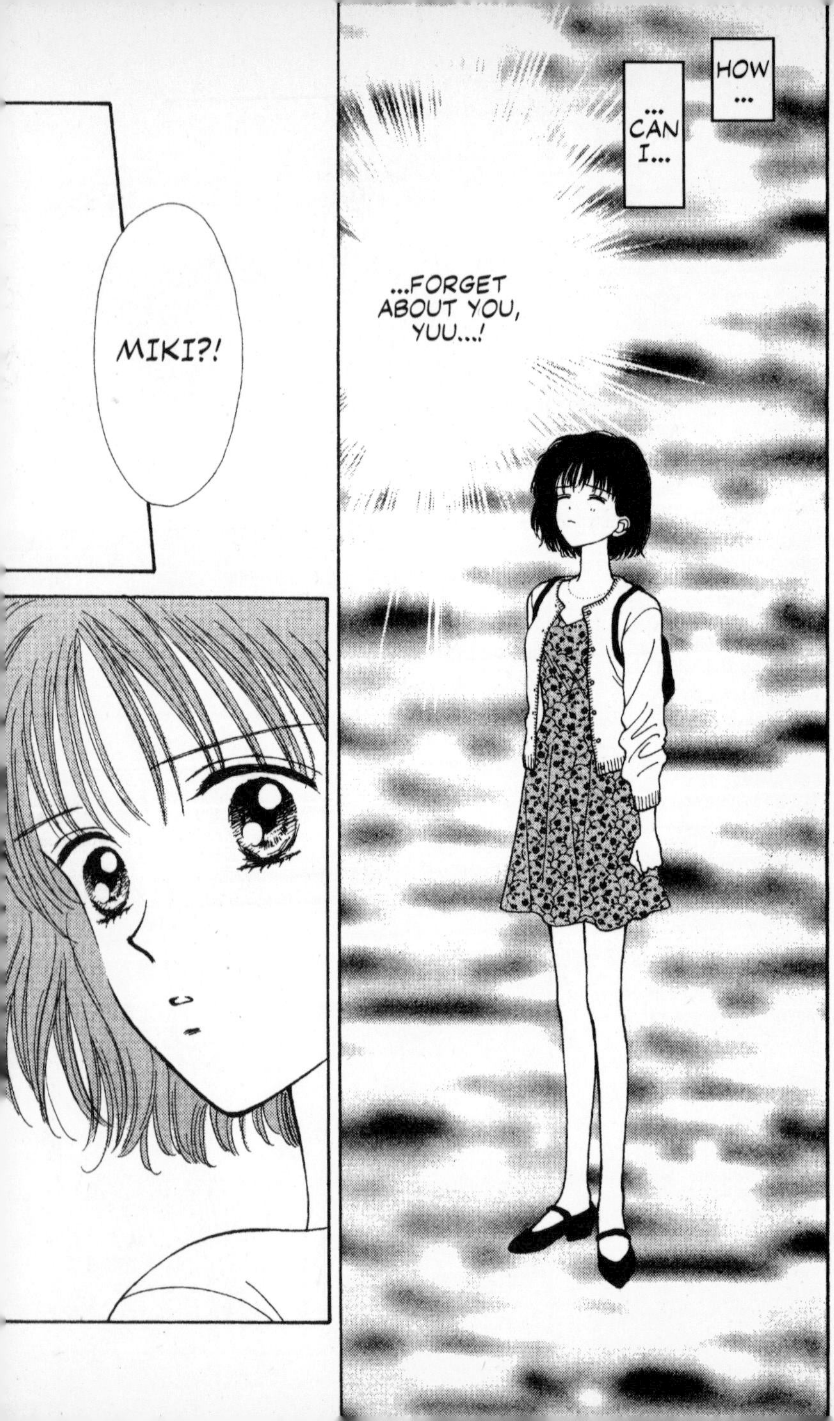
HOW ...
... CAN I...
...FORGET ABOUT YOU, YUU...!
MIKI?!

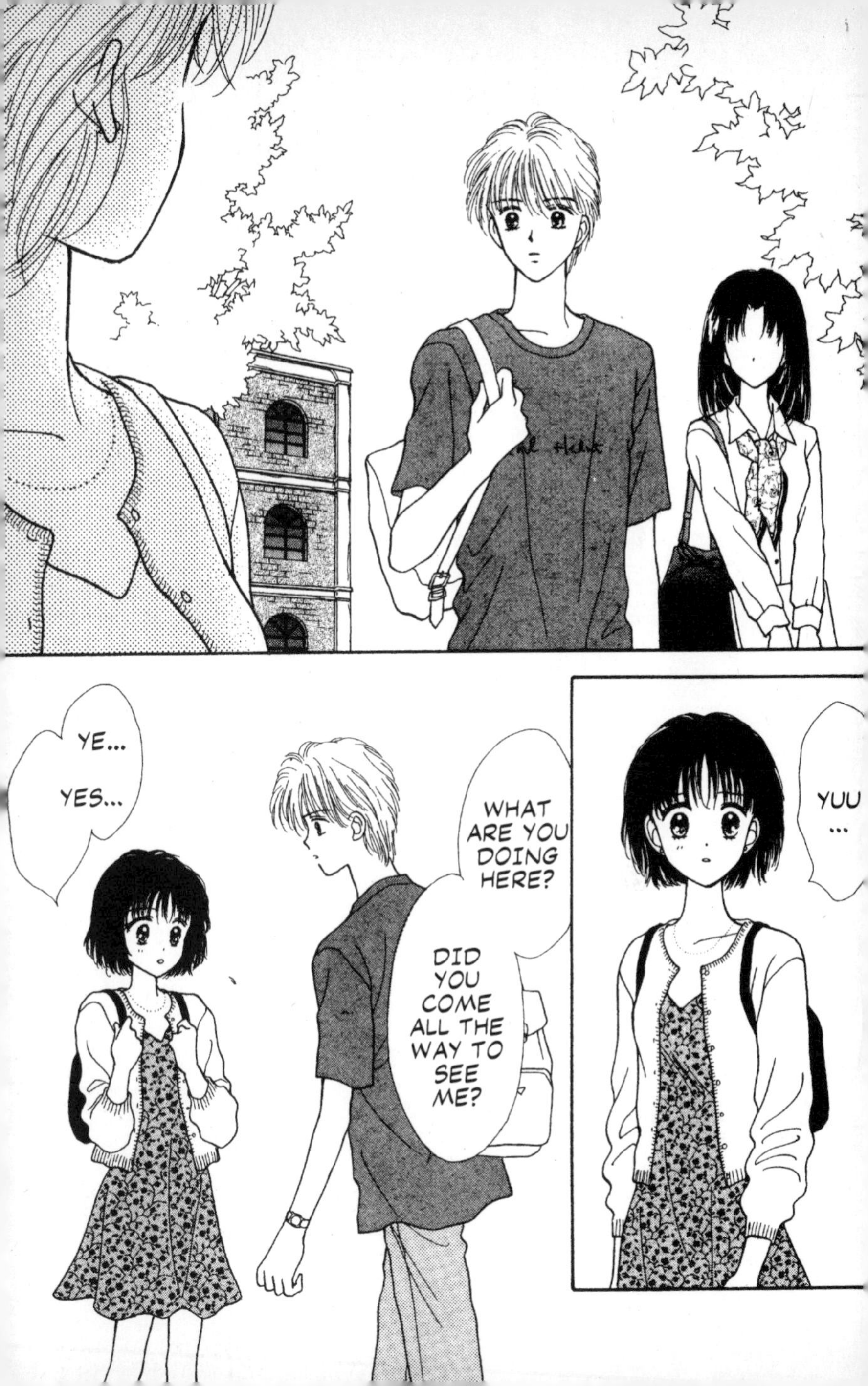
YUU ...
WHAT ARE YOU DOING HERE?
DID YOU COME ALL THE WAY TO SEE ME?
YE... YES...

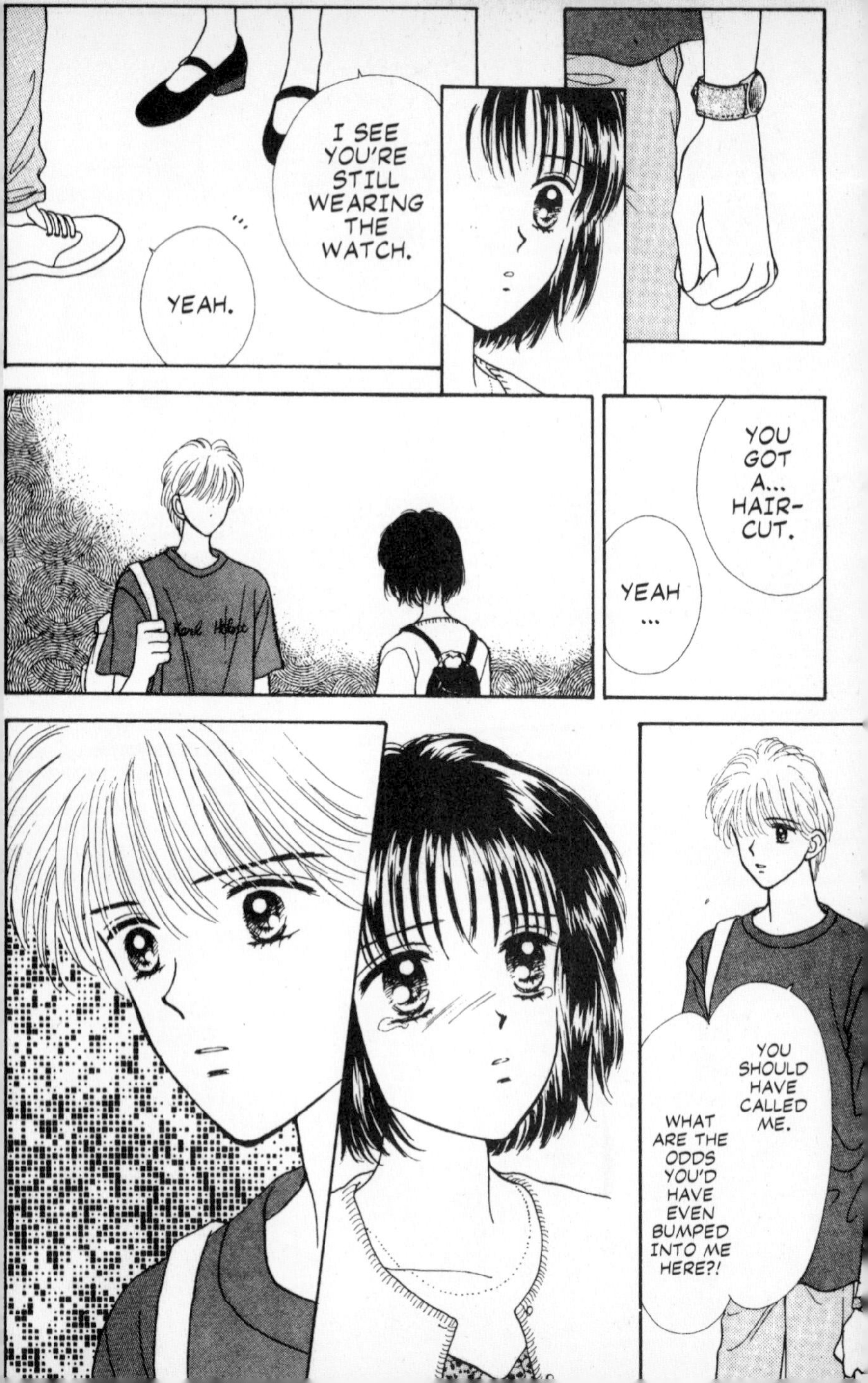
I SEE YOU'RE STILL WEARING THE WATCH.
YEAH.
YOU GOT A... HAIR-CUT.
YEAH ...
YOU SHOULD HAVE CALLED ME.
WHAT ARE THE ODDS YOU'D HAVE EVEN BUMPED INTO ME HERE?!

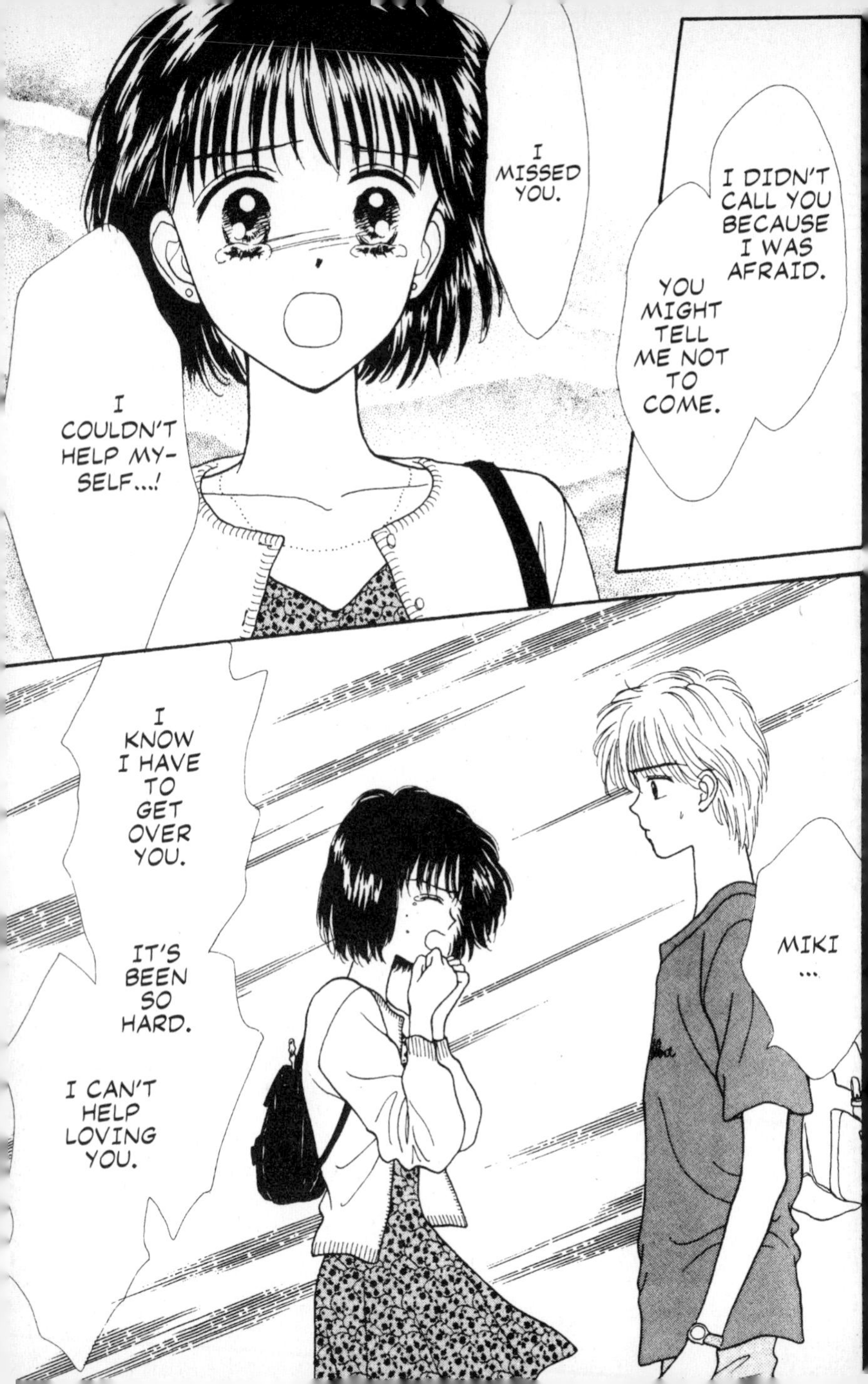
I DIDN'T CALL YOU BECAUSE I WAS AFRAID.
YOU MIGHT TELL ME NOT TO COME.
I MISSED YOU.
I COULDN'T HELP MY-SELF...!
I KNOW I HAVE TO GET OVER YOU.
IT'S BEEN SO HARD.
I CAN'T HELP LOVING YOU.
MIKI ...

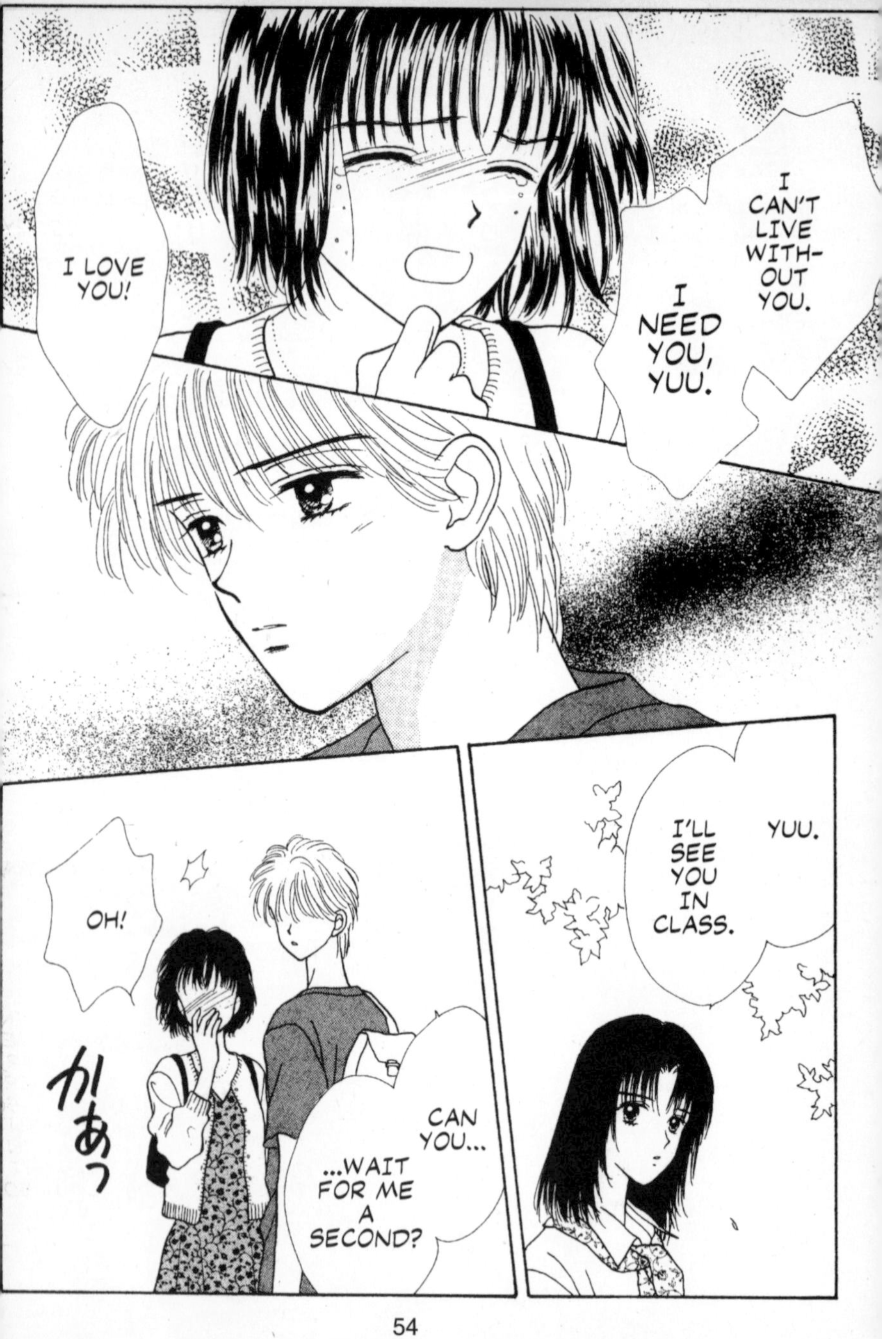
I CAN'T LIVE WITH-OUT YOU.
I NEED YOU, YUU.
I LOVE YOU!
YUU.
I'LL SEE YOU IN CLASS.
OH!
かあっ
CAN YOU...
...WAIT FOR ME A SECOND?

FREE TALK ④

It's a good thing that the anime was so popular that they decided to extend it. But I really needed to know how long the anime would last in order to figure out how extended the original story should be. A more talented writer wouldn't have had a problem coming up with great ideas but it was hard for someone who's a bit inexperienced like me. Anyway, it was quite a relief that I could finish the original story about the same time as the anime (sigh of relief). That's the only thing that truly bothered me but I was a bit stressed out about who in the story goes in the anime. (Laugh!) There were some personality differences in the characters between the original and the anime. I tried to convince myself that it is only natural that different people would make even the same characters differently.

(To be Continued in Free Talk 5)

SHE'S ... ...NOT JUST A FRIEND.

I'M SORRY ...

I DIDN'T KNOW YOU WERE WITH A FRIEND.

THIS IS SAHO TAKAYAMA

WE ARE IN THE SAME SEMINAR TOGETHER WE HAVE SO MUCH IN COMMON AND GET ALONG SO WELL.

SHE'S MY GIRLFRIEND.

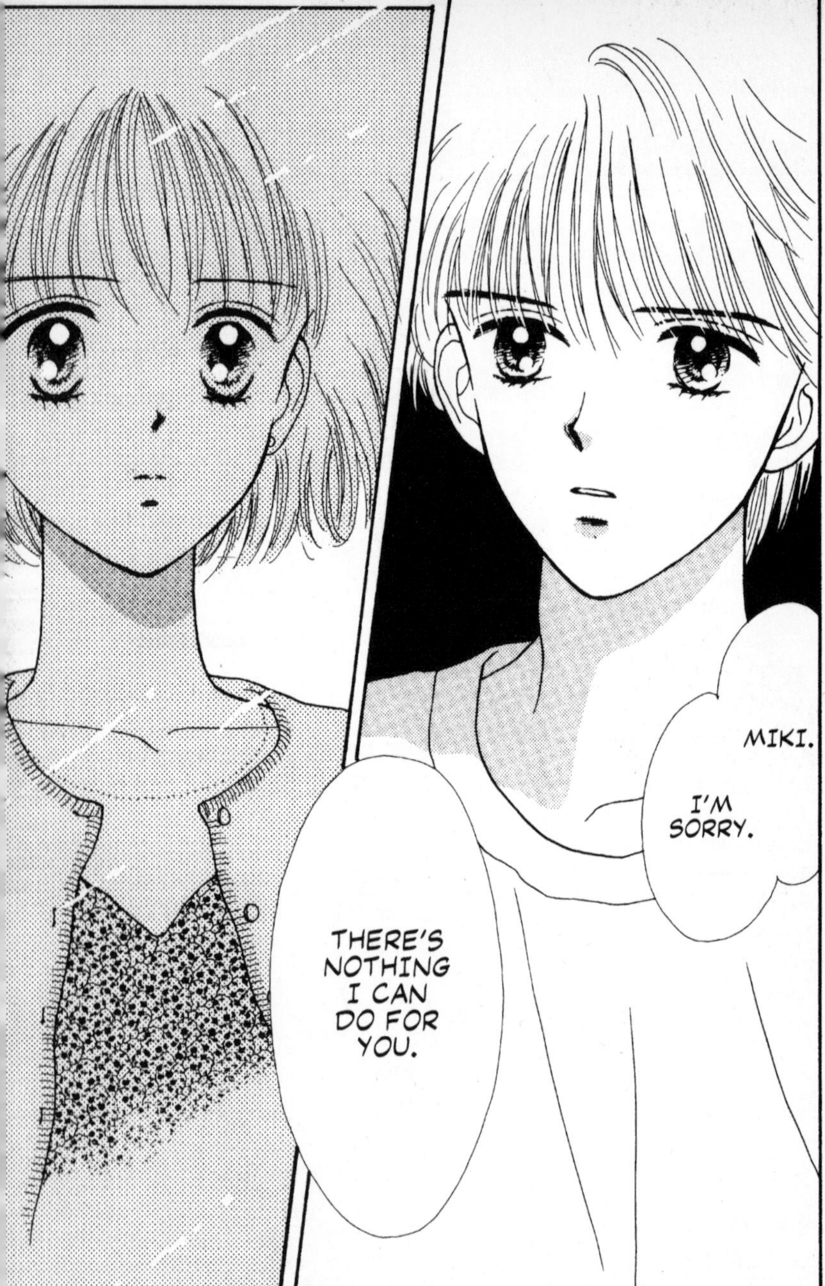
MIKI.
I'M SORRY.
THERE'S NOTHING I CAN DO FOR YOU.

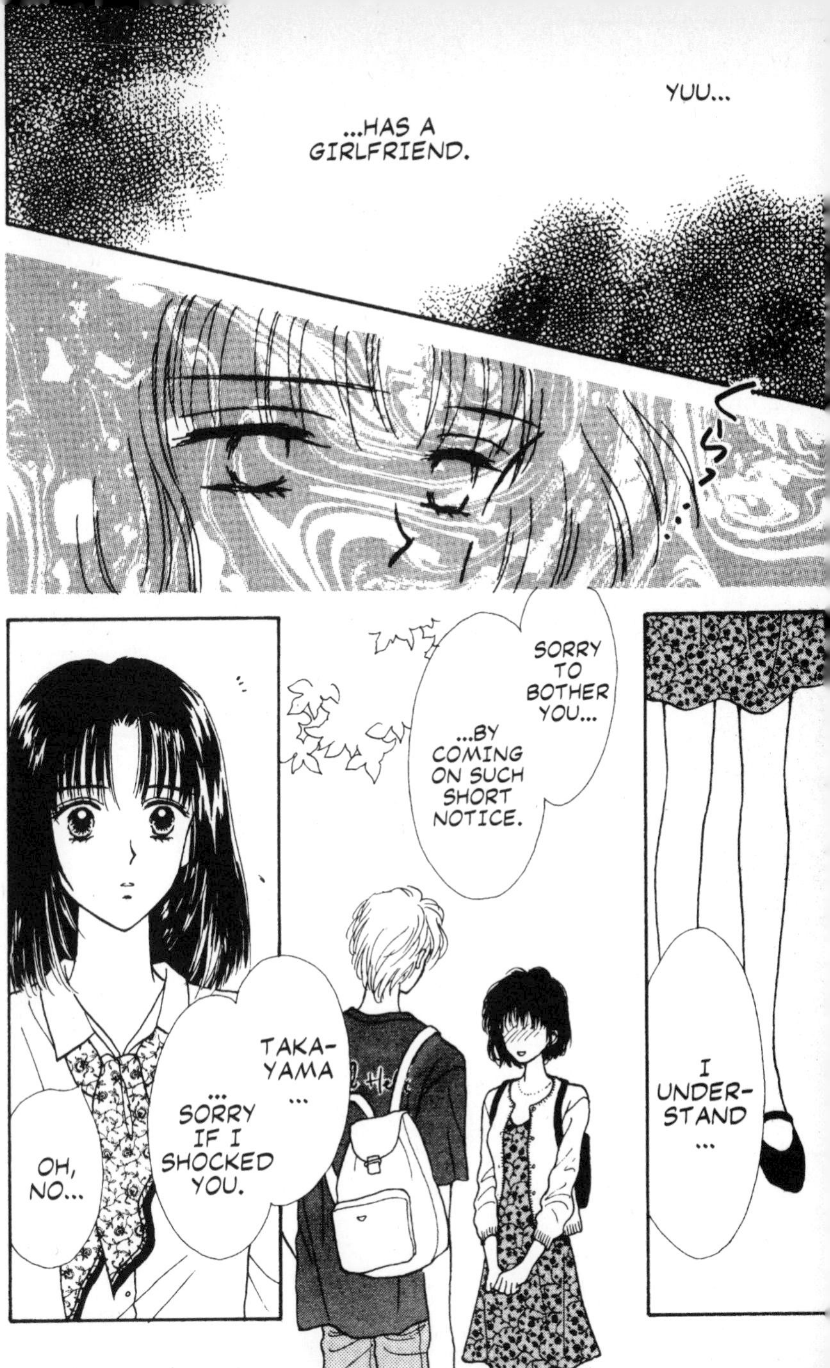
YUU...
...HAS A GIRLFRIEND.
I UNDER-STAND...
SORRY TO BOTHER YOU...
...BY COMING ON SUCH SHORT NOTICE.
TAKA-YAMA... ...SORRY IF I SHOCKED YOU.
OH, NO...

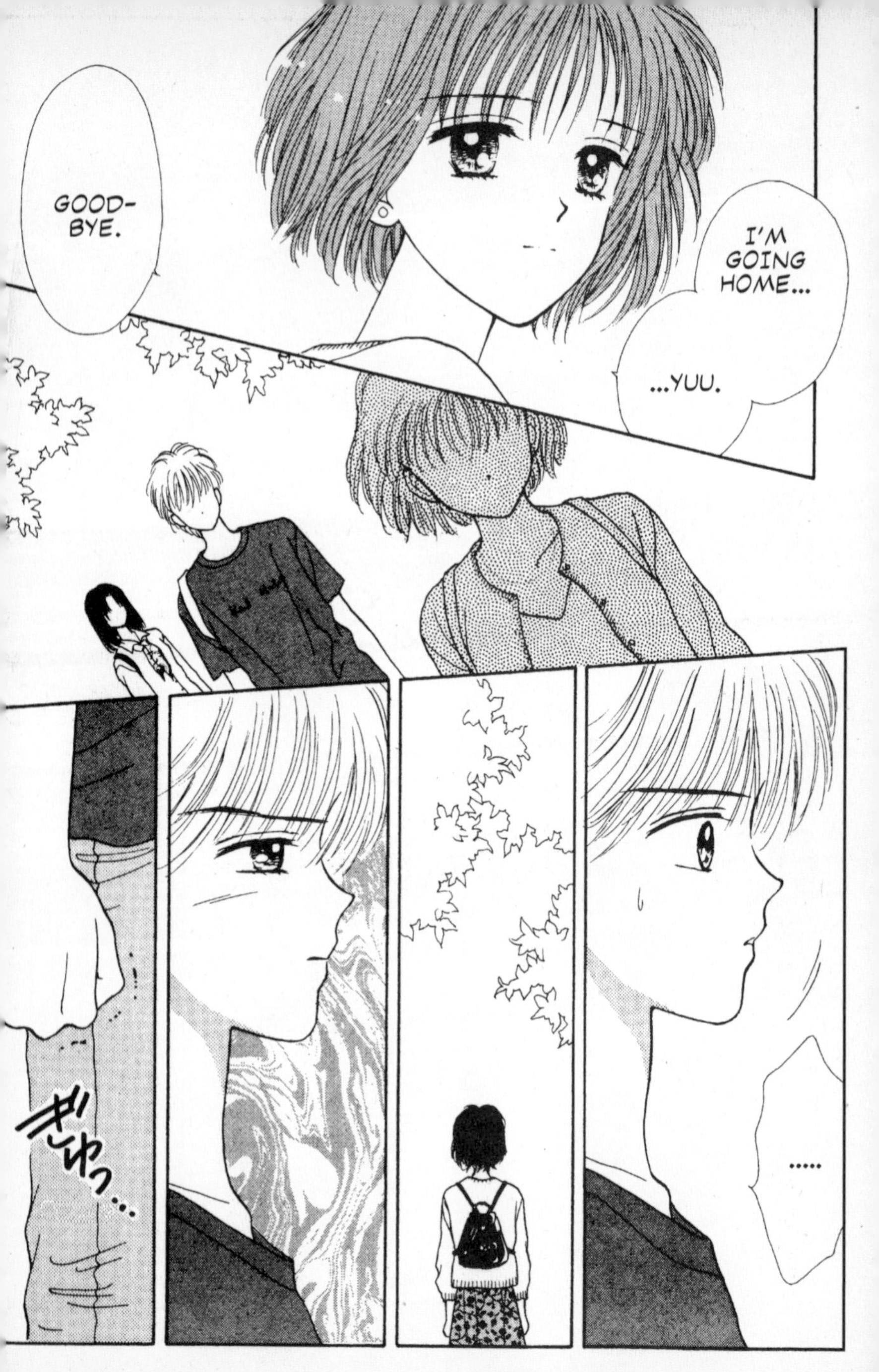
I'M GOING HOME...
...YUU.
GOOD-BYE.
.....
ぎゅっ...

FREE TALK ⑤

But there are some occasions that I absolutely hated the way the anime version went. I would like to take this opportunity to tell you what I really felt about the anime. The thing I hated the most is that they emphasized kissing scenes so much! There are a lot more kissing scenes. (They even had those scenes with different combinations of people from the original story.) And those kissing scenes were quite long and the characters obsessively think back on them. It was just too much. I really hated the way they did it. When I talked to Touru Huruya, the voice of Nachan, about how I felt about all the kissing scenes, he laughed it off and said, "Without those kissing scenes, it won't be Marlamade Boy!" (LOL!) The first kiss between Miki and Yuu at the nurse's office lasted 12 seconds. I intended to make it just a brief flash. Although Yuu kisses Miki exclusively in the comic version, he is forcefully kissed by Arimi, Suzu, and Jenny in the anime.

(To be continued in Free Talk 6)

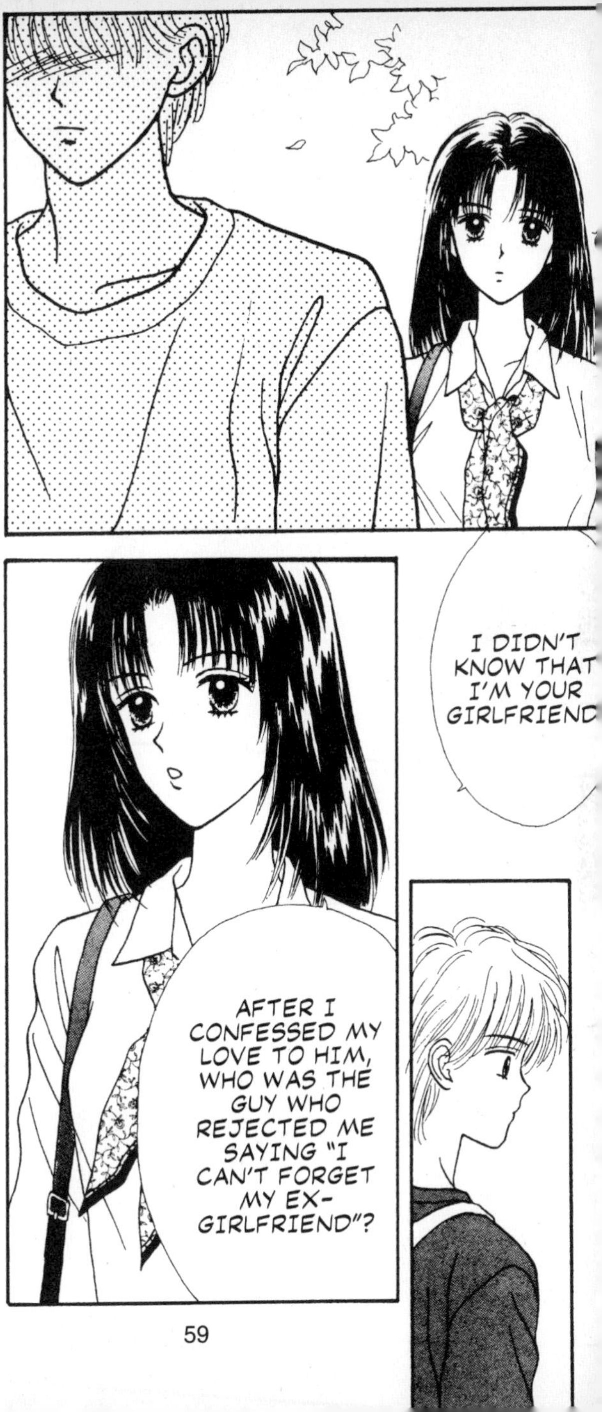
I DIDN'T KNOW THAT I'M YOUR GIRLFRIEND
AFTER I CONFESSED MY LOVE TO HIM, WHO WAS THE GUY WHO REJECTED ME SAYING "I CAN'T FORGET MY EX-GIRLFRIEND"?

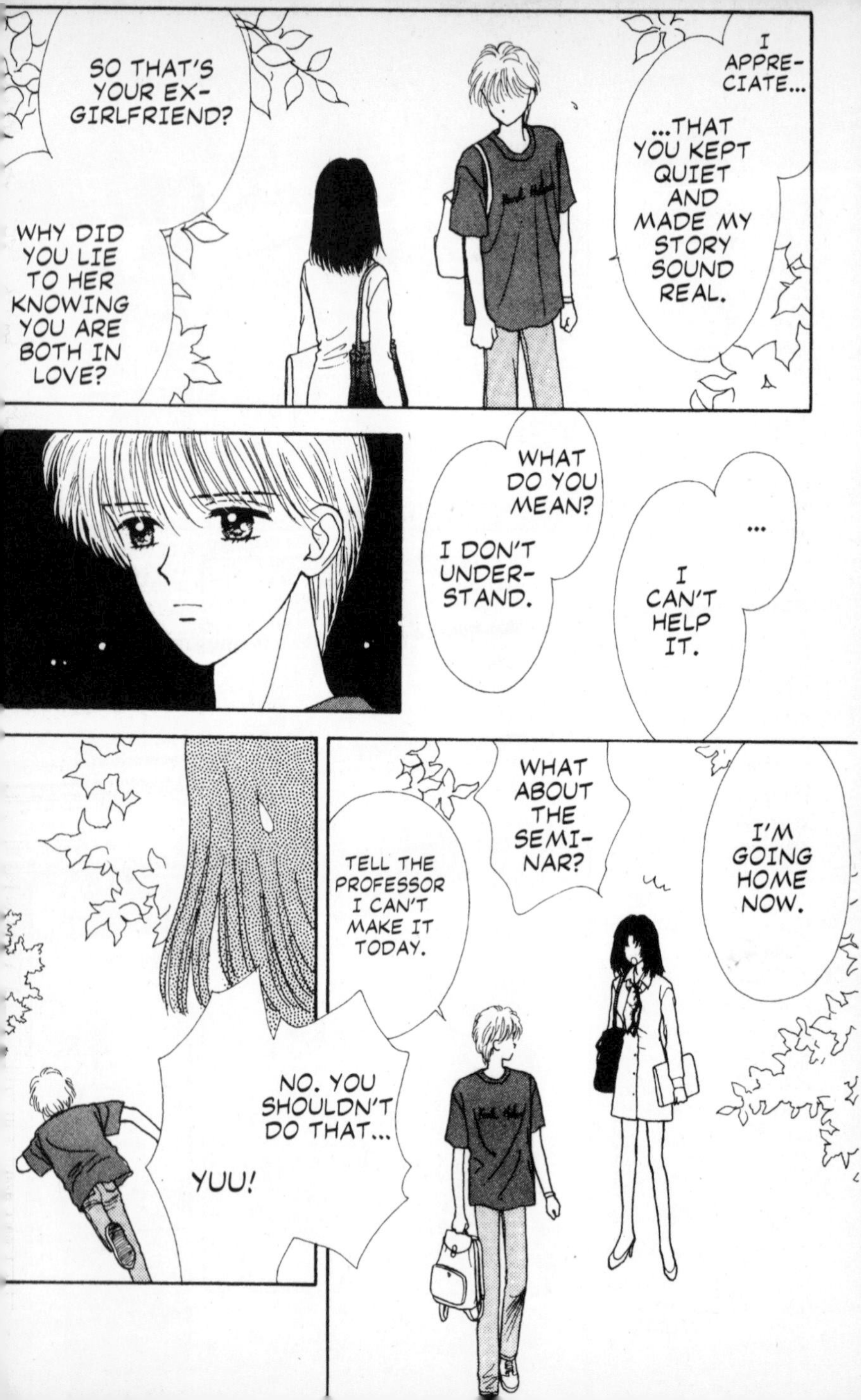
I APPRECIATE...
...THAT YOU KEPT QUIET AND MADE MY STORY SOUND REAL.
SO THAT'S YOUR EX-GIRLFRIEND?
WHY DID YOU LIE TO HER KNOWING YOU ARE BOTH IN LOVE?
...
I CAN'T HELP IT.
WHAT DO YOU MEAN?
I DON'T UNDERSTAND.
I'M GOING HOME NOW.
WHAT ABOUT THE SEMINAR?
TELL THE PROFESSOR I CAN'T MAKE IT TODAY.
NO. YOU SHOULDN'T DO THAT...
YUU!

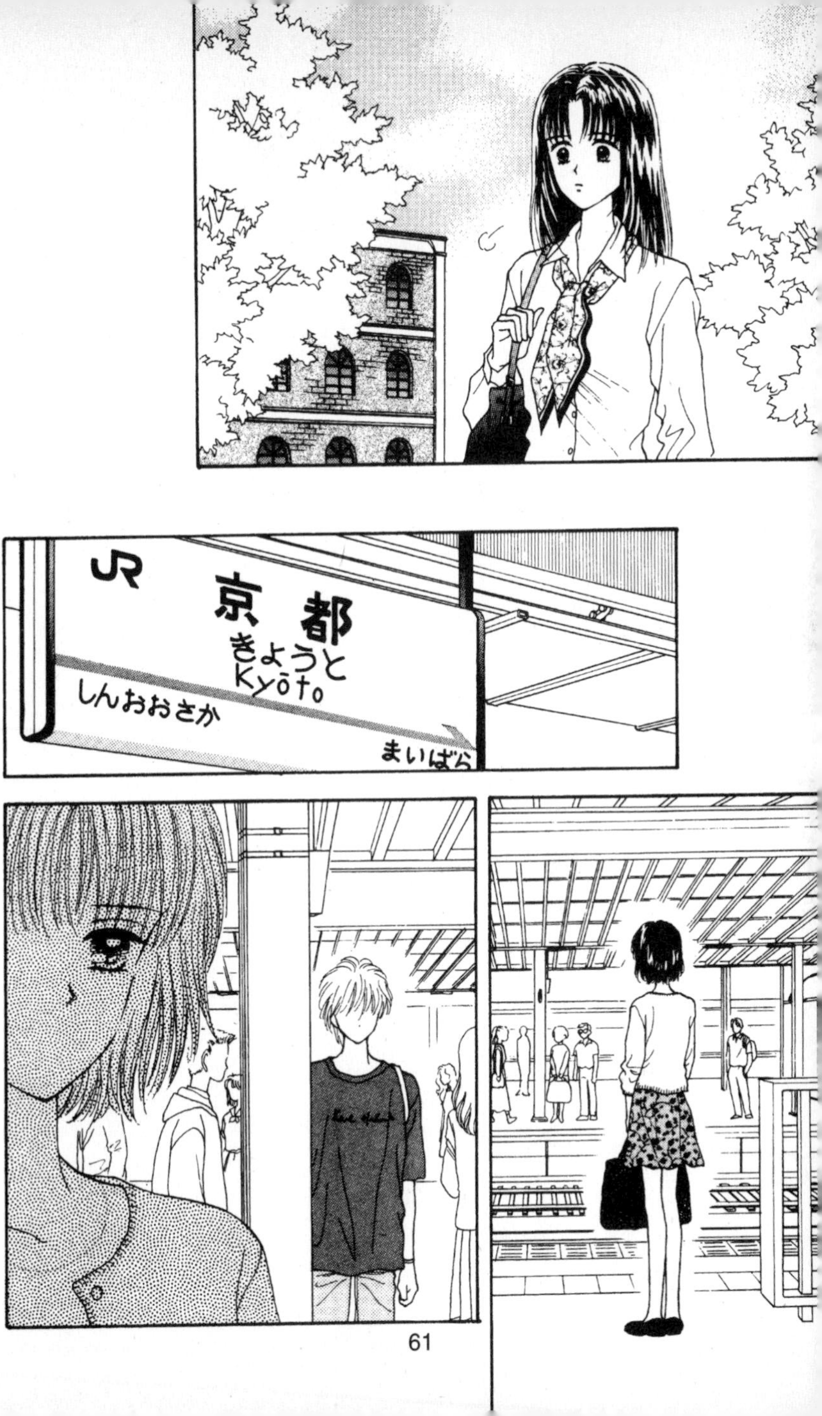
JR
京都
きょうと
Kyōto
しんおおさか
まいばら

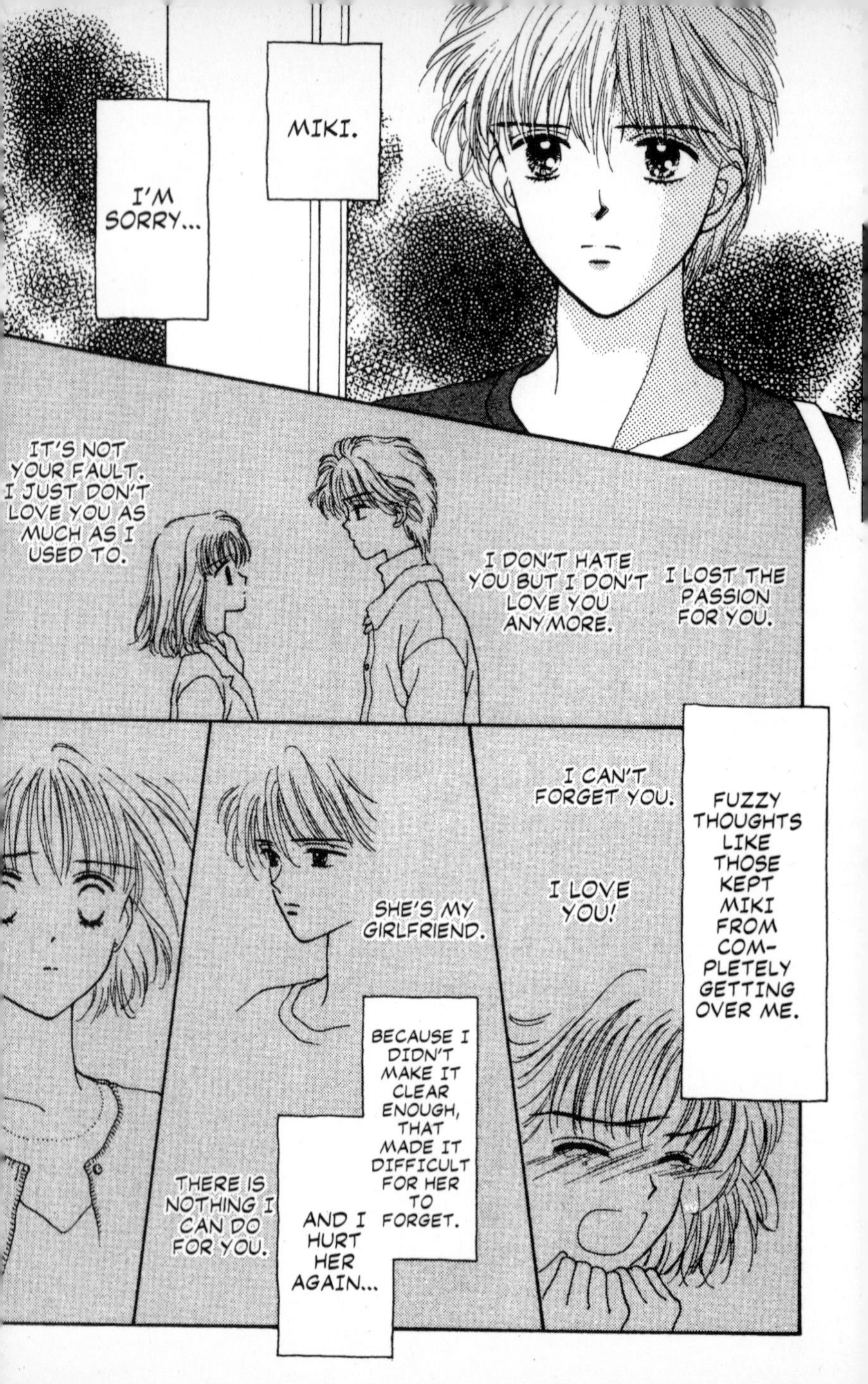
MIKI.
I'M SORRY...
I LOST THE PASSION FOR YOU.
I DON'T HATE YOU BUT I DON'T LOVE YOU ANYMORE.
IT'S NOT YOUR FAULT. I JUST DON'T LOVE YOU AS MUCH AS I USED TO.
FUZZY THOUGHTS LIKE THOSE KEPT MIKI FROM COM-PLETELY GETTING OVER ME.
I CAN'T FORGET YOU.
I LOVE YOU!
SHE'S MY GIRLFRIEND.
BECAUSE I DIDN'T MAKE IT CLEAR ENOUGH, THAT MADE IT DIFFICULT FOR HER TO FORGET.
AND I HURT HER AGAIN...
THERE IS NOTHING I CAN DO FOR YOU.

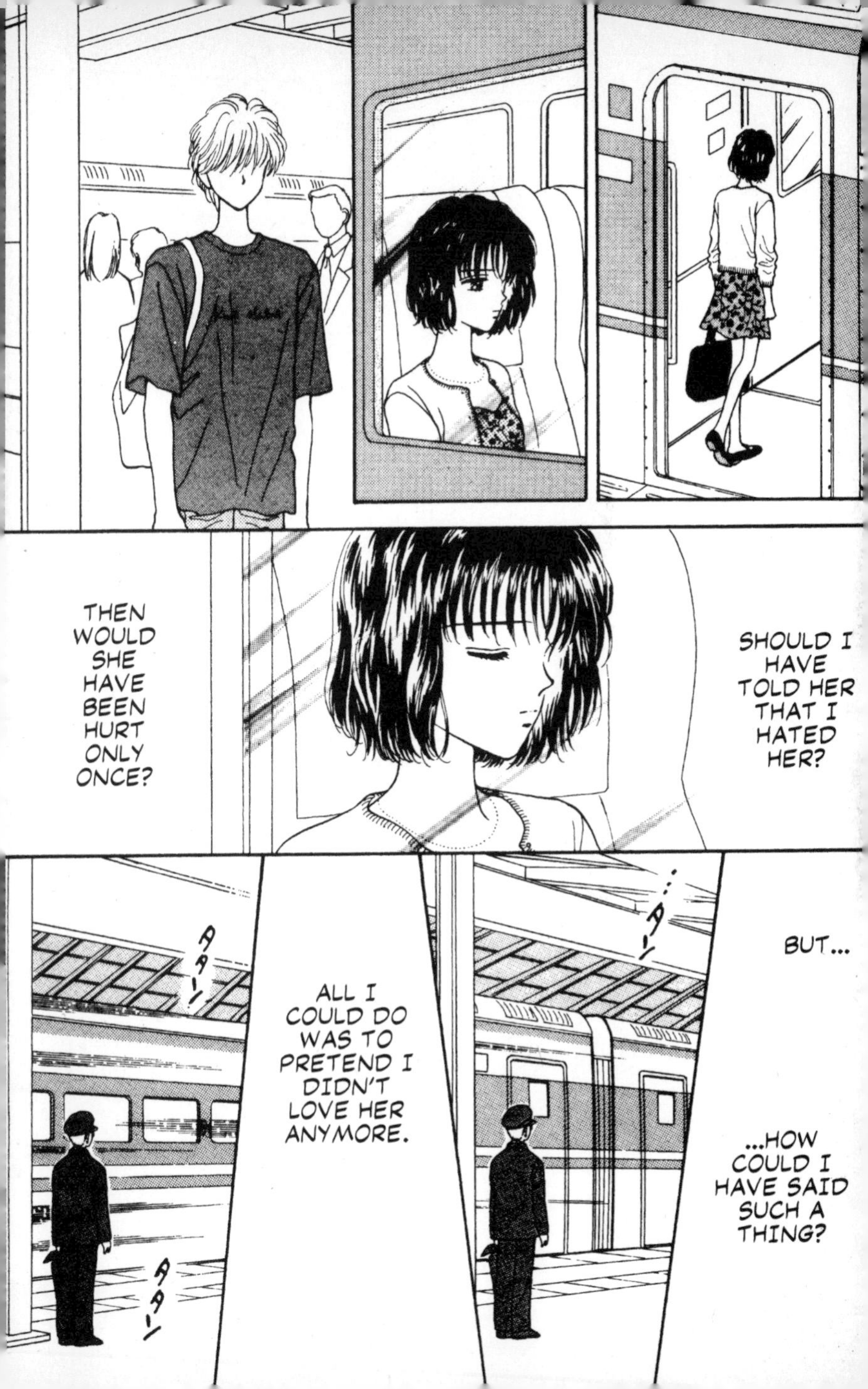
SHOULD I HAVE TOLD HER THAT I HATED HER?
THEN WOULD SHE HAVE BEEN HURT ONLY ONCE?
BUT...
...HOW COULD I HAVE SAID SUCH A THING?
...A!
ALL I COULD DO WAS TO PRETEND I DIDN'T LOVE HER ANYMORE.
AA!
AA!

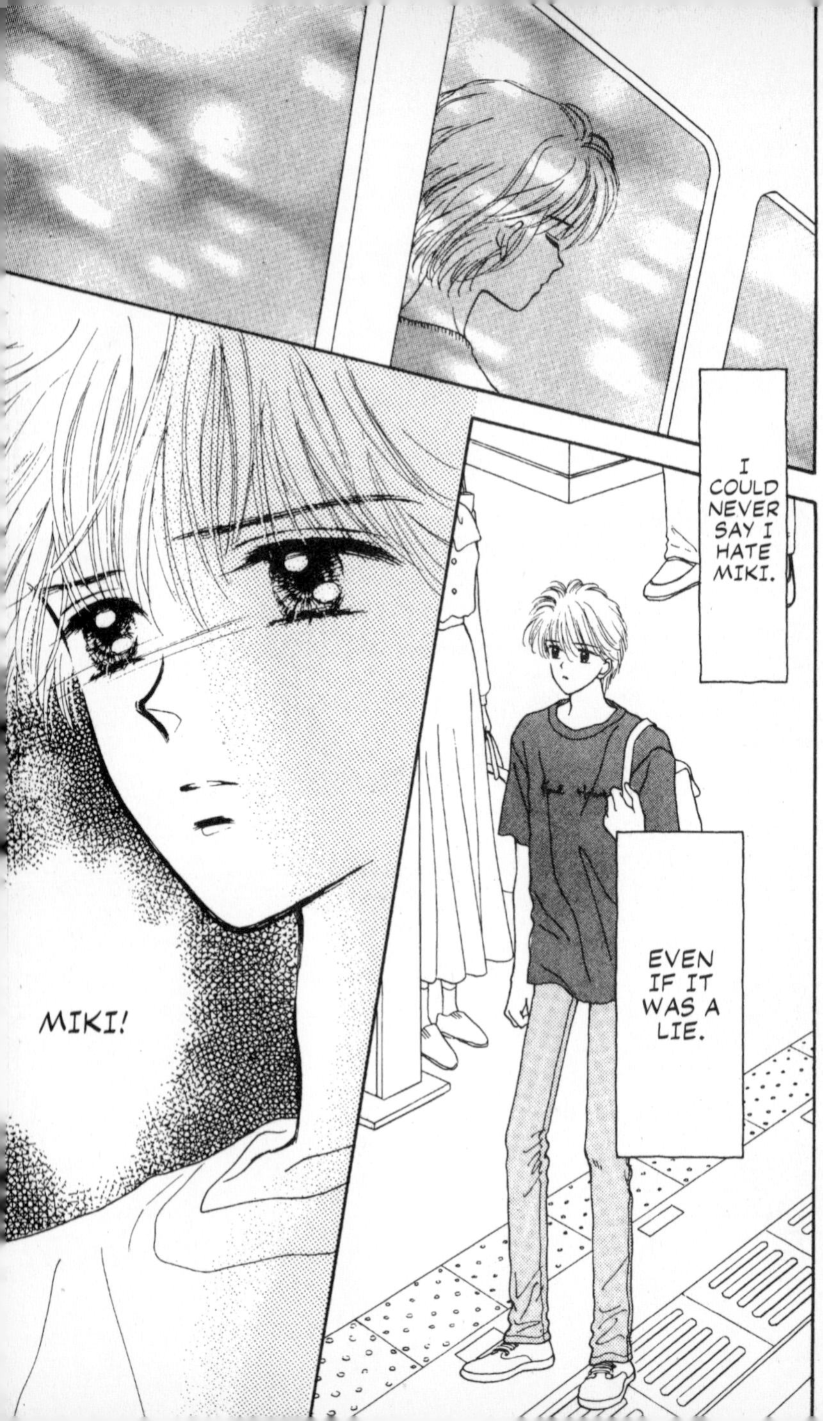
I COULD NEVER SAY I HATE MIKI.
EVEN IF IT WAS A LIE.
MIKI!

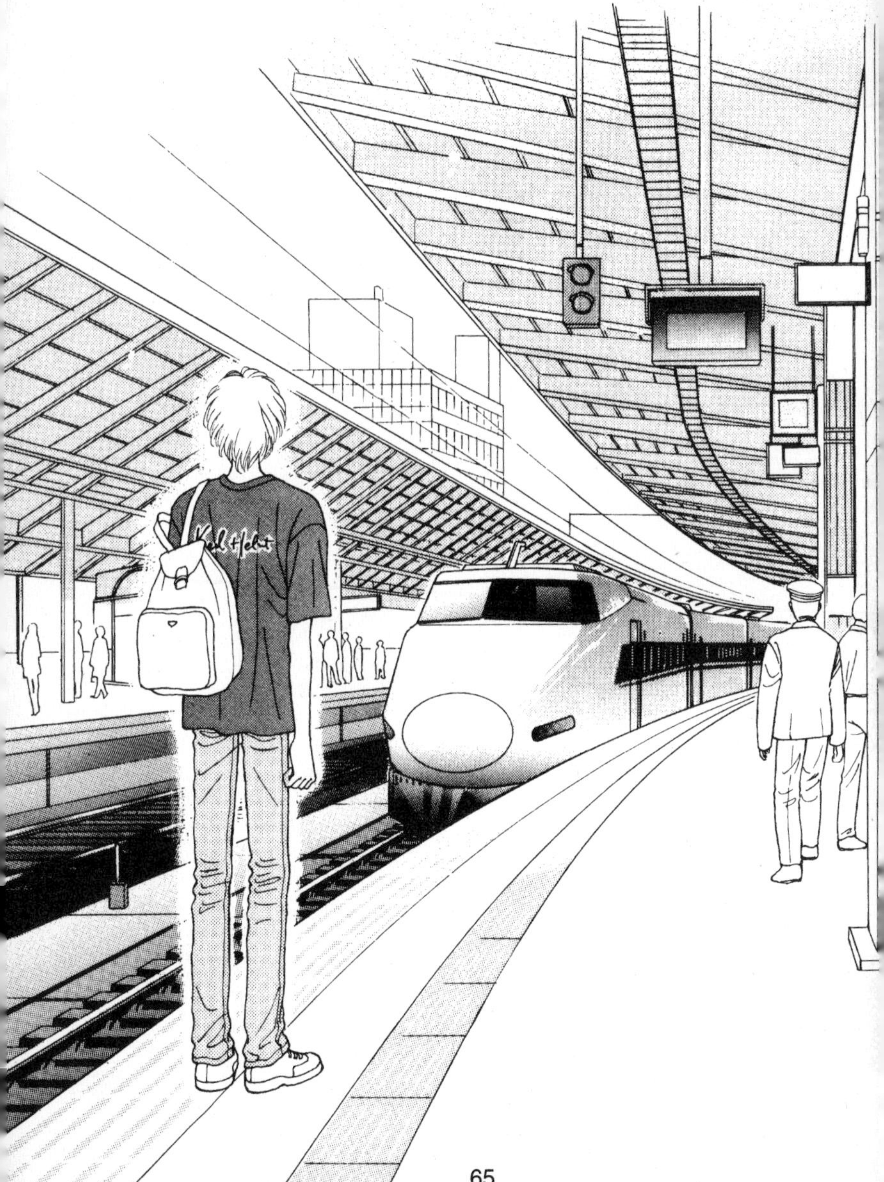

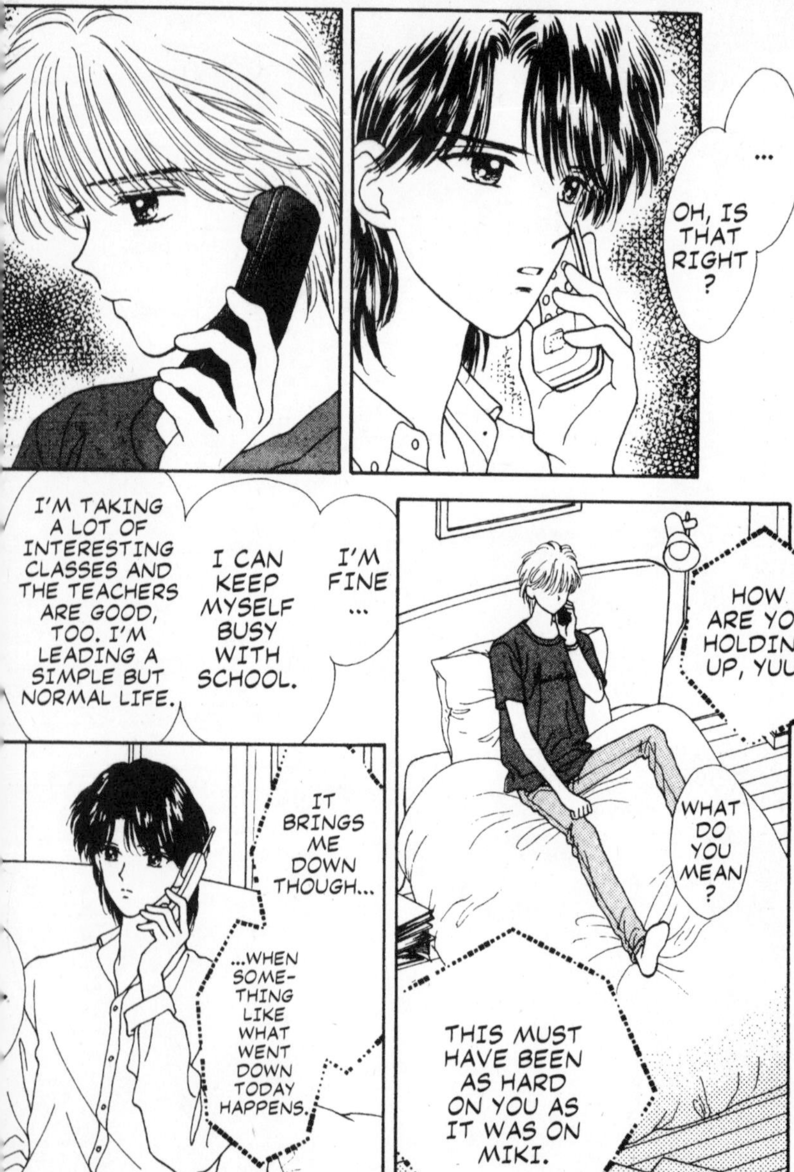
... OH, IS THAT RIGHT?
HOW ARE YOU HOLDING UP, YUU?
WHAT DO YOU MEAN?
THIS MUST HAVE BEEN AS HARD ON YOU AS IT WAS ON MIKI.
I'M FINE ...
I CAN KEEP MYSELF BUSY WITH SCHOOL.
I'M TAKING A LOT OF INTERESTING CLASSES AND THE TEACHERS ARE GOOD, TOO. I'M LEADING A SIMPLE BUT NORMAL LIFE.
IT BRINGS ME DOWN THOUGH...
...WHEN SOMETHING LIKE WHAT WENT DOWN TODAY HAPPENS.

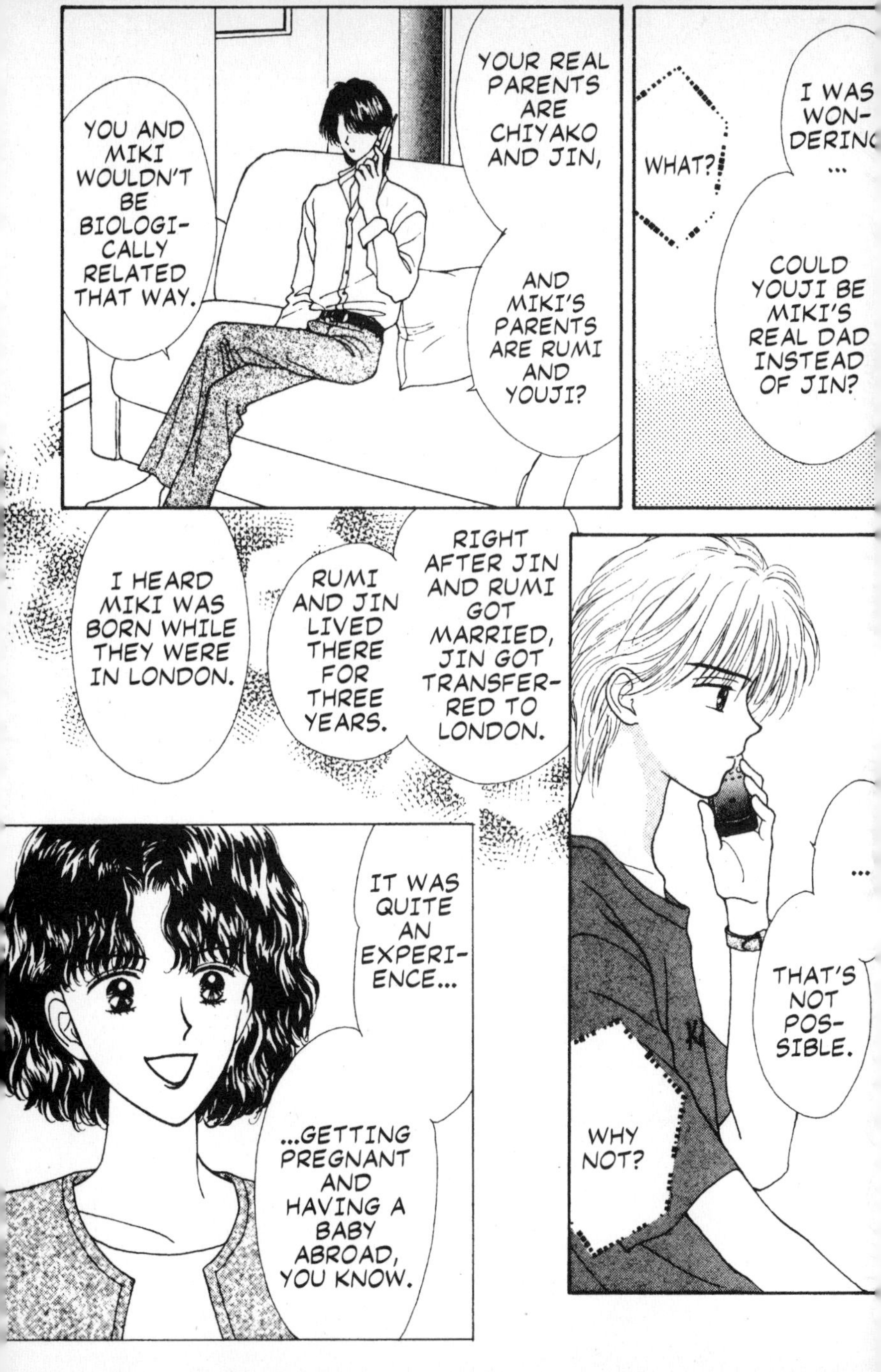
I WAS WON-DERING...
COULD YOUJI BE MIKI'S REAL DAD INSTEAD OF JIN?
WHAT?
YOUR REAL PARENTS ARE CHIYAKO AND JIN,
AND MIKI'S PARENTS ARE RUMI AND YOUJI?
YOU AND MIKI WOULDN'T BE BIOLOGI-CALLY RELATED THAT WAY.
...
THAT'S NOT POS-SIBLE.
WHY NOT?
RIGHT AFTER JIN AND RUMI GOT MARRIED, JIN GOT TRANSFER-RED TO LONDON.
RUMI AND JIN LIVED THERE FOR THREE YEARS.
I HEARD MIKI WAS BORN WHILE THEY WERE IN LONDON.
IT WAS QUITE AN EXPERI-ENCE...
...GETTING PREGNANT AND HAVING A BABY ABROAD, YOU KNOW.

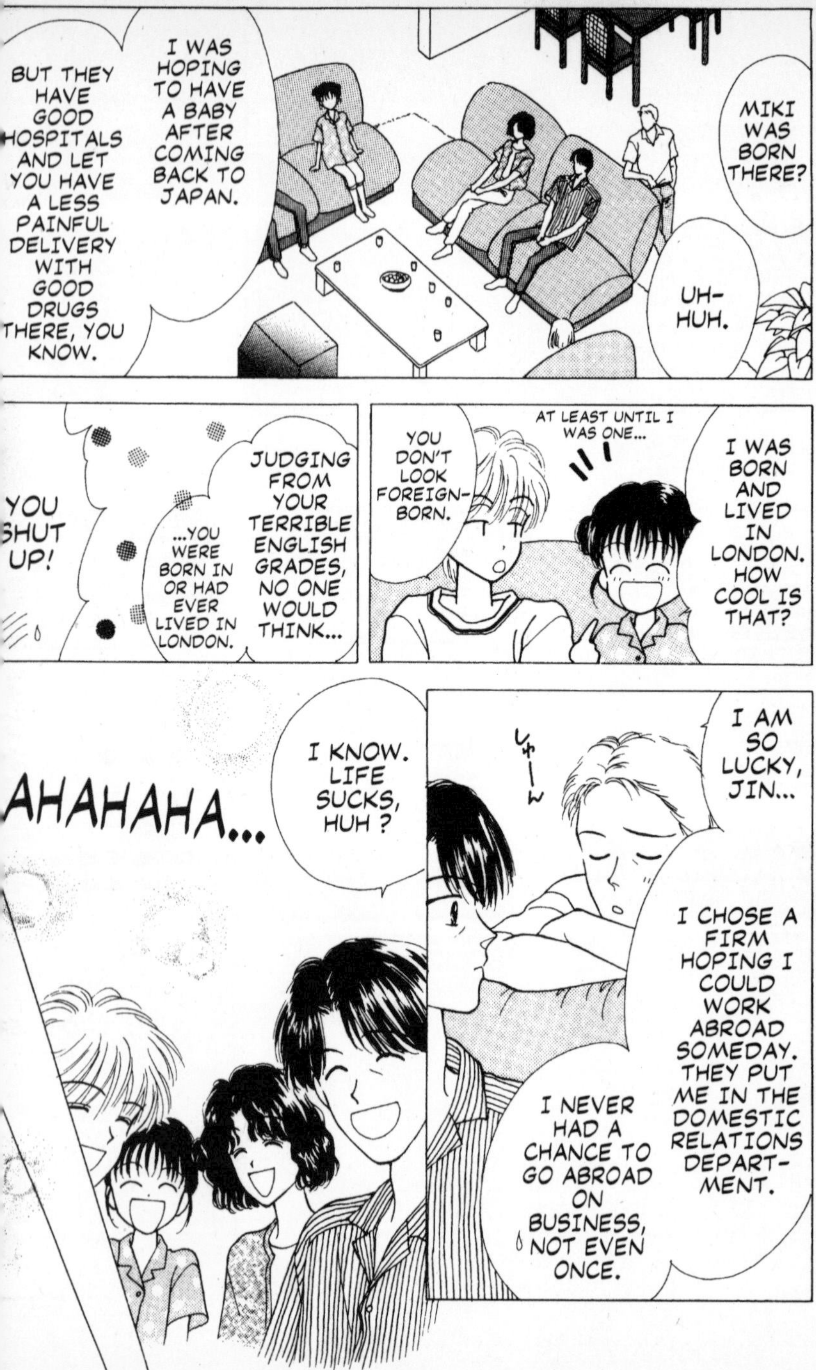
MIKI WAS BORN THERE?
UH-HUH.
I WAS HOPING TO HAVE A BABY AFTER COMING BACK TO JAPAN.
BUT THEY HAVE GOOD HOSPITALS AND LET YOU HAVE A LESS PAINFUL DELIVERY WITH GOOD DRUGS THERE, YOU KNOW.
I WAS BORN AND LIVED IN LONDON. HOW COOL IS THAT?
AT LEAST UNTIL I WAS ONE...
YOU DON'T LOOK FOREIGN-BORN.
JUDGING FROM YOUR TERRIBLE ENGLISH GRADES, NO ONE WOULD THINK...
...YOU WERE BORN IN OR HAD EVER LIVED IN LONDON.
YOU SHUT UP!
I AM SO LUCKY, JIN...
しゅーん
I CHOSE A FIRM HOPING I COULD WORK ABROAD SOMEDAY. THEY PUT ME IN THE DOMESTIC RELATIONS DEPART-MENT.
I NEVER HAD A CHANCE TO GO ABROAD ON BUSINESS, NOT EVEN ONCE.
I KNOW. LIFE SUCKS, HUH ?
AHAHAHA...

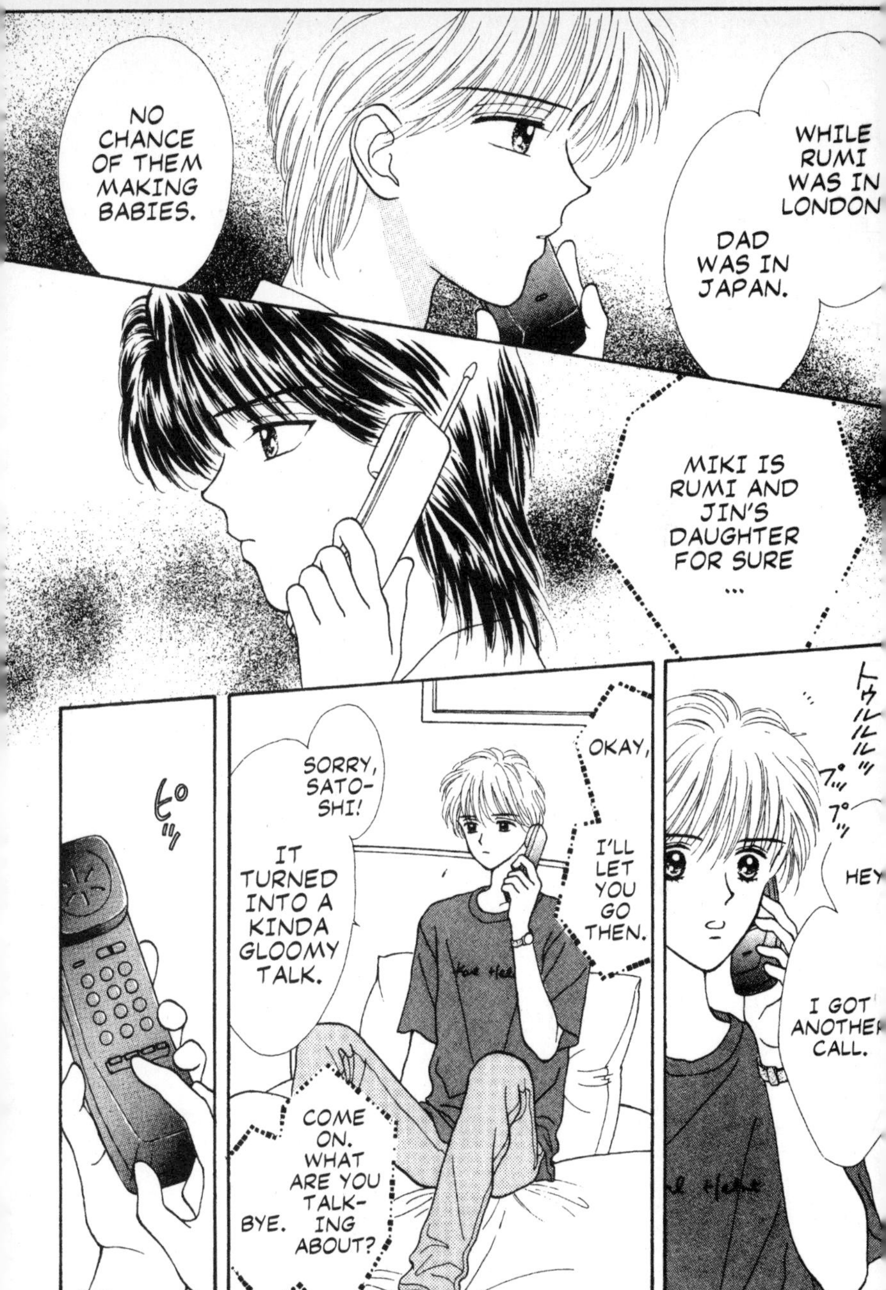
WHILE RUMI WAS IN LONDON
DAD WAS IN JAPAN.
NO CHANCE OF THEM MAKING BABIES.
MIKI IS RUMI AND JIN'S DAUGHTER FOR SURE ...
トゥルルルッ
プッ プッ
HEY
I GOT ANOTHER CALL.
OKAY,
I'LL LET YOU GO THEN.
SORRY, SATO-SHI!
IT TURNED INTO A KINDA GLOOMY TALK.
COME ON. WHAT ARE YOU TALK-ING ABOUT?
BYE.
ピッ

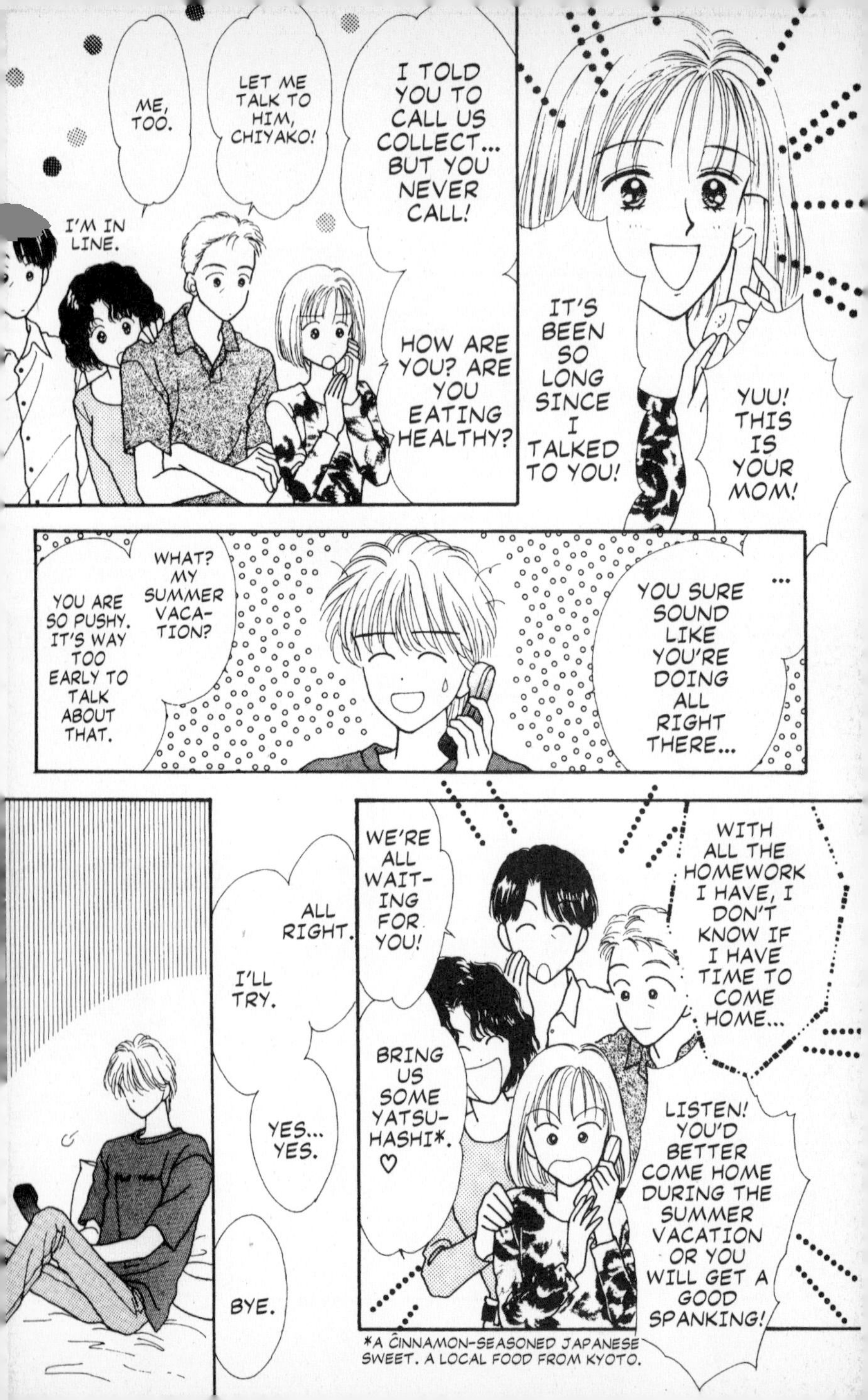
YUU! THIS IS YOUR MOM!
IT'S BEEN SO LONG SINCE I TALKED TO YOU!
I TOLD YOU TO CALL US COLLECT... BUT YOU NEVER CALL!
HOW ARE YOU? ARE YOU EATING HEALTHY?
LET ME TALK TO HIM, CHIYAKO!
ME, TOO.
I'M IN LINE.
...
YOU SURE SOUND LIKE YOU'RE DOING ALL RIGHT THERE...
WHAT? MY SUMMER VACATION?
YOU ARE SO PUSHY. IT'S WAY TOO EARLY TO TALK ABOUT THAT.
WITH ALL THE HOMEWORK I HAVE, I DON'T KNOW IF I HAVE TIME TO COME HOME...
LISTEN! YOU'D BETTER COME HOME DURING THE SUMMER VACATION OR YOU WILL GET A GOOD SPANKING!
WE'RE ALL WAITING FOR YOU!
BRING US SOME YATSUHASHI*. ♡
ALL RIGHT.
I'LL TRY.
YES... YES.
BYE.

*A CINNAMON-SEASONED JAPANESE SWEET. A LOCAL FOOD FROM KYOTO.

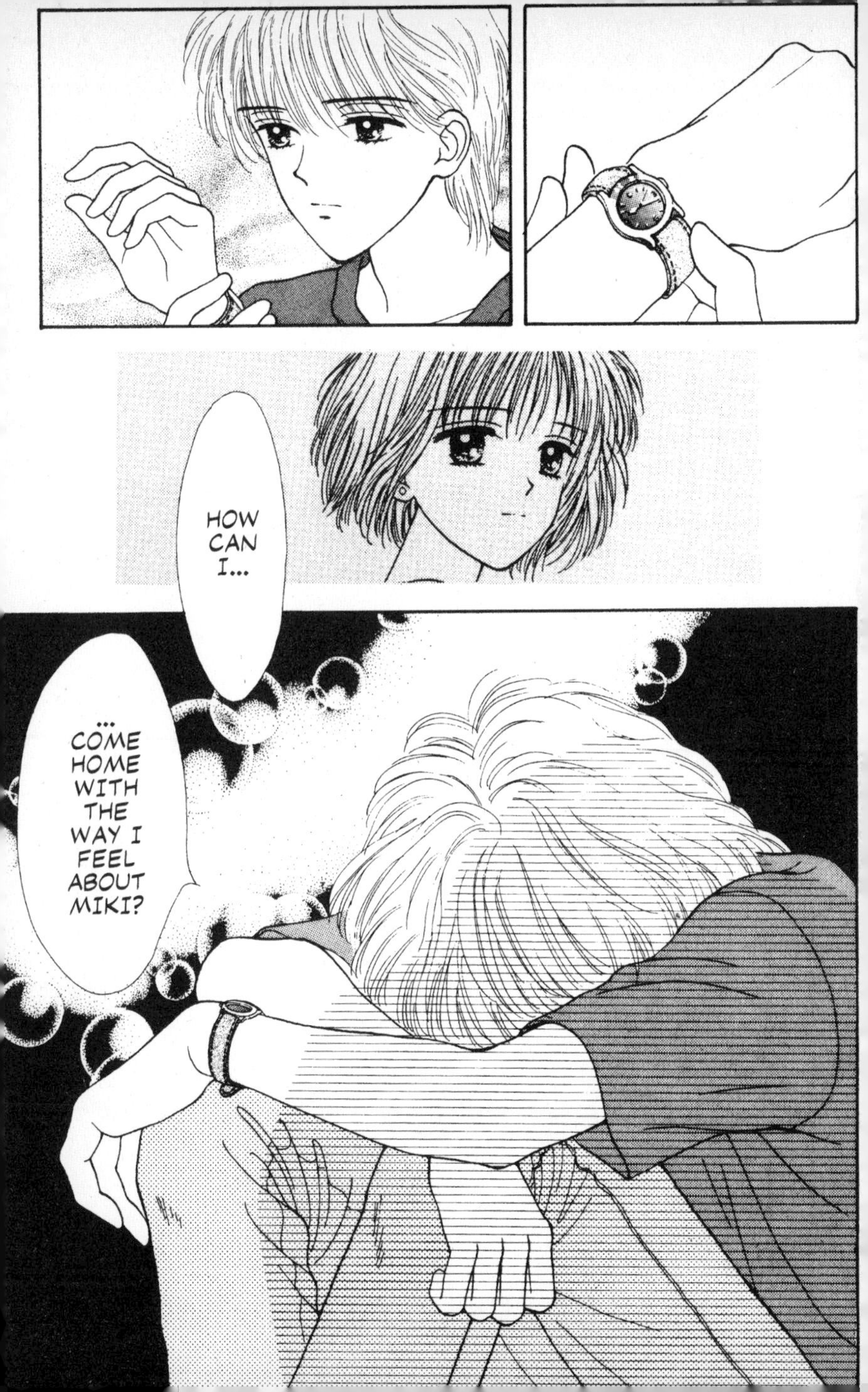
HOW CAN I...
... COME HOME WITH THE WAY I FEEL ABOUT MIKI?

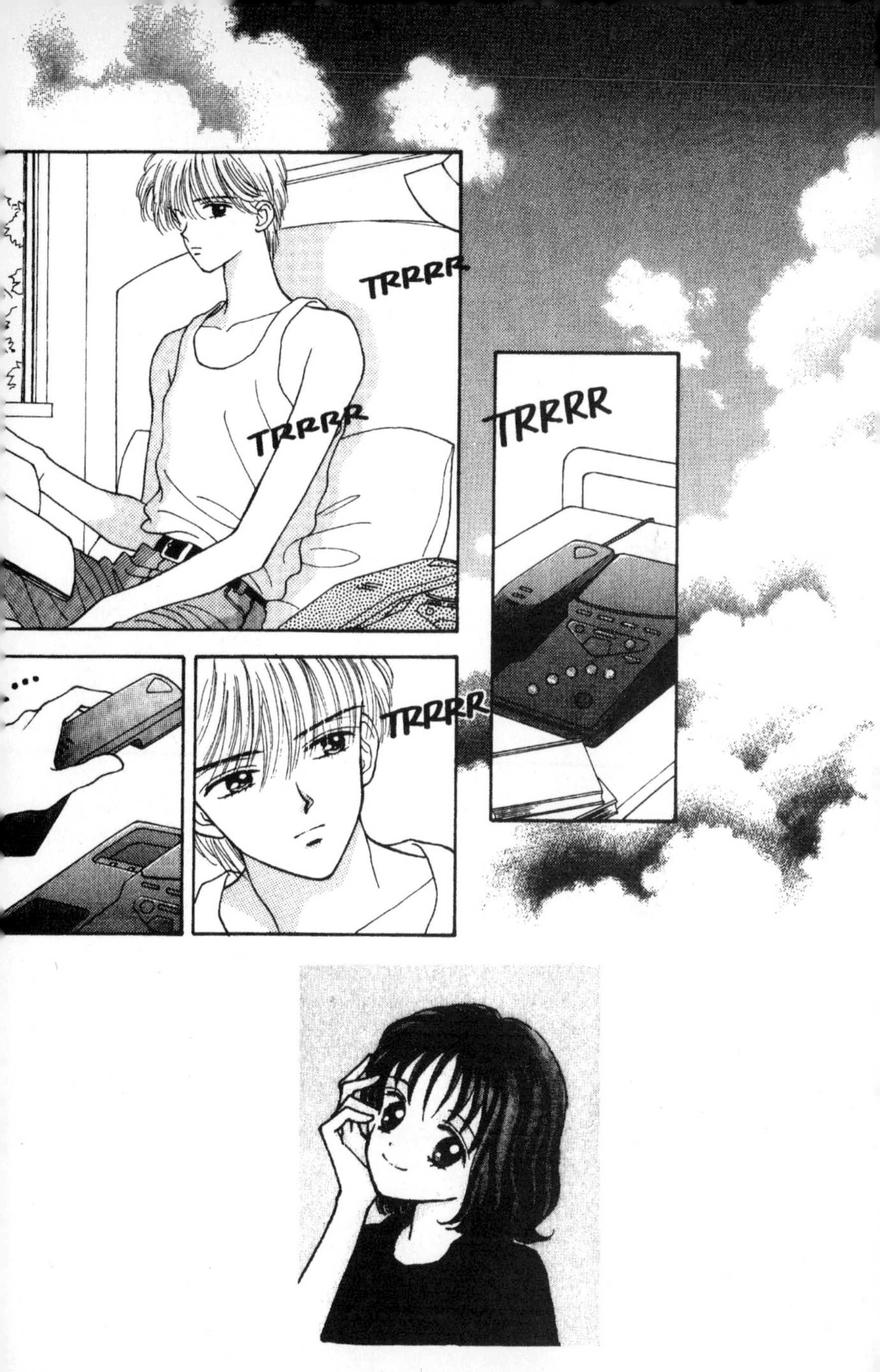
TRRRR
TRRRR
TRRRR
TRRRR
...

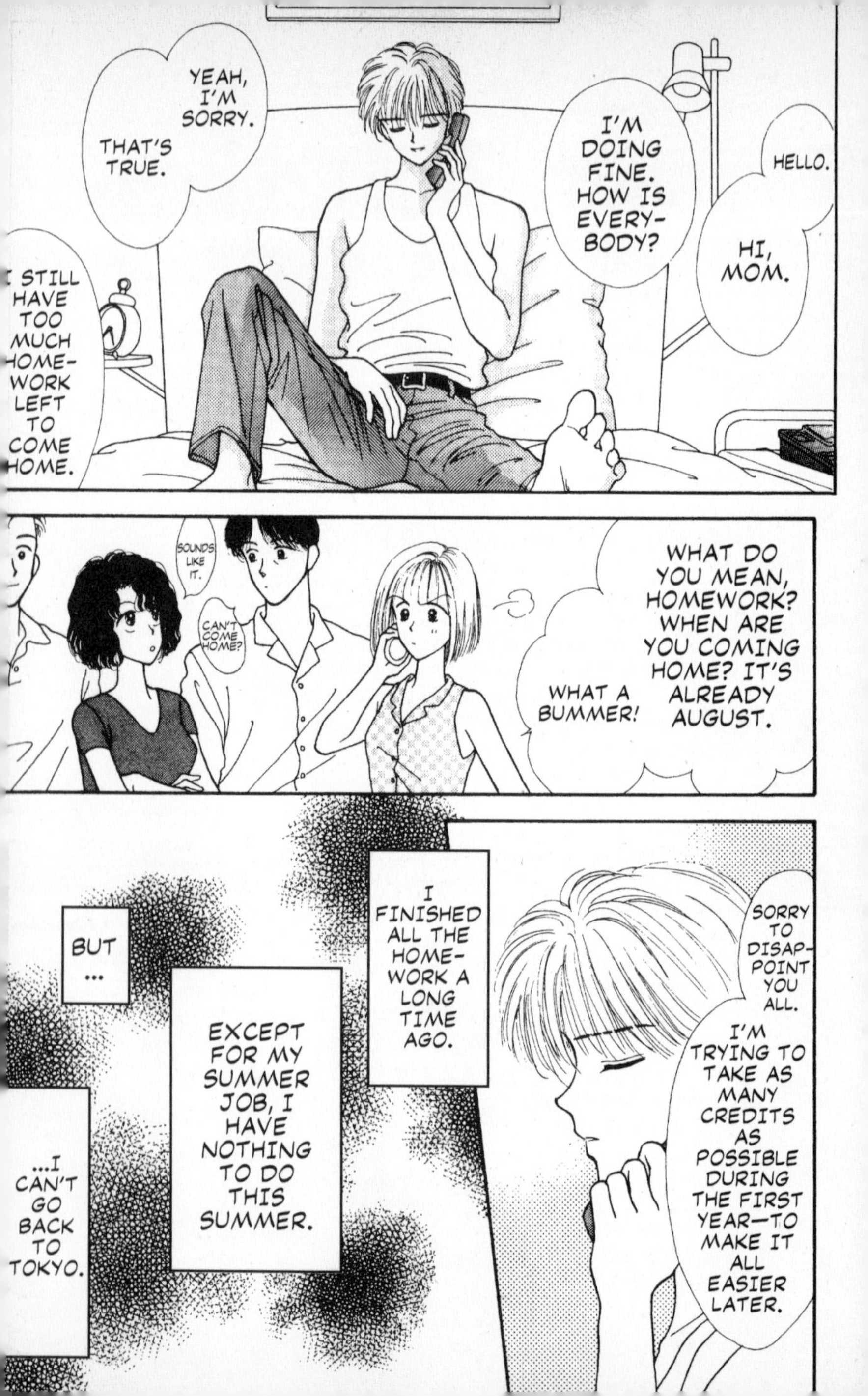
HELLO.
HI, MOM.
I'M DOING FINE. HOW IS EVERYBODY?
YEAH, I'M SORRY.
THAT'S TRUE.
I STILL HAVE TOO MUCH HOMEWORK LEFT TO COME HOME.
WHAT DO YOU MEAN, HOMEWORK? WHEN ARE YOU COMING HOME? IT'S ALREADY AUGUST.
WHAT A BUMMER!
CAN'T COME HOME?
SOUNDS LIKE IT.
SORRY TO DISAPPOINT YOU ALL.
I'M TRYING TO TAKE AS MANY CREDITS AS POSSIBLE DURING THE FIRST YEAR—TO MAKE IT ALL EASIER LATER.
I FINISHED ALL THE HOMEWORK A LONG TIME AGO.
BUT ...
EXCEPT FOR MY SUMMER JOB, I HAVE NOTHING TO DO THIS SUMMER.
...I CAN'T GO BACK TO TOKYO.

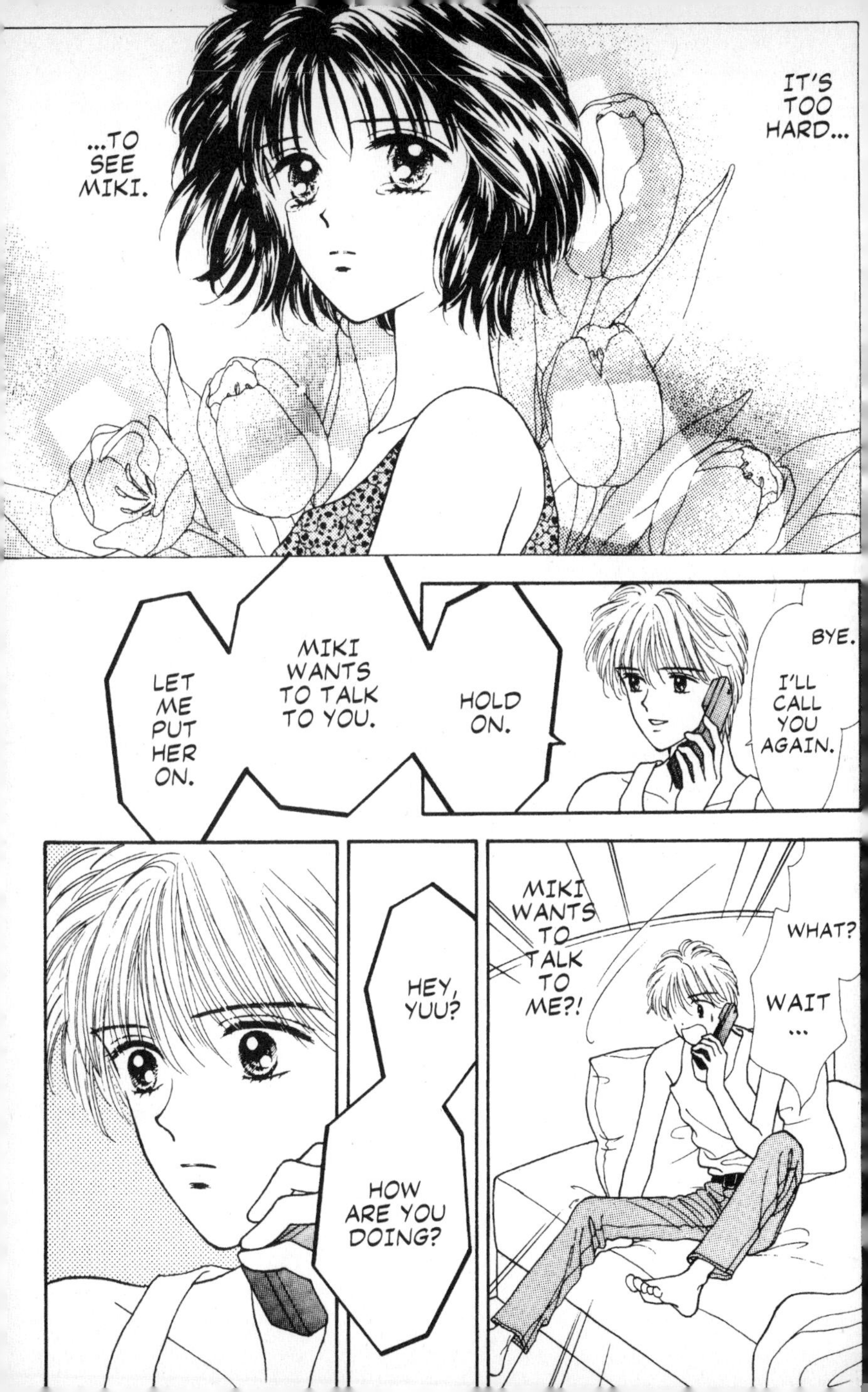
IT'S TOO HARD...
...TO SEE MIKI.
BYE.
I'LL CALL YOU AGAIN.
HOLD ON.
MIKI WANTS TO TALK TO YOU.
LET ME PUT HER ON.
WHAT?
WAIT...
MIKI WANTS TO TALK TO ME?!
HEY, YUU?
HOW ARE YOU DOING?

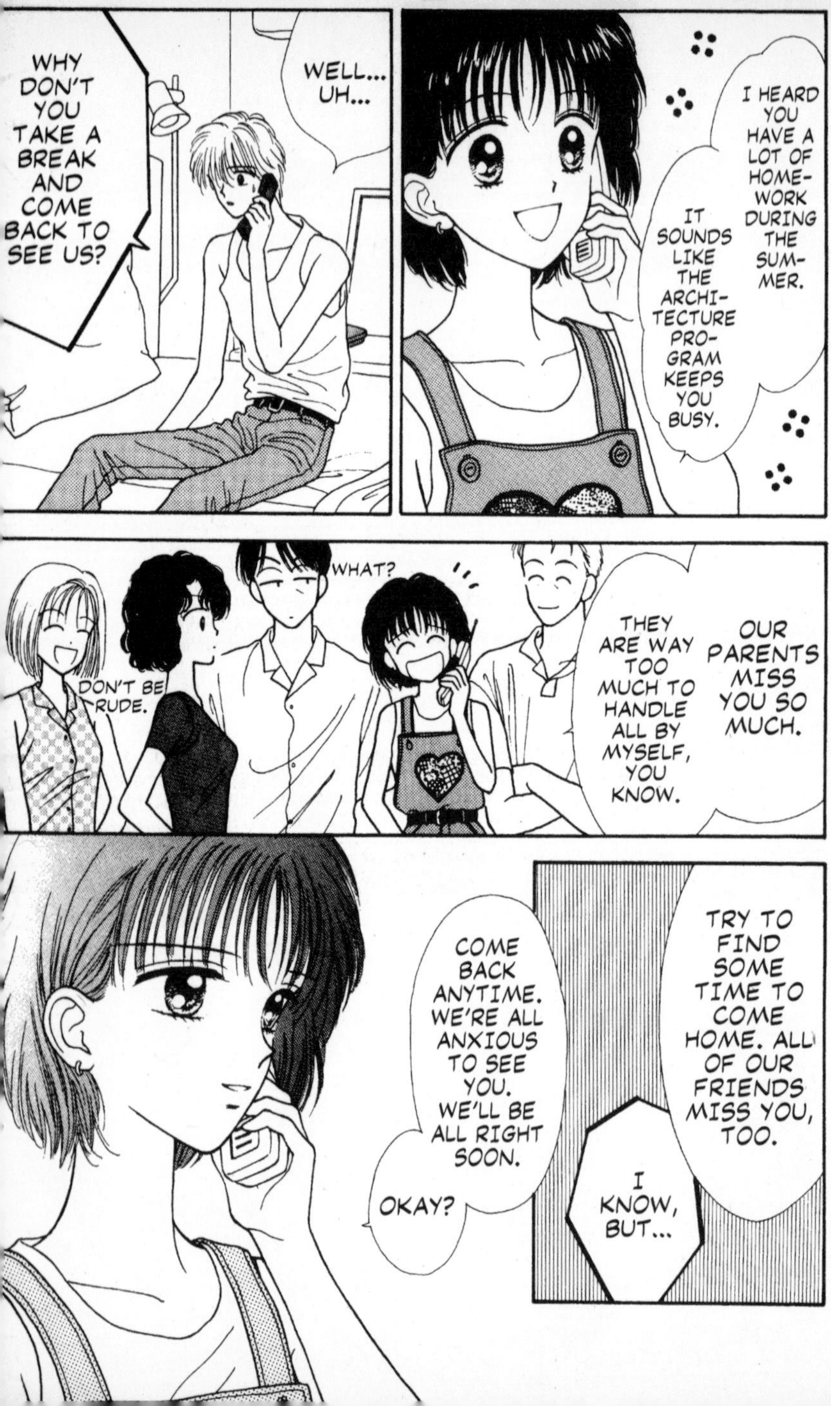
I HEARD YOU HAVE A LOT OF HOMEWORK DURING THE SUMMER.
IT SOUNDS LIKE THE ARCHITECTURE PROGRAM KEEPS YOU BUSY.
WELL... UH...
WHY DON'T YOU TAKE A BREAK AND COME BACK TO SEE US?
OUR PARENTS MISS YOU SO MUCH.
THEY ARE WAY TOO MUCH TO HANDLE ALL BY MYSELF, YOU KNOW.
WHAT?
DON'T BE RUDE.
TRY TO FIND SOME TIME TO COME HOME. ALL OF OUR FRIENDS MISS YOU, TOO.
I KNOW, BUT...
COME BACK ANYTIME. WE'RE ALL ANXIOUS TO SEE YOU. WE'LL BE ALL RIGHT SOON.
OKAY?

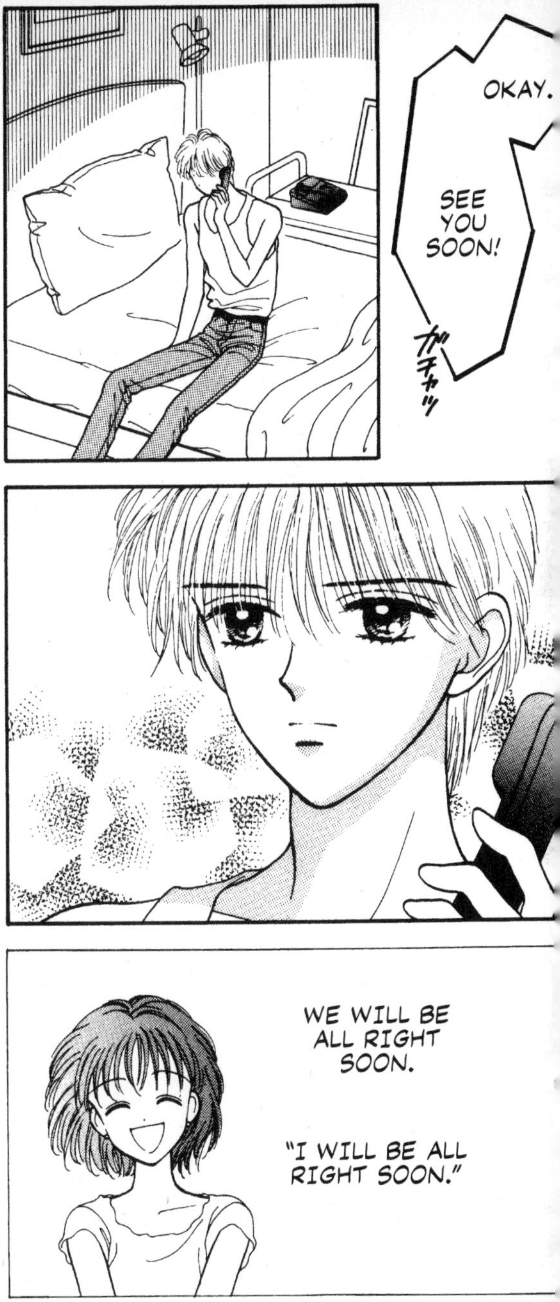
OKAY.
SEE YOU SOON!
ガチャッ
WE WILL BE ALL RIGHT SOON.
"I WILL BE ALL RIGHT SOON."
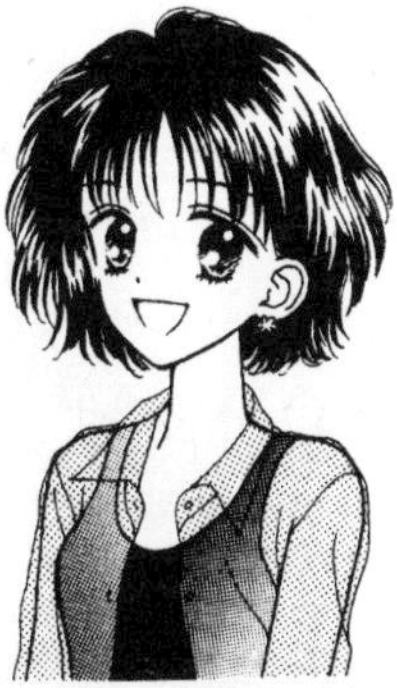

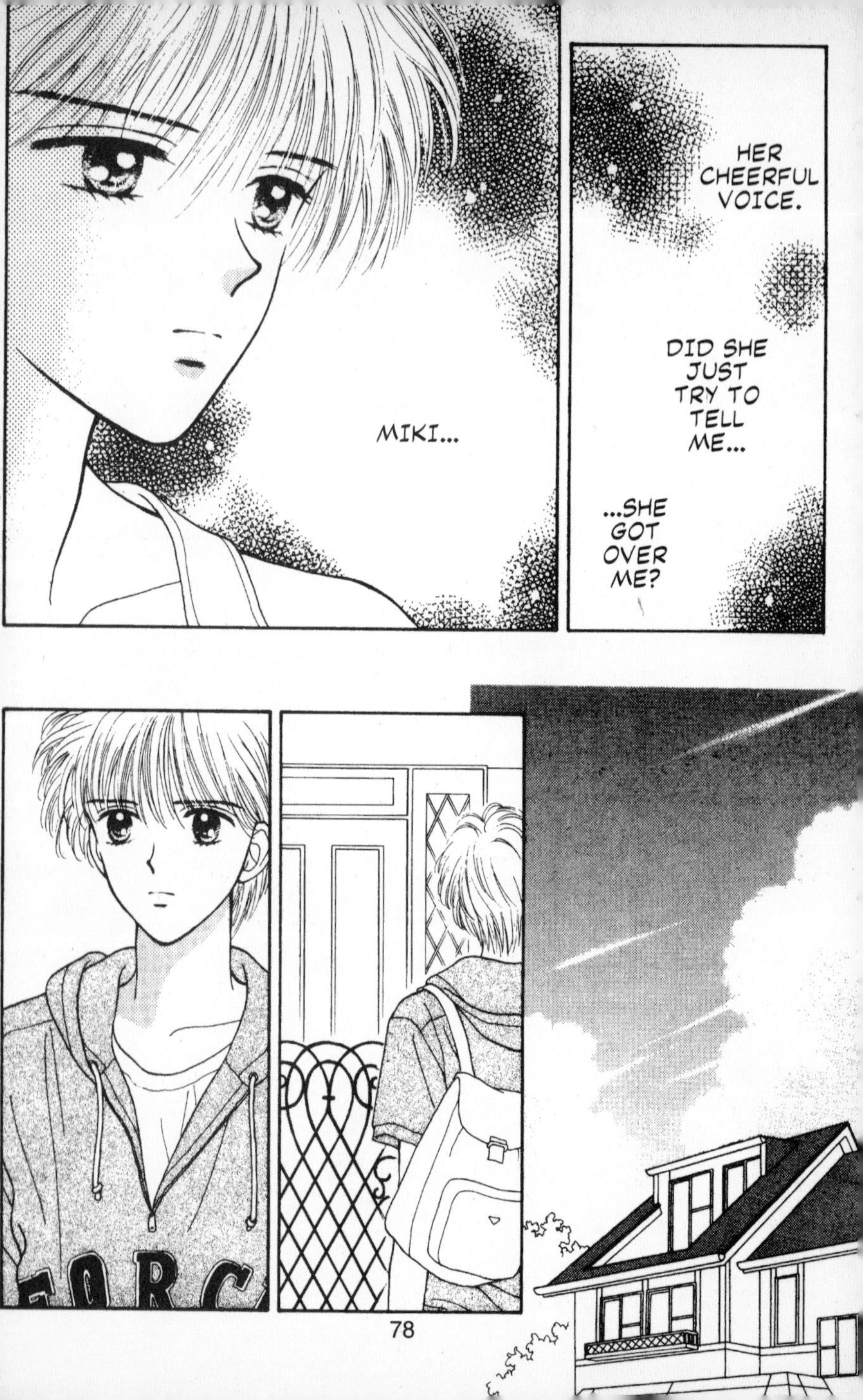
HER CHEERFUL VOICE.
DID SHE JUST TRY TO TELL ME...
...SHE GOT OVER ME?
MIKI...

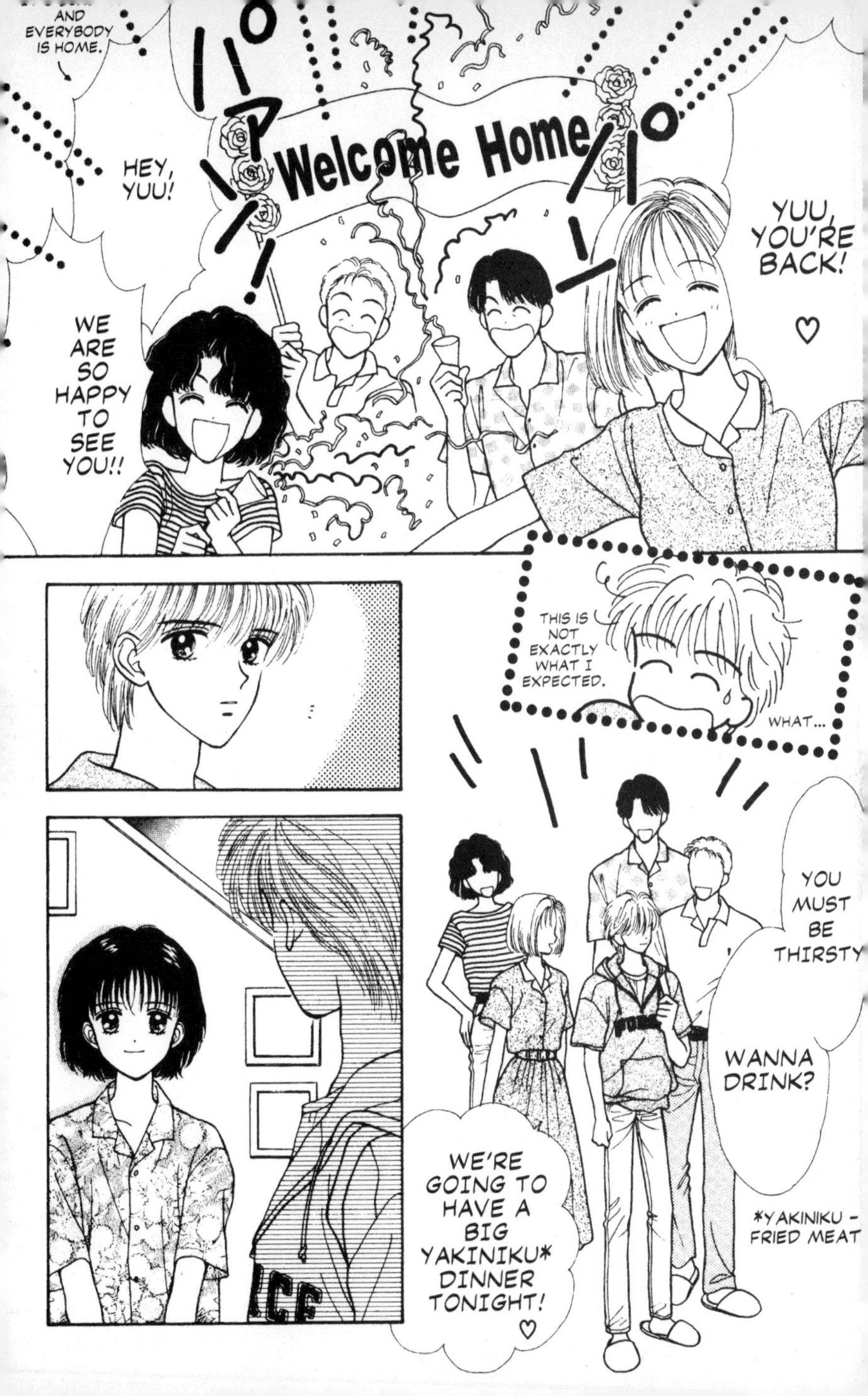
AND EVERYBODY IS HOME.
YUU, YOU'RE BACK! ♡
Welcome Home
HEY, YUU!
WE ARE SO HAPPY TO SEE YOU!!
WHAT...
THIS IS NOT EXACTLY WHAT I EXPECTED.
YOU MUST BE THIRSTY
WANNA DRINK?
WE'RE GOING TO HAVE A BIG YAKINIKU* DINNER TONIGHT! ♡
*YAKINIKU - FRIED MEAT

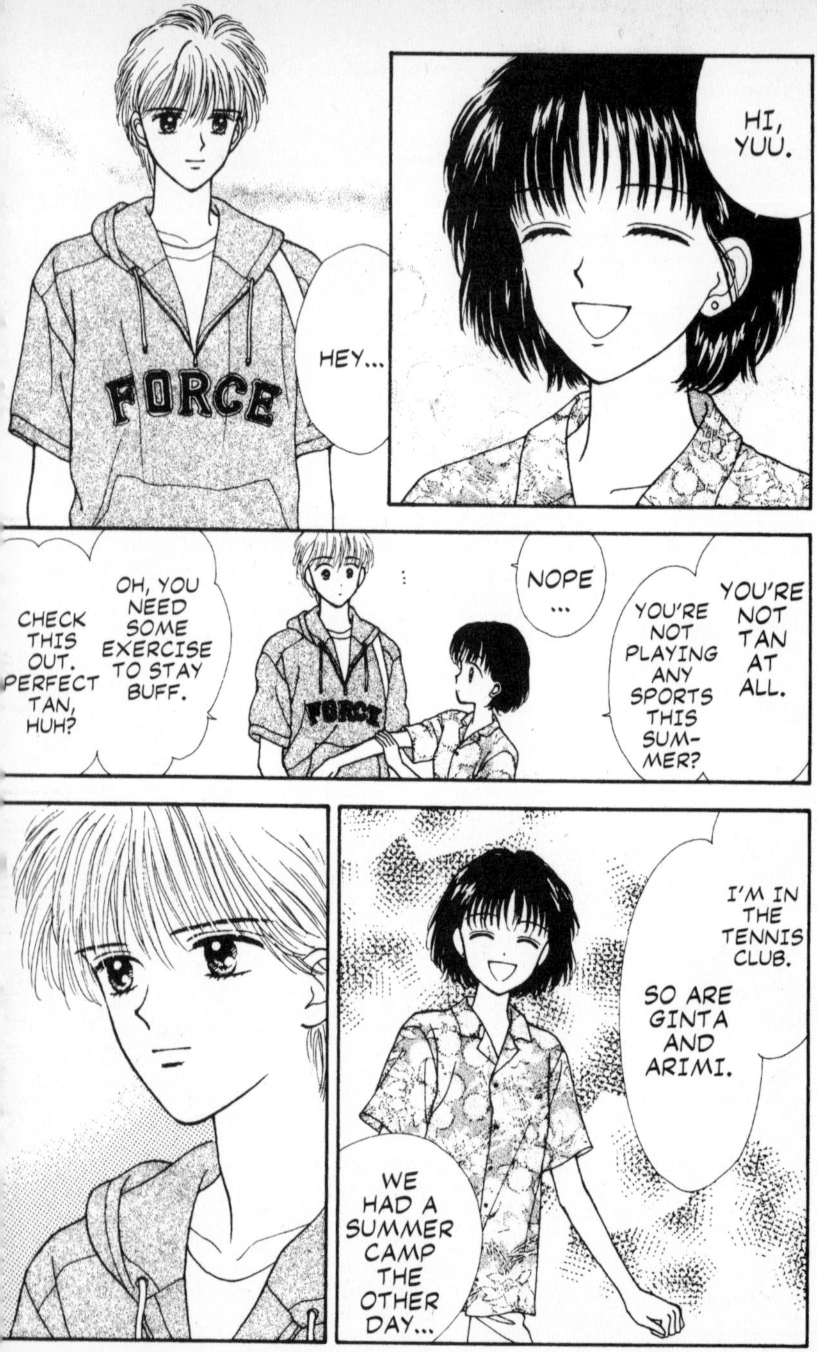
HI, YUU.
HEY...
YOU'RE NOT TAN AT ALL.
YOU'RE NOT PLAYING ANY SPORTS THIS SUMMER?
NOPE...
OH, YOU NEED SOME EXERCISE TO STAY BUFF.
CHECK THIS OUT. PERFECT TAN, HUH?
I'M IN THE TENNIS CLUB.
SO ARE GINTA AND ARIMI.
WE HAD A SUMMER CAMP THE OTHER DAY...
FORCE

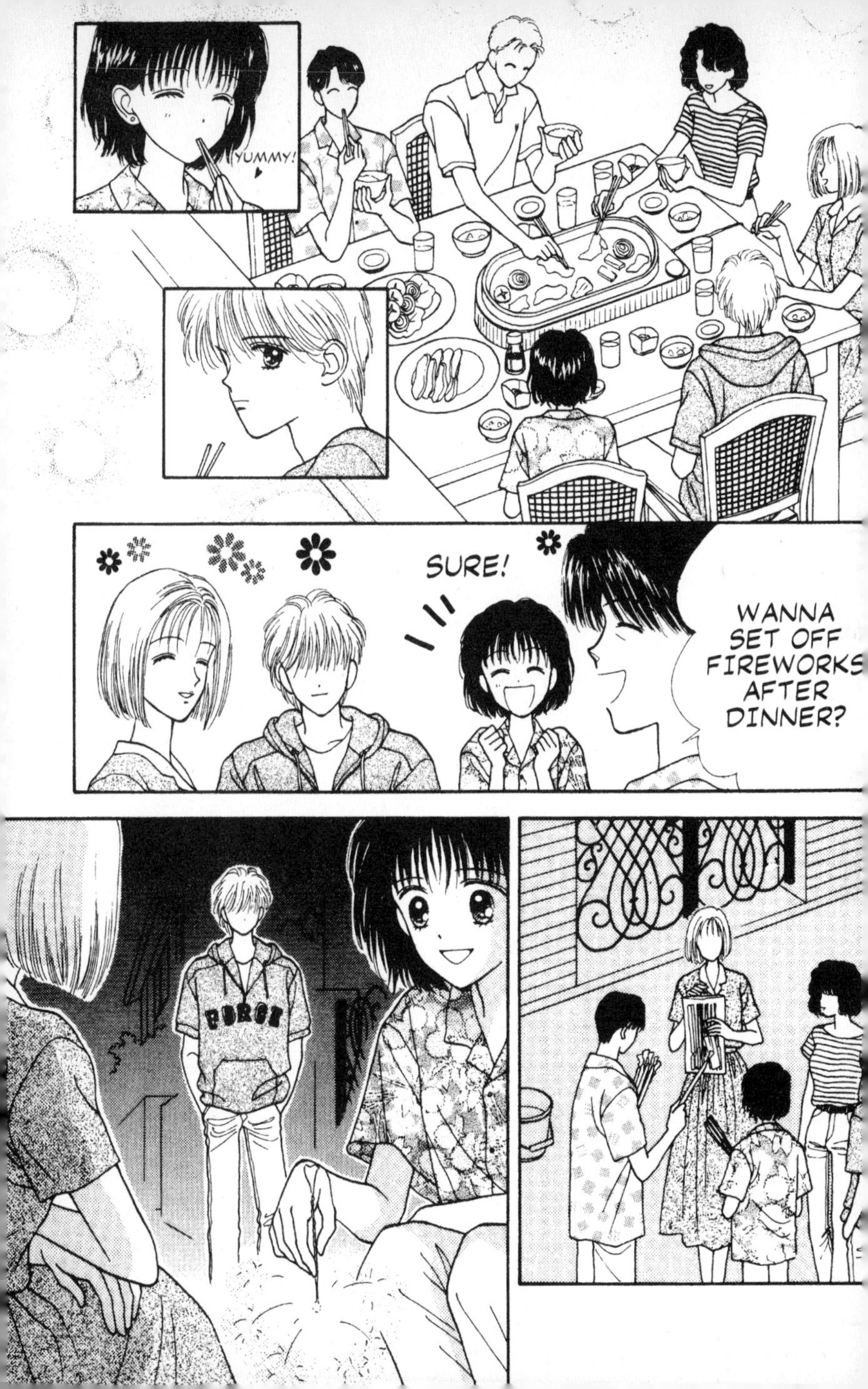
YUMMY!
WANNA SET OFF FIREWORKS AFTER DINNER?
SURE!

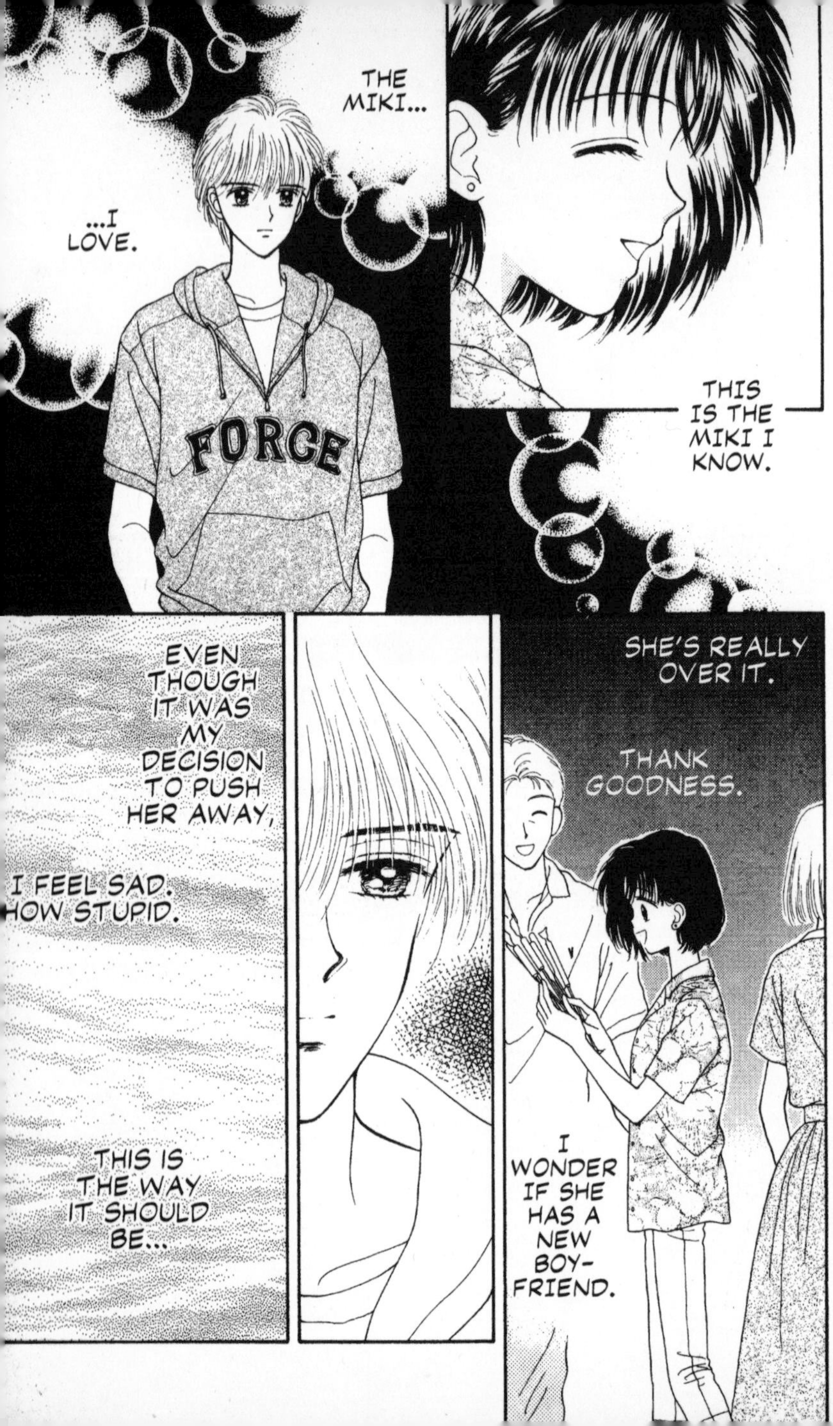
THIS IS THE MIKI I KNOW.
THE MIKI...
...I LOVE.
SHE'S REALLY OVER IT.
THANK GOODNESS.
I WONDER IF SHE HAS A NEW BOY-FRIEND.
EVEN THOUGH IT WAS MY DECISION TO PUSH HER AWAY,
I FEEL SAD. HOW STUPID.
THIS IS THE WAY IT SHOULD BE...

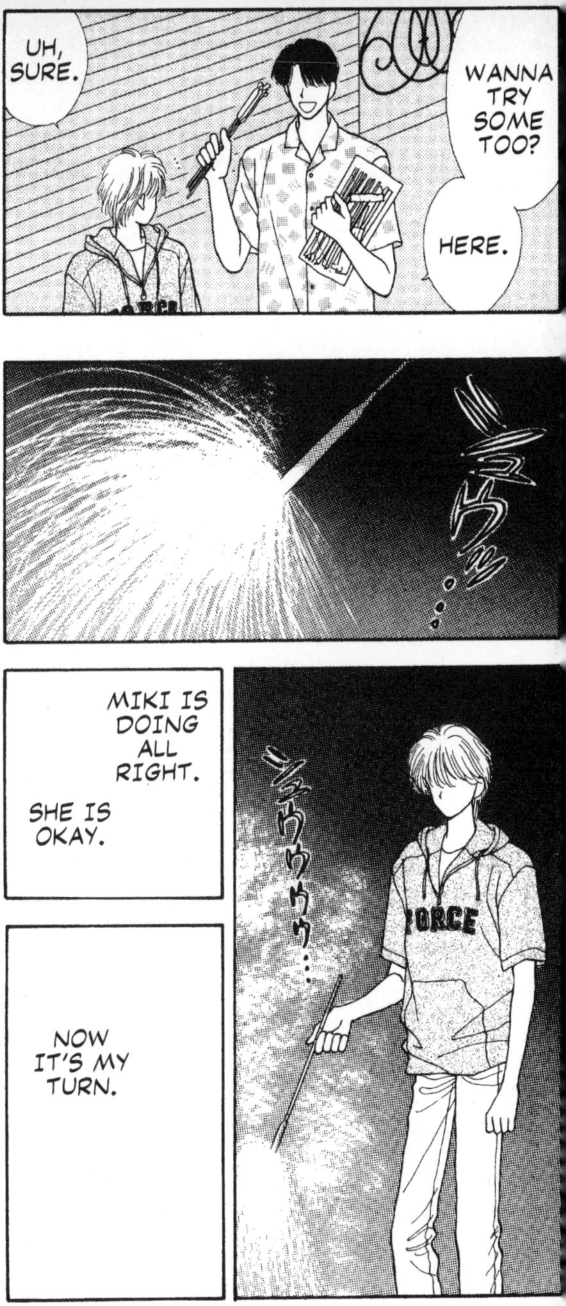
WANNA TRY SOME TOO?
HERE.
UH, SURE.
MIKI IS DOING ALL RIGHT.
SHE IS OKAY.
NOW IT'S MY TURN.

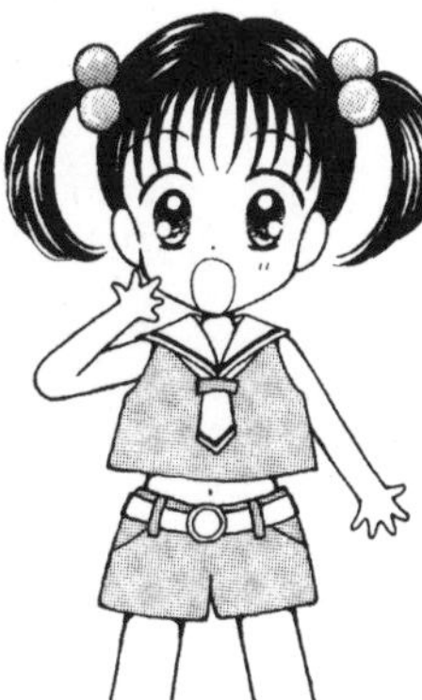

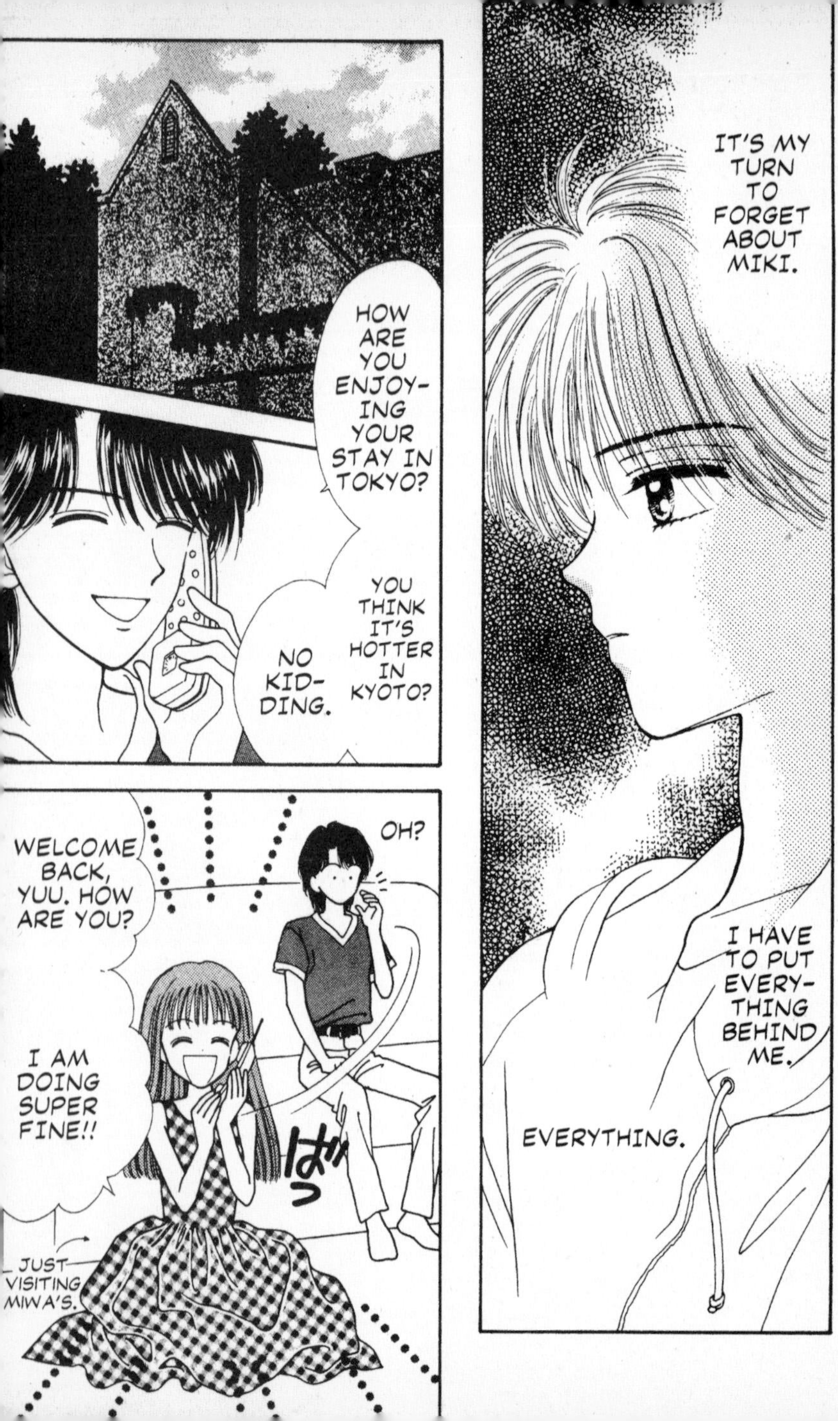
IT'S MY TURN TO FORGET ABOUT MIKI.
I HAVE TO PUT EVERYTHING BEHIND ME.
EVERYTHING.
HOW ARE YOU ENJOYING YOUR STAY IN TOKYO?
YOU THINK IT'S HOTTER IN KYOTO?
NO KIDDING.
OH?
WELCOME BACK, YUU. HOW ARE YOU?
I AM DOING SUPER FINE!!
ばっ
JUST VISITING MIWA'S.

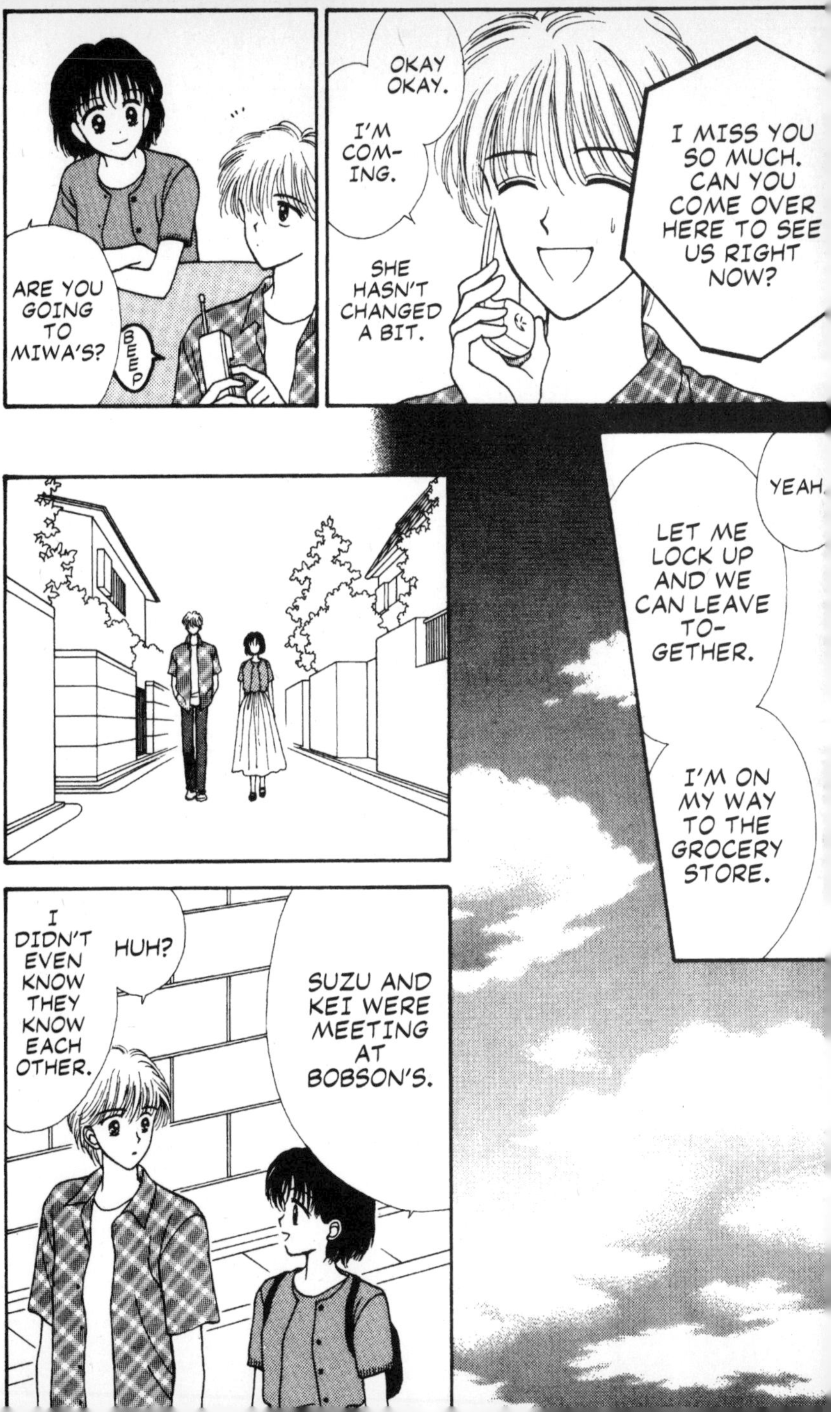
I MISS YOU SO MUCH. CAN YOU COME OVER HERE TO SEE US RIGHT NOW?
OKAY OKAY.
I'M COMING.
SHE HASN'T CHANGED A BIT.
BEEP
ARE YOU GOING TO MIWA'S?
YEAH.
LET ME LOCK UP AND WE CAN LEAVE TO-GETHER.
I'M ON MY WAY TO THE GROCERY STORE.
SUZU AND KEI WERE MEETING AT BOBSON'S.
HUH?
I DIDN'T EVEN KNOW THEY KNOW EACH OTHER.

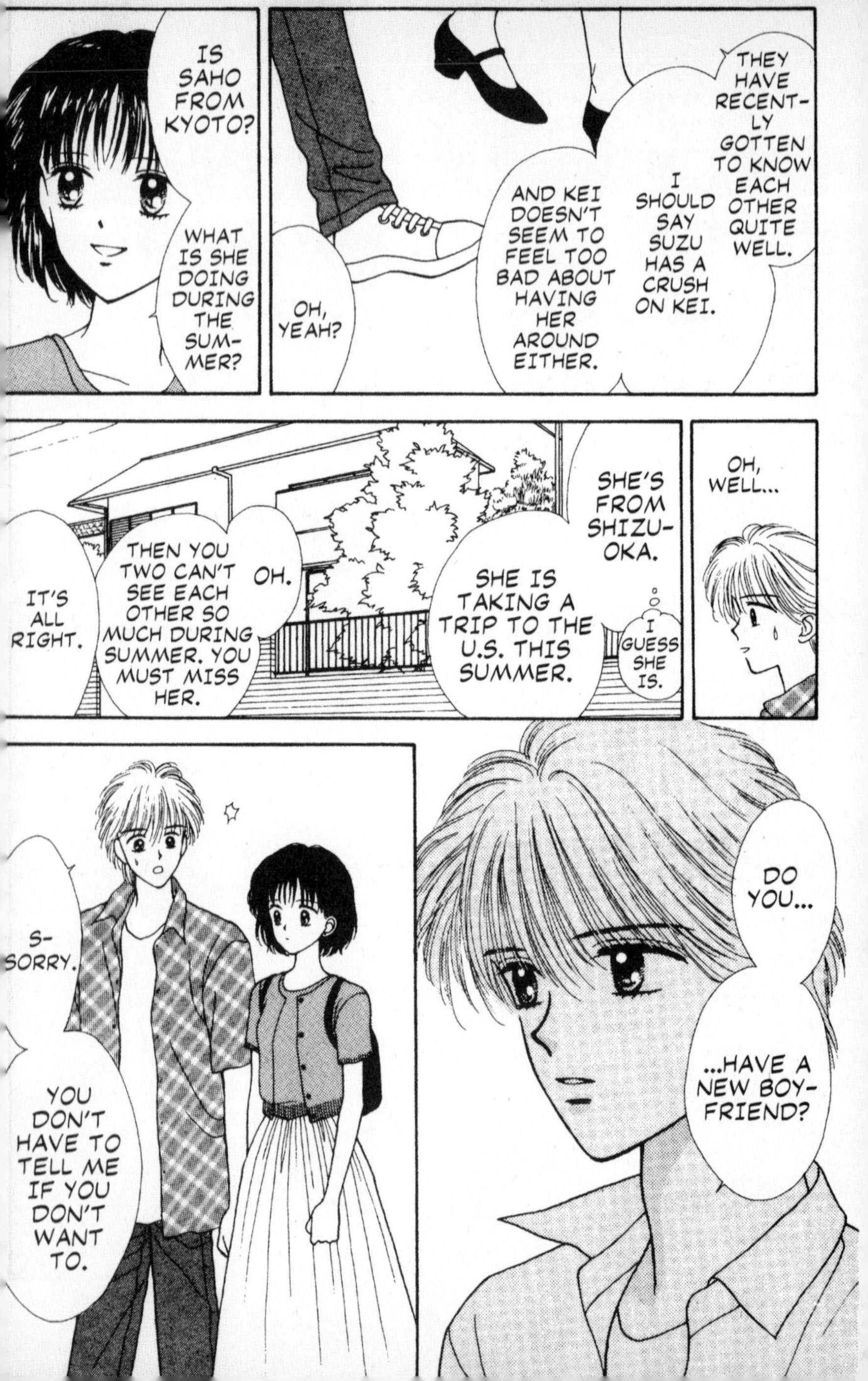
THEY HAVE RECENTLY GOTTEN TO KNOW EACH OTHER QUITE WELL.
I SHOULD SAY SUZU HAS A CRUSH ON KEI.
AND KEI DOESN'T SEEM TO FEEL TOO BAD ABOUT HAVING HER AROUND EITHER.
OH, YEAH?
IS SAHO FROM KYOTO?
WHAT IS SHE DOING DURING THE SUMMER?
OH, WELL...
SHE'S FROM SHIZUOKA.
I GUESS SHE IS.
SHE IS TAKING A TRIP TO THE U.S. THIS SUMMER.
OH.
THEN YOU TWO CAN'T SEE EACH OTHER SO MUCH DURING SUMMER. YOU MUST MISS HER.
IT'S ALL RIGHT.
DO YOU...
...HAVE A NEW BOYFRIEND?
S-SORRY.
YOU DON'T HAVE TO TELL ME IF YOU DON'T WANT TO.

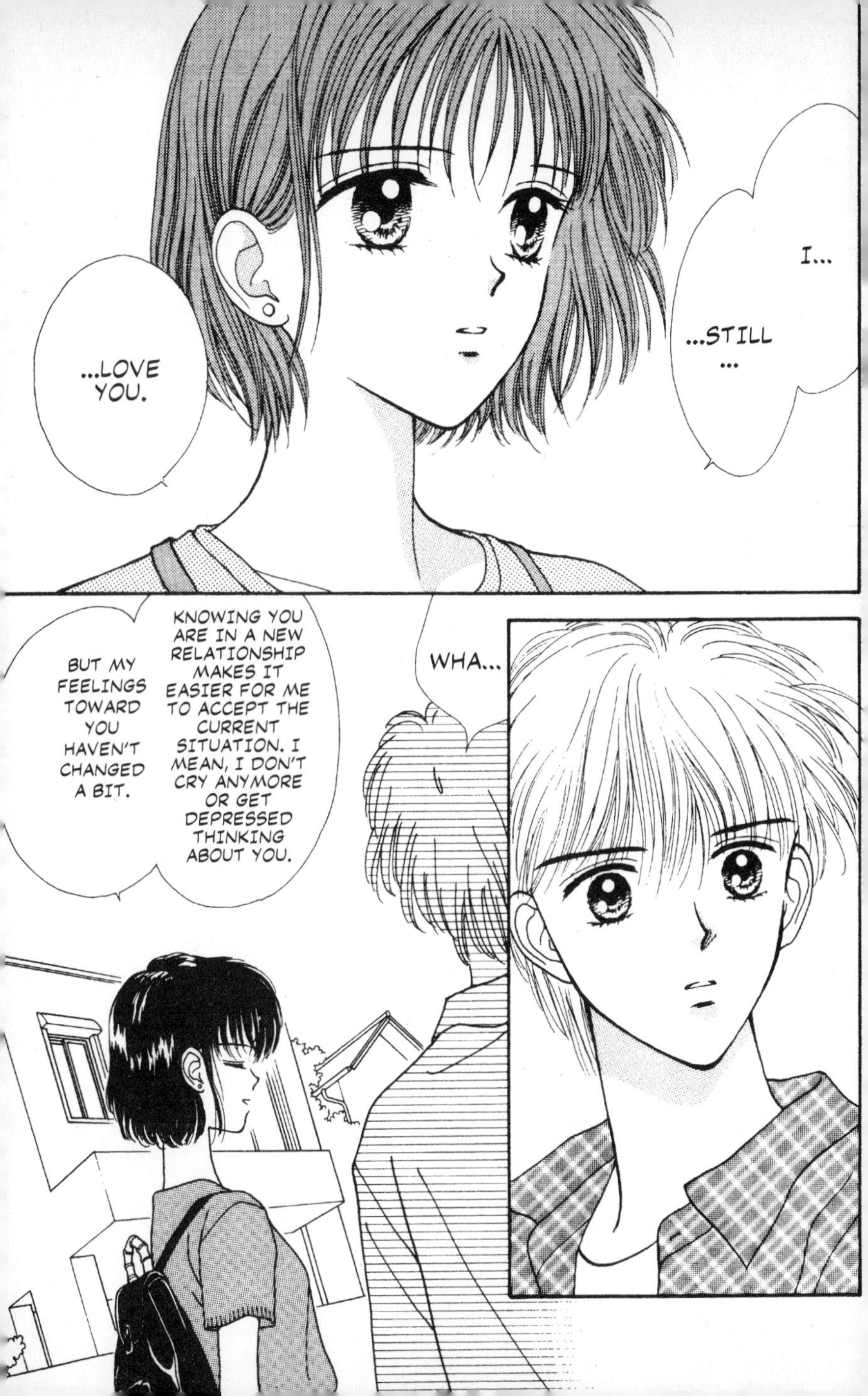
I...
...STILL ...
...LOVE YOU.
WHA...
KNOWING YOU ARE IN A NEW RELATIONSHIP MAKES IT EASIER FOR ME TO ACCEPT THE CURRENT SITUATION. I MEAN, I DON'T CRY ANYMORE OR GET DEPRESSED THINKING ABOUT YOU.
BUT MY FEELINGS TOWARD YOU HAVEN'T CHANGED A BIT.

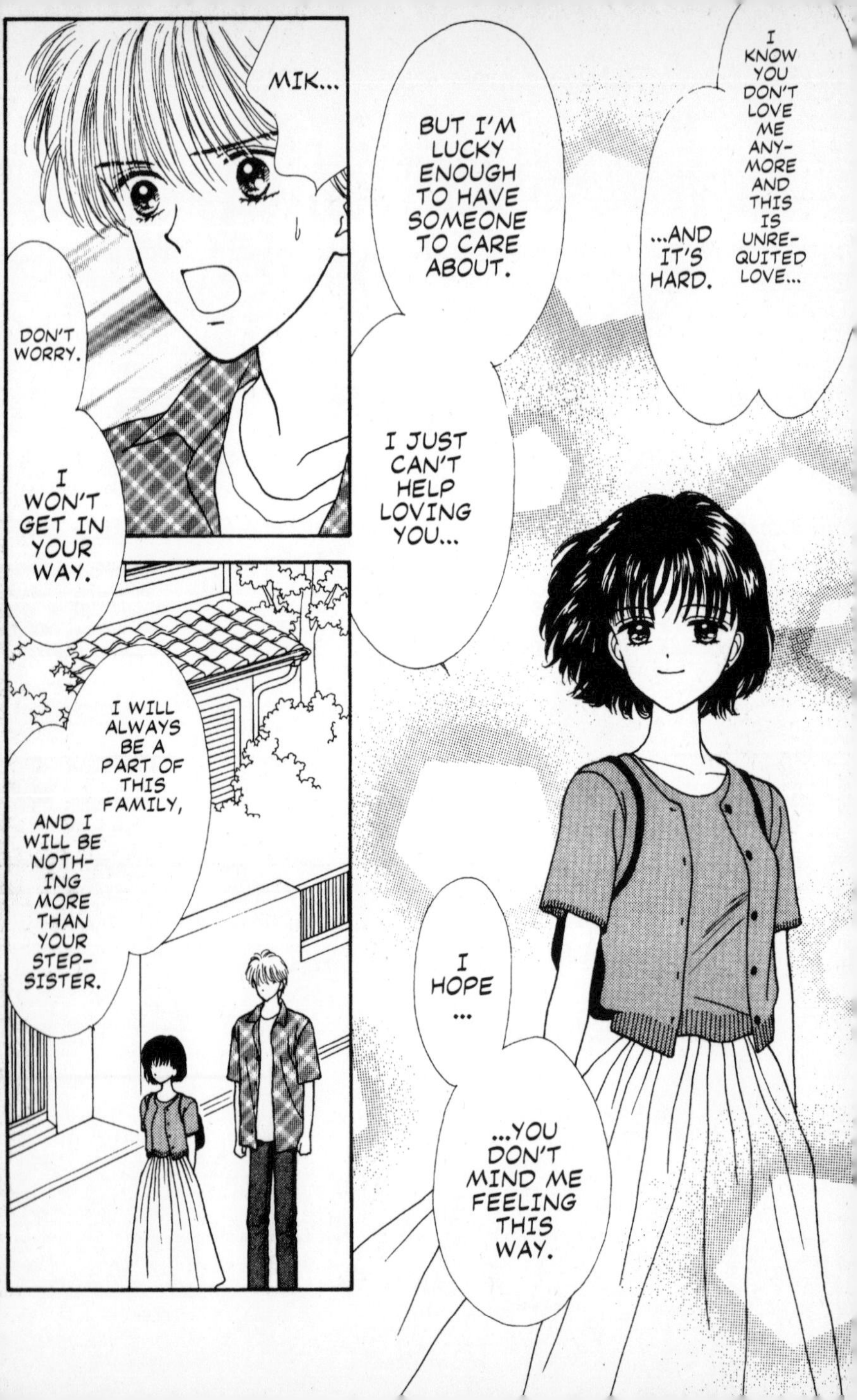
I KNOW YOU DON'T LOVE ME ANYMORE AND THIS IS UNREQUITED LOVE...
...AND IT'S HARD.
BUT I'M LUCKY ENOUGH TO HAVE SOMEONE TO CARE ABOUT.
I JUST CAN'T HELP LOVING YOU...
I HOPE...
...YOU DON'T MIND ME FEELING THIS WAY.
MIK...
DON'T WORRY.
I WON'T GET IN YOUR WAY.
I WILL ALWAYS BE A PART OF THIS FAMILY,
AND I WILL BE NOTHING MORE THAN YOUR STEPSISTER.

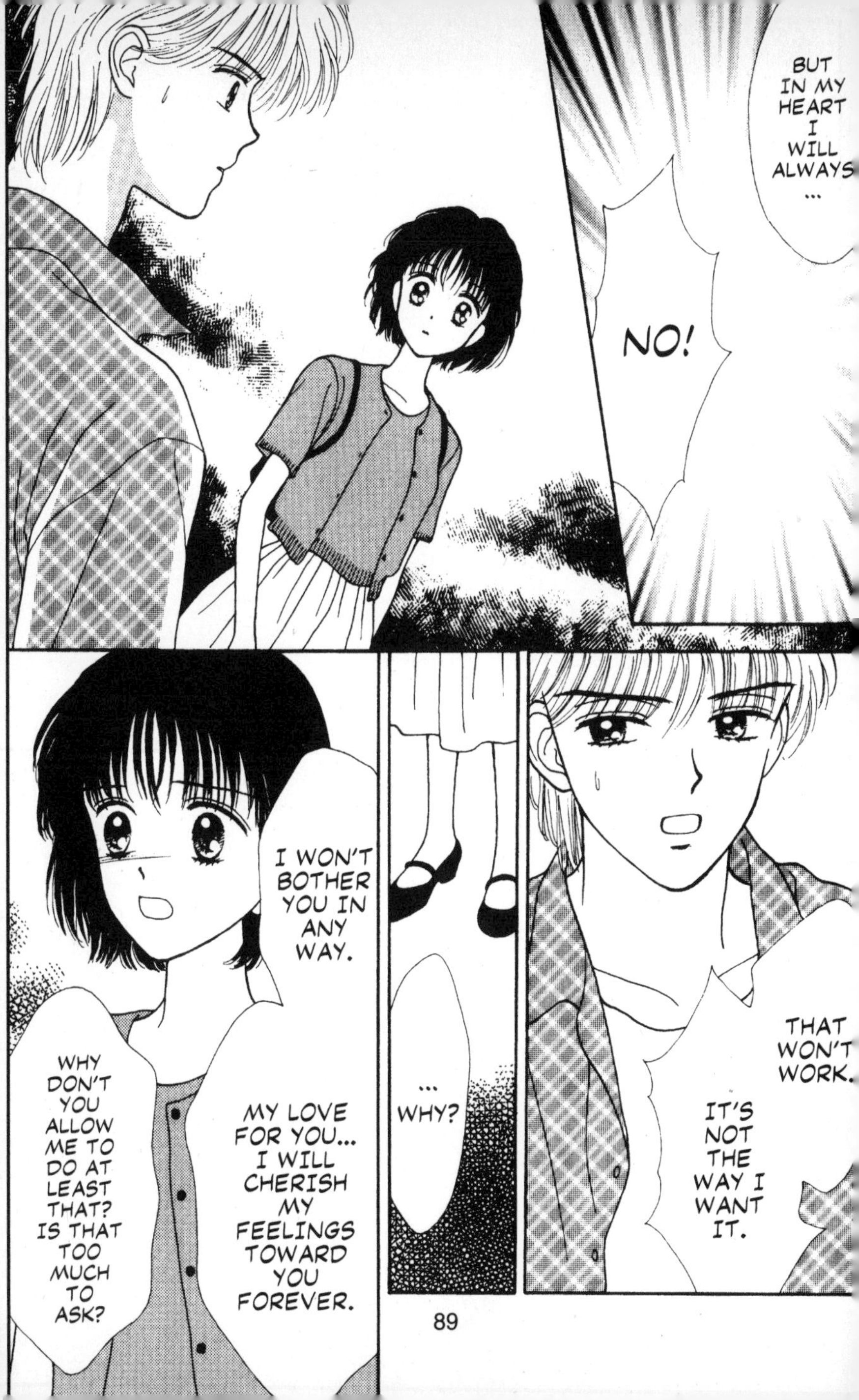

BUT IN MY HEART I WILL ALWAYS...
NO!
THAT WON'T WORK.
IT'S NOT THE WAY I WANT IT.
... WHY?
I WON'T BOTHER YOU IN ANY WAY.
MY LOVE FOR YOU... I WILL CHERISH MY FEELINGS TOWARD YOU FOREVER.
WHY DON'T YOU ALLOW ME TO DO AT LEAST THAT? IS THAT TOO MUCH TO ASK?

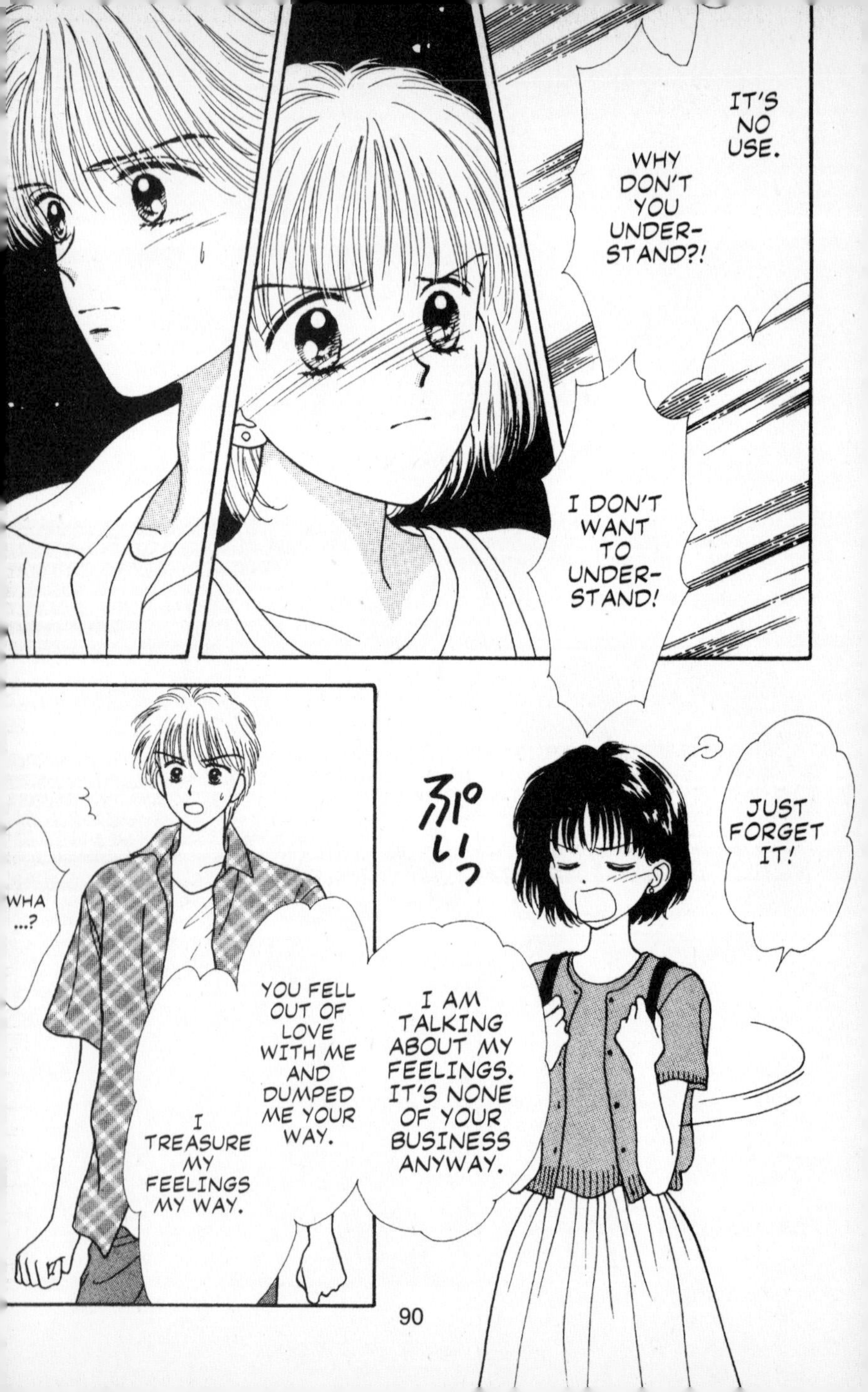
IT'S NO USE.
WHY DON'T YOU UNDER-STAND?!
I DON'T WANT TO UNDER-STAND!
JUST FORGET IT!
ぷいっ
I AM TALKING ABOUT MY FEELINGS. IT'S NONE OF YOUR BUSINESS ANYWAY.
YOU FELL OUT OF LOVE WITH ME AND DUMPED ME YOUR WAY.
I TREASURE MY FEELINGS MY WAY.
WHA ...?

FREE TALK ⑥

Yuu is always kissed by the girls in public. Miki allows Yuu to kiss her for as long as 12 seconds, only to sit up right after that and say, "What in the world did he do to me?" I can't help thinking, "What's up with you, Miki?! You could have said something or stopped him if that's not what you had desired!" I wish I could tell Yuu to duck their kisses if he really doesn't want them! My goodness, I am criticizing the behaviors of the very characters I created! (LOL!) I don't like the way Miki is dressed in the anime, either. She wears a combination of pink and light blue quite often (and I hate that combination). They almost look like the theme colors. Miki is dressed like that probably 70 percent of the time. I also hate the way all the foreign characters speak perfect Japanese. It destroys the exotic image of those characters.

(To be continued in Free Talk 7)

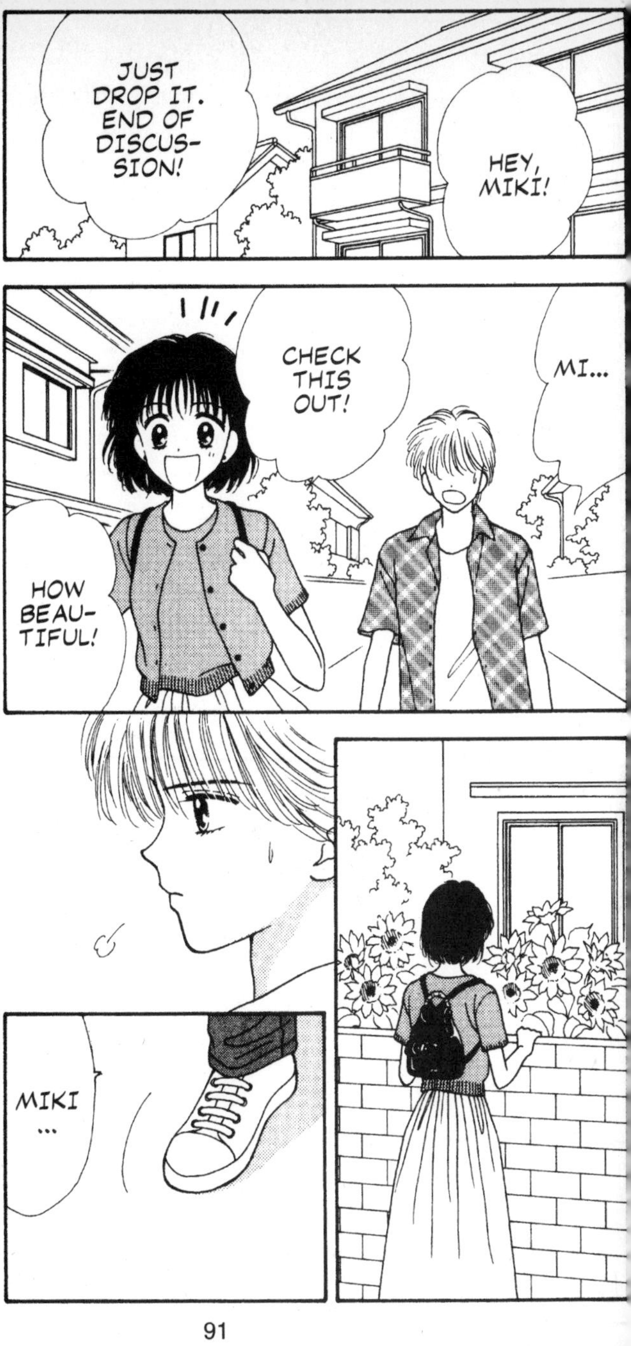
HEY, MIKI!
JUST DROP IT. END OF DISCUSSION!
MI...
CHECK THIS OUT!
HOW BEAUTIFUL!
MIKI ...

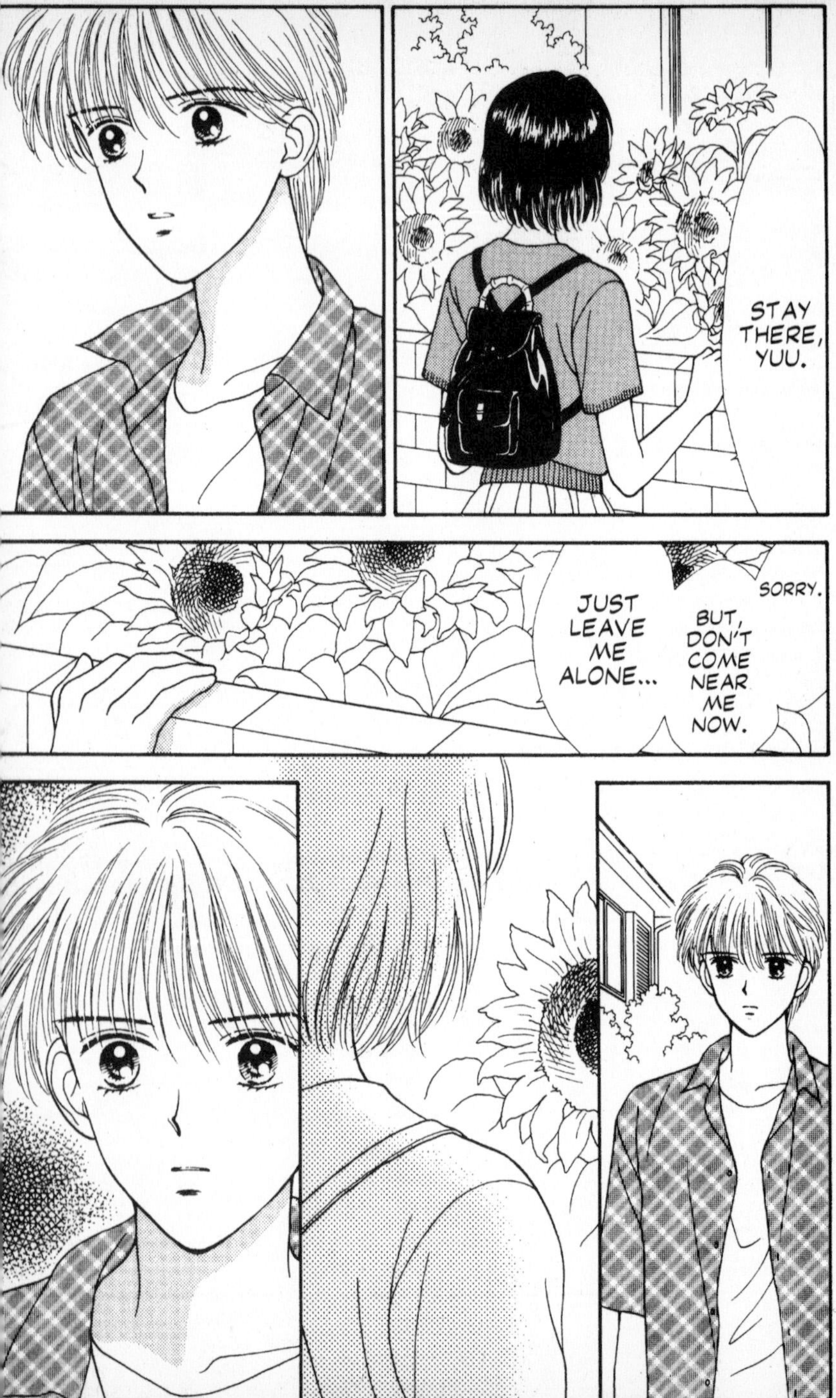
STAY THERE, YUU.
SORRY.
BUT, DON'T COME NEAR ME NOW.
JUST LEAVE ME ALONE...

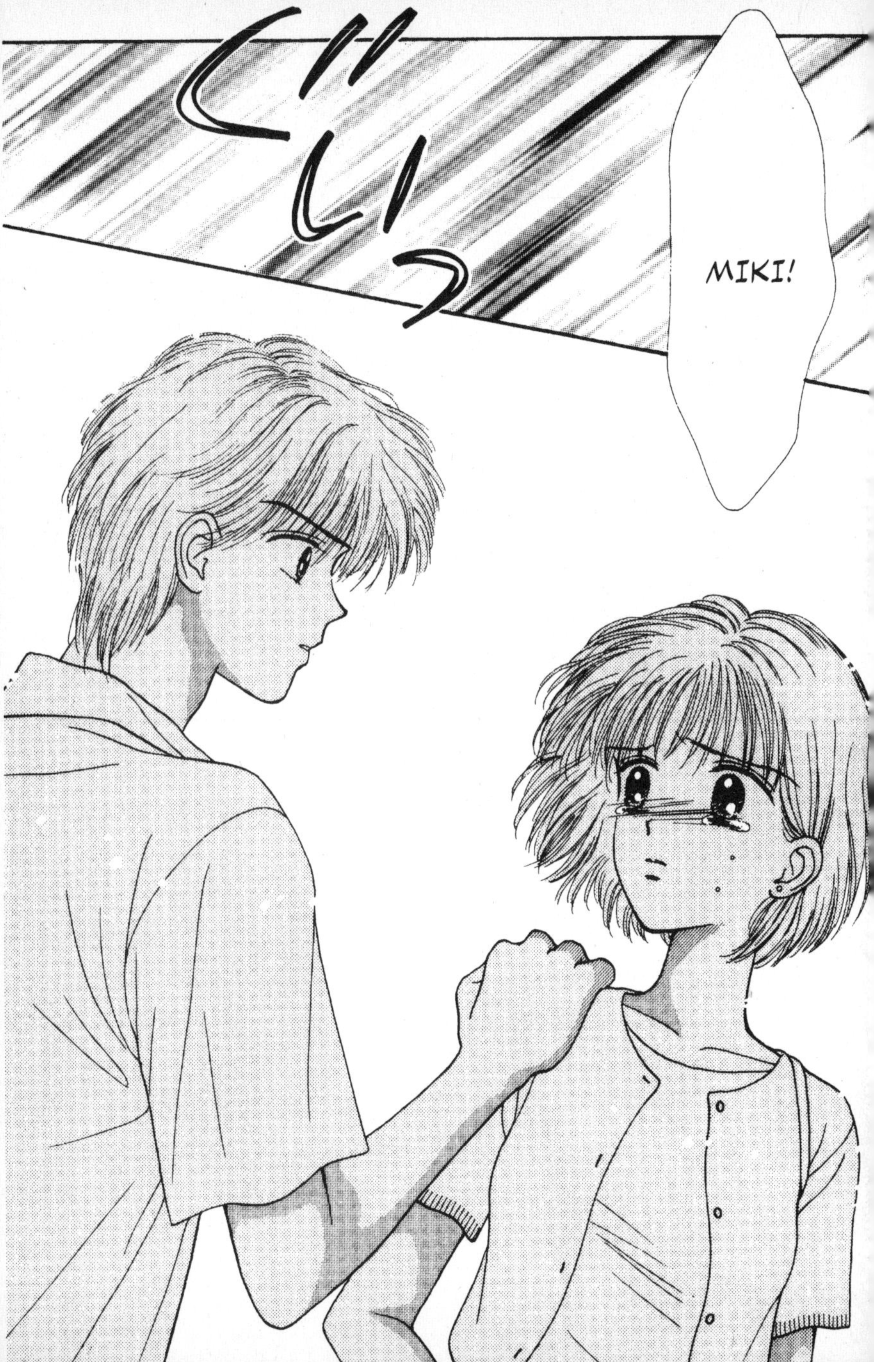
MIKI!
ぐいっ

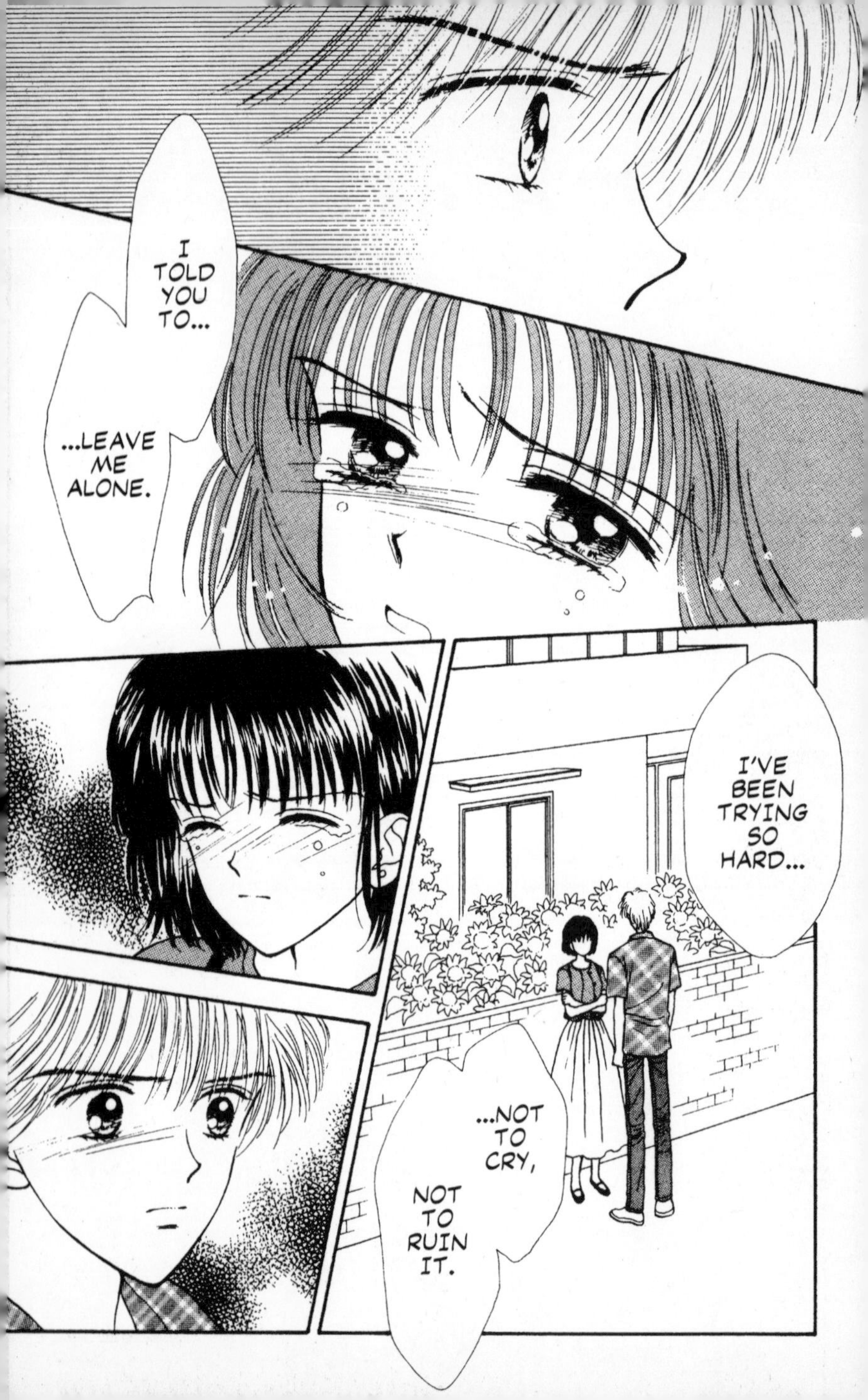
I TOLD YOU TO...
...LEAVE ME ALONE.
I'VE BEEN TRYING SO HARD...
...NOT TO CRY,
NOT TO RUIN IT.

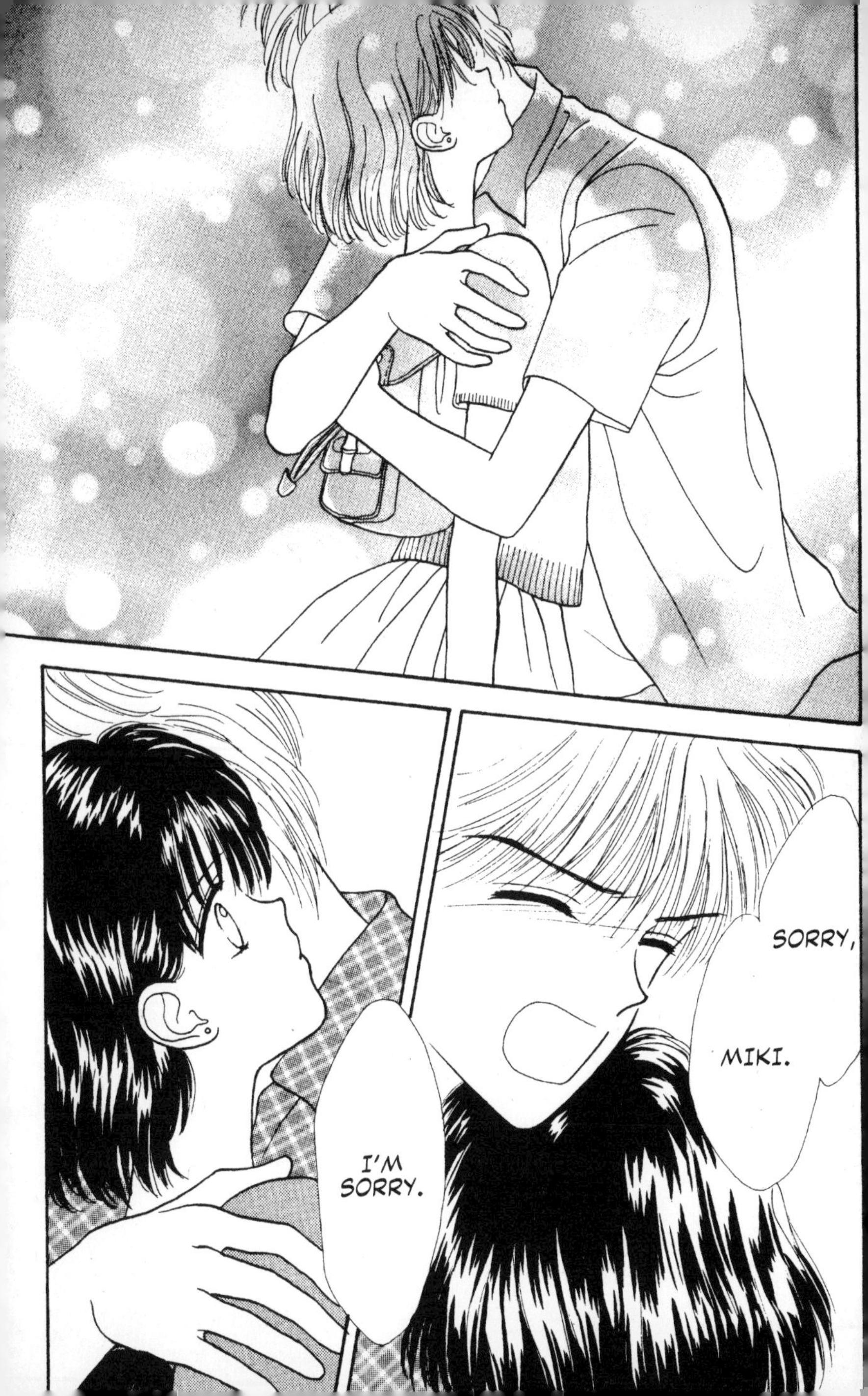
SORRY, MIKI.
I'M SORRY.

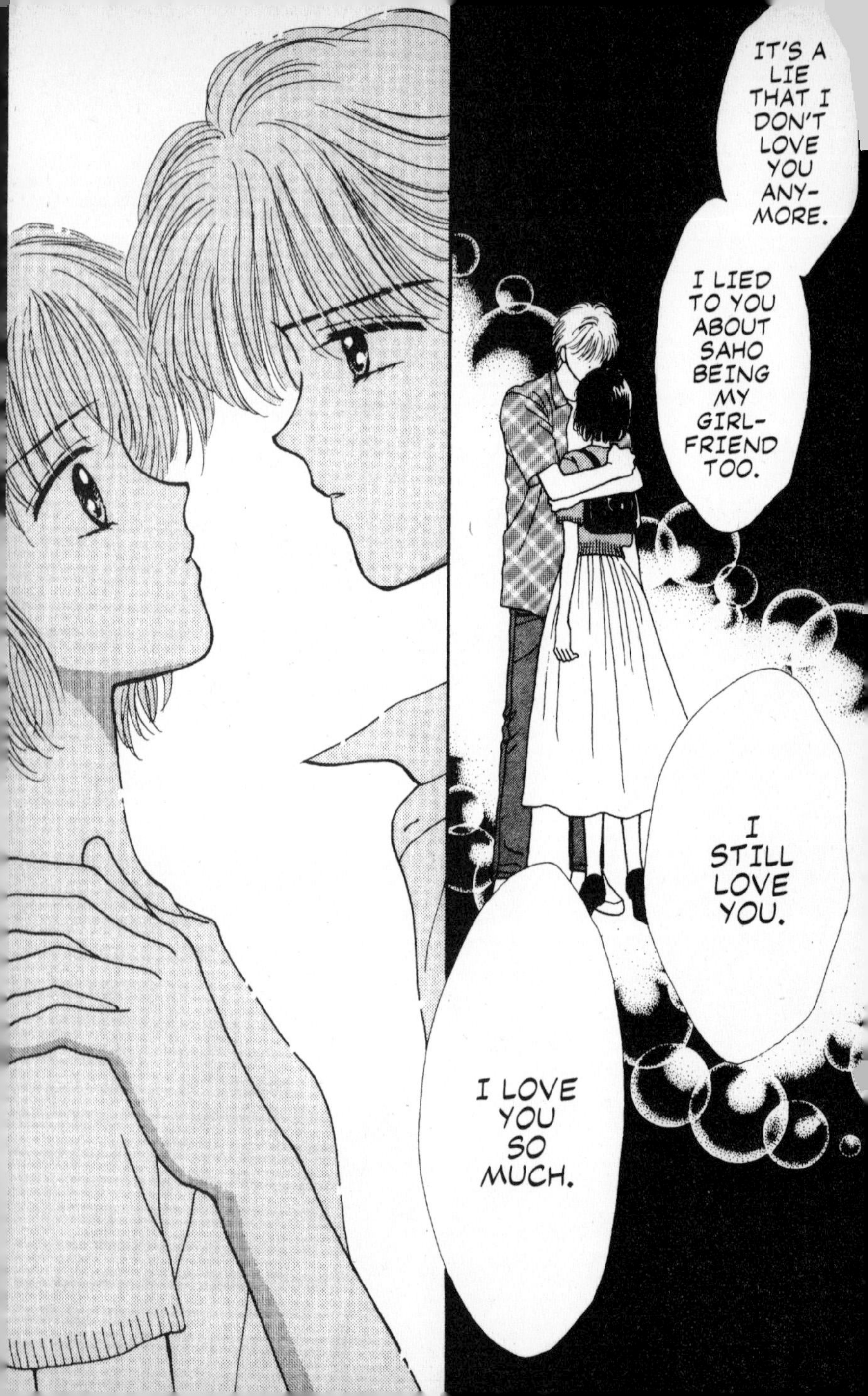
IT'S A LIE THAT I DON'T LOVE YOU ANY-MORE.
I LIED TO YOU ABOUT SAHO BEING MY GIRL-FRIEND TOO.
I STILL LOVE YOU.
I LOVE YOU SO MUCH.

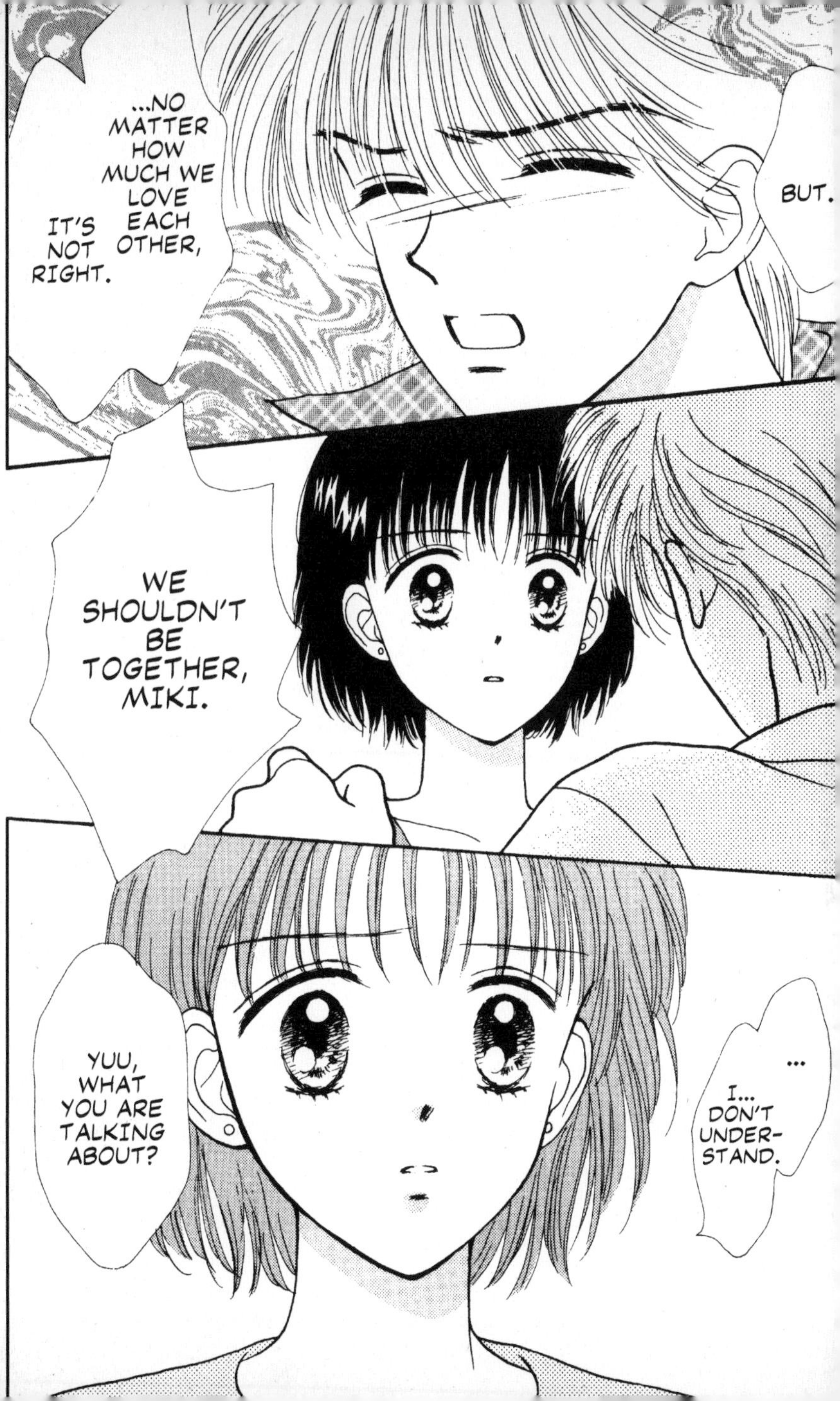
BUT.
...NO MATTER HOW MUCH WE LOVE EACH OTHER,
IT'S NOT RIGHT.
WE SHOULDN'T BE TOGETHER, MIKI.
...
I... DON'T UNDER-STAND.
YUU, WHAT YOU ARE TALKING ABOUT?

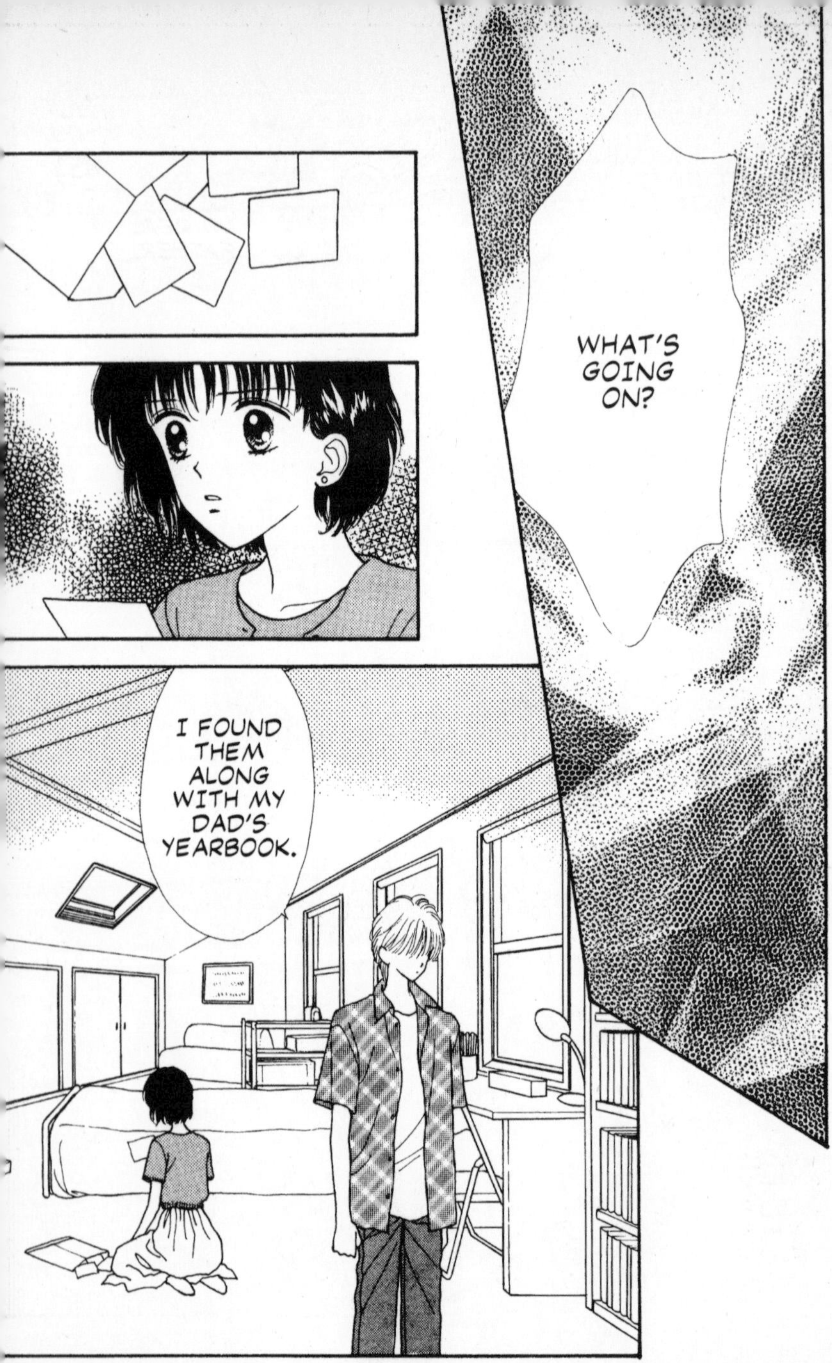
WHAT'S GOING ON?
I FOUND THEM ALONG WITH MY DAD'S YEARBOOK.

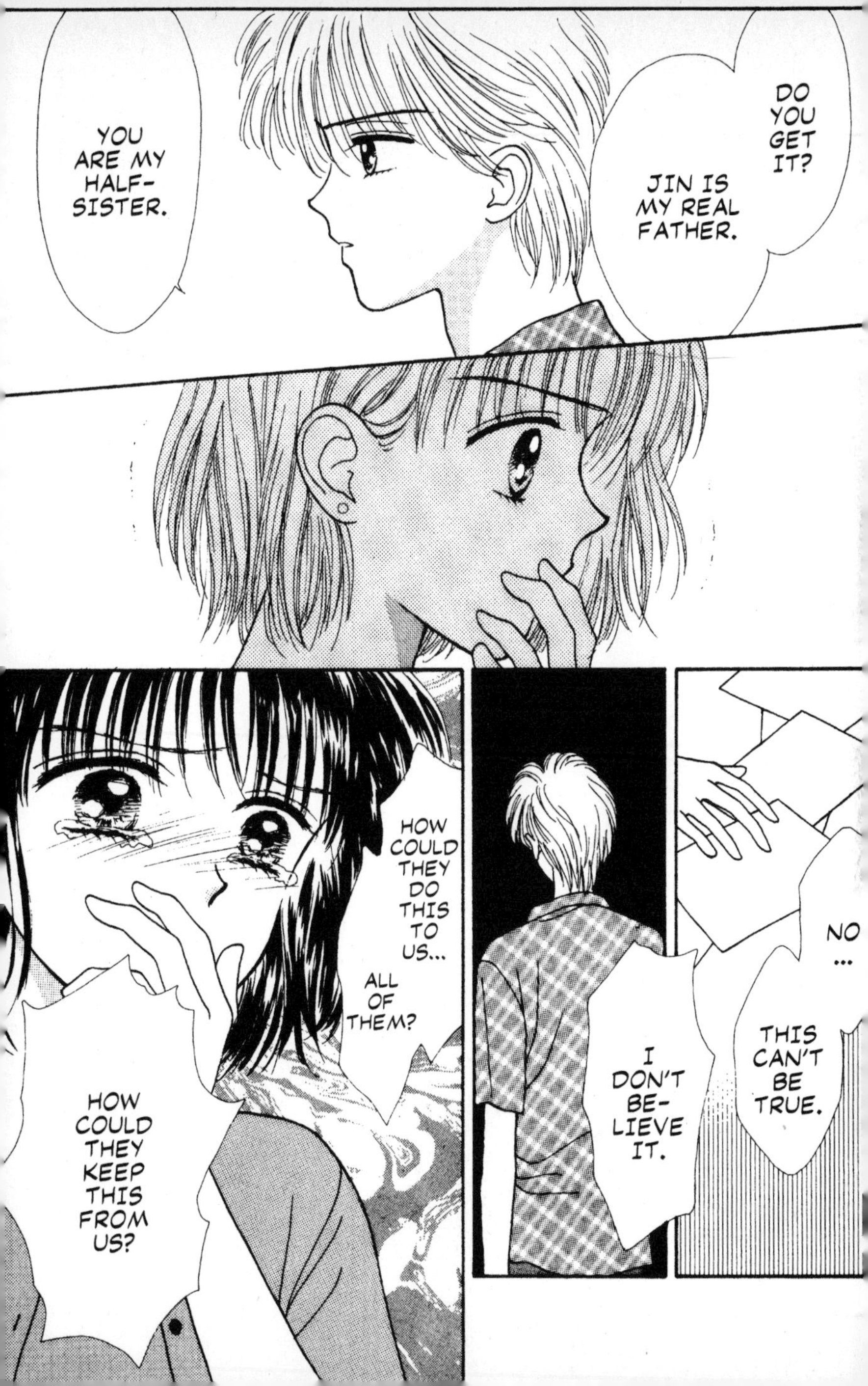
DO YOU GET IT?
JIN IS MY REAL FATHER.
YOU ARE MY HALF-SISTER.
NO...
THIS CAN'T BE TRUE.
I DON'T BE-LIEVE IT.
HOW COULD THEY DO THIS TO US...
ALL OF THEM?
HOW COULD THEY KEEP THIS FROM US?

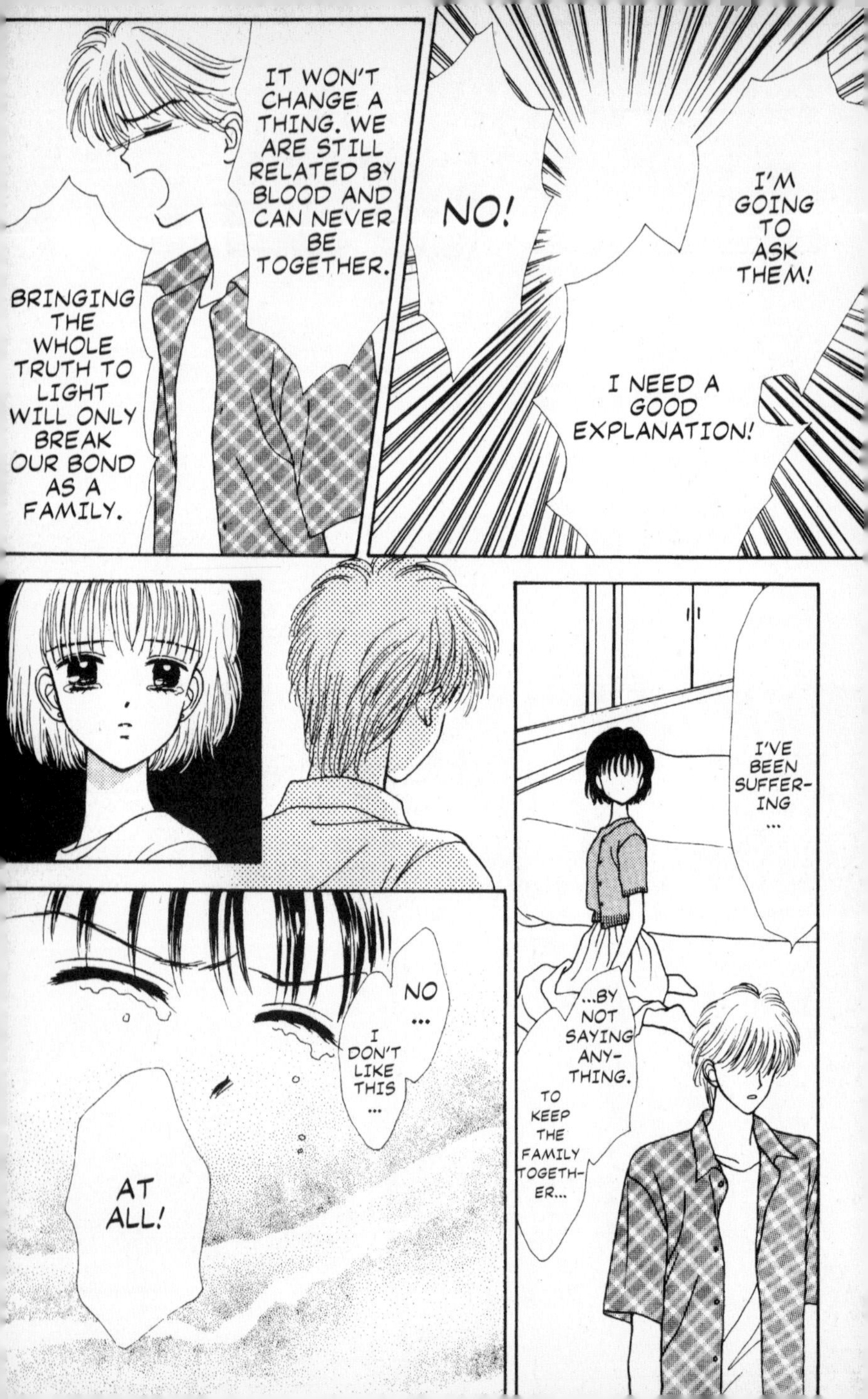

IT WON'T CHANGE A THING. WE ARE STILL RELATED BY BLOOD AND CAN NEVER BE TOGETHER.
BRINGING THE WHOLE TRUTH TO LIGHT WILL ONLY BREAK OUR BOND AS A FAMILY.
I'M GOING TO ASK THEM!
NO!
I NEED A GOOD EXPLANATION!
I'VE BEEN SUFFERING...
...BY NOT SAYING ANYTHING.
TO KEEP THE FAMILY TOGETHER...
NO...
I DON'T LIKE THIS...
AT ALL!

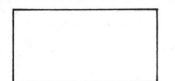

WHAT? MIKI DOESN'T WANT DINNER?

NO. SHE SAYS SHE DOESN'T FEEL WELL.

SHE SAYS ALL SHE NEEDS IS A LITTLE REST.

THE SUMMER HEAT HAS HER ALL MESSED UP.

NOOOOOO...

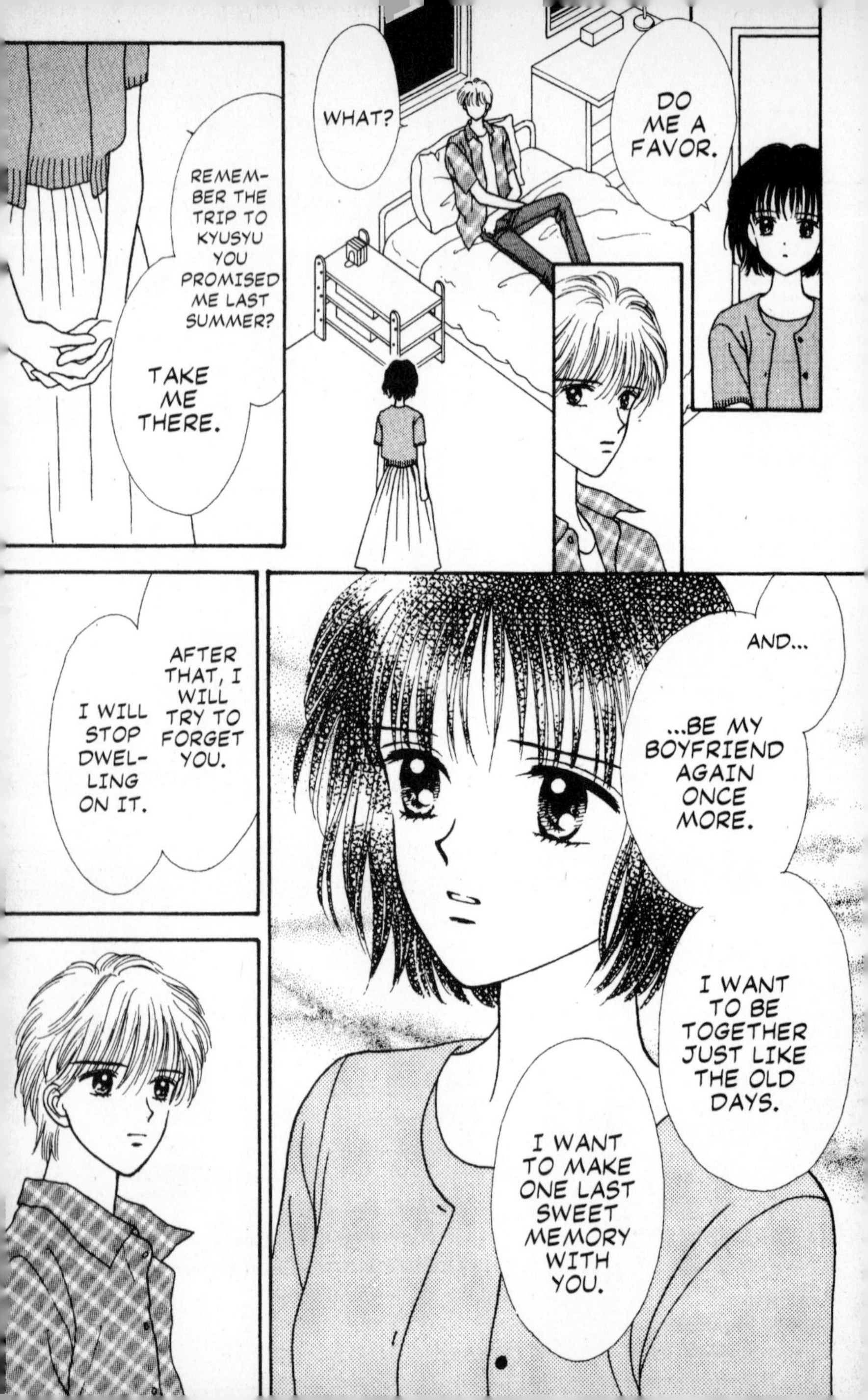
DO ME A FAVOR.
WHAT?
REMEMBER THE TRIP TO KYUSYU YOU PROMISED ME LAST SUMMER?
TAKE ME THERE.
AND...
...BE MY BOYFRIEND AGAIN ONCE MORE.
I WANT TO BE TOGETHER JUST LIKE THE OLD DAYS.
I WANT TO MAKE ONE LAST SWEET MEMORY WITH YOU.
AFTER THAT, I WILL TRY TO FORGET YOU.
I WILL STOP DWELLING ON IT.

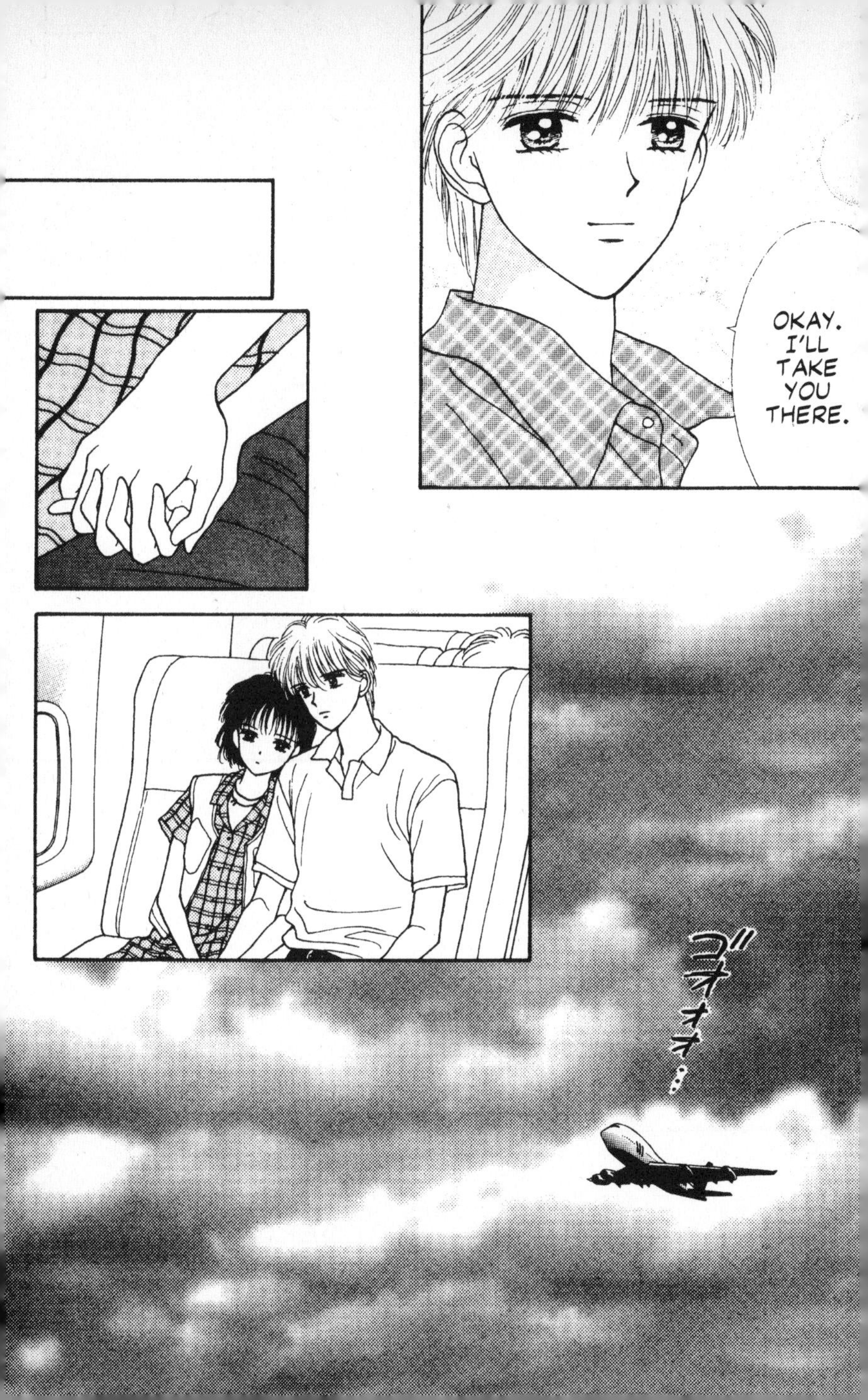
OKAY. I'LL TAKE YOU THERE.
ゴオオオ…

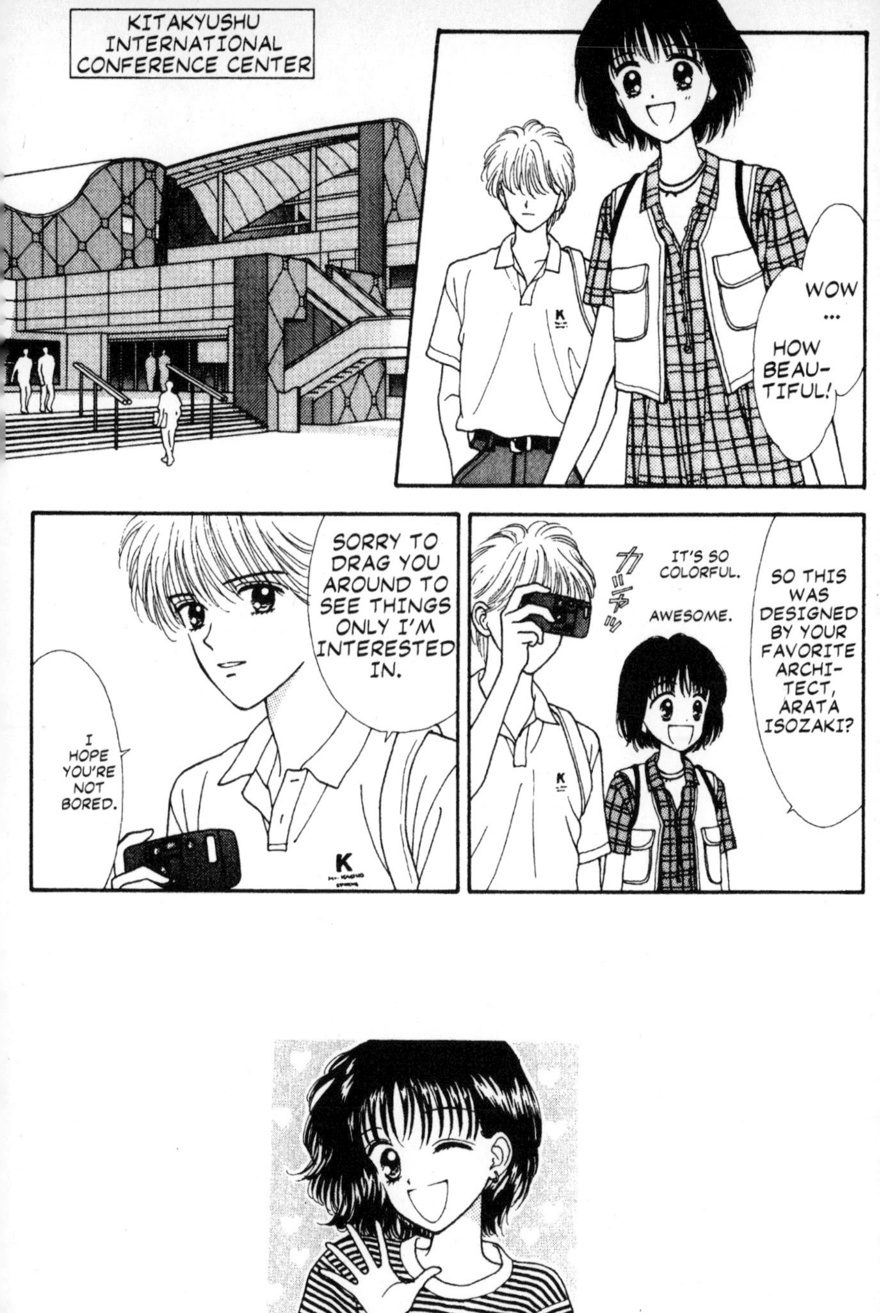
KITAKYUSHU INTERNATIONAL CONFERENCE CENTER
WOW... HOW BEAUTIFUL!
SO THIS WAS DESIGNED BY YOUR FAVORITE ARCHITECT, ARATA ISOZAKI?
カシャッ
IT'S SO COLORFUL.
AWESOME.
SORRY TO DRAG YOU AROUND TO SEE THINGS ONLY I'M INTERESTED IN.
I HOPE YOU'RE NOT BORED.

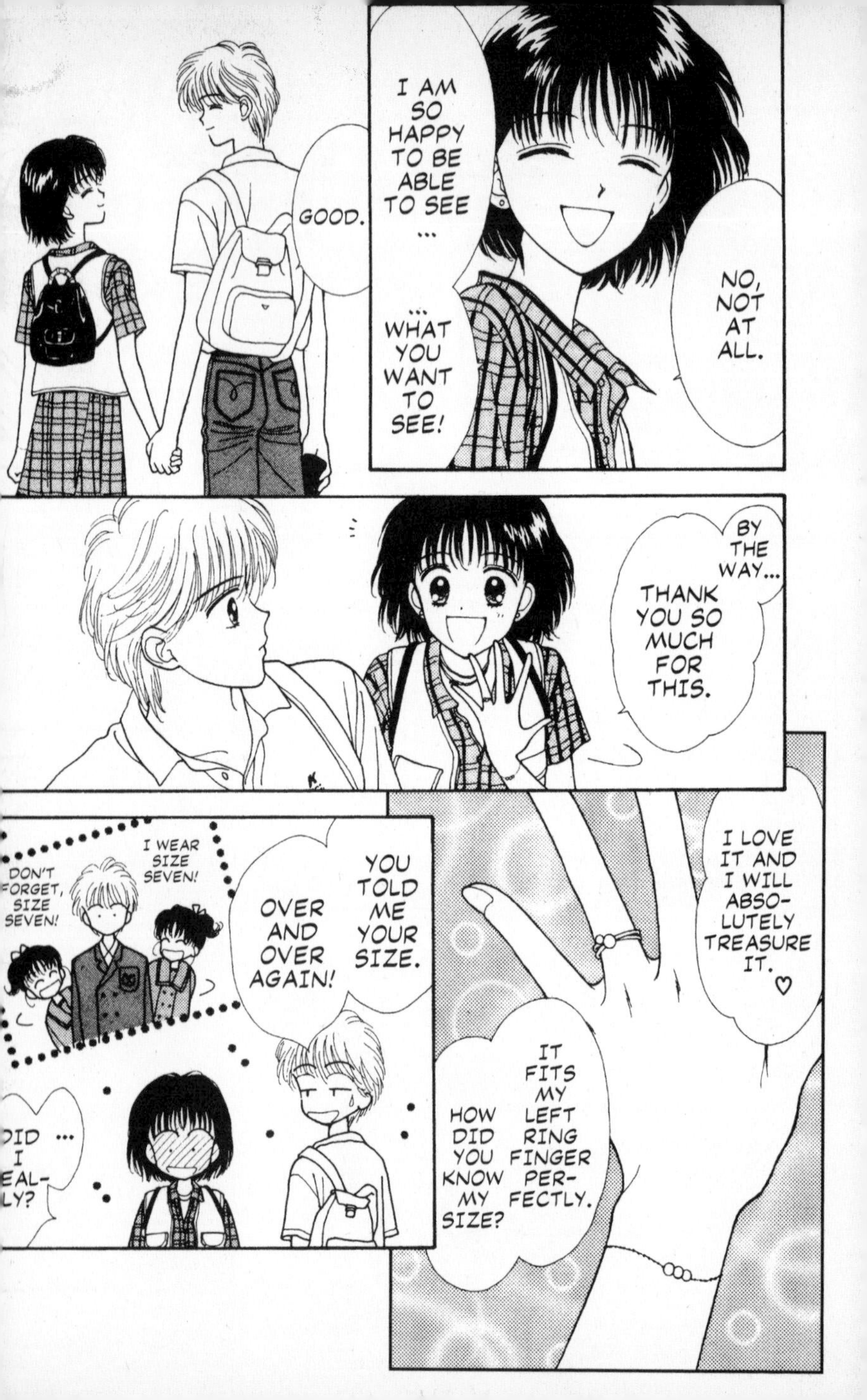
NO, NOT AT ALL.
I AM SO HAPPY TO BE ABLE TO SEE ... ... WHAT YOU WANT TO SEE!
GOOD.
BY THE WAY...
THANK YOU SO MUCH FOR THIS.
I LOVE IT AND I WILL ABSOLUTELY TREASURE IT. ♡
IT FITS MY LEFT RING FINGER PERFECTLY.
HOW DID YOU KNOW MY SIZE?
YOU TOLD ME YOUR SIZE.
OVER AND OVER AGAIN!
I WEAR SIZE SEVEN!
DON'T FORGET, SIZE SEVEN!
DID I REALLY? ...

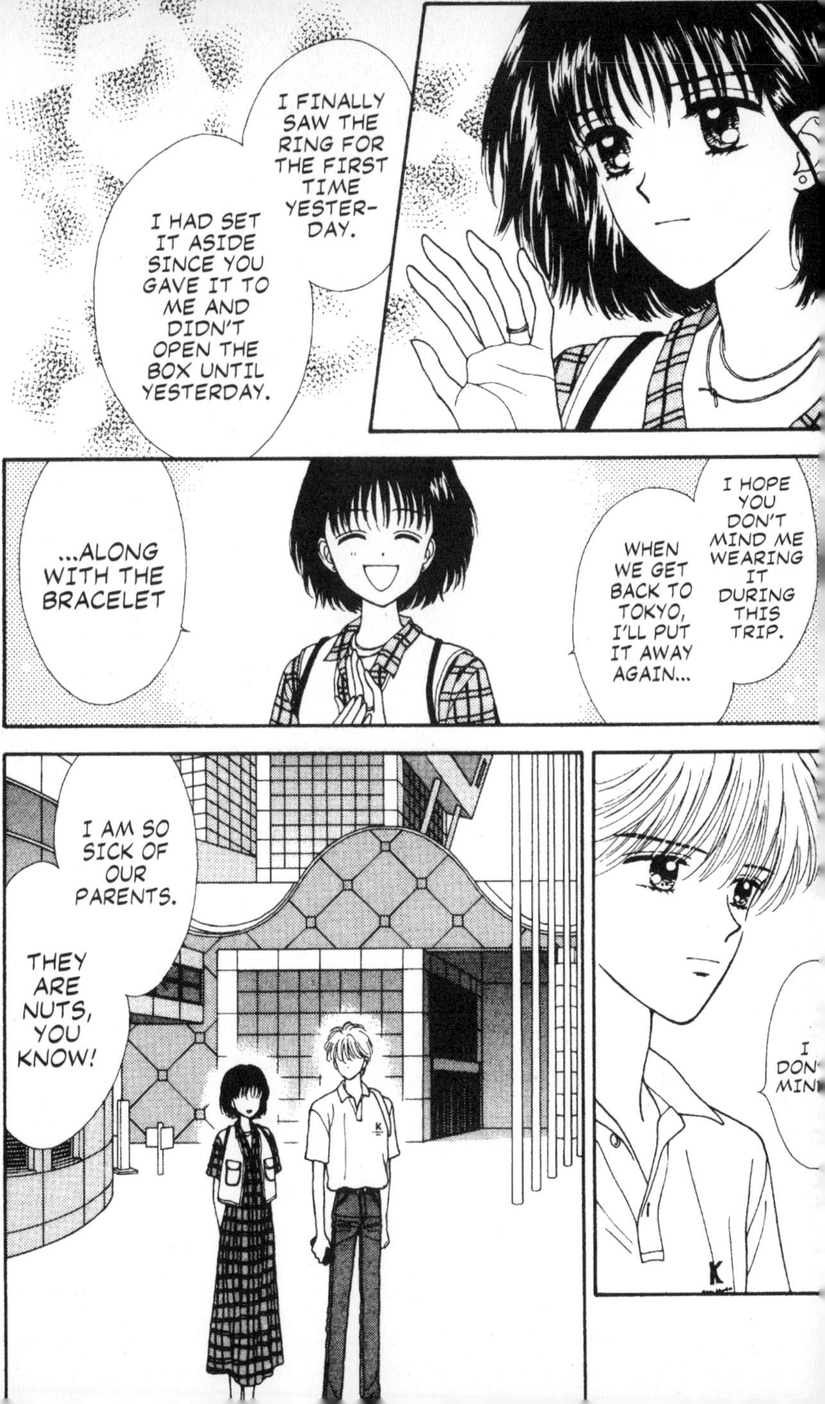
I FINALLY SAW THE RING FOR THE FIRST TIME YESTER-DAY.
I HAD SET IT ASIDE SINCE YOU GAVE IT TO ME AND DIDN'T OPEN THE BOX UNTIL YESTERDAY.
I HOPE YOU DON'T MIND ME WEARING IT DURING THIS TRIP.
WHEN WE GET BACK TO TOKYO, I'LL PUT IT AWAY AGAIN...
...ALONG WITH THE BRACELET
I AM SO SICK OF OUR PARENTS.
THEY ARE NUTS, YOU KNOW!

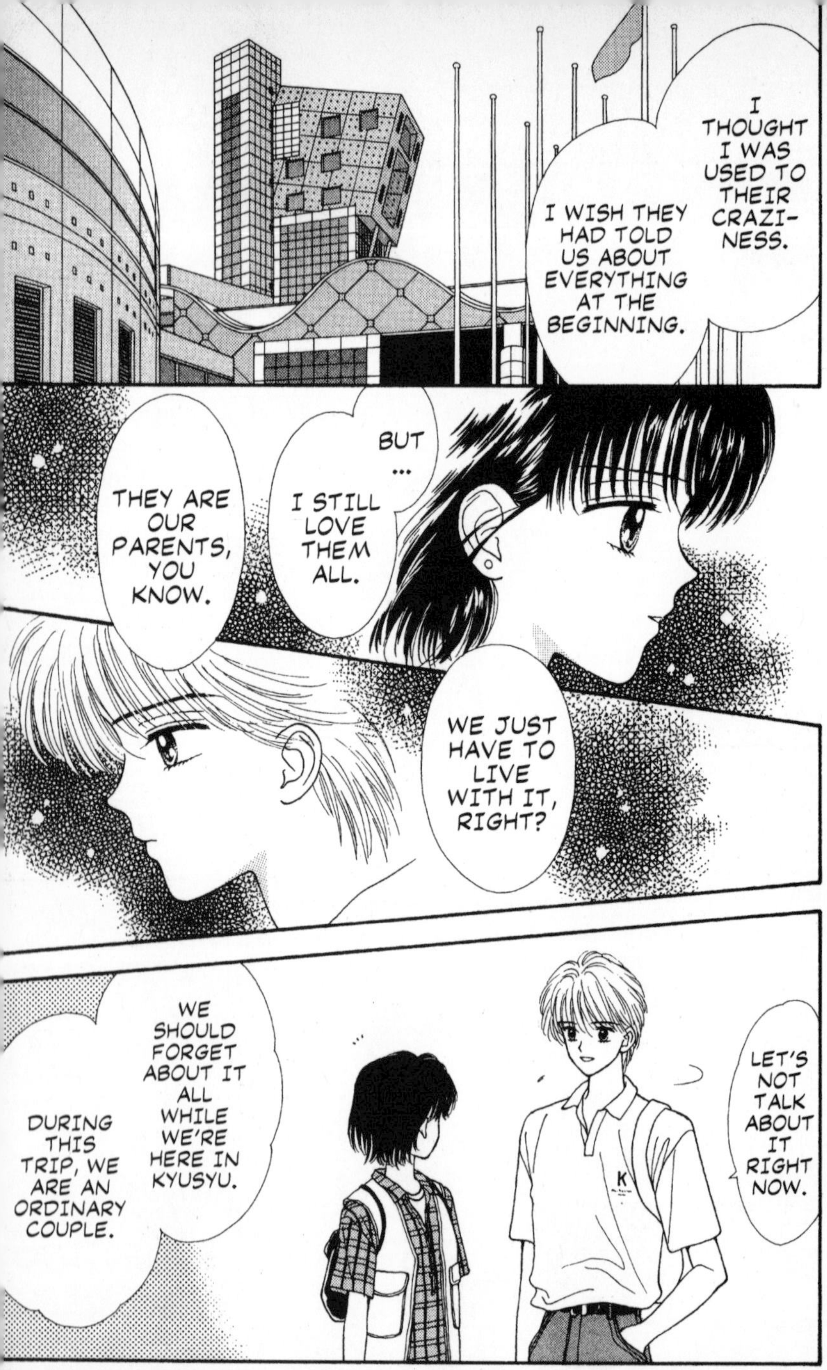
I THOUGHT I WAS USED TO THEIR CRAZINESS.
I WISH THEY HAD TOLD US ABOUT EVERYTHING AT THE BEGINNING.
BUT ... I STILL LOVE THEM ALL.
THEY ARE OUR PARENTS, YOU KNOW.
WE JUST HAVE TO LIVE WITH IT, RIGHT?
LET'S NOT TALK ABOUT IT RIGHT NOW.
WE SHOULD FORGET ABOUT IT ALL WHILE WE'RE HERE IN KYUSYU.
DURING THIS TRIP, WE ARE AN ORDINARY COUPLE.

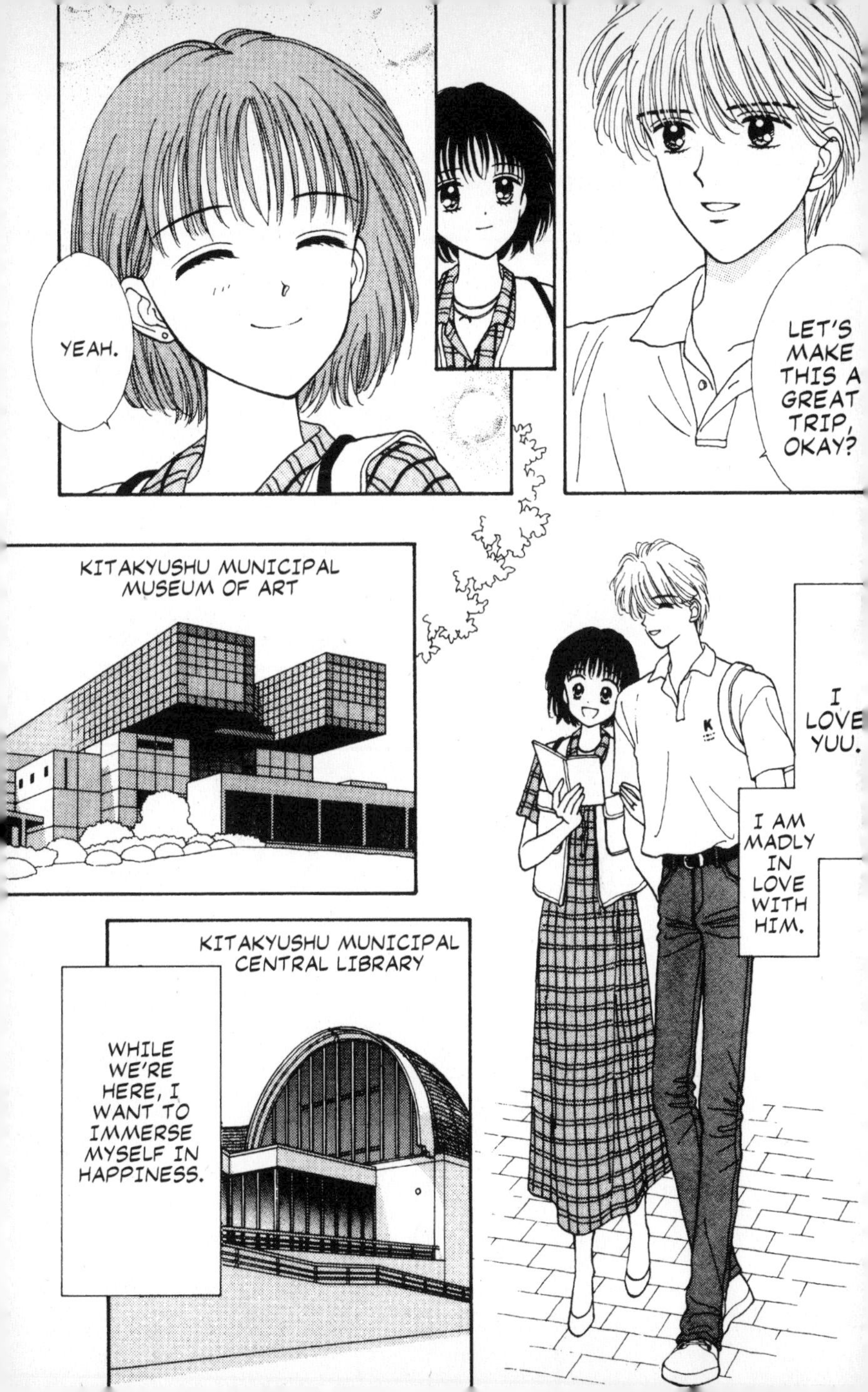
LET'S MAKE THIS A GREAT TRIP, OKAY?
YEAH.
I LOVE YUU.
I AM MADLY IN LOVE WITH HIM.
KITAKYUSHU MUNICIPAL MUSEUM OF ART
KITAKYUSHU MUNICIPAL CENTRAL LIBRARY
WHILE WE'RE HERE, I WANT TO IMMERSE MYSELF IN HAPPINESS.

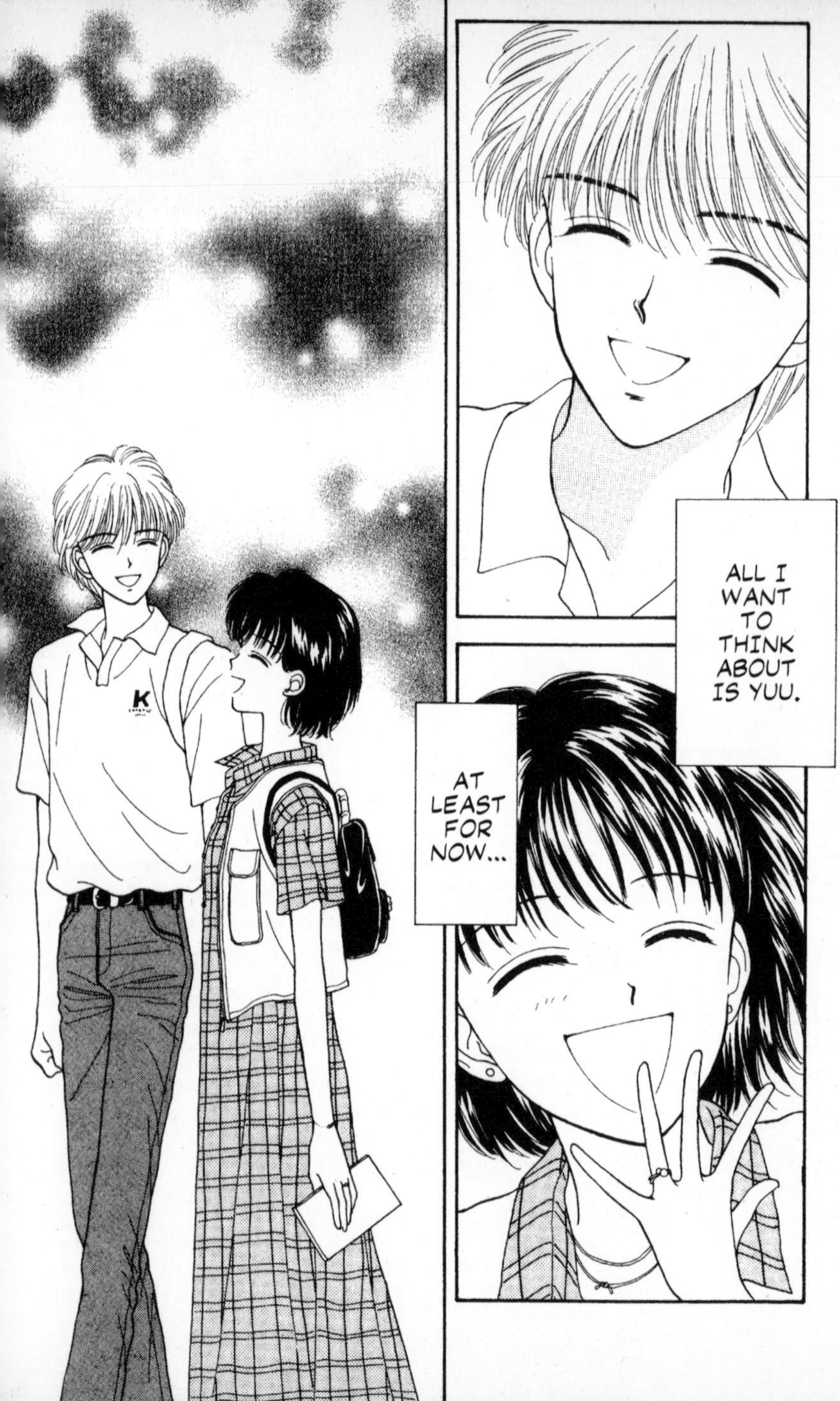
ALL I WANT TO THINK ABOUT IS YUU.
AT LEAST FOR NOW...

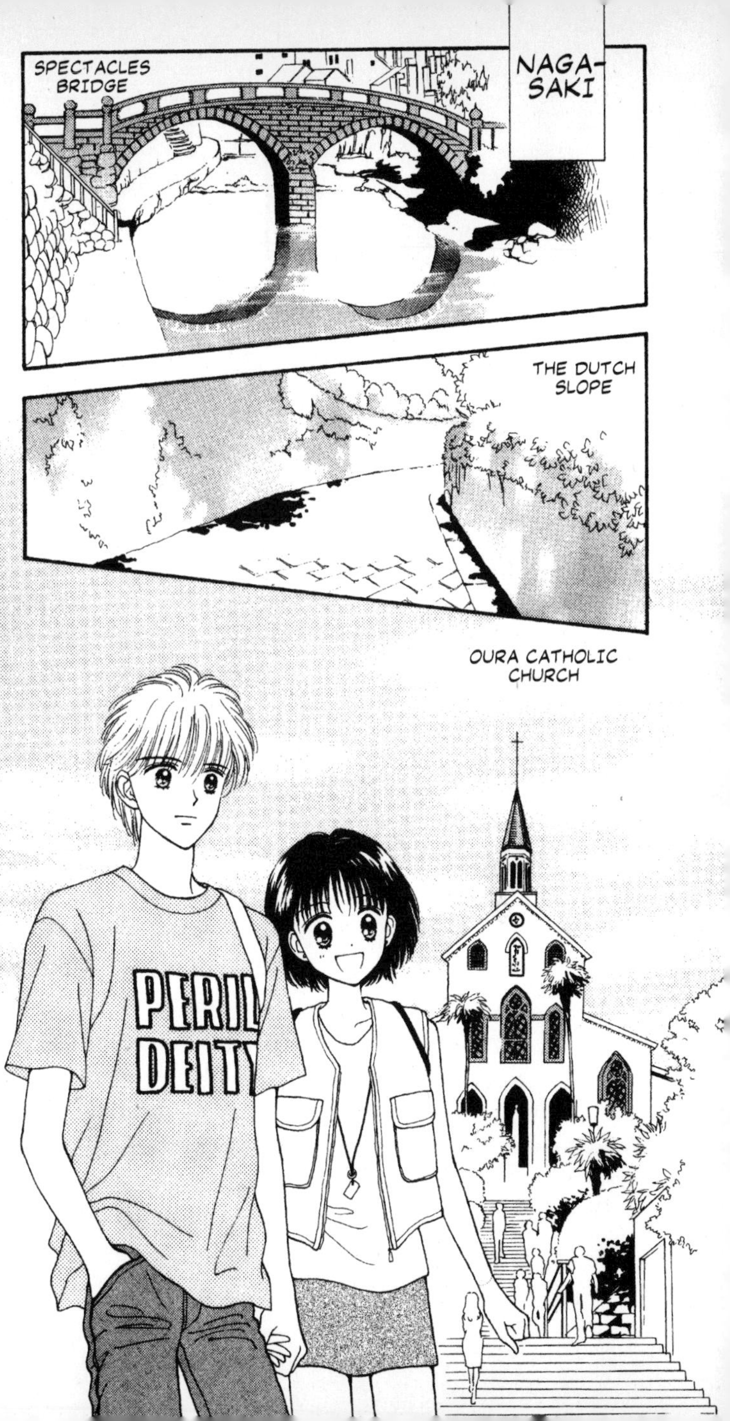
NAGA-SAKI
SPECTACLES BRIDGE
THE DUTCH SLOPE
OURA CATHOLIC CHURCH
PERIL DEITY

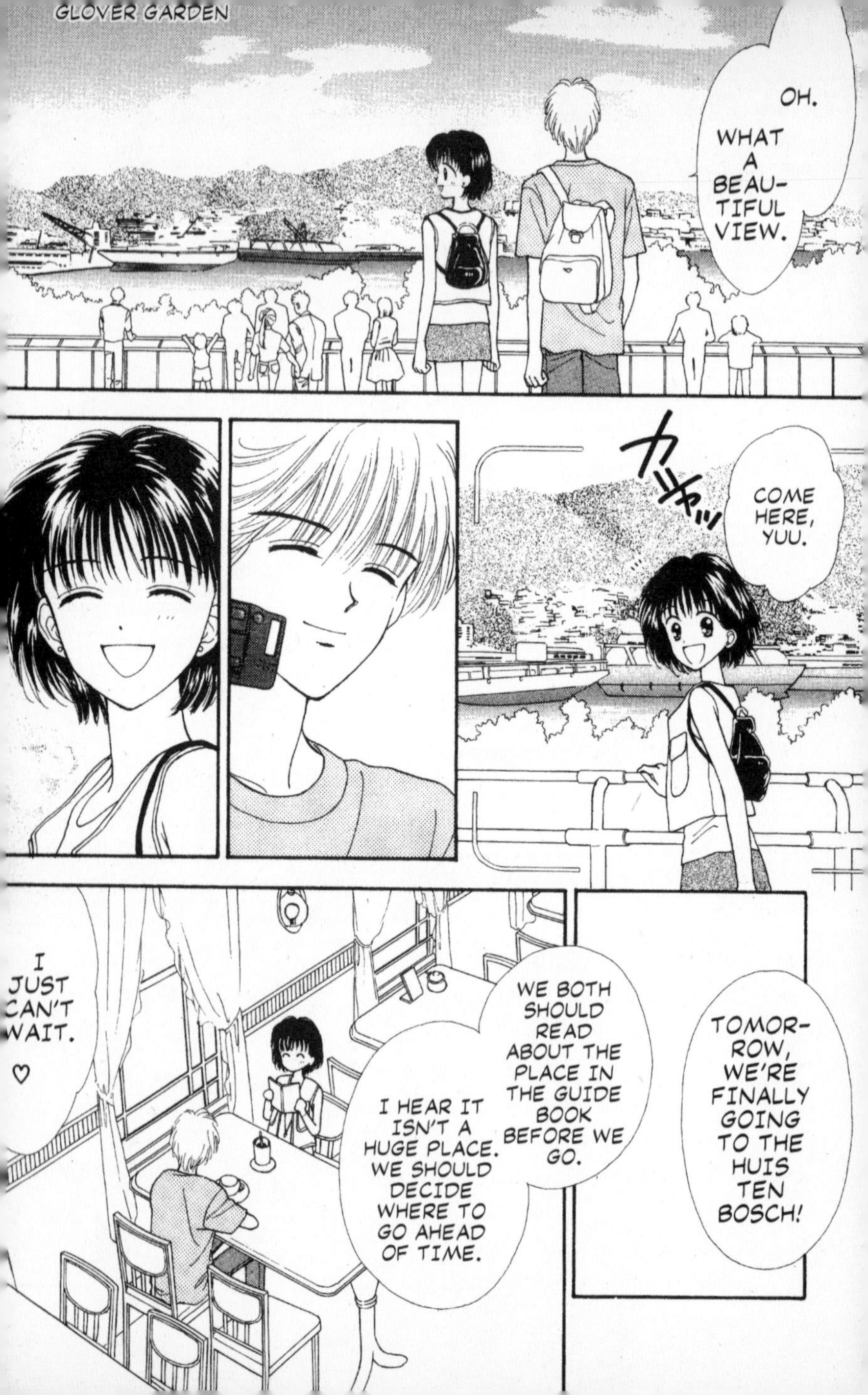
GLOVER GARDEN
OH. WHAT A BEAUTIFUL VIEW.
カチャッ
COME HERE, YUU.
TOMORROW, WE'RE FINALLY GOING TO THE HUIS TEN BOSCH!
WE BOTH SHOULD READ ABOUT THE PLACE IN THE GUIDE BOOK BEFORE WE GO.
I HEAR IT ISN'T A HUGE PLACE. WE SHOULD DECIDE WHERE TO GO AHEAD OF TIME.
I JUST CAN'T WAIT. ♡

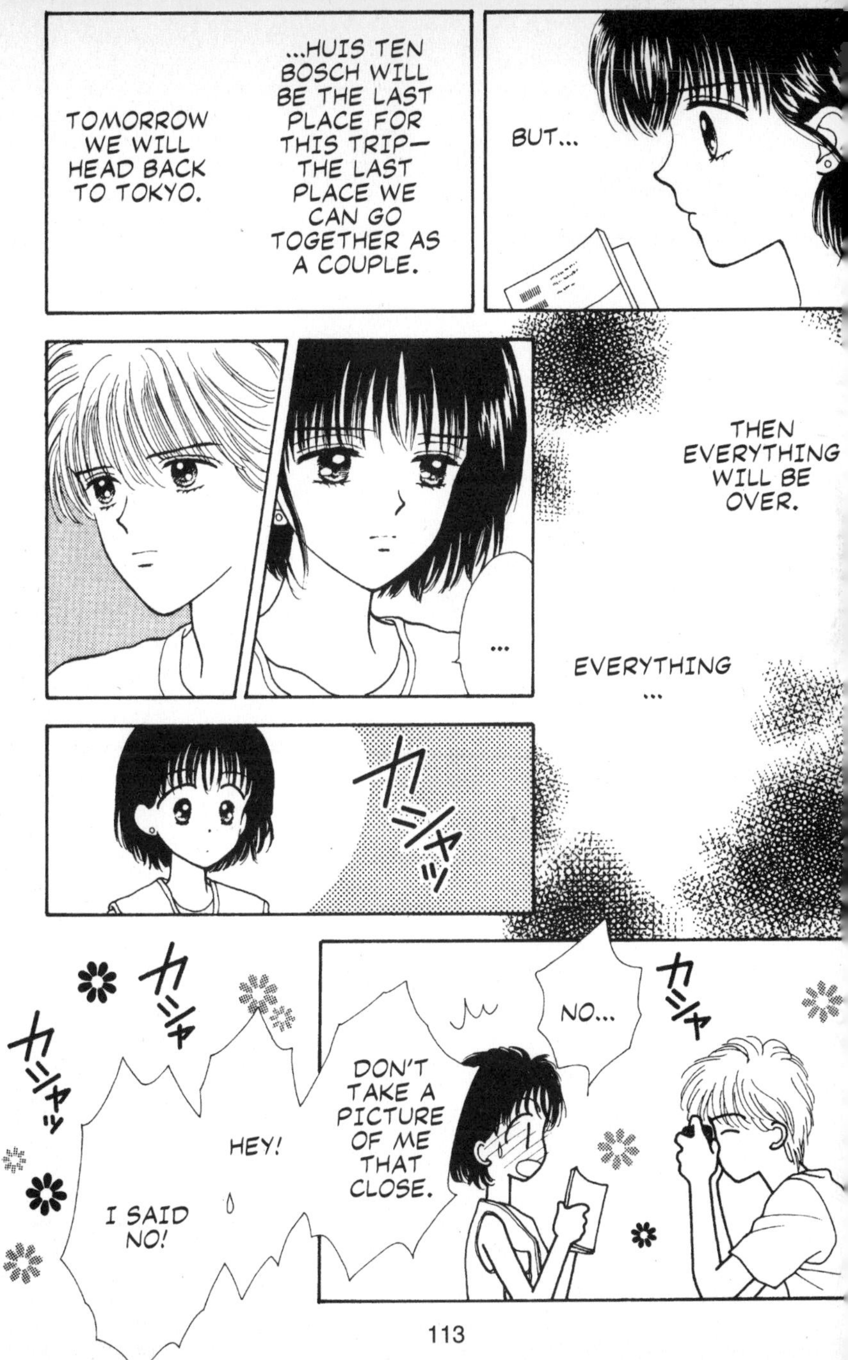
TOMORROW WE WILL HEAD BACK TO TOKYO.
...HUIS TEN BOSCH WILL BE THE LAST PLACE FOR THIS TRIP—THE LAST PLACE WE CAN GO TOGETHER AS A COUPLE.
BUT...
THEN EVERYTHING WILL BE OVER.
...
EVERYTHING ...
カシャッ
カシャ
NO...
DON'T TAKE A PICTURE OF ME THAT CLOSE.
カシャ
カシャッ
HEY!
I SAID NO!

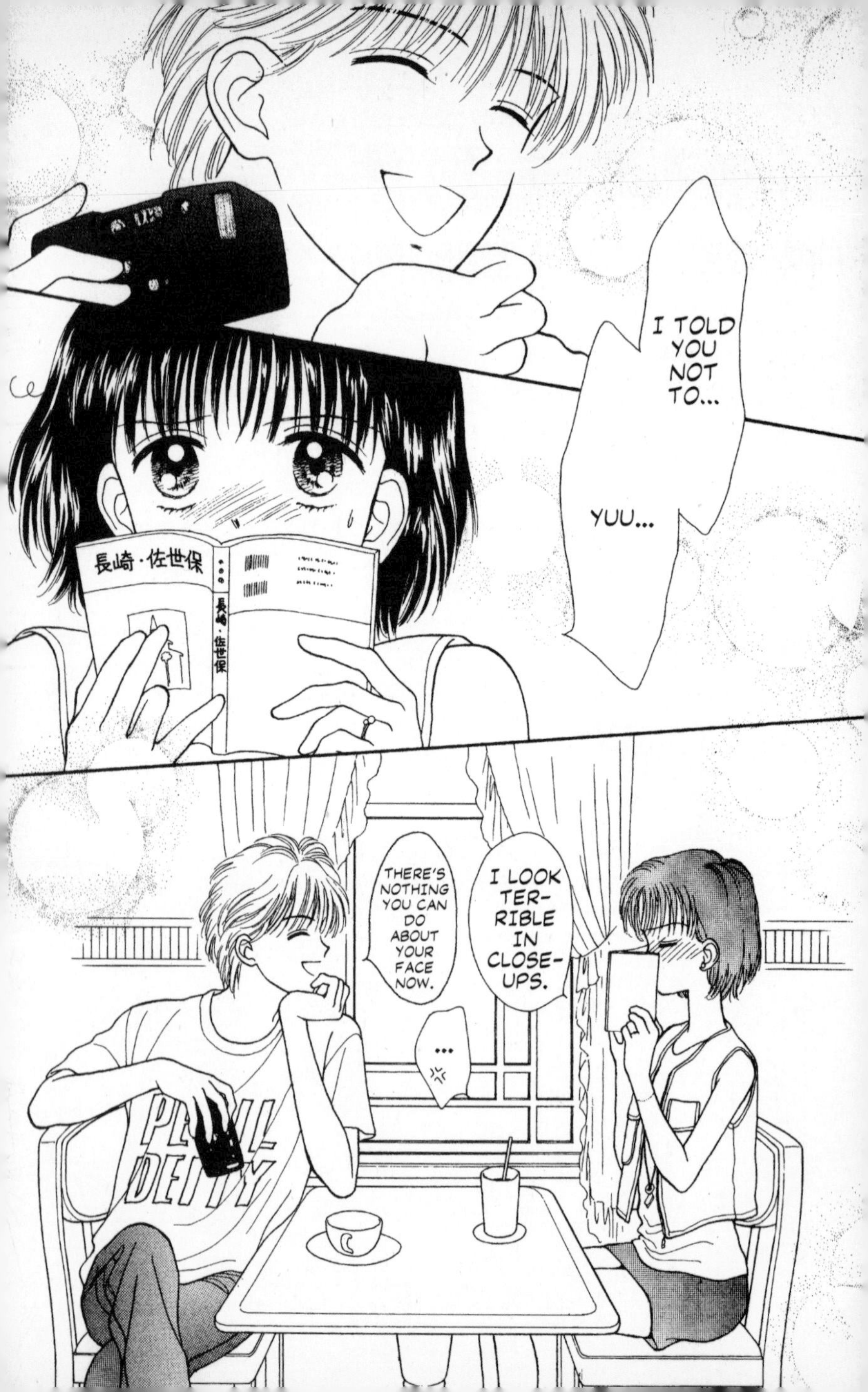
I TOLD YOU NOT TO...
YUU...
長崎・佐世保
I LOOK TER-RIBLE IN CLOSE-UPS.
THERE'S NOTHING YOU CAN DO ABOUT YOUR FACE NOW.
...

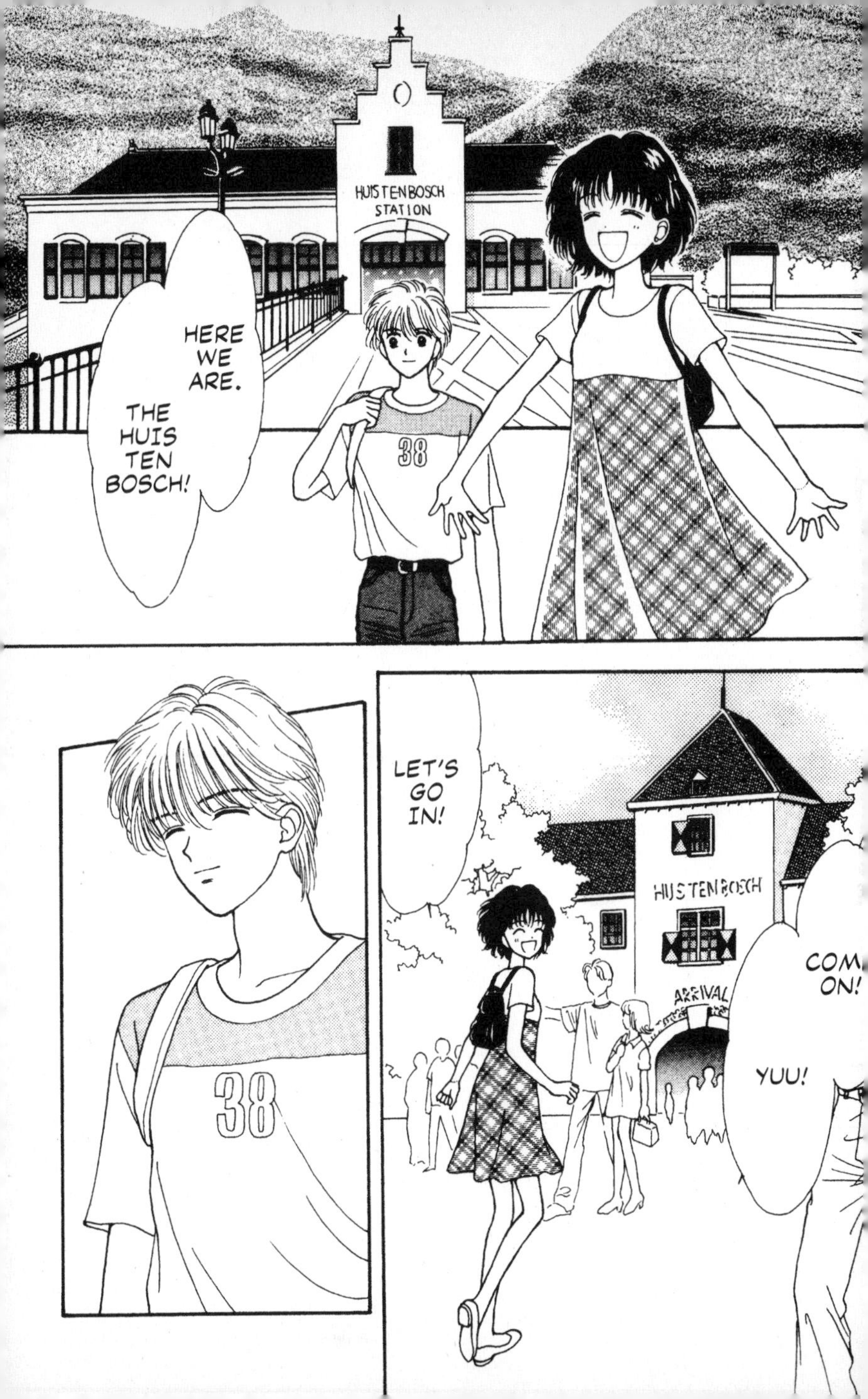
HUISTENBOSCH STATION
HERE WE ARE.
THE HUIS TEN BOSCH!
LET'S GO IN!
HUSTENBOSCH
ARRIVAL
COM ON!
YUU!

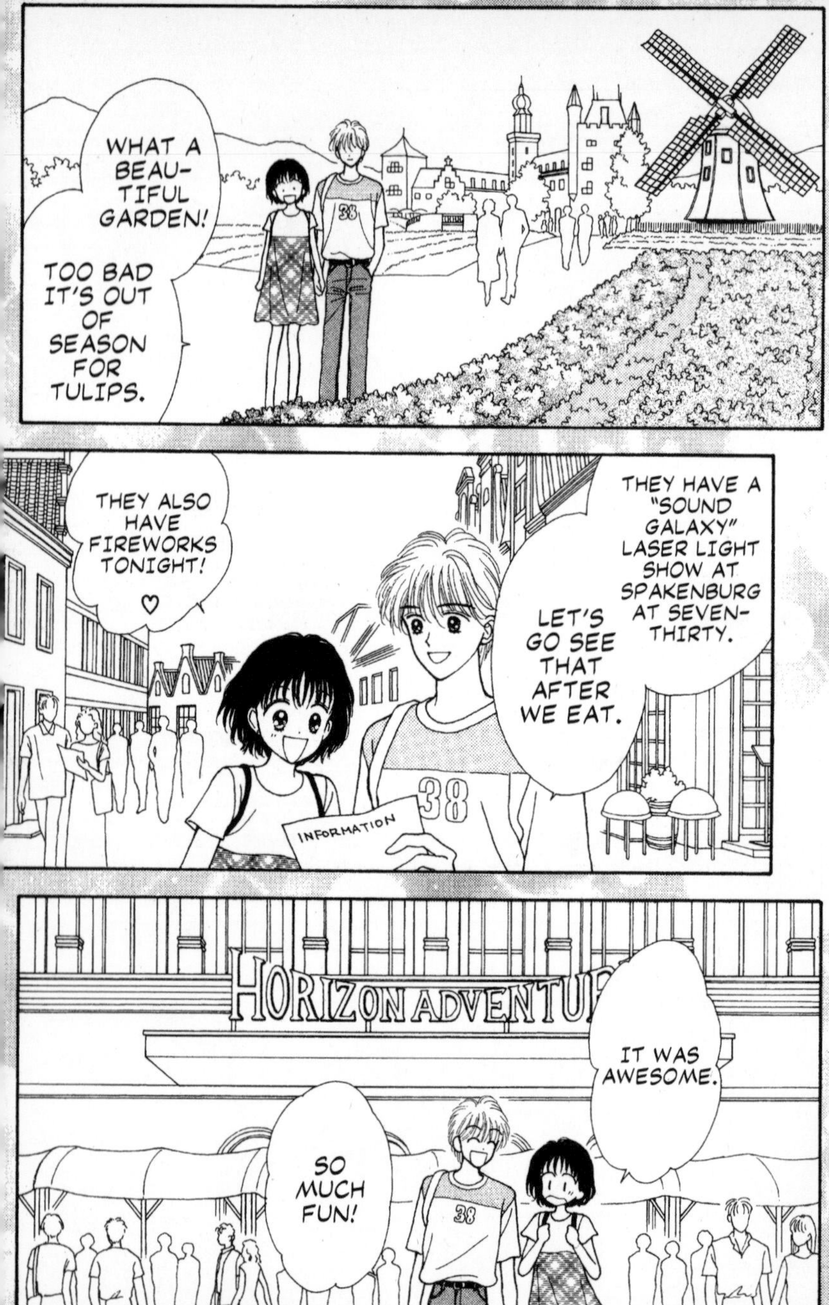
WHAT A BEAU-TIFUL GARDEN!
TOO BAD IT'S OUT OF SEASON FOR TULIPS.
THEY HAVE A "SOUND GALAXY" LASER LIGHT SHOW AT SPAKENBURG AT SEVEN-THIRTY.
LET'S GO SEE THAT AFTER WE EAT.
THEY ALSO HAVE FIREWORKS TONIGHT! ♡
INFORMATION
HORIZON ADVENTU
IT WAS AWESOME.
SO MUCH FUN!

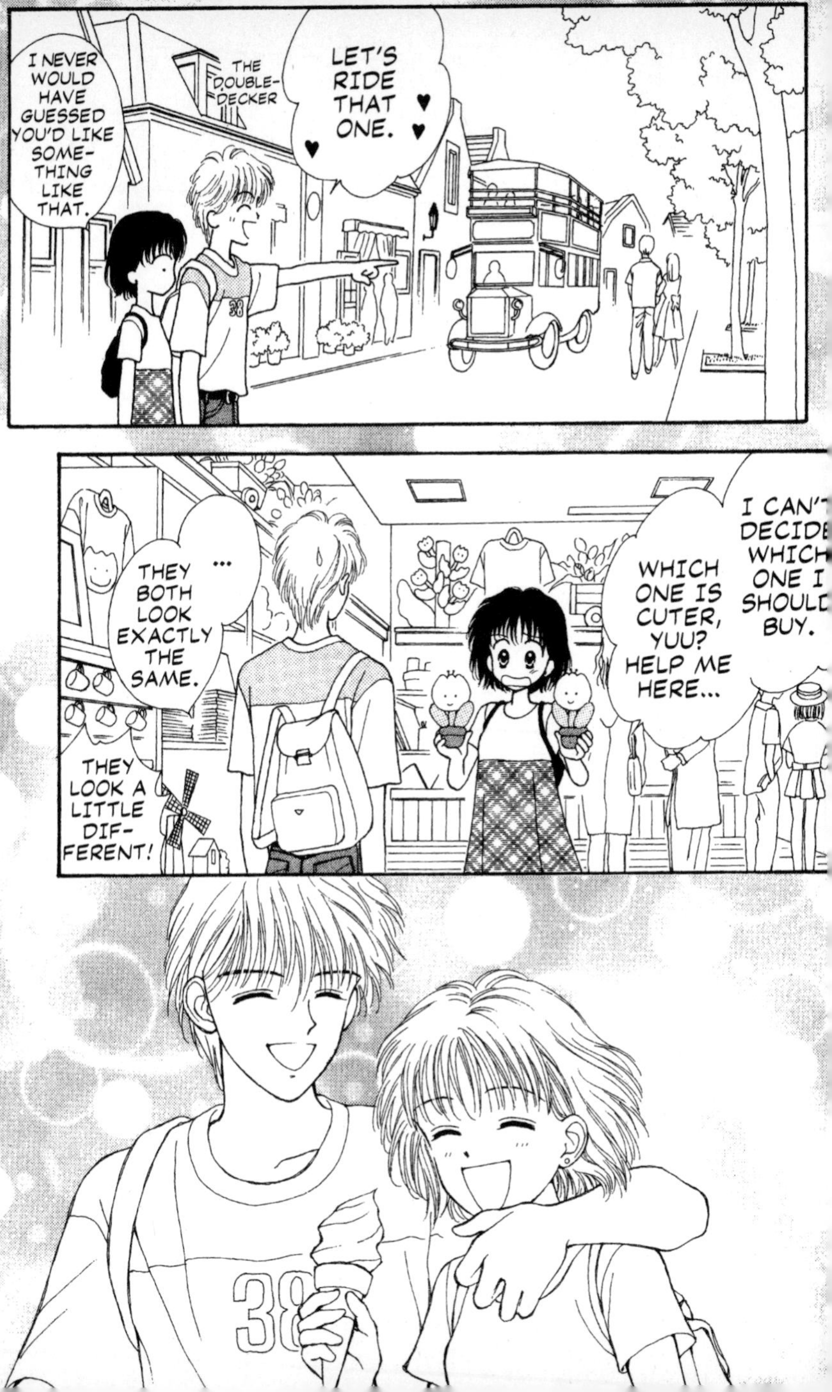
LET'S RIDE THAT ONE. ♥ ♥ ♥
THE DOUBLE-DECKER
I NEVER WOULD HAVE GUESSED YOU'D LIKE SOME-THING LIKE THAT.
I CAN'T DECIDE WHICH ONE I SHOULD BUY.
WHICH ONE IS CUTER, YUU? HELP ME HERE...
...
THEY BOTH LOOK EXACTLY THE SAME.
THEY LOOK A LITTLE DIF-FERENT!

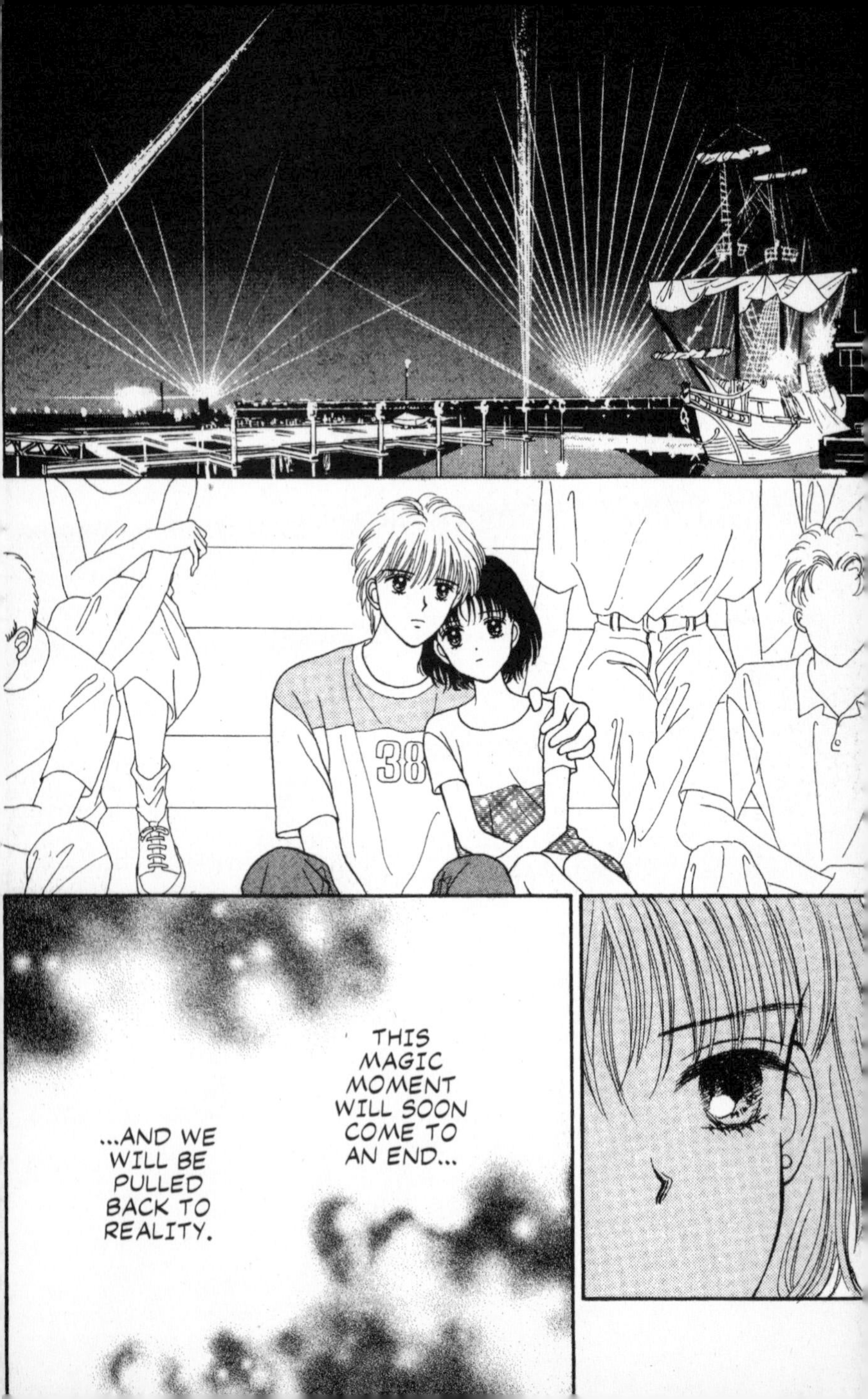
THIS MAGIC MOMENT WILL SOON COME TO AN END...
...AND WE WILL BE PULLED BACK TO REALITY.

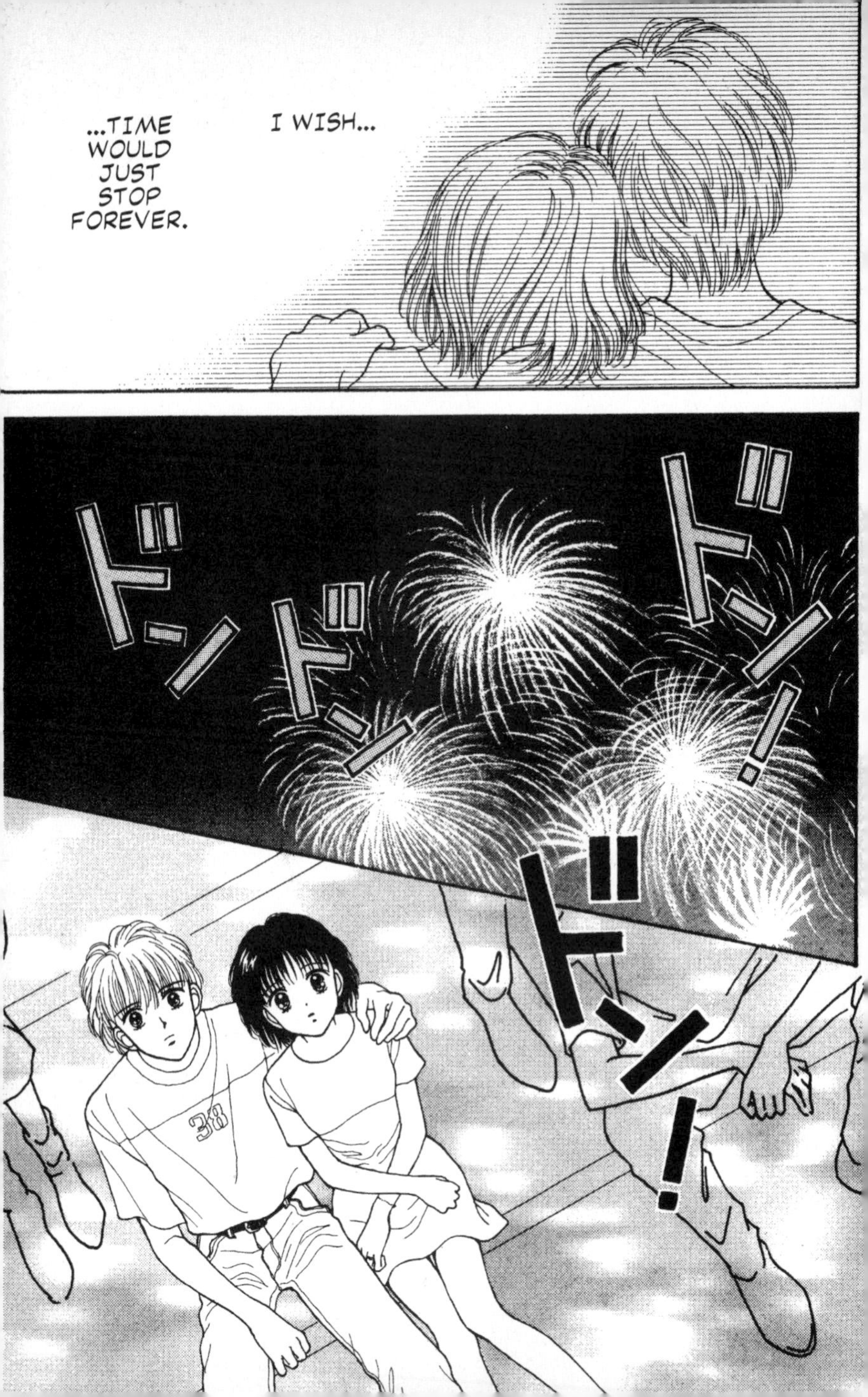
I WISH...
...TIME WOULD JUST STOP FOREVER.
ドーン!
ドーン
ドーン
ドン!

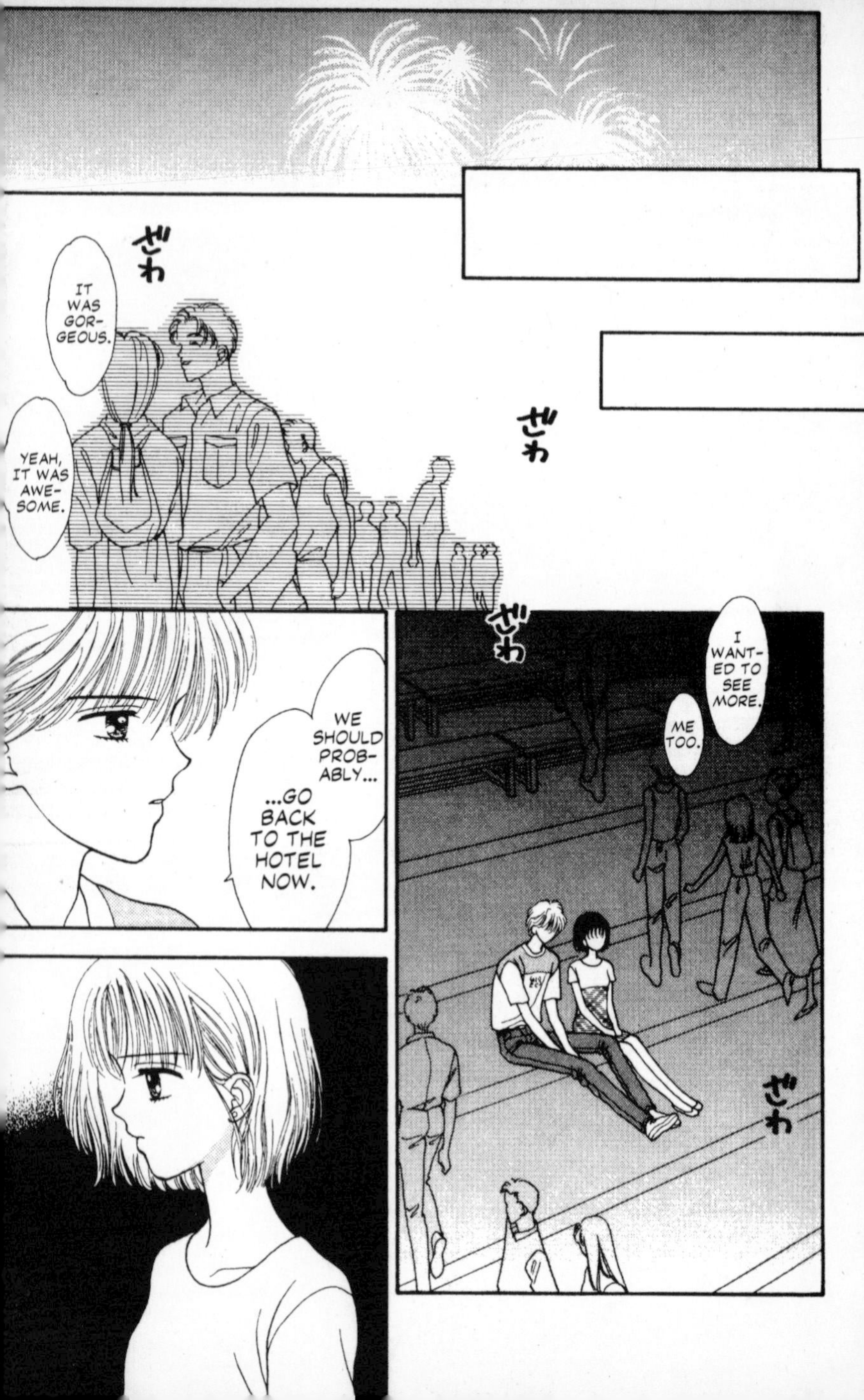
ざわ
ざわ
IT WAS GORGEOUS.
YEAH, IT WAS AWESOME.
ざわ
I WANTED TO SEE MORE.
ME TOO.
ざわ
WE SHOULD PROBABLY...
...GO BACK TO THE HOTEL NOW.

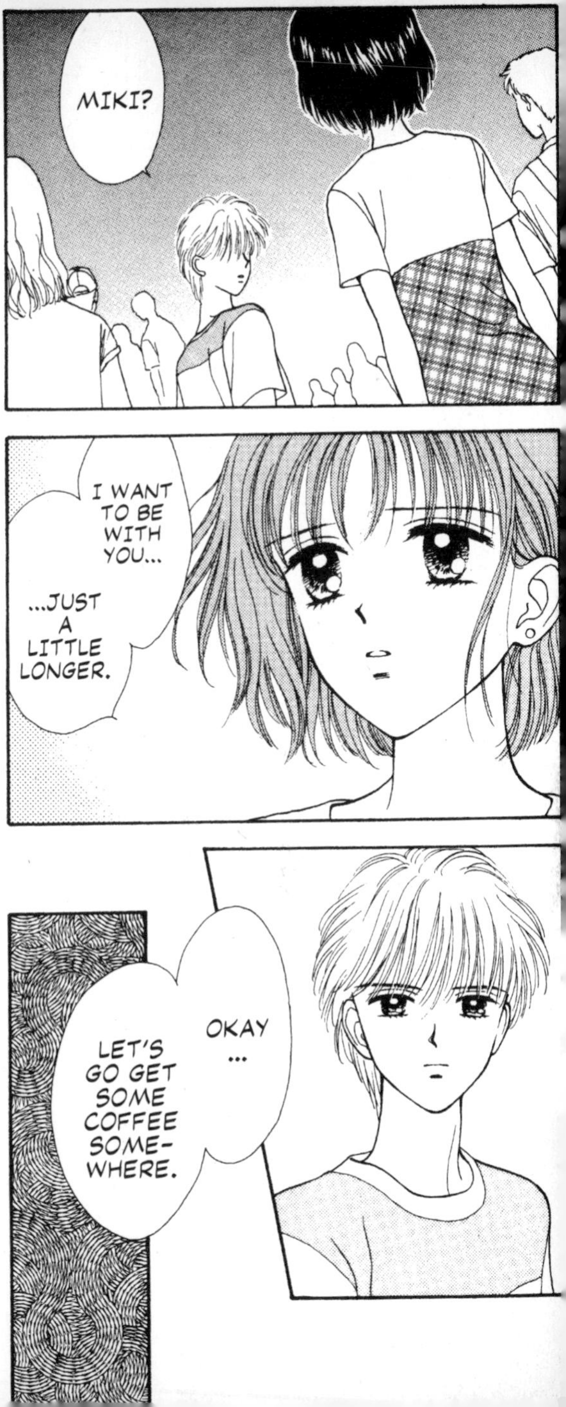
MIKI?
I WANT TO BE WITH YOU...
...JUST A LITTLE LONGER.
OKAY...
LET'S GO GET SOME COFFEE SOME-WHERE.

FREE TALK ⑦

A lot of mangas and animes often have a hero who is sent to a foreign country and all the native people there speak perfect Japanese. That kind of thing really turns me off and it's so sad that Marmalade Boy the anime turned out to be one of them. Anyway, I had some disagreements with the anime staff but I dared not say anything. I thought it would make their job easier if I stayed out of their business. I convinced myself that I should just appreciate the fact they were turning my story into an anime and I was not supposed to complain about how they developed their story. After the TV series was over, I started to wonder if I did the right thing about remaining silent. I wondered if the anime staff would have appreciated my input to some degree. It probably wouldn't have been such a big deal for them if I had complained about the story. They could have changed things if I had asked. Now that I look back, I think everything was great just the way it was. I finally came to the conclusion that the anime was created by the anime staff for the anime viewers and it was wonderful the way it was.

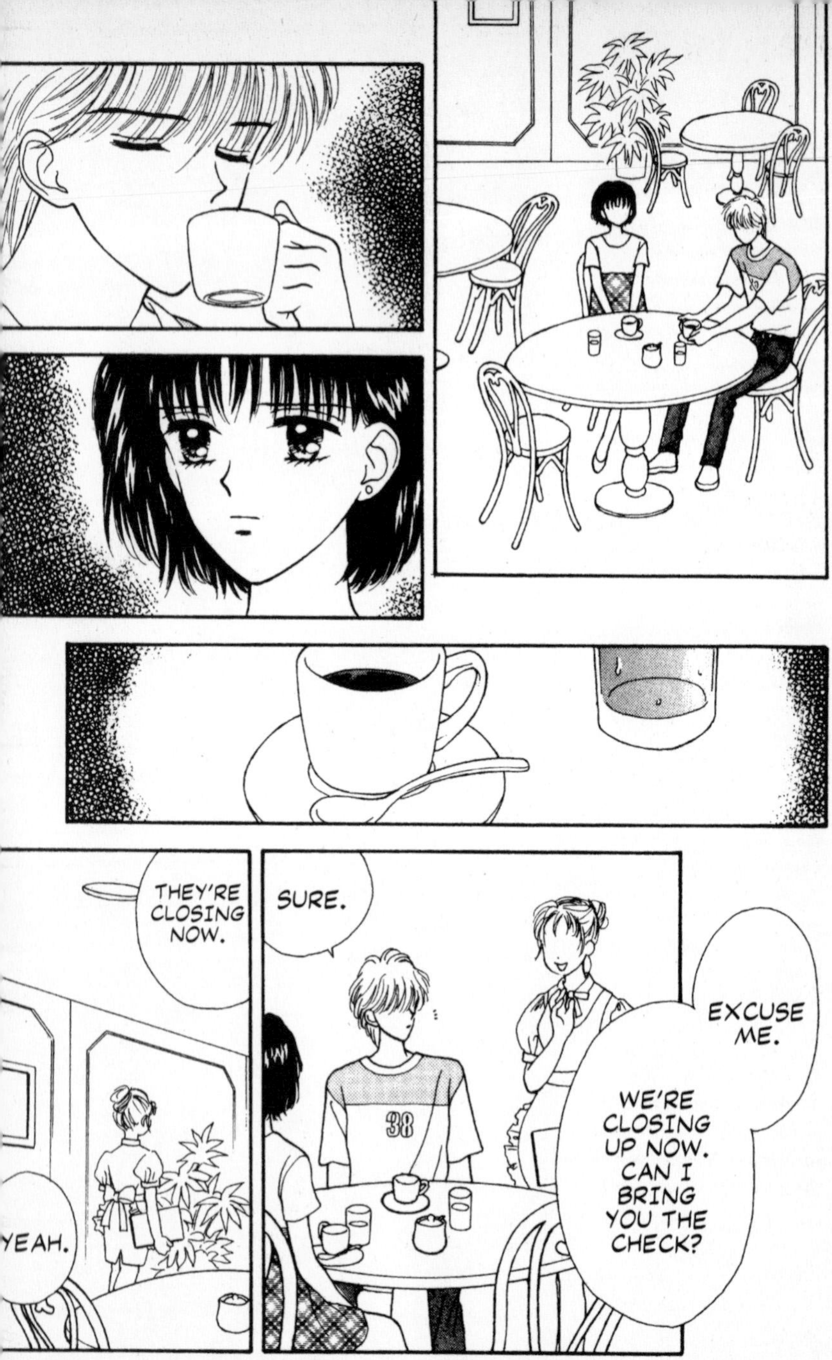
EXCUSE ME.
WE'RE CLOSING UP NOW. CAN I BRING YOU THE CHECK?
SURE.
THEY'RE CLOSING NOW.
YEAH.

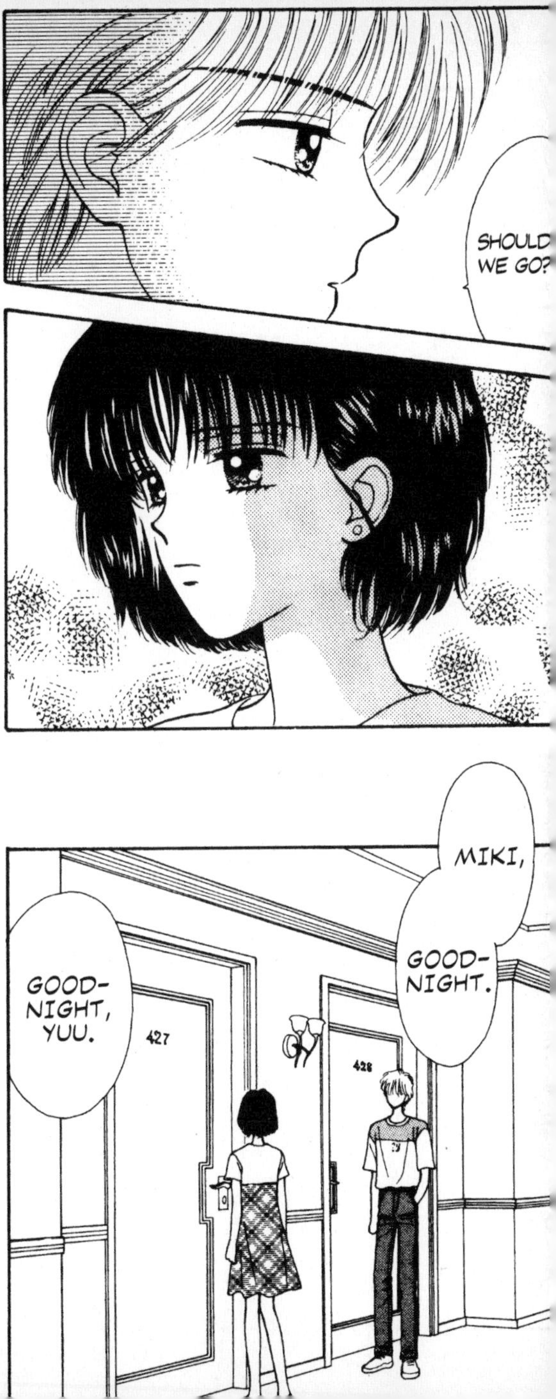
SHOULD WE GO?
MIKI, GOOD-NIGHT.
428
427
GOOD-NIGHT, YUU.

FREE TALK ⑧

I am satisfied with the anime version of Marmalade Boy overall. It has a lot of scenes I like and, most of all, it is so much fun to be able to see the story with motions, voices and music. Again, I am so happy that they made the anime. It was such a good experience for me too. Well, to change the subject, I had three months vacation after finishing writing Marmalade Boy and I could relax quite a bit during that period. However, I still had some stuff to take care of, so I could only truly relax for about a month or so. I tried to write back to fans who had sent me letters and bought post-cards. Although I tried to write to as many people as possible, I could only write to 50 fans before I had to start working on the next story. I will try to make it a habit of writing back to my fans more often, little by little. I finally got to reply to a fan who sent me a letter three years ago. I hope she doesn't feel that I was too late or say, "I'm not reading her manga anymore."

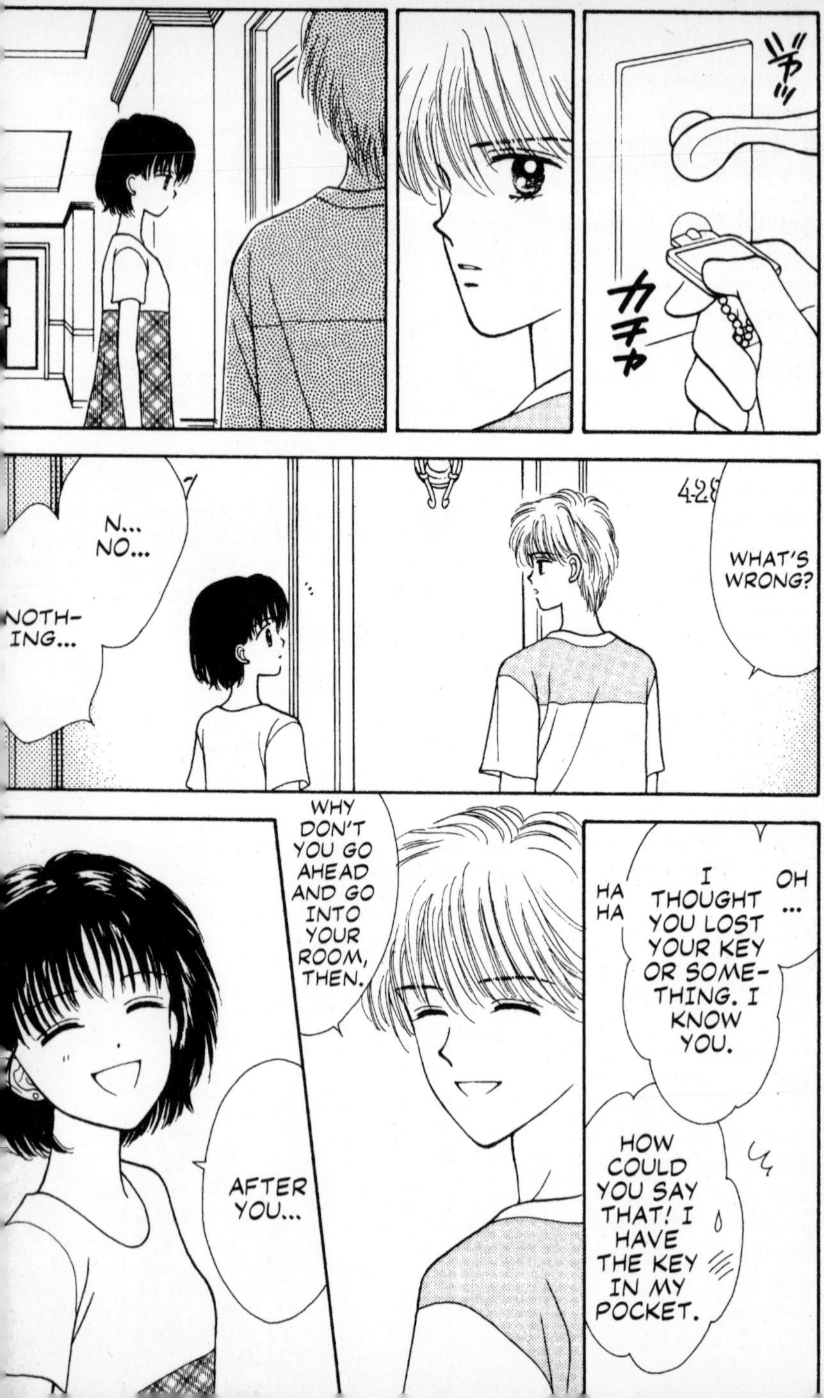
ガッ
カチャ
4-28
WHAT'S WRONG?
N... NO... NOTHING...
OH ...
I THOUGHT YOU LOST YOUR KEY OR SOMETHING. I KNOW YOU.
HA HA
HOW COULD YOU SAY THAT! I HAVE THE KEY IN MY POCKET.
WHY DON'T YOU GO AHEAD AND GO INTO YOUR ROOM, THEN.
AFTER YOU...

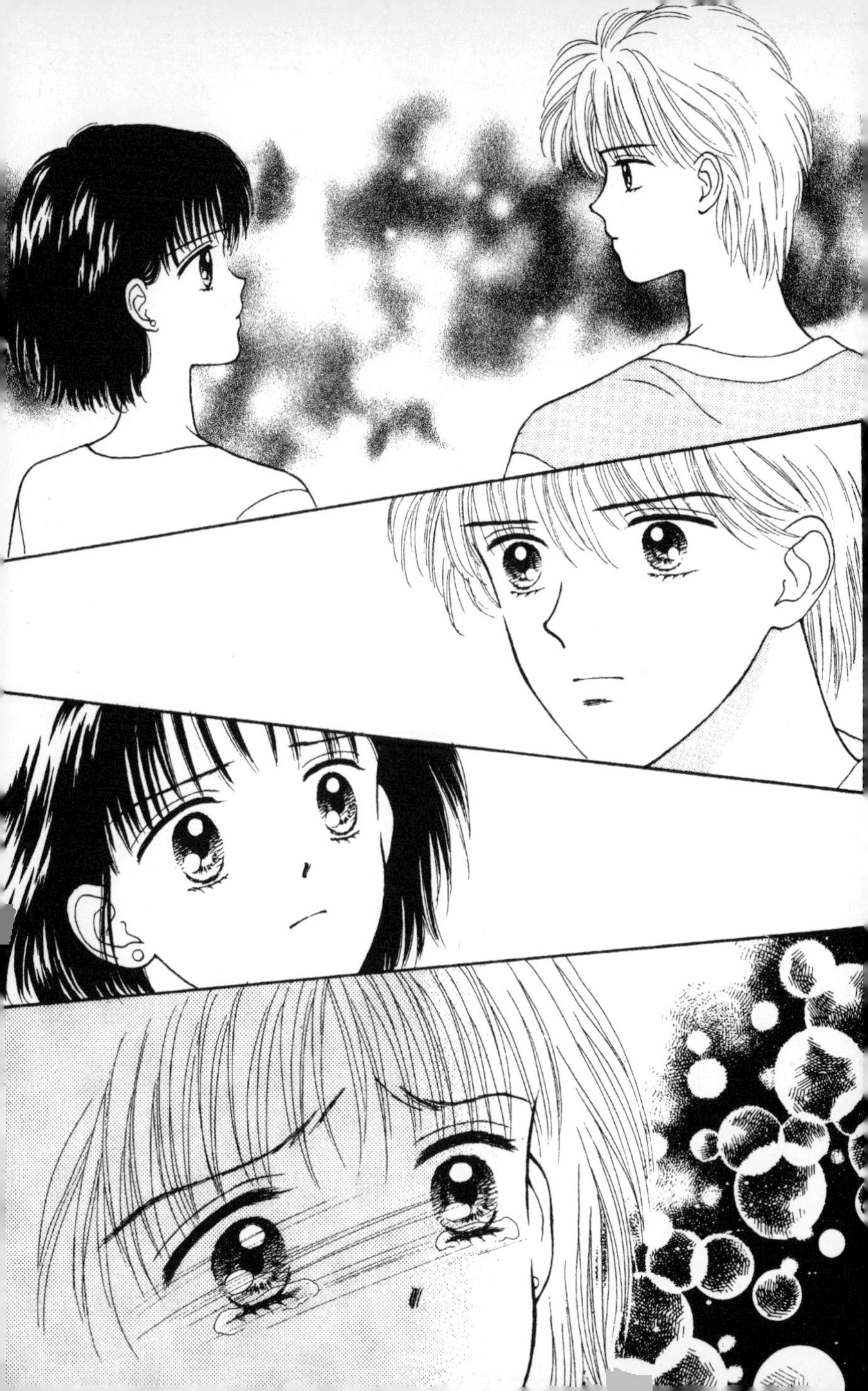

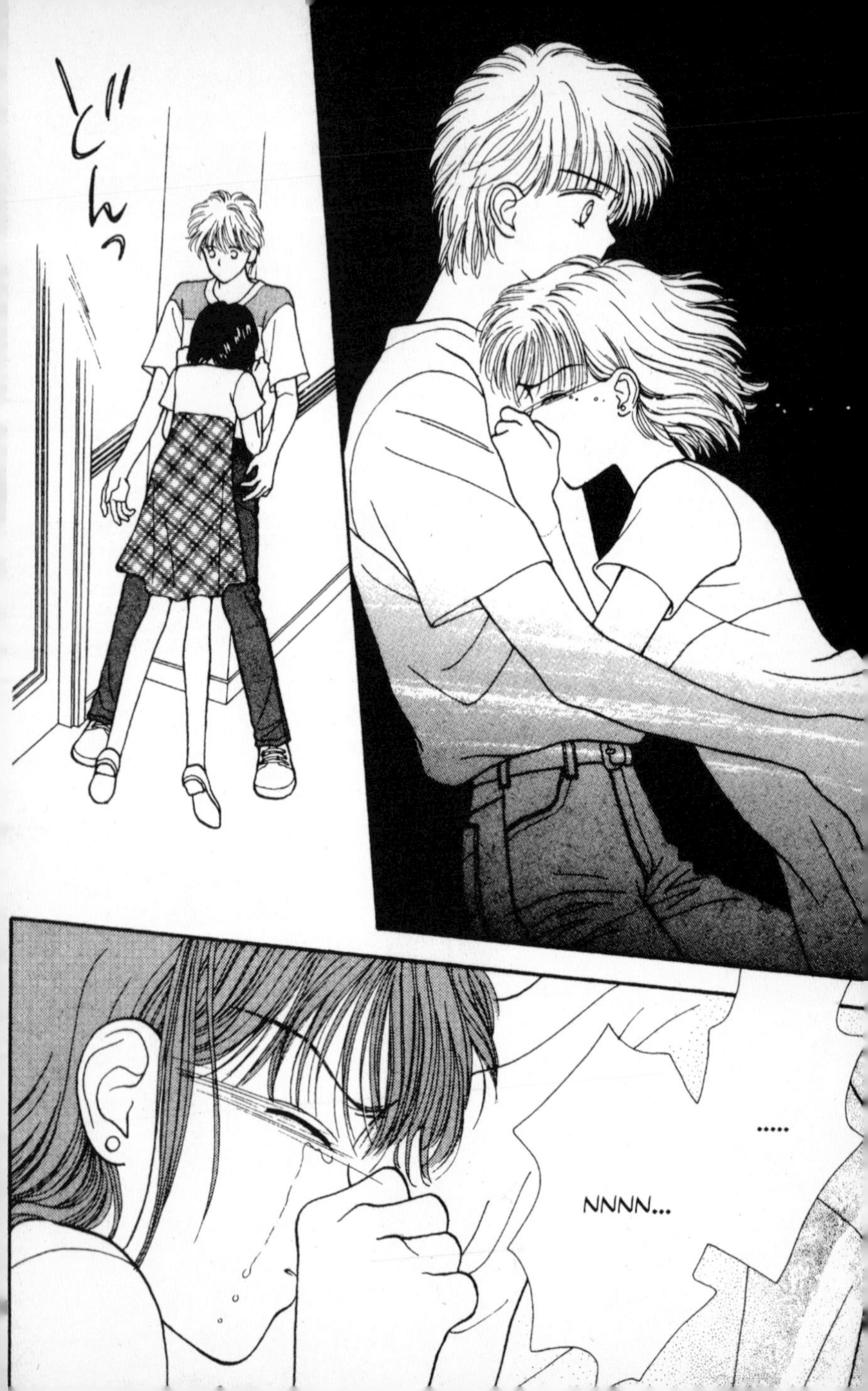
どんっ
.....
NNNN...

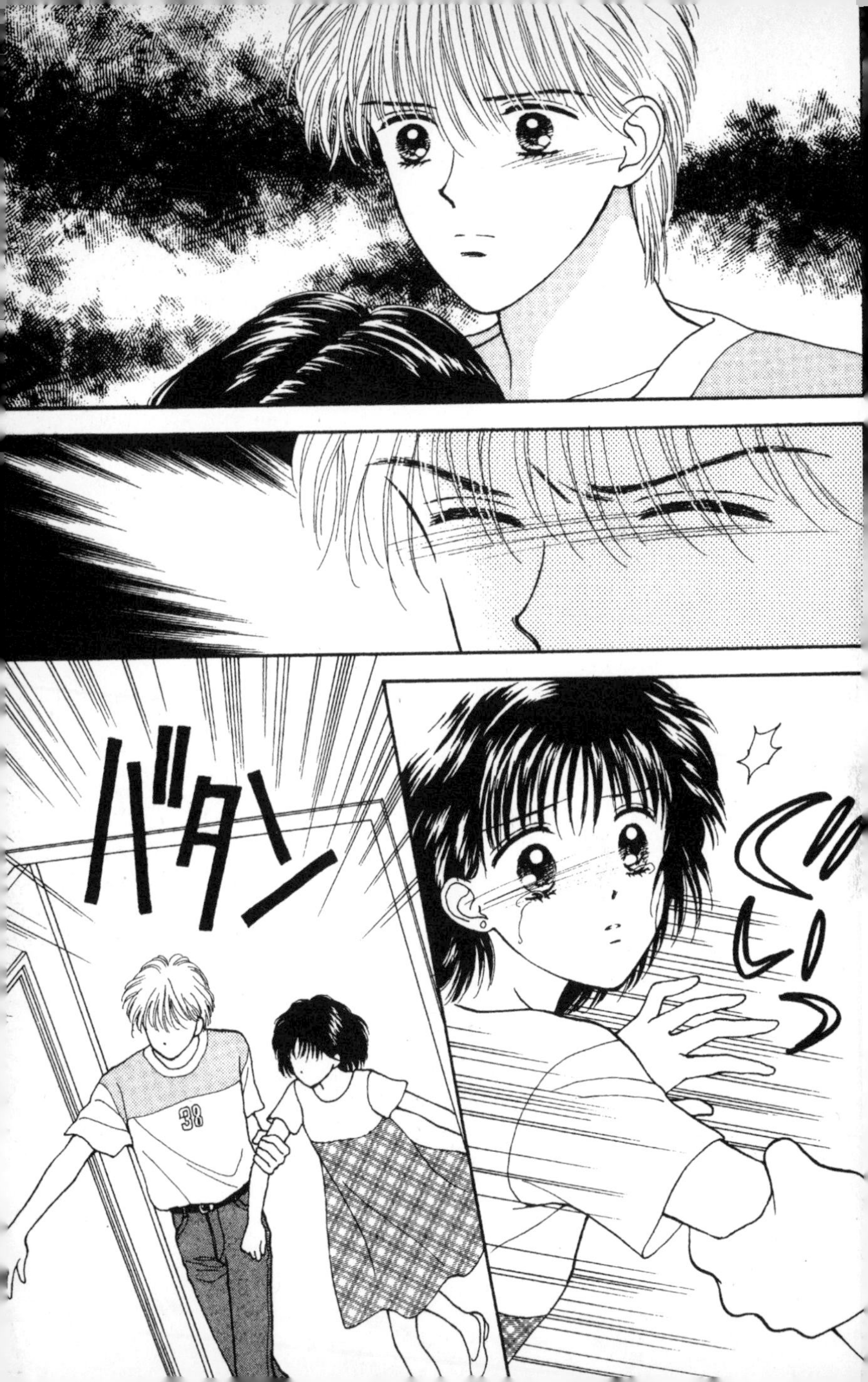
ぐいっ
バタン

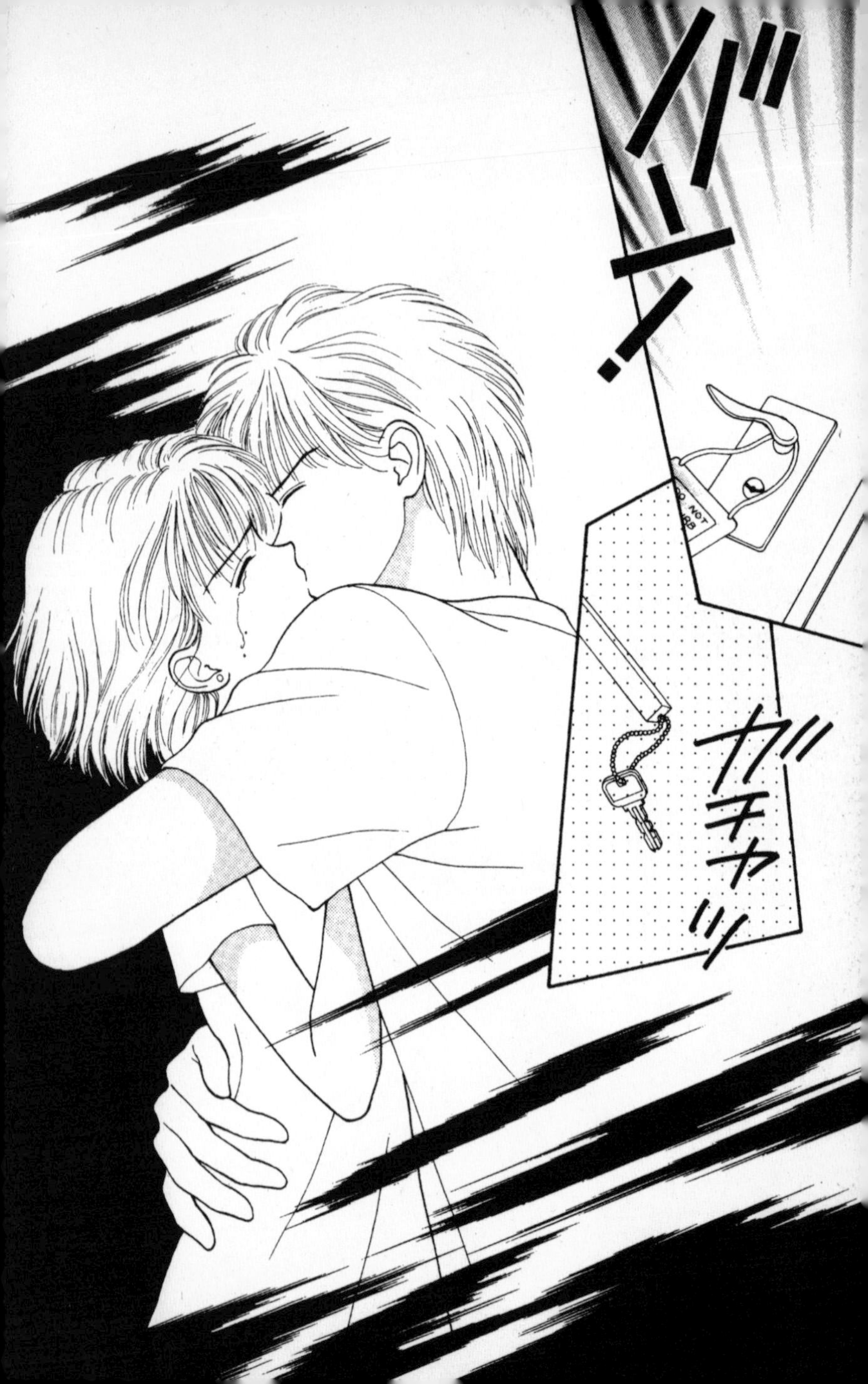
バーン!!
DO NOT
ガチャッ

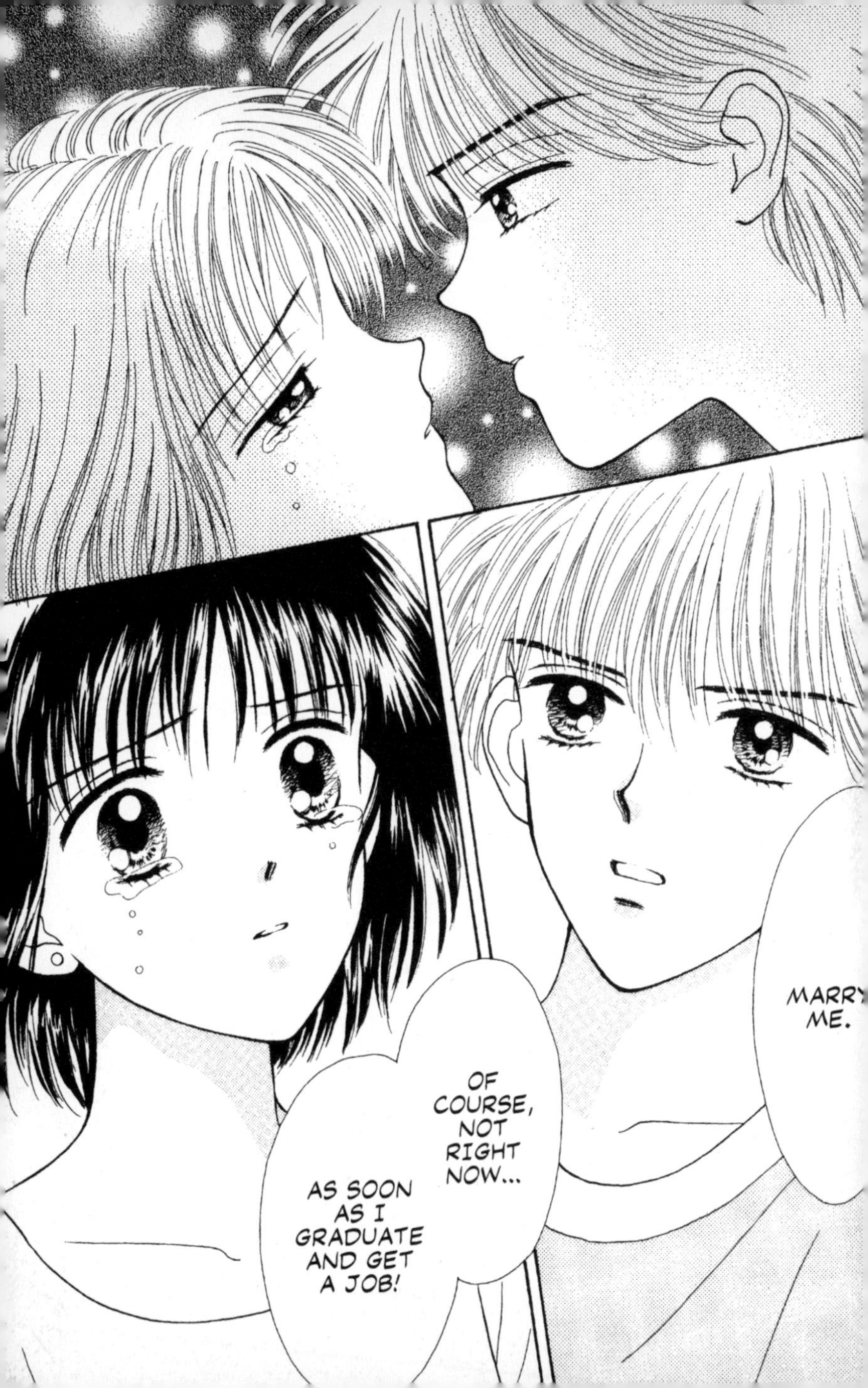
MARRY ME.
OF COURSE, NOT RIGHT NOW...
AS SOON AS I GRADUATE AND GET A JOB!

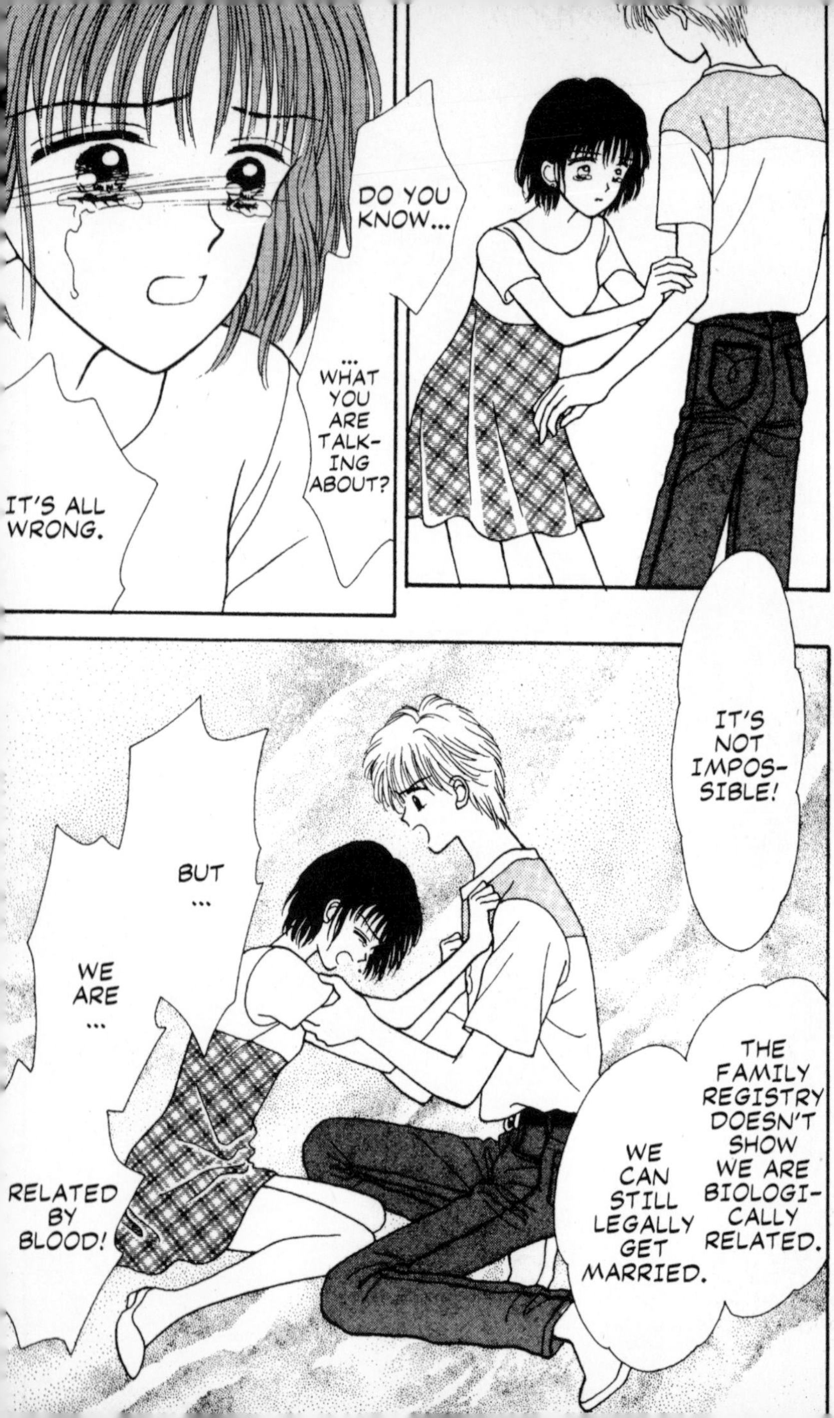

DO YOU KNOW...
...WHAT YOU ARE TALKING ABOUT?
IT'S ALL WRONG.
IT'S NOT IMPOSSIBLE!
THE FAMILY REGISTRY DOESN'T SHOW WE ARE BIOLOGICALLY RELATED.
WE CAN STILL LEGALLY GET MARRIED.
BUT...
WE ARE...
RELATED BY BLOOD!

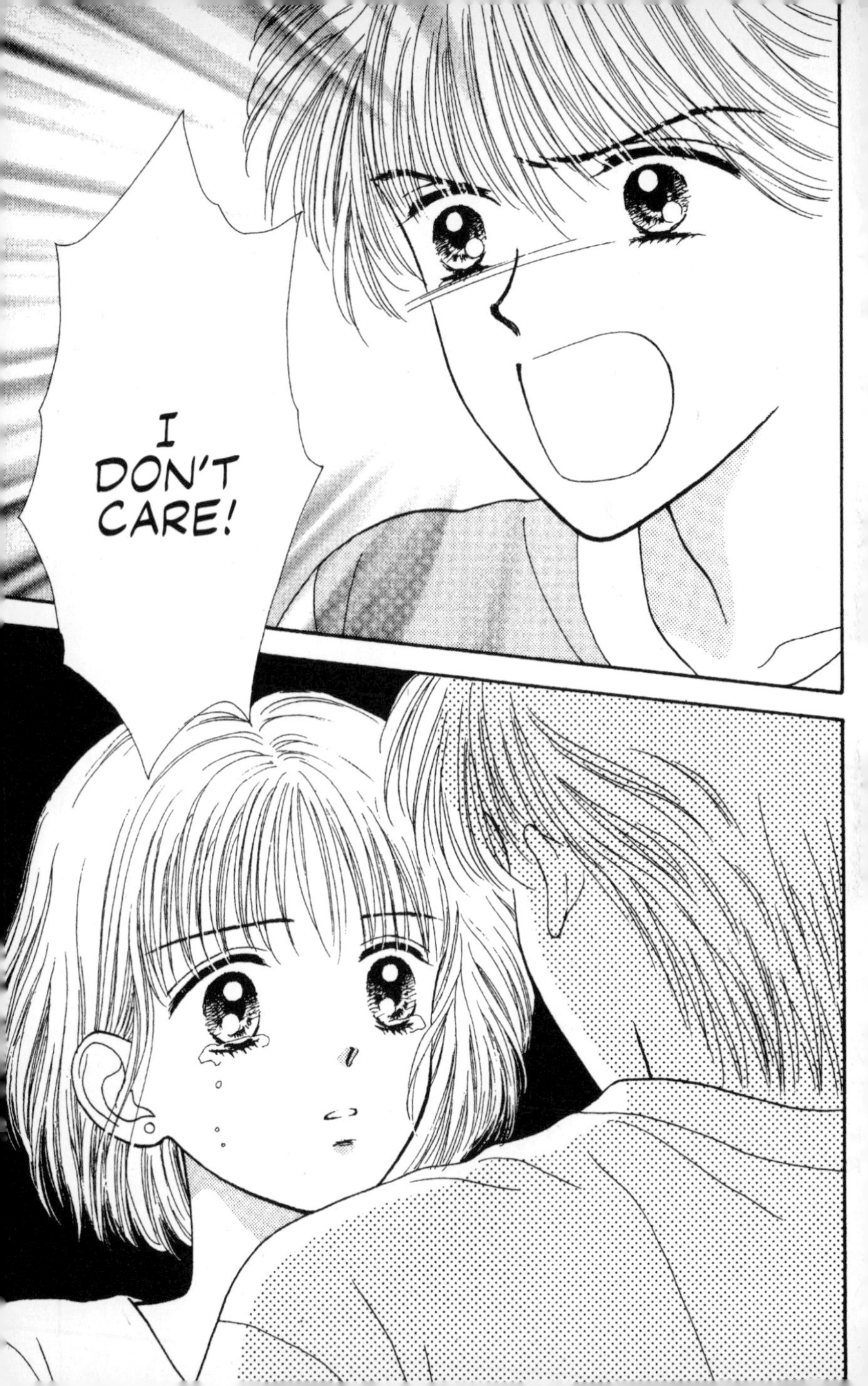
I DON'T CARE!

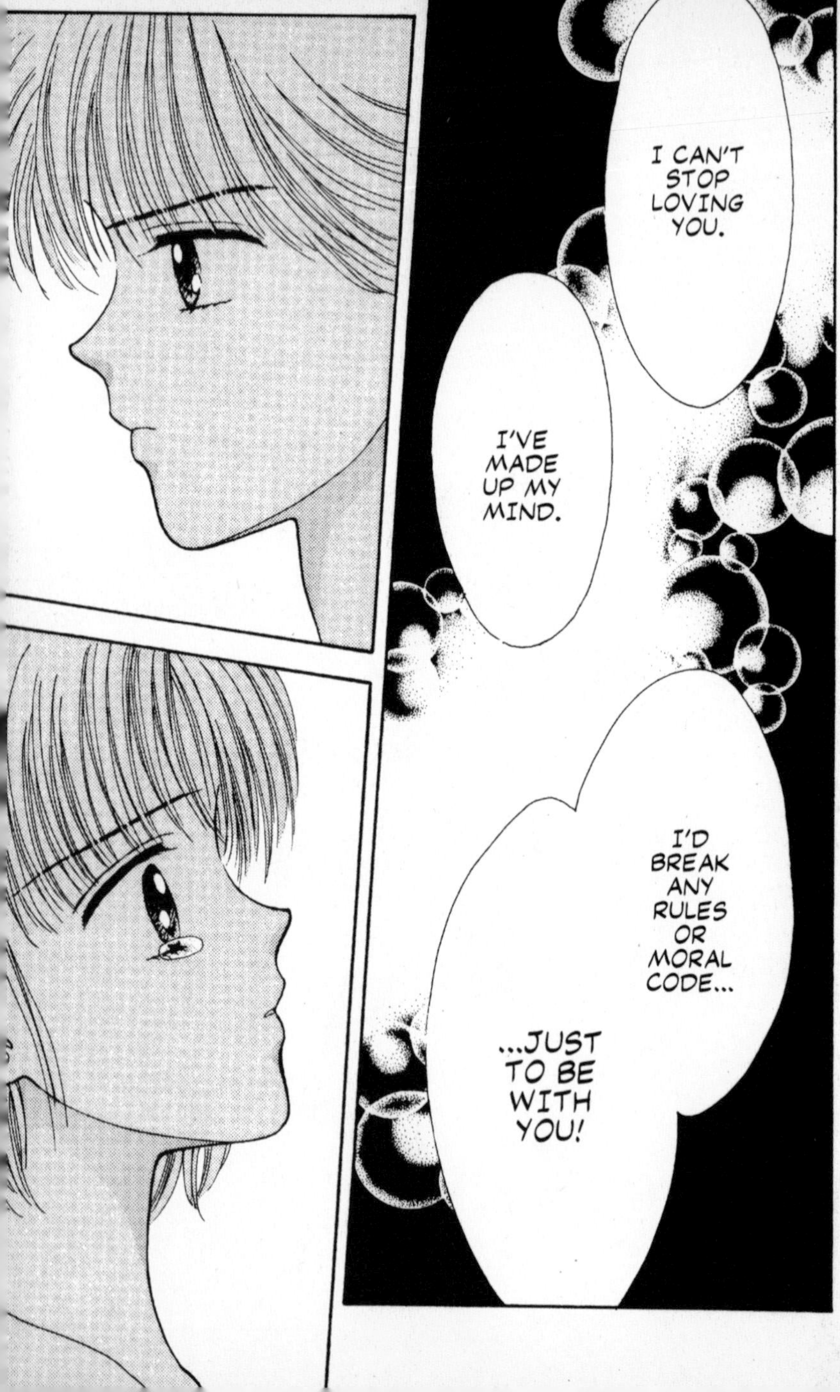
I CAN'T STOP LOVING YOU.
I'VE MADE UP MY MIND.
I'D BREAK ANY RULES OR MORAL CODE...
...JUST TO BE WITH YOU!

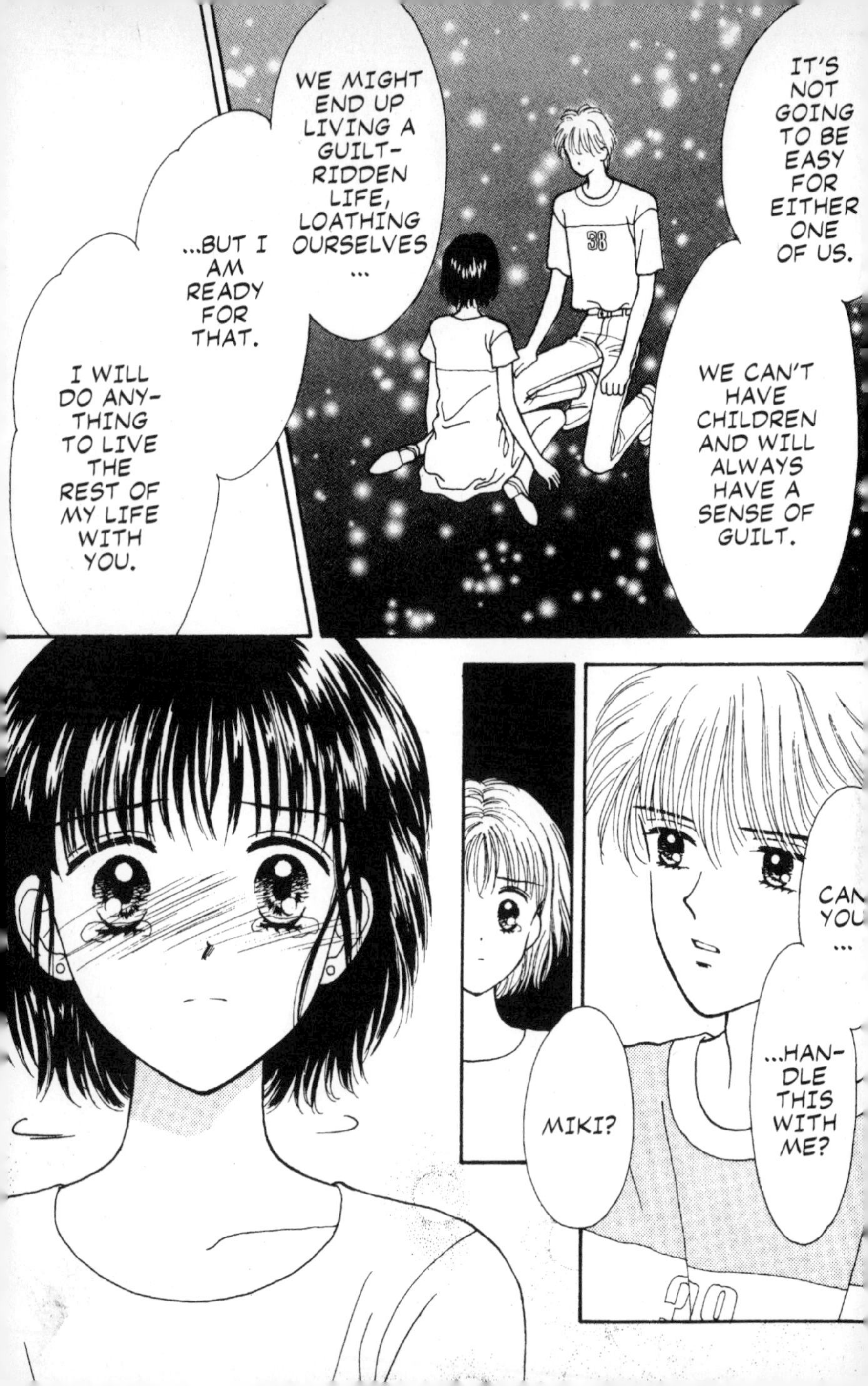
IT'S NOT GOING TO BE EASY FOR EITHER ONE OF US.
WE CAN'T HAVE CHILDREN AND WILL ALWAYS HAVE A SENSE OF GUILT.
WE MIGHT END UP LIVING A GUILT-RIDDEN LIFE, LOATHING OURSELVES ...
...BUT I AM READY FOR THAT.
I WILL DO ANY-THING TO LIVE THE REST OF MY LIFE WITH YOU.
CAN YOU ...
...HAN-DLE THIS WITH ME?
MIKI?

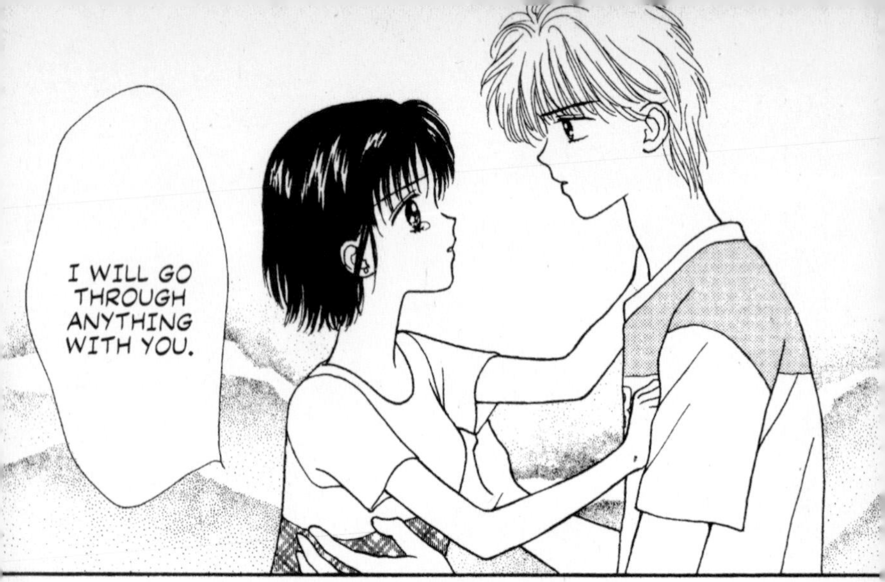
I WILL GO THROUGH ANYTHING WITH YOU.
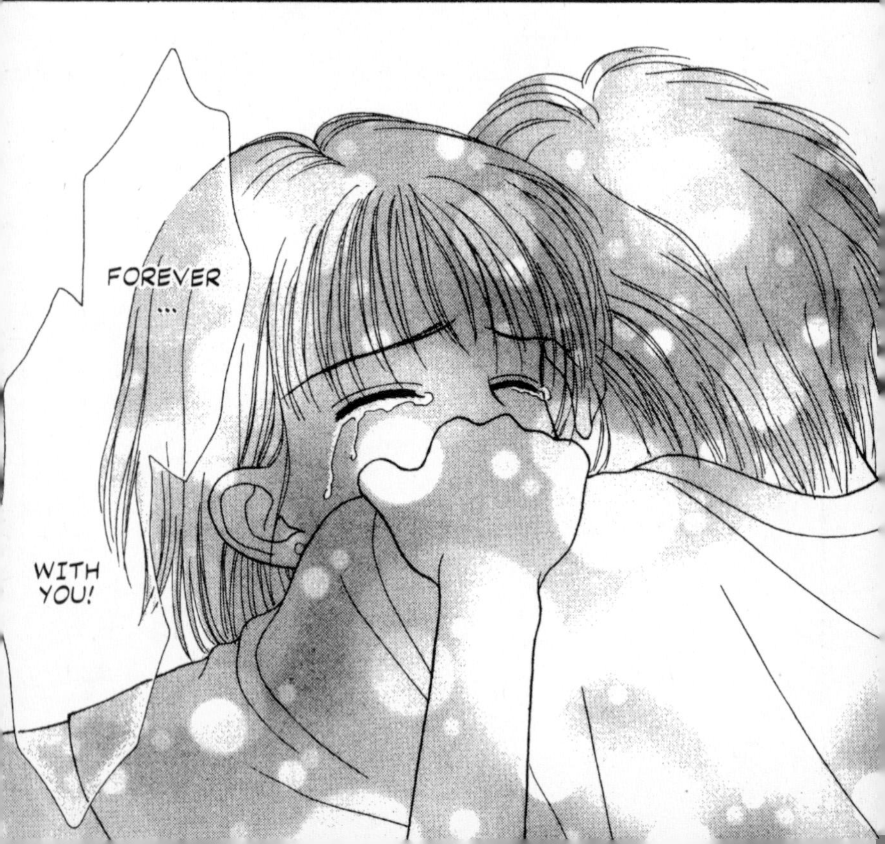
FOREVER ...
WITH YOU!

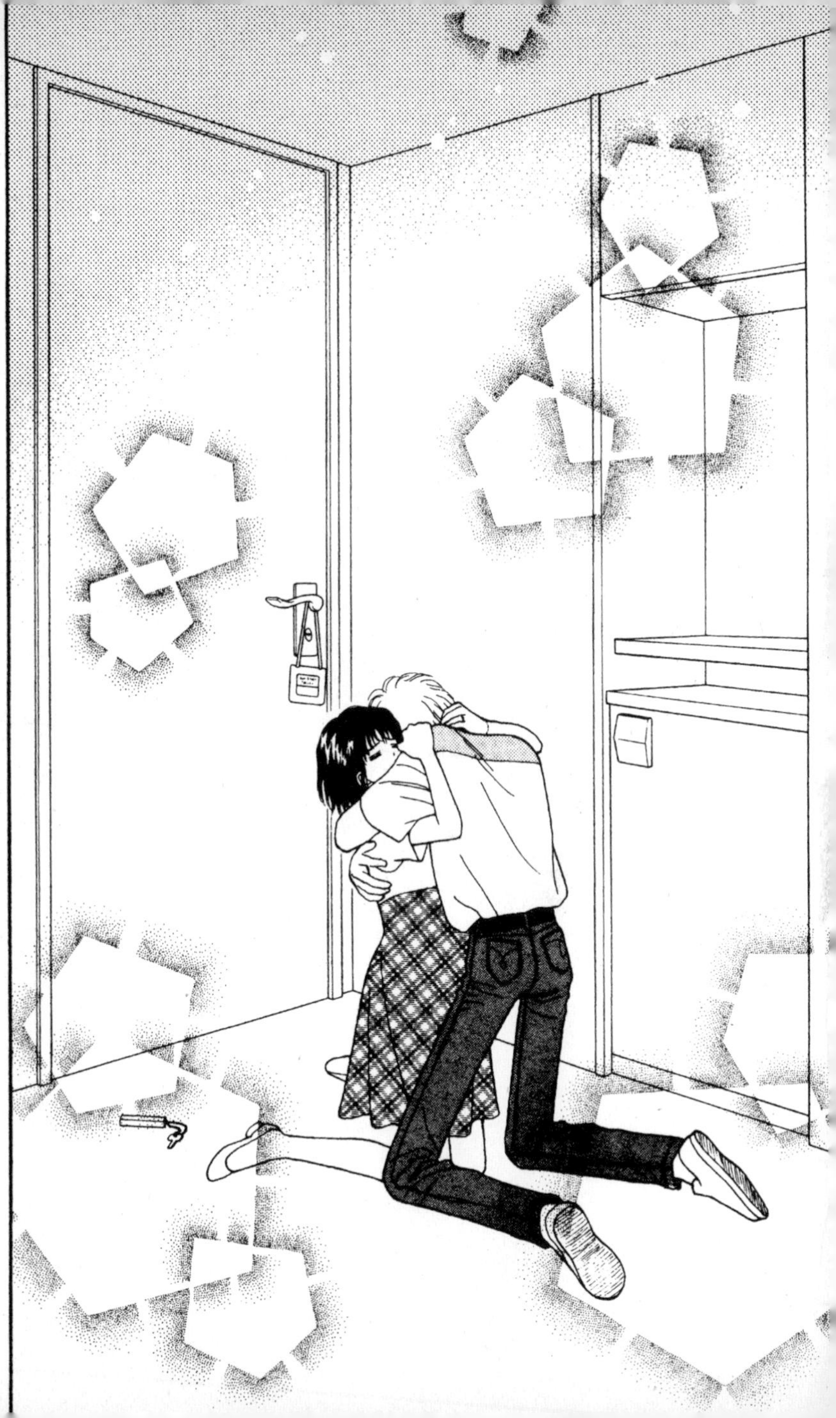

WHEN WE GET BACK HOME, LET'S TELL OUR PARENTS ABOUT US.

WHAT?

LET'S TELL THEM THAT WE KNOW WE ARE RELATED BY BLOOD BUT WE LOVE EACH OTHER AND WE CAN'T LIVE WITHOUT EACH OTHER. WE NEED TO ASK FOR THEIR APPROVAL.

DO YOU THINK THEY WILL APPROVE OUR MARRIAGE?

YOU NEVER KNOW. THEY MIGHT GIVE US THEIR PERMISSION PRETTY EASILY. WE ARE TALKING ABOUT OUR PARENTS, WHO ARE TOTALLY INSANE, YOU KNOW.

AFTER ALL, THE WHOLE PROBLEM STEMS FROM THEM HIDING SUCH AN IMPORTANT FACT FROM US.

BUT WHAT IF THEY DON'T GIVE US PERMISSION?

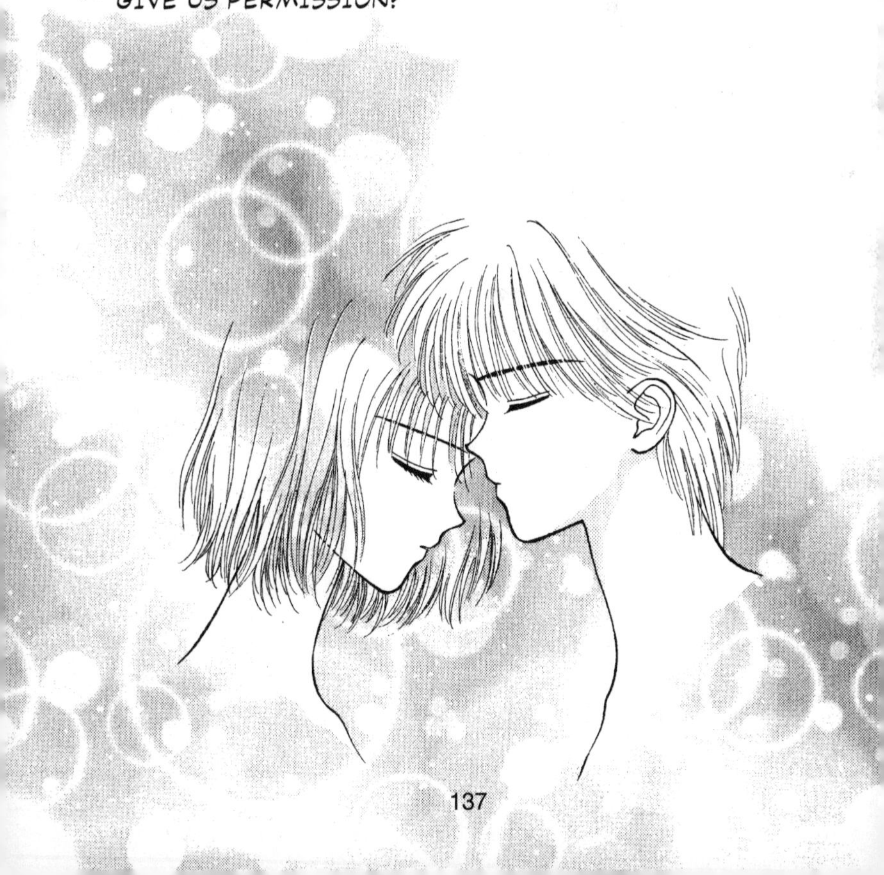

THEN WE'VE GOT TO...

...ELOPE OR SOMETHING.

WE HAVE SOMETHING TO TELL YOU.

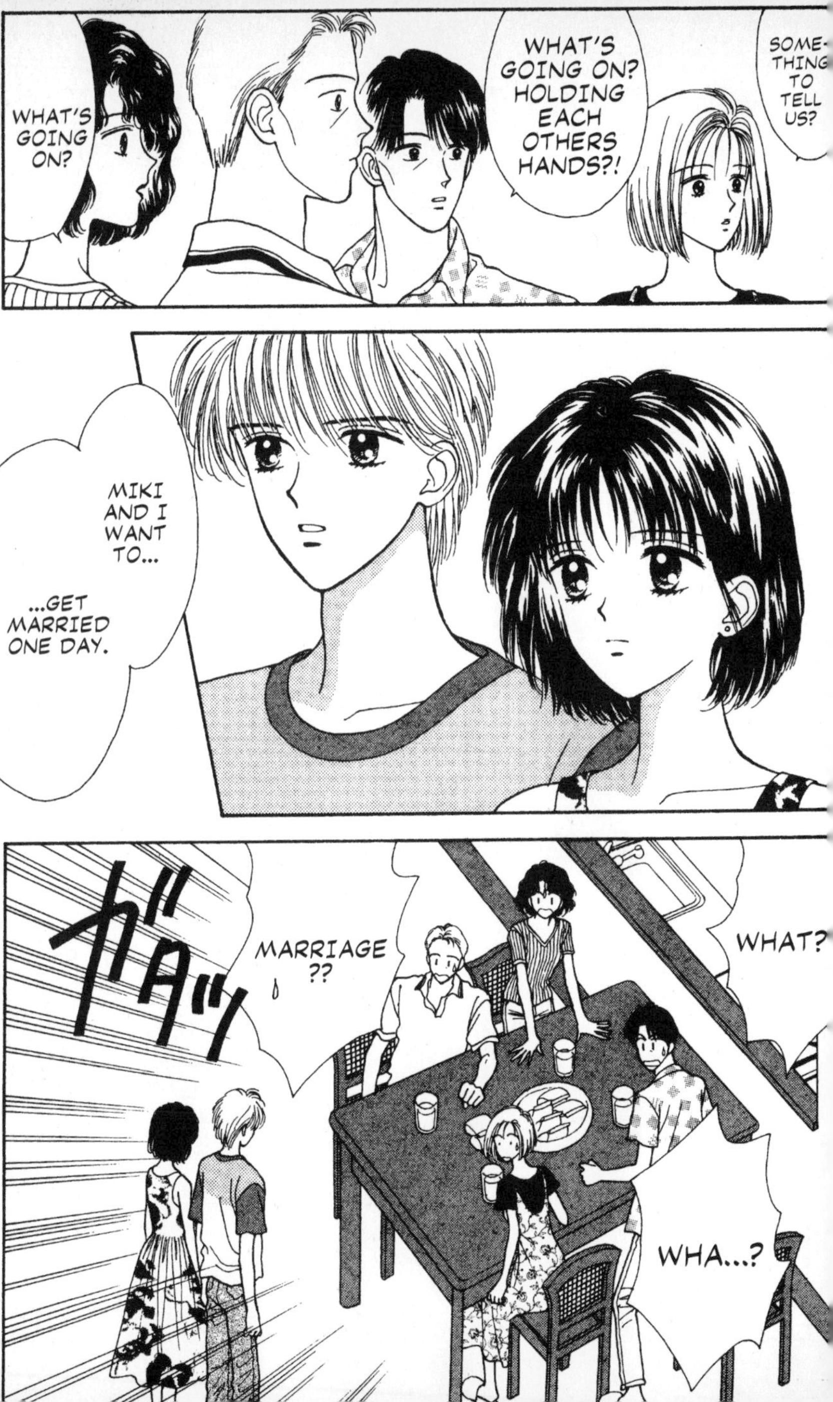
SOME-THING TO TELL US?
WHAT'S GOING ON? HOLDING EACH OTHERS HANDS?!
WHAT'S GOING ON?
MIKI AND I WANT TO...
...GET MARRIED ONE DAY.
WHAT?
MARRIAGE ??
WHA...?
ガタッ

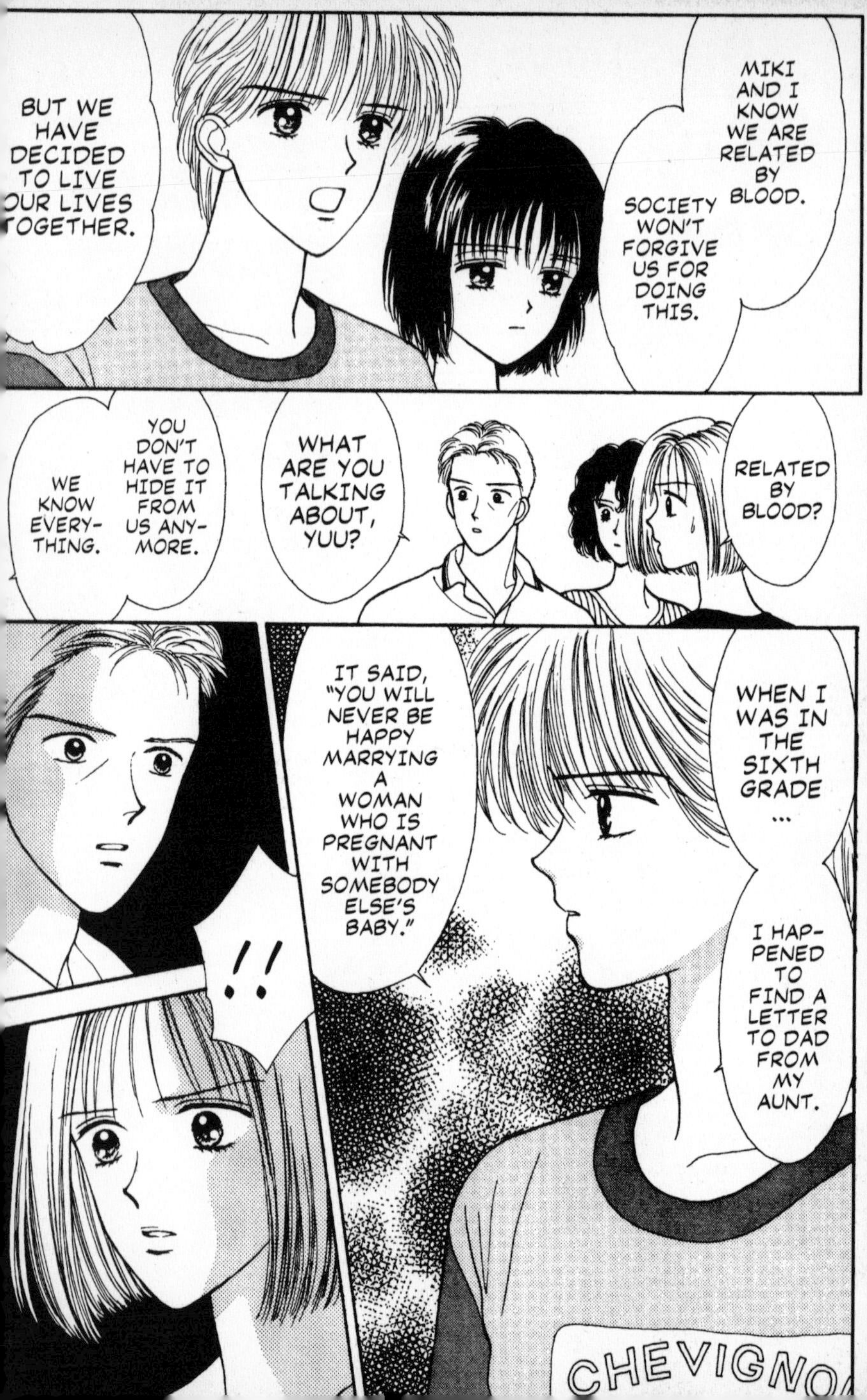
MIKI AND I KNOW WE ARE RELATED BY BLOOD.
SOCIETY WON'T FORGIVE US FOR DOING THIS.
BUT WE HAVE DECIDED TO LIVE OUR LIVES TOGETHER.
RELATED BY BLOOD?
WHAT ARE YOU TALKING ABOUT, YUU?
YOU DON'T HAVE TO HIDE IT FROM US ANYMORE.
WE KNOW EVERYTHING.
WHEN I WAS IN THE SIXTH GRADE ...
I HAPPENED TO FIND A LETTER TO DAD FROM MY AUNT.
IT SAID, "YOU WILL NEVER BE HAPPY MARRYING A WOMAN WHO IS PREGNANT WITH SOMEBODY ELSE'S BABY."
!!
CHEVIGNO

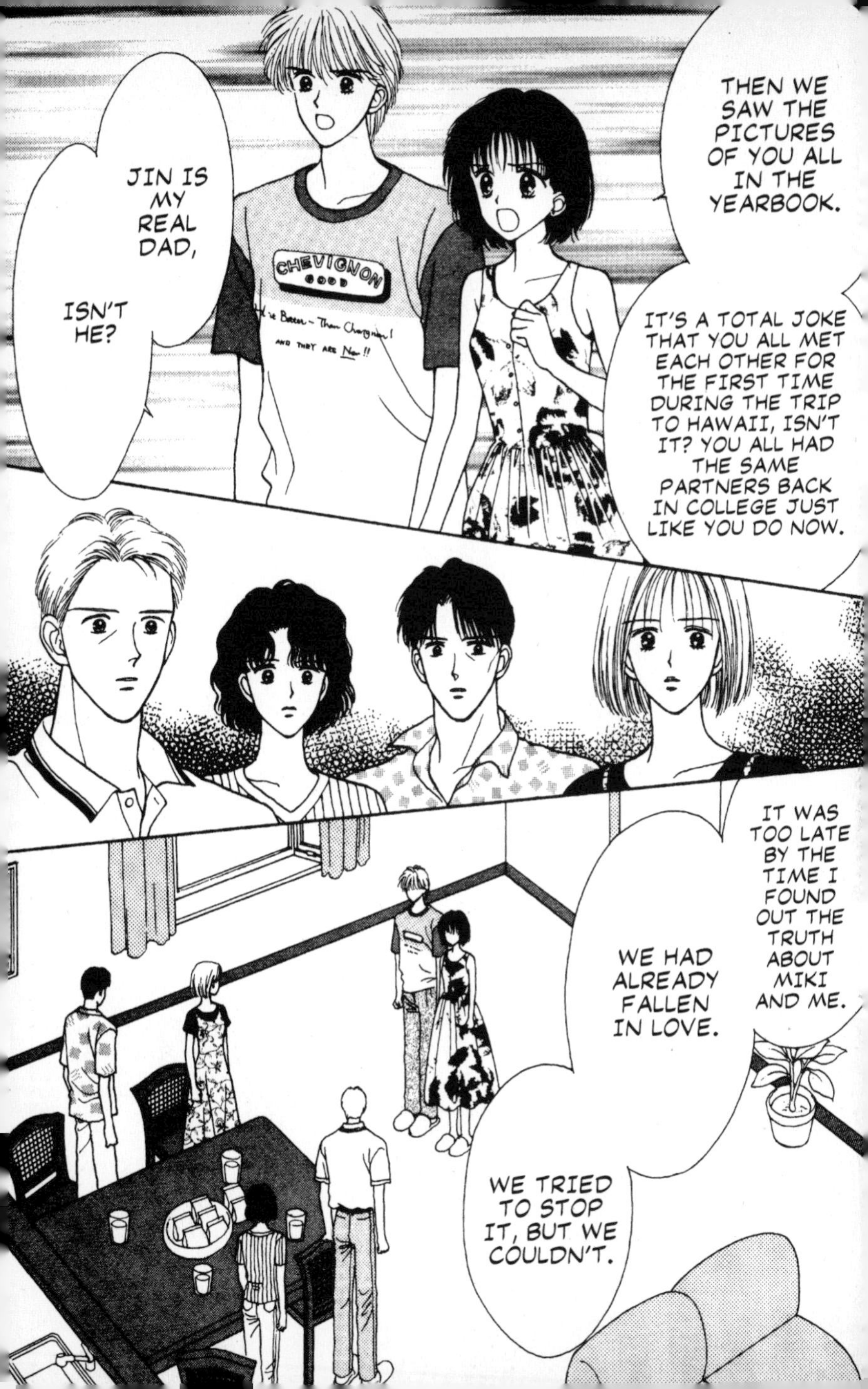
THEN WE SAW THE PICTURES OF YOU ALL IN THE YEARBOOK.
IT'S A TOTAL JOKE THAT YOU ALL MET EACH OTHER FOR THE FIRST TIME DURING THE TRIP TO HAWAII, ISN'T IT? YOU ALL HAD THE SAME PARTNERS BACK IN COLLEGE JUST LIKE YOU DO NOW.
CHEVIGNON
JIN IS MY REAL DAD,
ISN'T HE?
IT WAS TOO LATE BY THE TIME I FOUND OUT THE TRUTH ABOUT MIKI AND ME.
WE HAD ALREADY FALLEN IN LOVE.
WE TRIED TO STOP IT, BUT WE COULDN'T.

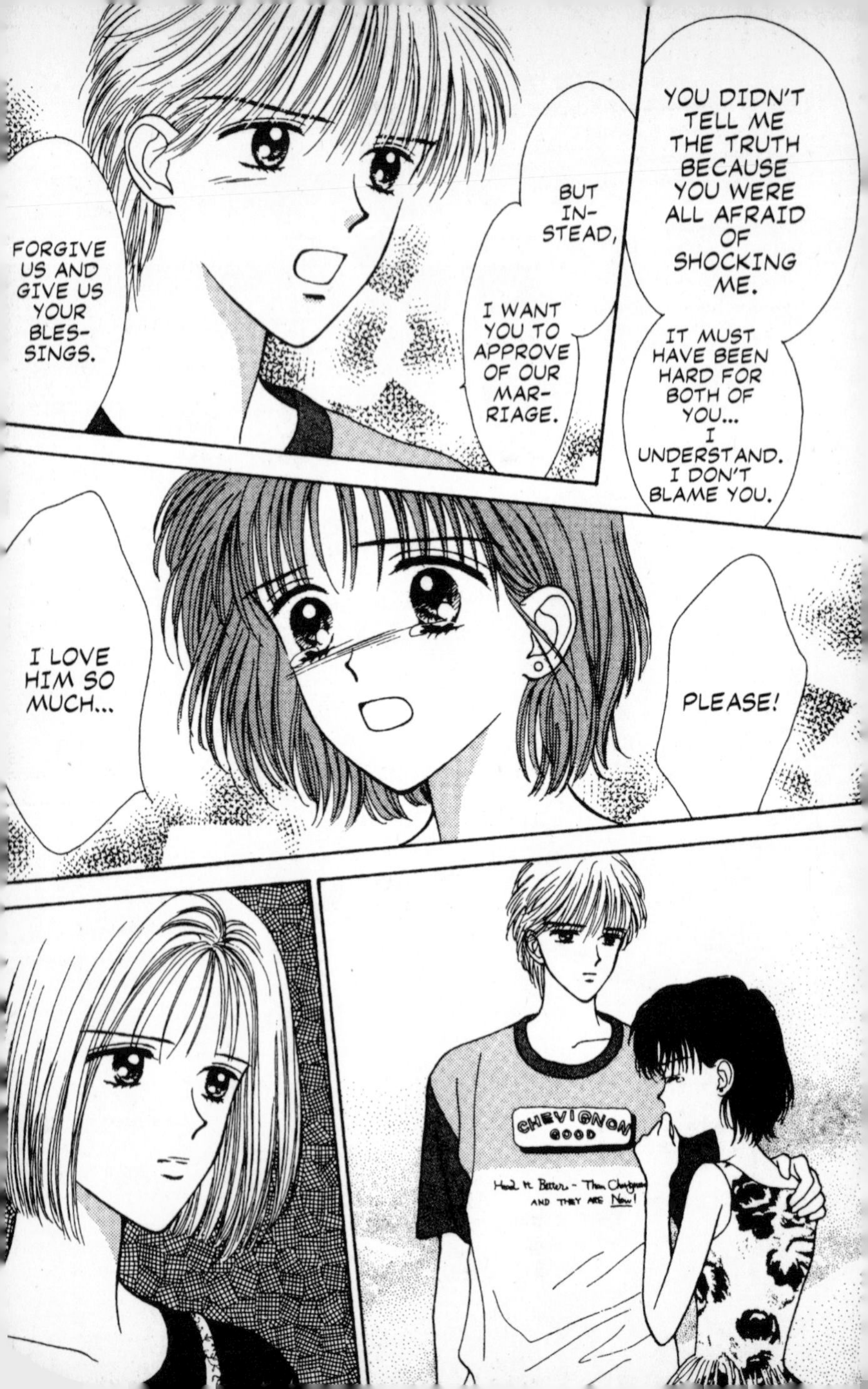
YOU DIDN'T TELL ME THE TRUTH BECAUSE YOU WERE ALL AFRAID OF SHOCKING ME.
IT MUST HAVE BEEN HARD FOR BOTH OF YOU... I UNDERSTAND. I DON'T BLAME YOU.
BUT IN-STEAD,
I WANT YOU TO APPROVE OF OUR MAR-RIAGE.
FORGIVE US AND GIVE US YOUR BLES-SINGS.
PLEASE!
I LOVE HIM SO MUCH...
CHEVIGNON
GOOD
AND THEY ARE Now!

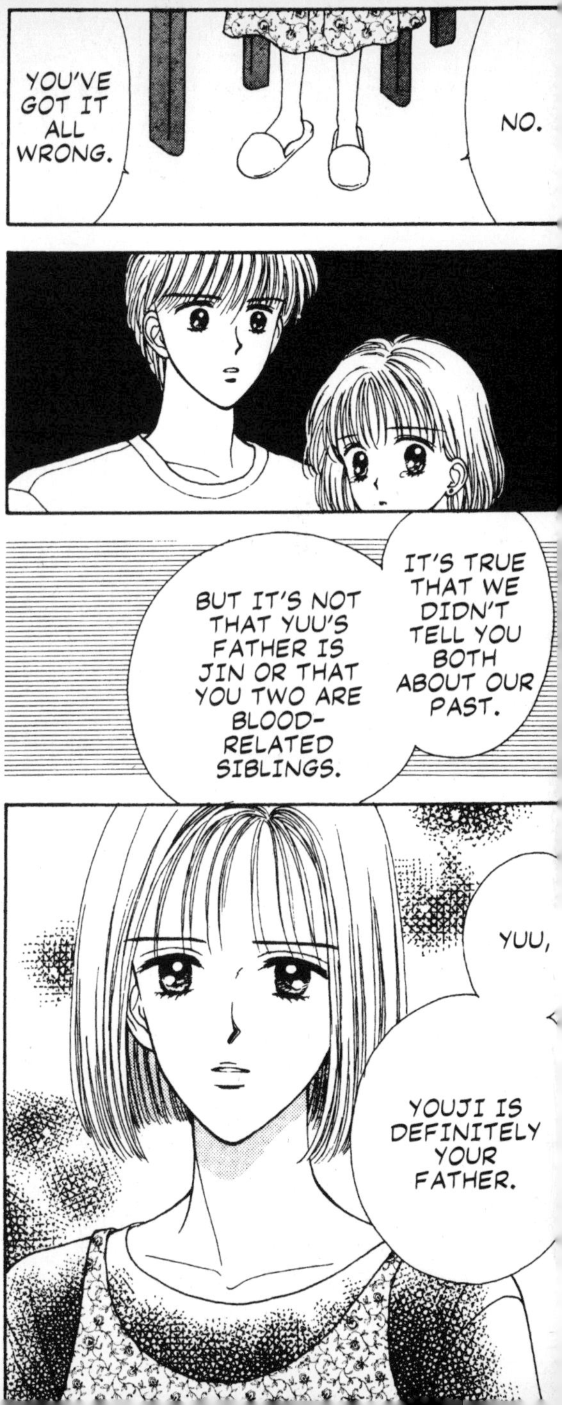
NO.
YOU'VE GOT IT ALL WRONG.
IT'S TRUE THAT WE DIDN'T TELL YOU BOTH ABOUT OUR PAST.
BUT IT'S NOT THAT YUU'S FATHER IS JIN OR THAT YOU TWO ARE BLOOD-RELATED SIBLINGS.
YUU,
YOUJI IS DEFINITELY YOUR FATHER.

FREE TALK ⑨

During my break, I took a trip to New York for about 10 days with Naoko Takeuchi, the author of Sailor Moon.

One day in August, I was talking to Takeuchi-san on the phone...

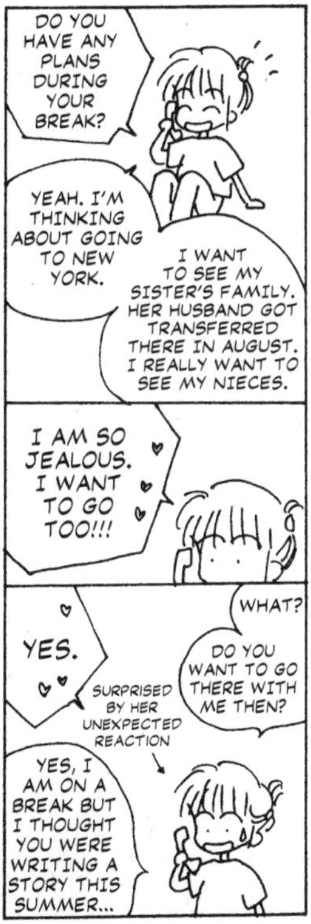
DO YOU HAVE ANY PLANS DURING YOUR BREAK?
YEAH. I'M THINKING ABOUT GOING TO NEW YORK.
I WANT TO SEE MY SISTER'S FAMILY. HER HUSBAND GOT TRANSFERRED THERE IN AUGUST. I REALLY WANT TO SEE MY NIECES.
I AM SO JEALOUS. I WANT TO GO TOO!!!
WHAT?
DO YOU WANT TO GO THERE WITH ME THEN?
YES.
SURPRISED BY HER UNEXPECTED REACTION
YES, I AM ON A BREAK BUT I THOUGHT YOU WERE WRITING A STORY THIS SUMMER...

With all the work she has, she never forgets to enjoy her life. I wish I was as energetic as she is.

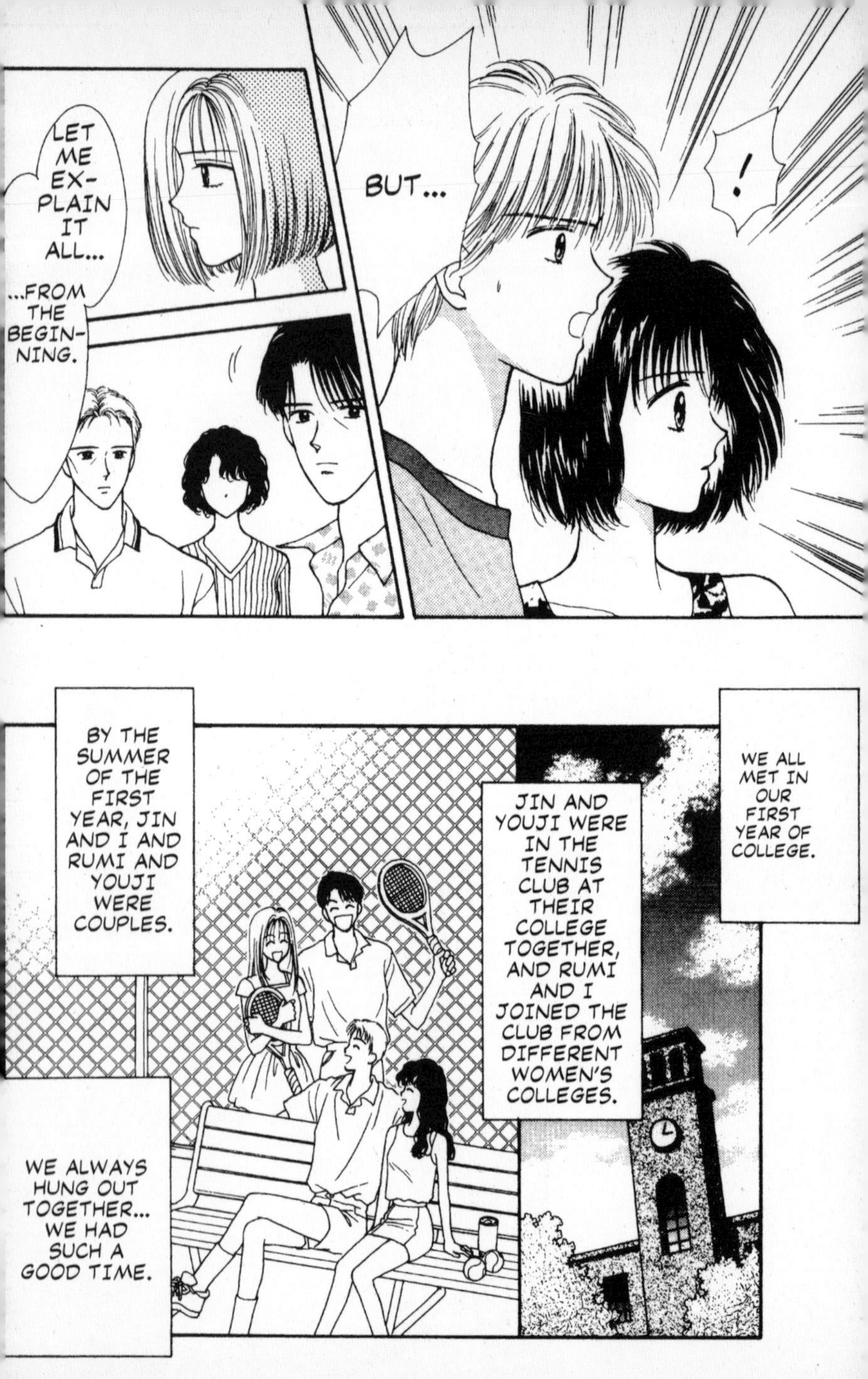
!
BUT...
LET ME EX-PLAIN IT ALL...
...FROM THE BEGIN-NING.
WE ALL MET IN OUR FIRST YEAR OF COLLEGE.
JIN AND YOUJI WERE IN THE TENNIS CLUB AT THEIR COLLEGE TOGETHER, AND RUMI AND I JOINED THE CLUB FROM DIFFERENT WOMEN'S COLLEGES.
BY THE SUMMER OF THE FIRST YEAR, JIN AND I AND RUMI AND YOUJI WERE COUPLES.
WE ALWAYS HUNG OUT TOGETHER... WE HAD SUCH A GOOD TIME.

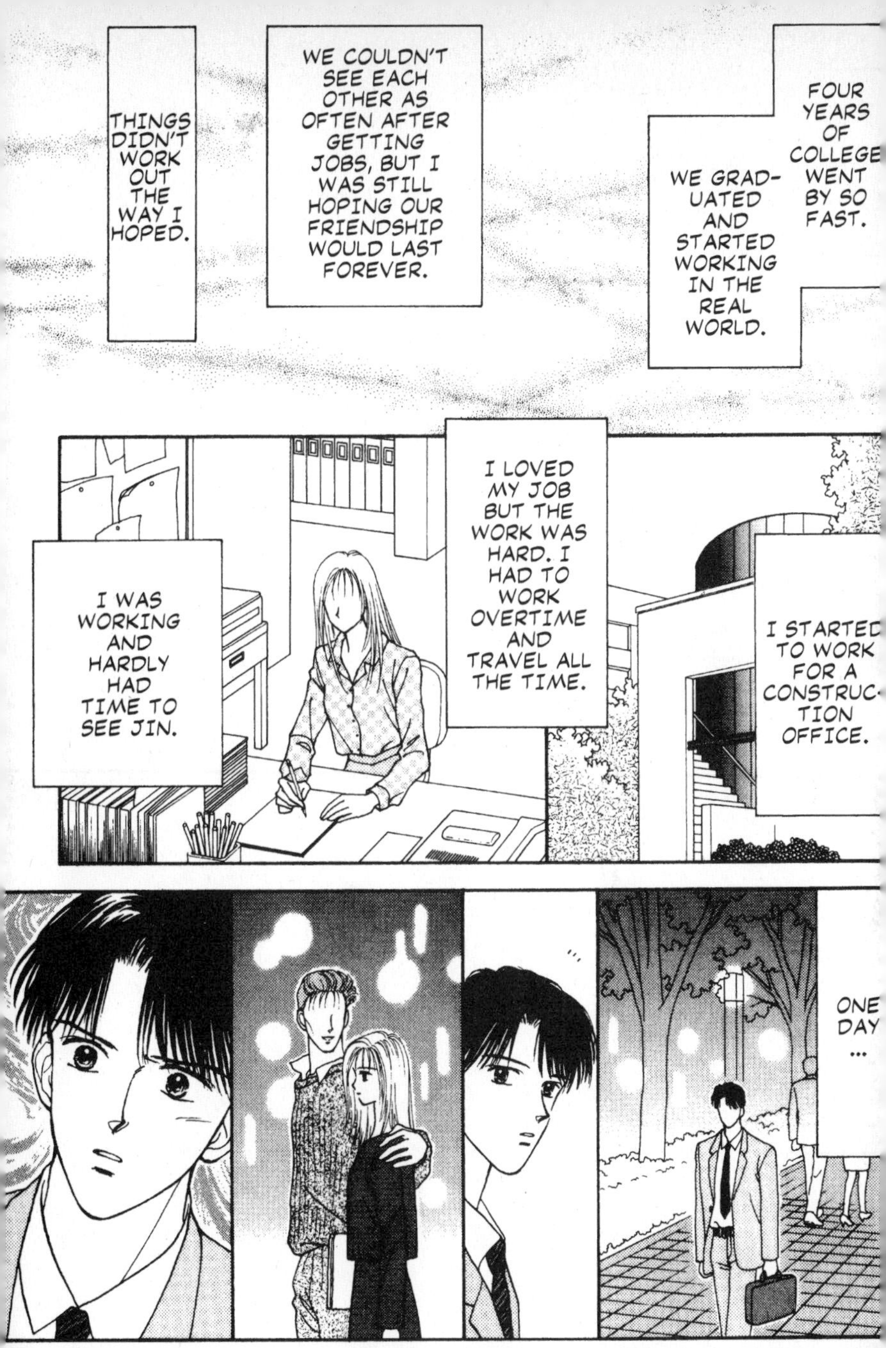
FOUR YEARS OF COLLEGE WENT BY SO FAST.
WE GRADUATED AND STARTED WORKING IN THE REAL WORLD.
WE COULDN'T SEE EACH OTHER AS OFTEN AFTER GETTING JOBS, BUT I WAS STILL HOPING OUR FRIENDSHIP WOULD LAST FOREVER.
THINGS DIDN'T WORK OUT THE WAY I HOPED.
I STARTED TO WORK FOR A CONSTRUCTION OFFICE.
I LOVED MY JOB BUT THE WORK WAS HARD. I HAD TO WORK OVERTIME AND TRAVEL ALL THE TIME.
I WAS WORKING AND HARDLY HAD TIME TO SEE JIN.
ONE DAY ...
...

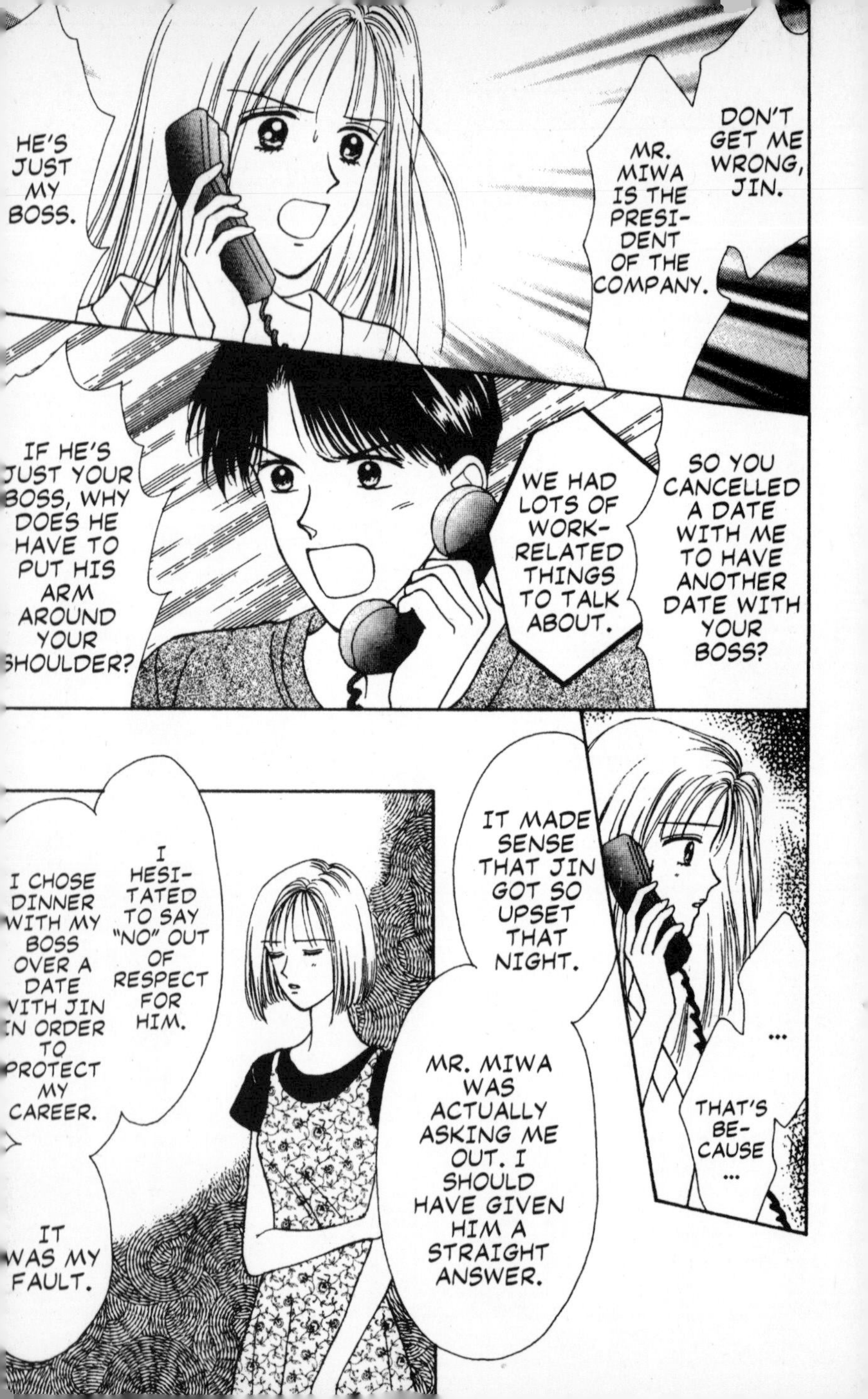
DON'T GET ME WRONG, JIN.
MR. MIWA IS THE PRESIDENT OF THE COMPANY.
HE'S JUST MY BOSS.
SO YOU CANCELLED A DATE WITH ME TO HAVE ANOTHER DATE WITH YOUR BOSS?
WE HAD LOTS OF WORK-RELATED THINGS TO TALK ABOUT.
IF HE'S JUST YOUR BOSS, WHY DOES HE HAVE TO PUT HIS ARM AROUND YOUR SHOULDER?
...
THAT'S BECAUSE ...
IT MADE SENSE THAT JIN GOT SO UPSET THAT NIGHT.
MR. MIWA WAS ACTUALLY ASKING ME OUT. I SHOULD HAVE GIVEN HIM A STRAIGHT ANSWER.
I HESITATED TO SAY "NO" OUT OF RESPECT FOR HIM.
I CHOSE DINNER WITH MY BOSS OVER A DATE WITH JIN IN ORDER TO PROTECT MY CAREER.
IT WAS MY FAULT.

FREE TALK ⑩

I was introduced to Takeuchi-san several years ago at a Kodansha party. At that time I was writing "Handsome Girl" and she was writing "Cherry Project". Since then, we have been good friends. Despite her small appearance, she is such an energetic person who enjoys life to the fullest but also always handles her work efficiently. She often asks me out for a meal and picks me up by her front porch. She takes me to a lot of nice restaurants. Because I can be lazy about leaving the house, I appreciate her taking me out. She is a lot fun to be with. While we were in New York, we went to my sister's house, museums, shopping in Soho and on 5th Avenue and so forth. The 10-day stay was too short, but I got to relax. I would love to go there again soon.

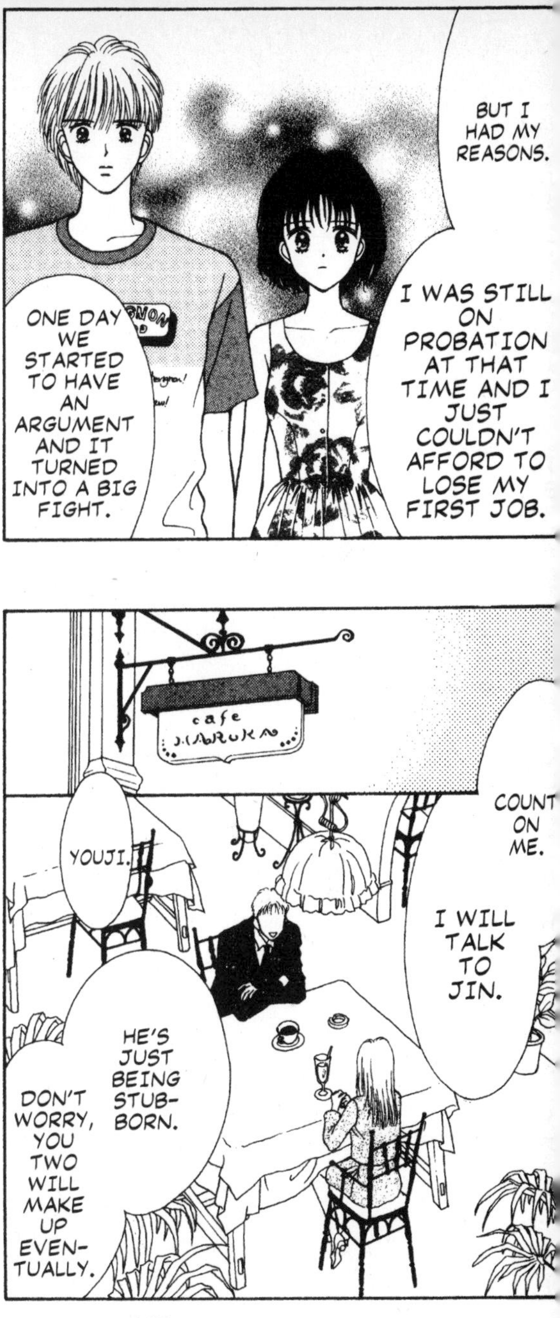
BUT I HAD MY REASONS.
I WAS STILL ON PROBATION AT THAT TIME AND I JUST COULDN'T AFFORD TO LOSE MY FIRST JOB.
ONE DAY WE STARTED TO HAVE AN ARGUMENT AND IT TURNED INTO A BIG FIGHT.
cafe
COUNT ON ME.
YOUJI.
I WILL TALK TO JIN.
HE'S JUST BEING STUB-BORN.
DON'T WORRY, YOU TWO WILL MAKE UP EVEN-TUALLY.

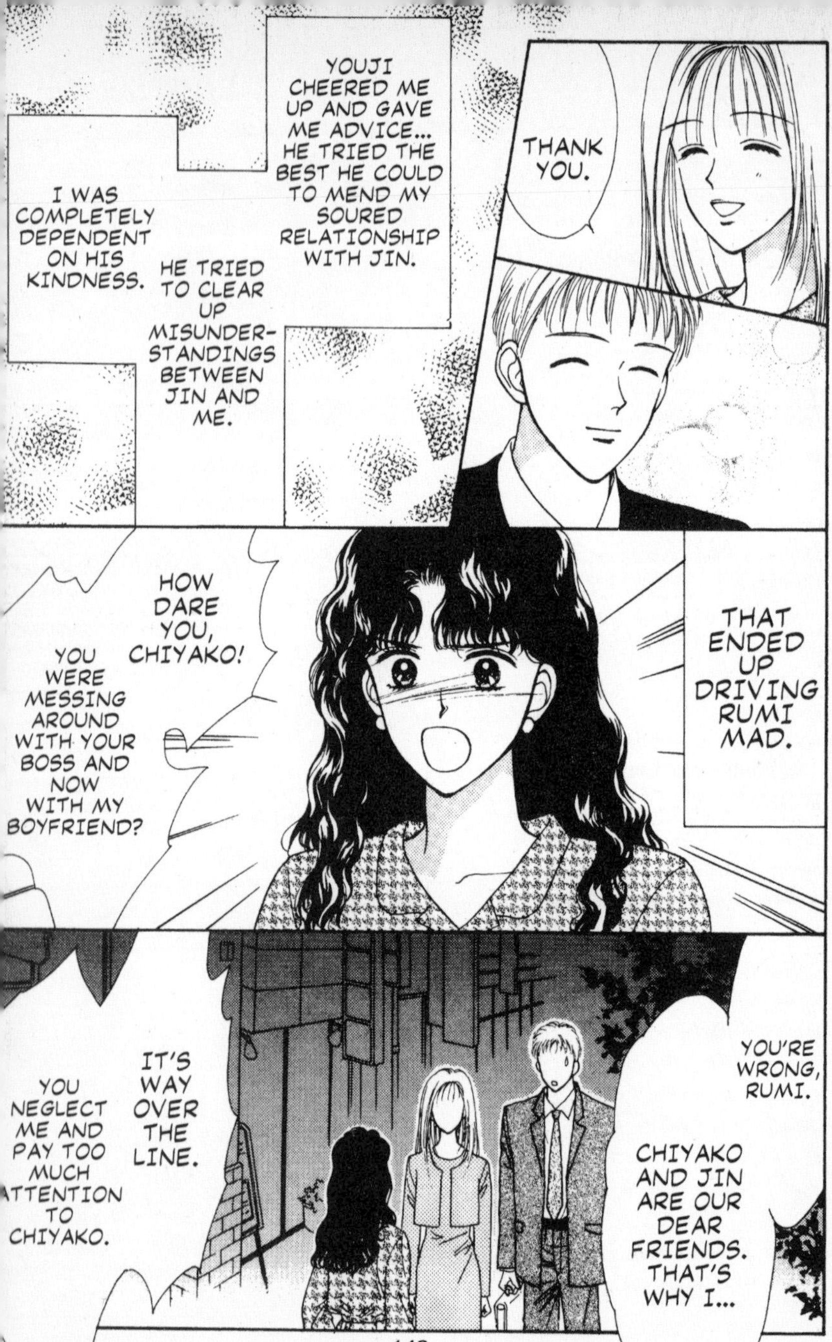
THANK YOU.
YOUJI CHEERED ME UP AND GAVE ME ADVICE... HE TRIED THE BEST HE COULD TO MEND MY SOURED RELATIONSHIP WITH JIN.
HE TRIED TO CLEAR UP MISUNDER-STANDINGS BETWEEN JIN AND ME.
I WAS COMPLETELY DEPENDENT ON HIS KINDNESS.
THAT ENDED UP DRIVING RUMI MAD.
HOW DARE YOU, CHIYAKO!
YOU WERE MESSING AROUND WITH YOUR BOSS AND NOW WITH MY BOYFRIEND?
YOU'RE WRONG, RUMI.
CHIYAKO AND JIN ARE OUR DEAR FRIENDS. THAT'S WHY I...
IT'S WAY OVER THE LINE.
YOU NEGLECT ME AND PAY TOO MUCH ATTENTION TO CHIYAKO.

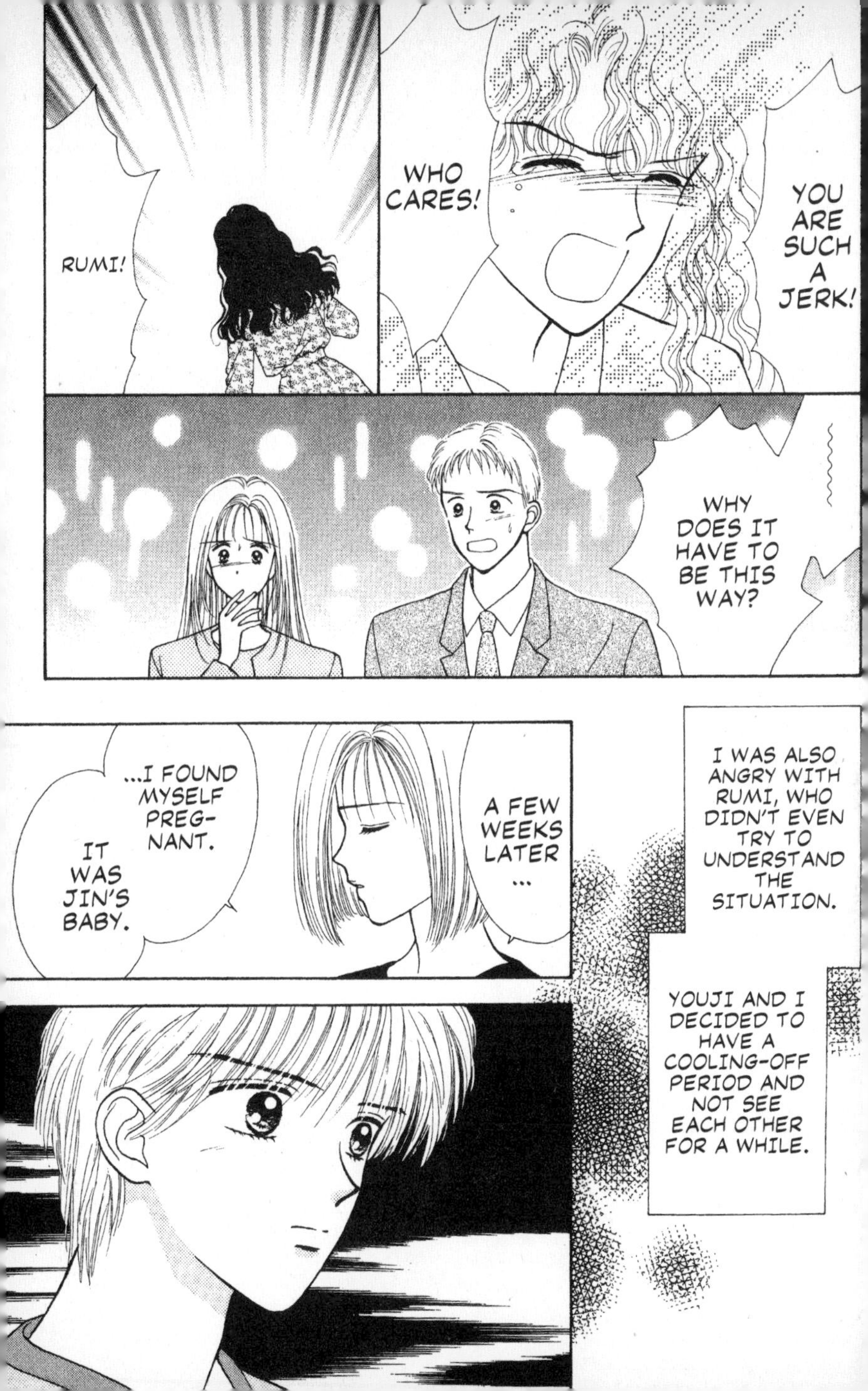
YOU ARE SUCH A JERK!
WHO CARES!
RUMI!
WHY DOES IT HAVE TO BE THIS WAY?
I WAS ALSO ANGRY WITH RUMI, WHO DIDN'T EVEN TRY TO UNDERSTAND THE SITUATION.
A FEW WEEKS LATER ...
...I FOUND MYSELF PREG-NANT.
IT WAS JIN'S BABY.
YOUJI AND I DECIDED TO HAVE A COOLING-OFF PERIOD AND NOT SEE EACH OTHER FOR A WHILE.

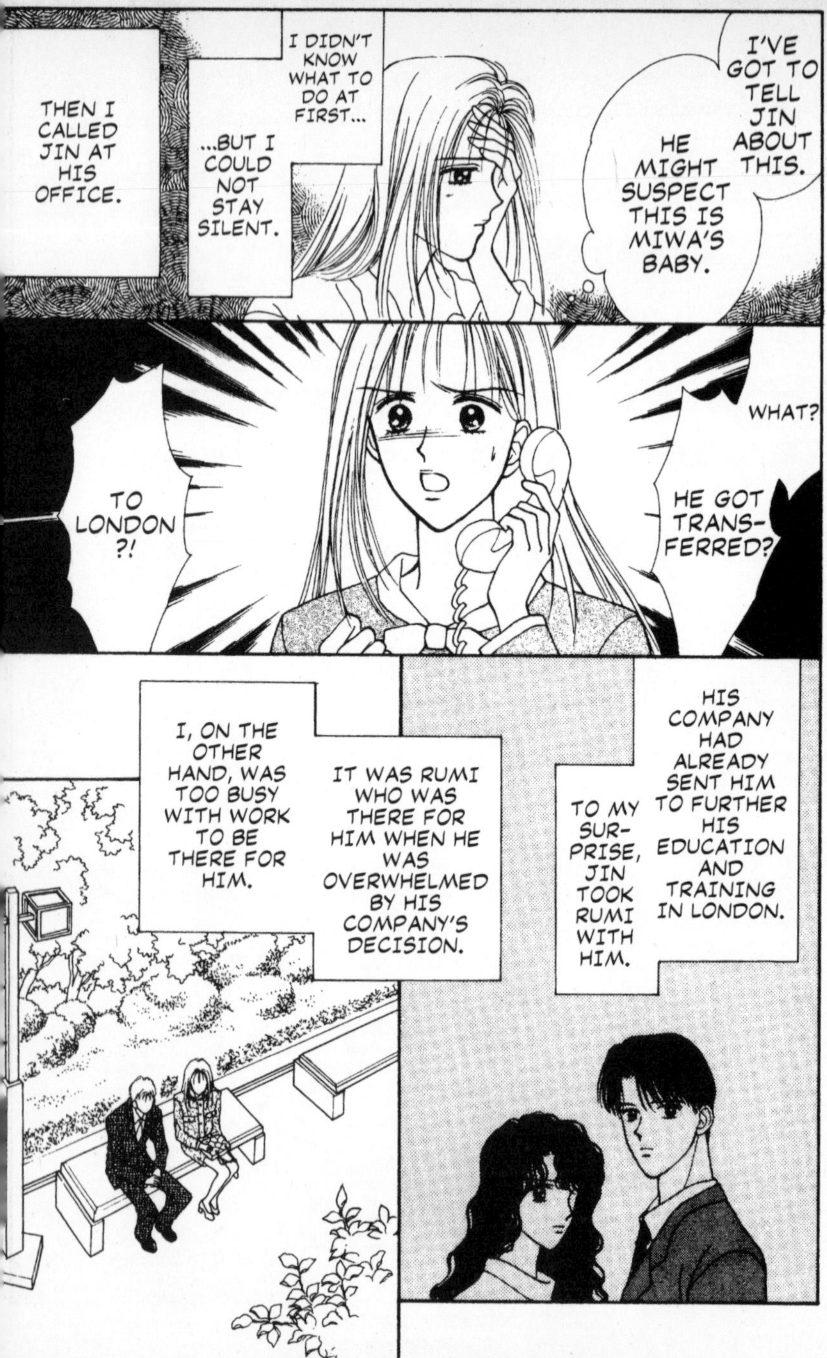

I'VE GOT TO TELL JIN ABOUT THIS.
HE MIGHT SUSPECT THIS IS MIWA'S BABY.
I DIDN'T KNOW WHAT TO DO AT FIRST...
...BUT I COULD NOT STAY SILENT.
THEN I CALLED JIN AT HIS OFFICE.
WHAT?
HE GOT TRANS-FERRED?
TO LONDON?!
HIS COMPANY HAD ALREADY SENT HIM TO FURTHER HIS EDUCATION AND TRAINING IN LONDON.
TO MY SUR-PRISE, JIN TOOK RUMI WITH HIM.
IT WAS RUMI WHO WAS THERE FOR HIM WHEN HE WAS OVERWHELMED BY HIS COMPANY'S DECISION.
I, ON THE OTHER HAND, WAS TOO BUSY WITH WORK TO BE THERE FOR HIM.

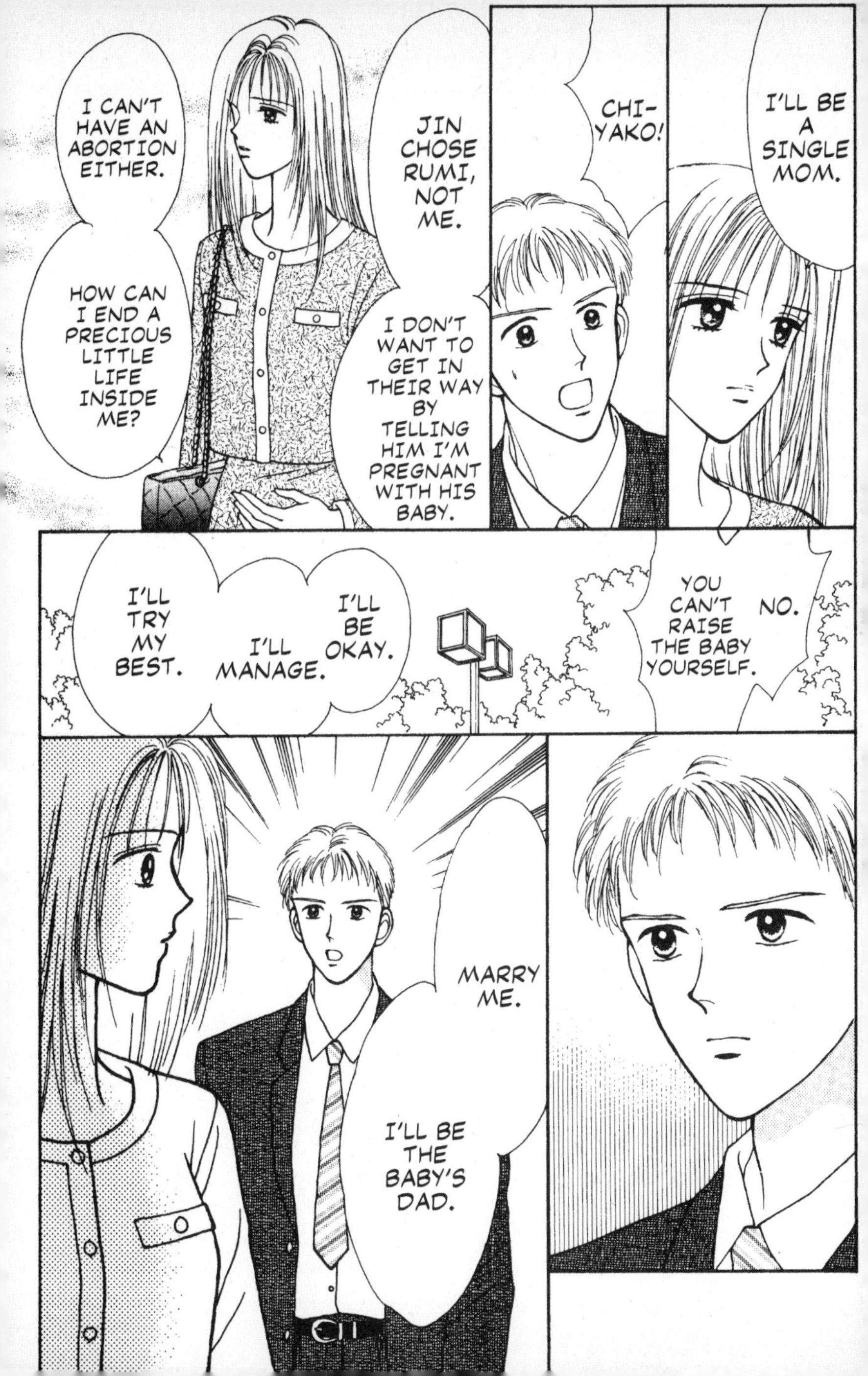
I'LL BE A SINGLE MOM.
CHI-YAKO!
JIN CHOSE RUMI, NOT ME.
I DON'T WANT TO GET IN THEIR WAY BY TELLING HIM I'M PREGNANT WITH HIS BABY.
I CAN'T HAVE AN ABORTION EITHER.
HOW CAN I END A PRECIOUS LITTLE LIFE INSIDE ME?
NO.
YOU CAN'T RAISE THE BABY YOURSELF.
I'LL BE OKAY.
I'LL MANAGE.
I'LL TRY MY BEST.
MARRY ME.
I'LL BE THE BABY'S DAD.

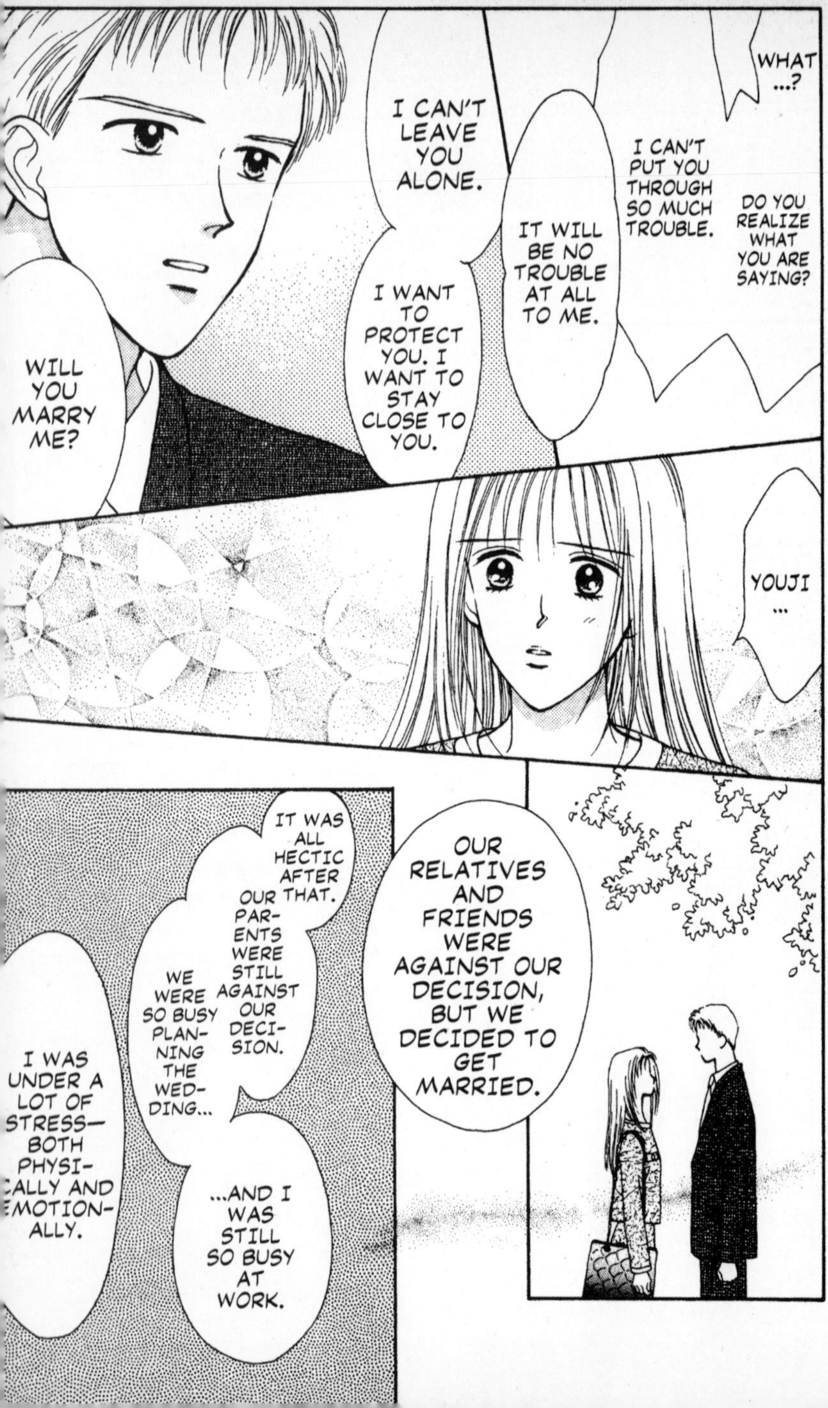

WHAT...?
DO YOU REALIZE WHAT YOU ARE SAYING?
I CAN'T PUT YOU THROUGH SO MUCH TROUBLE.
IT WILL BE NO TROUBLE AT ALL TO ME.
I CAN'T LEAVE YOU ALONE.
I WANT TO PROTECT YOU. I WANT TO STAY CLOSE TO YOU.
WILL YOU MARRY ME?
YOUJI...
OUR RELATIVES AND FRIENDS WERE AGAINST OUR DECISION, BUT WE DECIDED TO GET MARRIED.
IT WAS ALL HECTIC AFTER THAT.
OUR PARENTS WERE STILL AGAINST OUR DECISION.
WE WERE SO BUSY PLANNING THE WEDDING...
...AND I WAS STILL SO BUSY AT WORK.
I WAS UNDER A LOT OF STRESS—BOTH PHYSICALLY AND EMOTIONALLY.

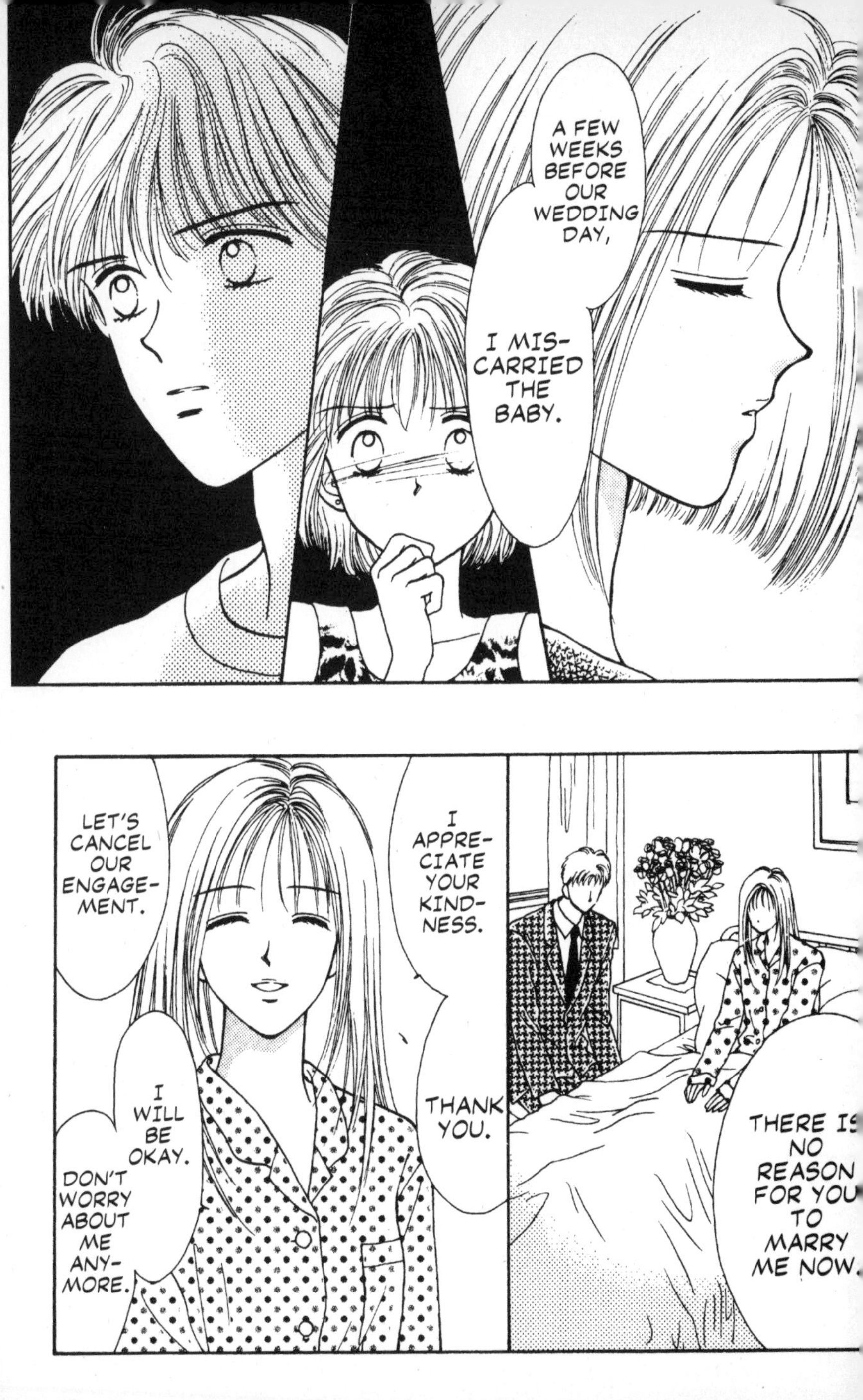
A FEW WEEKS BEFORE OUR WEDDING DAY,
I MIS-CARRIED THE BABY.
THERE IS NO REASON FOR YOU TO MARRY ME NOW.
I APPRECIATE YOUR KIND-NESS.
LET'S CANCEL OUR ENGAGE-MENT.
THANK YOU.
I WILL BE OKAY.
DON'T WORRY ABOUT ME ANY-MORE.

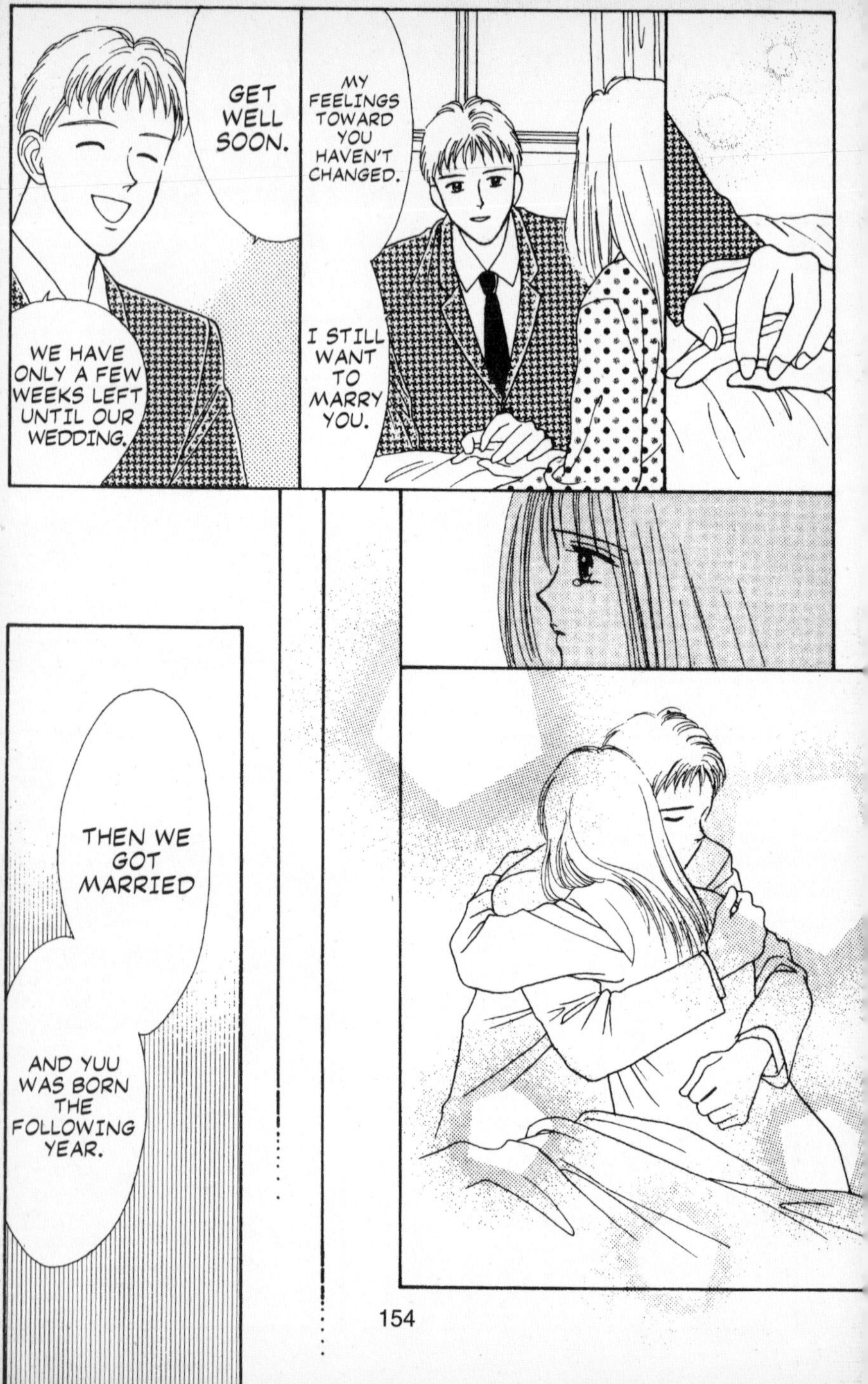
MY FEELINGS TOWARD YOU HAVEN'T CHANGED.
I STILL WANT TO MARRY YOU.
GET WELL SOON.
WE HAVE ONLY A FEW WEEKS LEFT UNTIL OUR WEDDING.
THEN WE GOT MARRIED
AND YUU WAS BORN THE FOLLOWING YEAR.

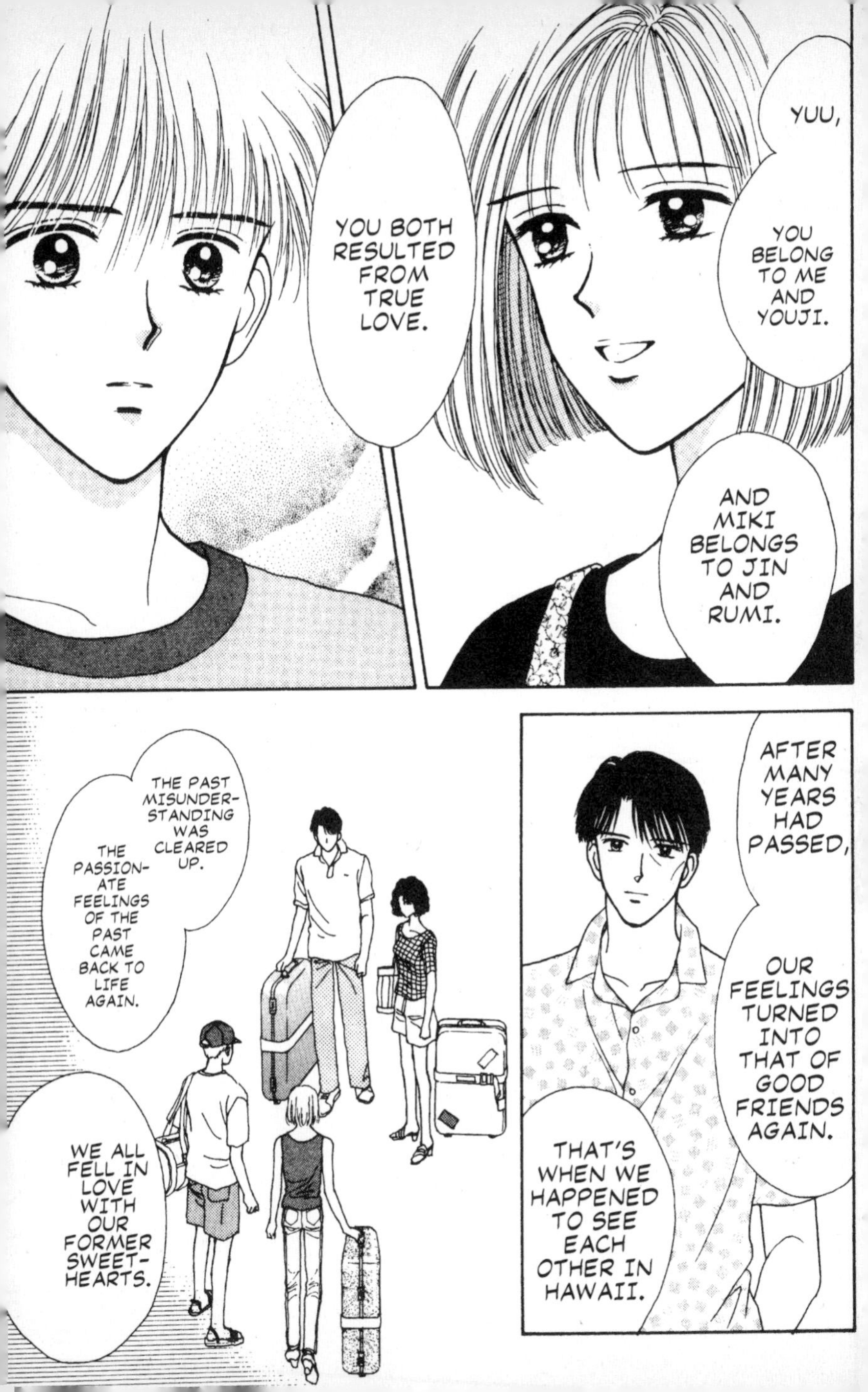
YUU,
YOU BELONG TO ME AND YOUJI.
AND MIKI BELONGS TO JIN AND RUMI.
YOU BOTH RESULTED FROM TRUE LOVE.
AFTER MANY YEARS HAD PASSED,
OUR FEELINGS TURNED INTO THAT OF GOOD FRIENDS AGAIN.
THAT'S WHEN WE HAPPENED TO SEE EACH OTHER IN HAWAII.
THE PAST MISUNDER-STANDING WAS CLEARED UP.
THE PASSION-ATE FEELINGS OF THE PAST CAME BACK TO LIFE AGAIN.
WE ALL FELL IN LOVE WITH OUR FORMER SWEET-HEARTS.

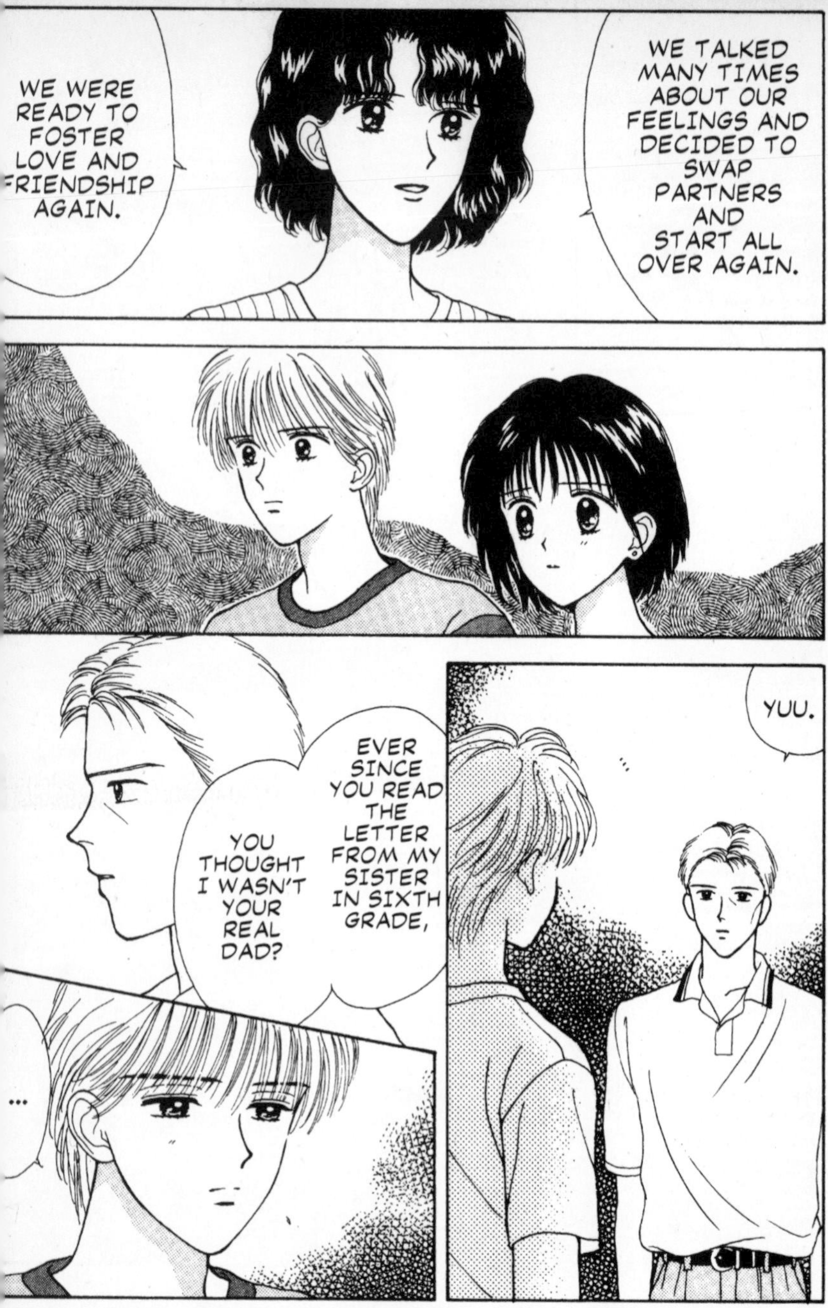
WE TALKED MANY TIMES ABOUT OUR FEELINGS AND DECIDED TO SWAP PARTNERS AND START ALL OVER AGAIN.
WE WERE READY TO FOSTER LOVE AND FRIENDSHIP AGAIN.
YUU.
EVER SINCE YOU READ THE LETTER FROM MY SISTER IN SIXTH GRADE,
YOU THOUGHT I WASN'T YOUR REAL DAD?
...

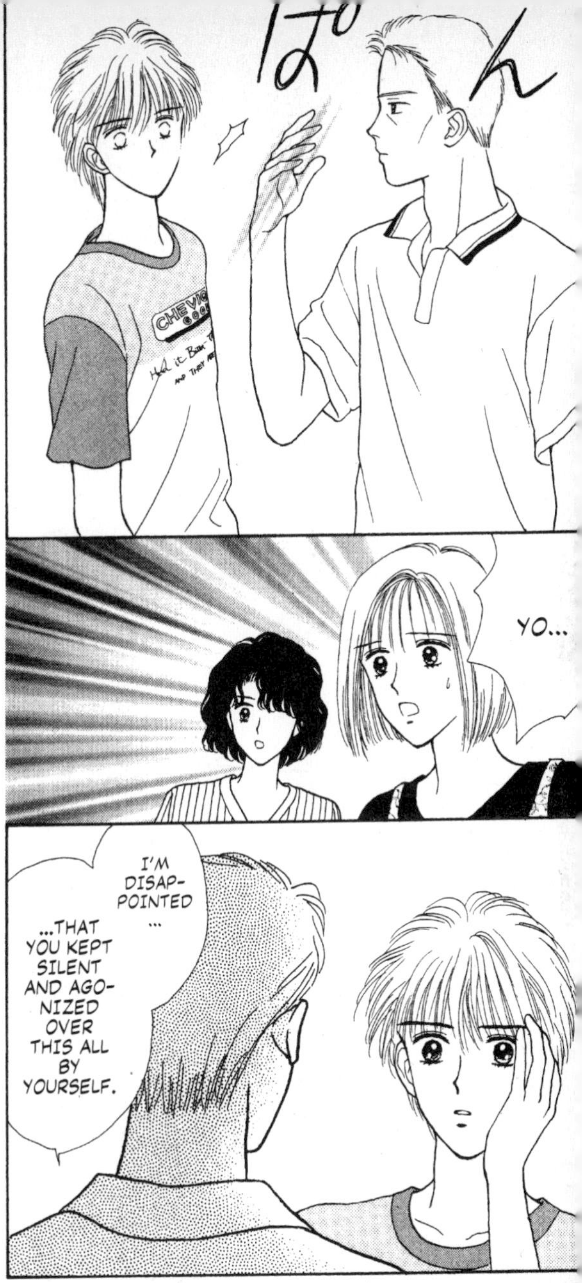
ぱん
YO...
I'M DISAP-POINTED ...
...THAT YOU KEPT SILENT AND AGO-NIZED OVER THIS ALL BY YOURSELF.

FREE TALK ⑪

I almost forgot to tell you! A reader who read the July issue of Ribon wrote to me saying that if Jin and Rumi stayed in London for three years during which Miki was born, it would be impossible for Jin and Chiyako to have a child after Chiyako lost her first child because Miki and Yuu are the same age. Let me clarify this. It would be impossible if Jin and Rumi had been there until Miki was just a year old. Miki was actually there until she was a little over a year old. Let's say that Miki was there until she was one year and six months old. (Yuu was born 10 months earlier than Miki.) The time for Rumi to conceive Miki and carry her to full term (10 months) and raise her until they come back to Japan (one year and six months) add up to be three years and one month. This adds up to over three years, leaving enough time for Jin and Chiyako to have Yuu. It might sound a little complicated but I gave this enough thought to make the story credible. Don't worry too much whether the story is believable or not. Thank you so much for supporting Marmalade Boy for such a long time. This volume contains the bonus pages at the end. Please enjoy them, too.

* Editor's note : In Japan, the normal length of full-term pregnancy is considered to be 10 months, not 9 months.

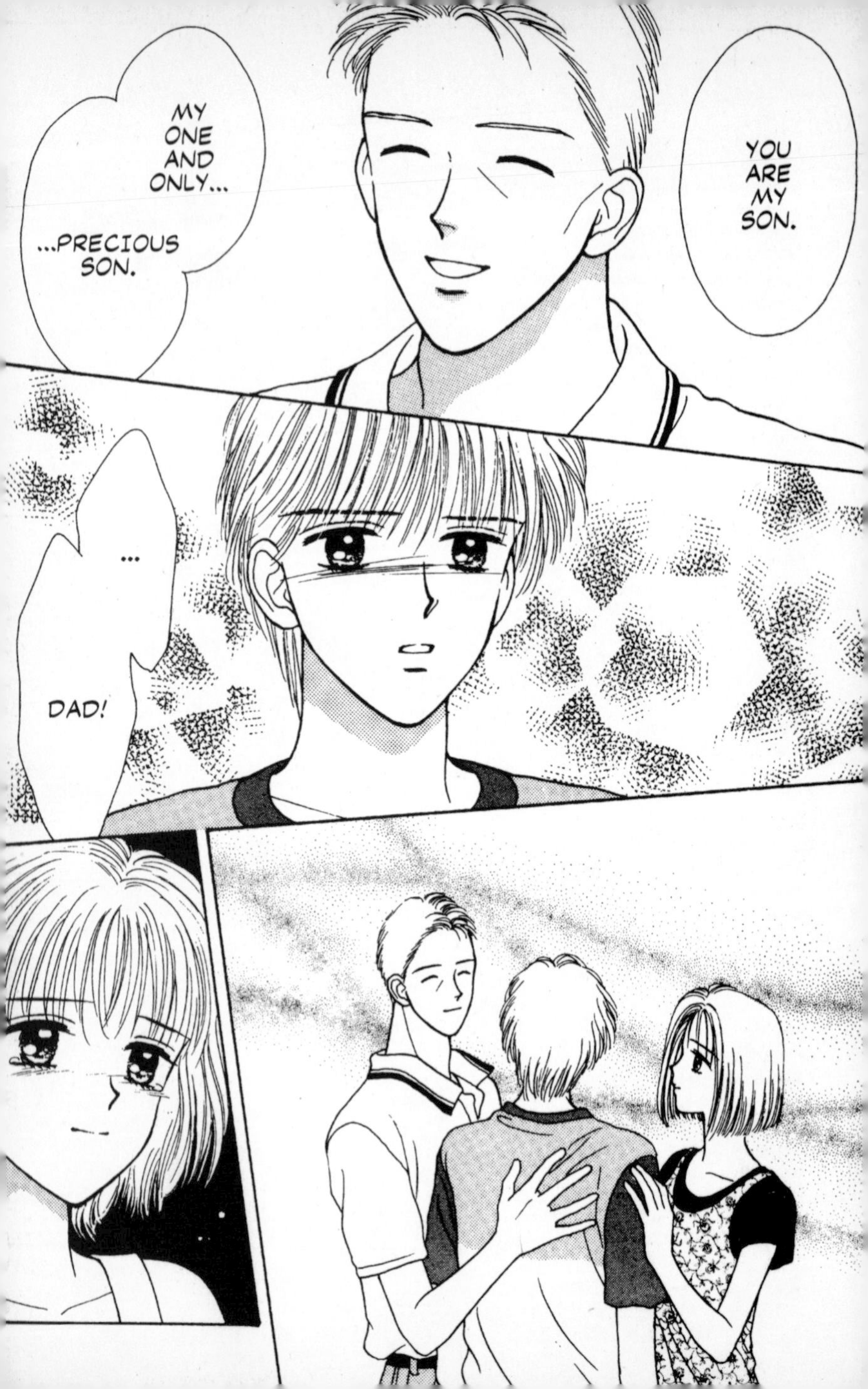
YOU ARE MY SON.
MY ONE AND ONLY...
...PRECIOUS SON.
...
DAD!

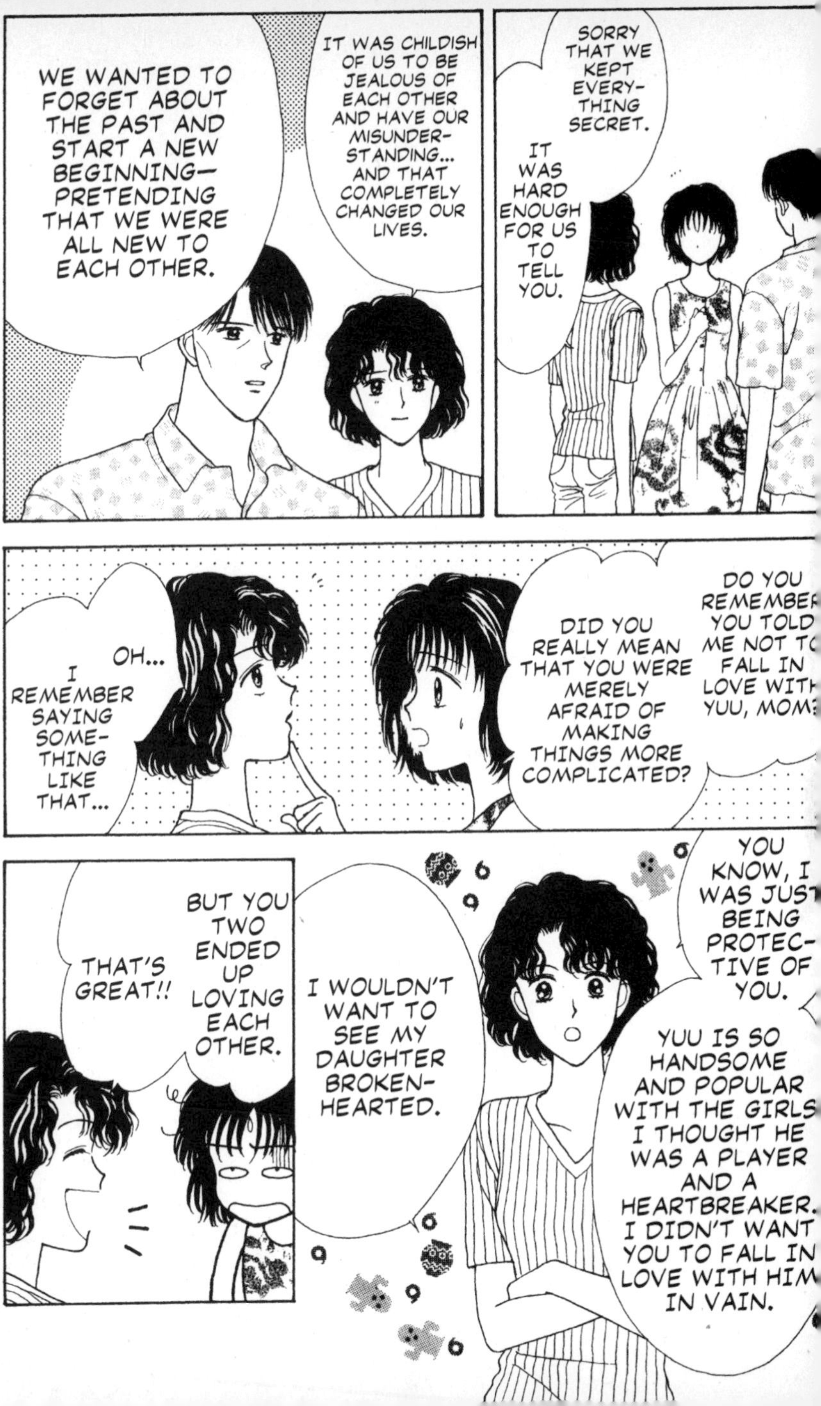
SORRY THAT WE KEPT EVERY-THING SECRET.
IT WAS HARD ENOUGH FOR US TO TELL YOU.
IT WAS CHILDISH OF US TO BE JEALOUS OF EACH OTHER AND HAVE OUR MISUNDER-STANDING... AND THAT COMPLETELY CHANGED OUR LIVES.
WE WANTED TO FORGET ABOUT THE PAST AND START A NEW BEGINNING— PRETENDING THAT WE WERE ALL NEW TO EACH OTHER.
DO YOU REMEMBER YOU TOLD ME NOT TO FALL IN LOVE WITH YUU, MOM?
DID YOU REALLY MEAN THAT YOU WERE MERELY AFRAID OF MAKING THINGS MORE COMPLICATED?
OH...
I REMEMBER SAYING SOME-THING LIKE THAT...
YOU KNOW, I WAS JUST BEING PROTEC-TIVE OF YOU.
YUU IS SO HANDSOME AND POPULAR WITH THE GIRLS I THOUGHT HE WAS A PLAYER AND A HEARTBREAKER. I DIDN'T WANT YOU TO FALL IN LOVE WITH HIM IN VAIN.
I WOULDN'T WANT TO SEE MY DAUGHTER BROKEN-HEARTED.
BUT YOU TWO ENDED UP LOVING EACH OTHER.
THAT'S GREAT!!

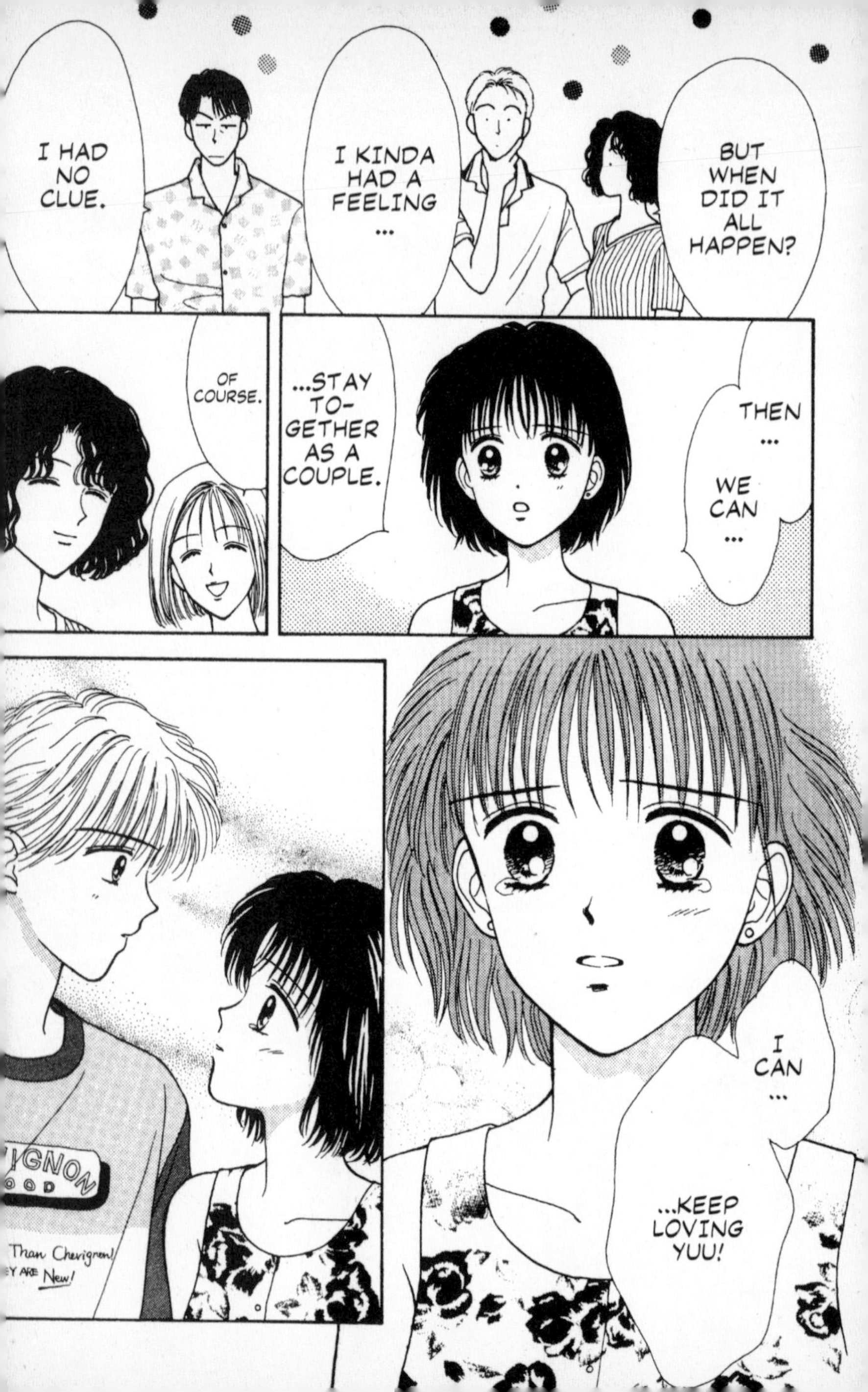
BUT WHEN DID IT ALL HAPPEN?
I KINDA HAD A FEELING ...
I HAD NO CLUE.
THEN ... WE CAN ...
...STAY TO-GETHER AS A COUPLE.
OF COURSE.
I CAN ...
...KEEP LOVING YUU!

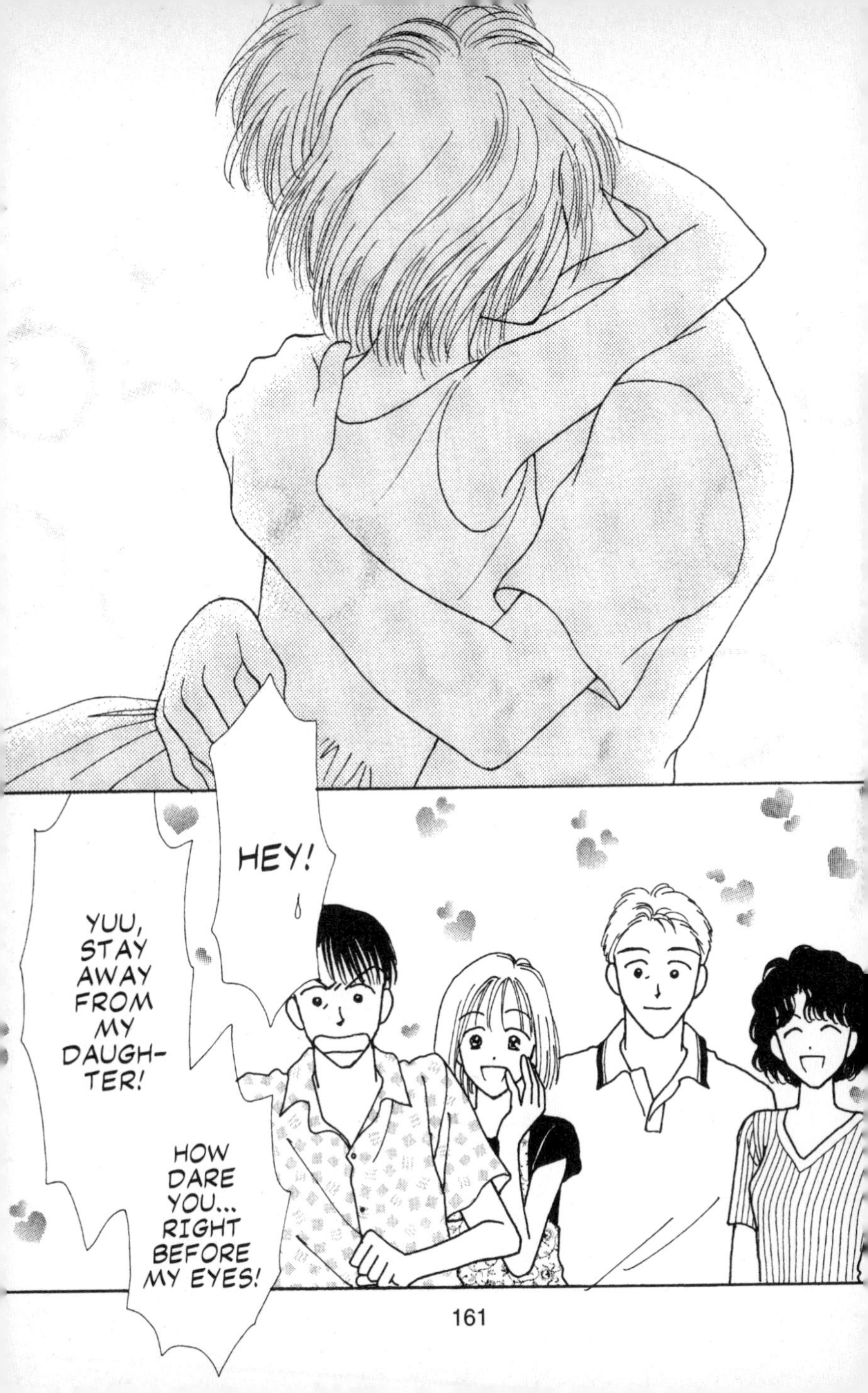
HEY!
YUU, STAY AWAY FROM MY DAUGHTER!
HOW DARE YOU... RIGHT BEFORE MY EYES!

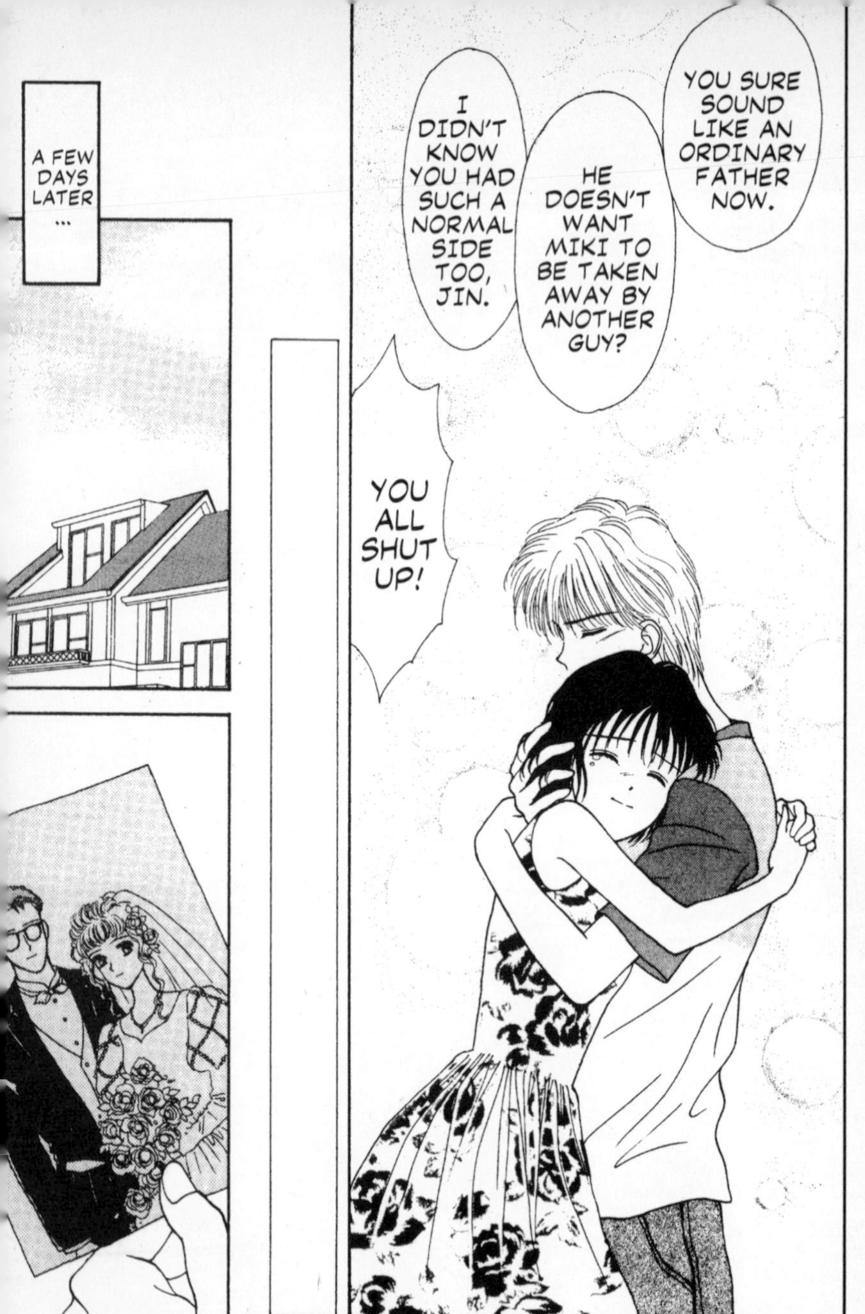
YOU SURE SOUND LIKE AN ORDINARY FATHER NOW.
HE DOESN'T WANT MIKI TO BE TAKEN AWAY BY ANOTHER GUY?
I DIDN'T KNOW YOU HAD SUCH A NORMAL SIDE TOO, JIN.
YOU ALL SHUT UP!
A FEW DAYS LATER ...

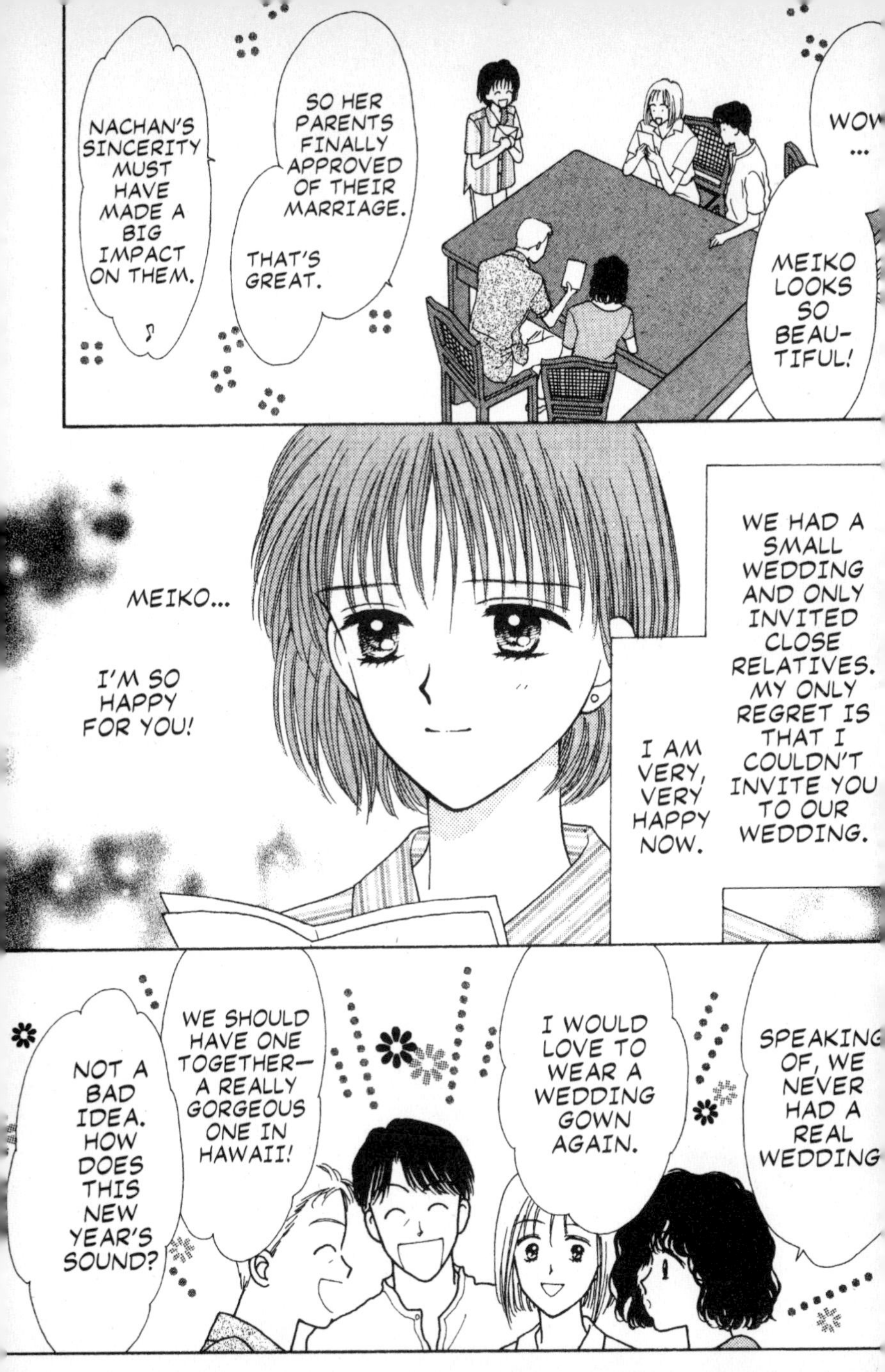
WOW ...
MEIKO LOOKS SO BEAU-TIFUL!
SO HER PARENTS FINALLY APPROVED OF THEIR MARRIAGE.
THAT'S GREAT.
NACHAN'S SINCERITY MUST HAVE MADE A BIG IMPACT ON THEM.
WE HAD A SMALL WEDDING AND ONLY INVITED CLOSE RELATIVES. MY ONLY REGRET IS THAT I COULDN'T INVITE YOU TO OUR WEDDING.
I AM VERY, VERY HAPPY NOW.
MEIKO...
I'M SO HAPPY FOR YOU!
SPEAKING OF, WE NEVER HAD A REAL WEDDING
I WOULD LOVE TO WEAR A WEDDING GOWN AGAIN.
WE SHOULD HAVE ONE TOGETHER— A REALLY GORGEOUS ONE IN HAWAII!
NOT A BAD IDEA. HOW DOES THIS NEW YEAR'S SOUND?

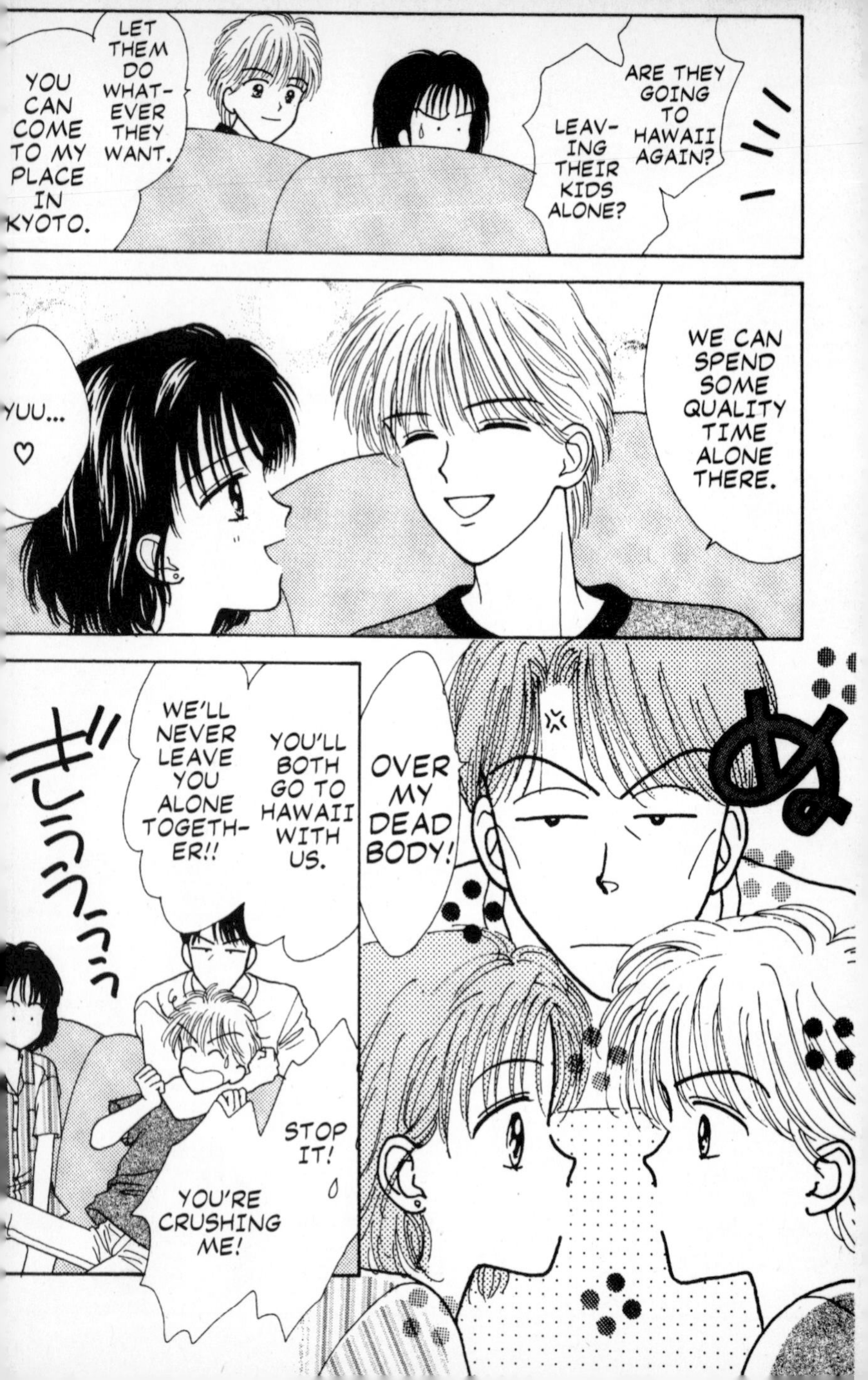

ARE THEY GOING TO HAWAII AGAIN?
LEAVING THEIR KIDS ALONE?
LET THEM DO WHATEVER THEY WANT.
YOU CAN COME TO MY PLACE IN KYOTO.
WE CAN SPEND SOME QUALITY TIME ALONE THERE.
YUU... ♡
ぬ
OVER MY DEAD BODY!
YOU'LL BOTH GO TO HAWAII WITH US.
WE'LL NEVER LEAVE YOU ALONE TOGETHER!!
ぎゅううう
STOP IT!
YOU'RE CRUSHING ME!

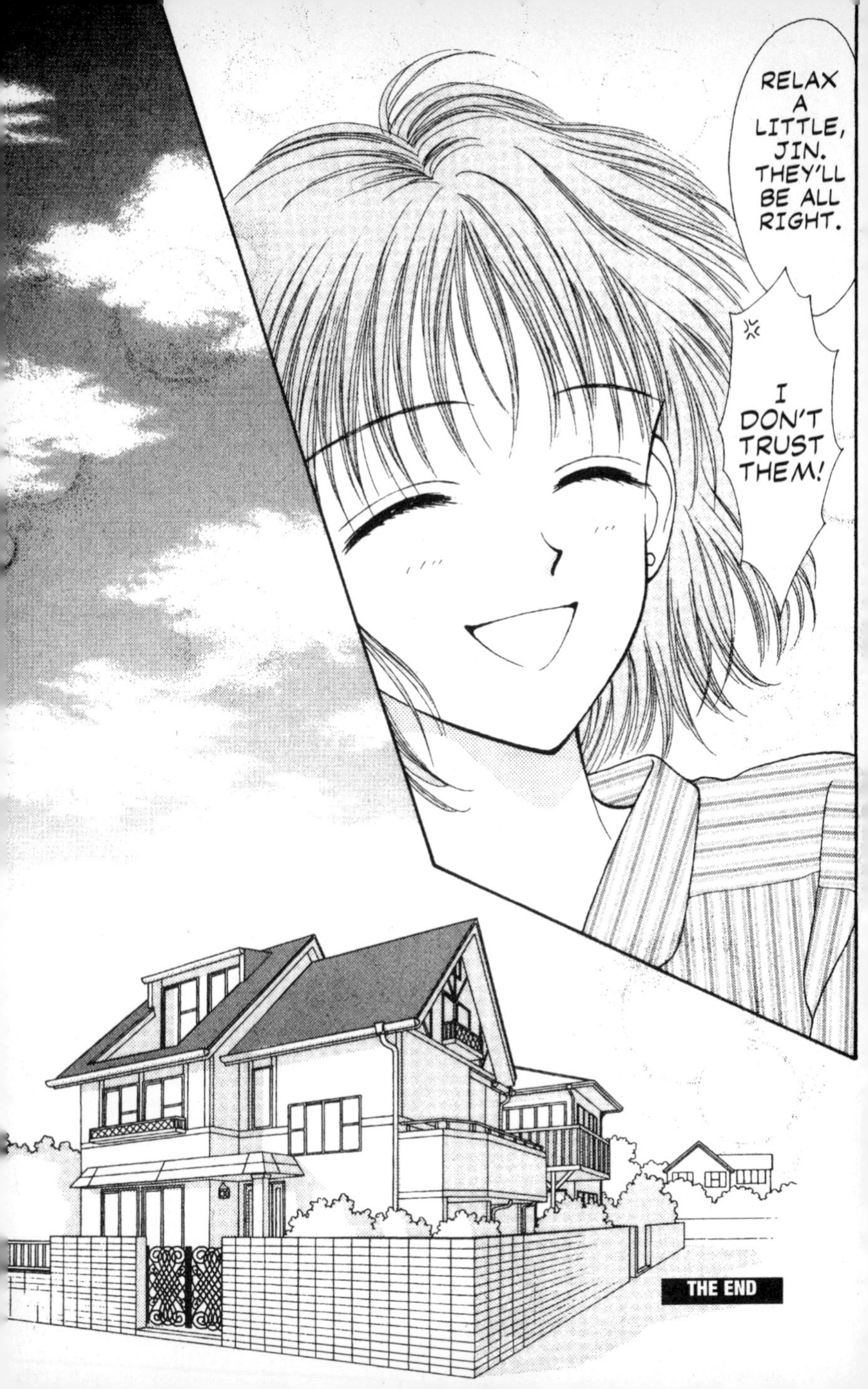
RELAX A LITTLE, JIN. THEY'LL BE ALL RIGHT.
I DON'T TRUST THEM!
THE END

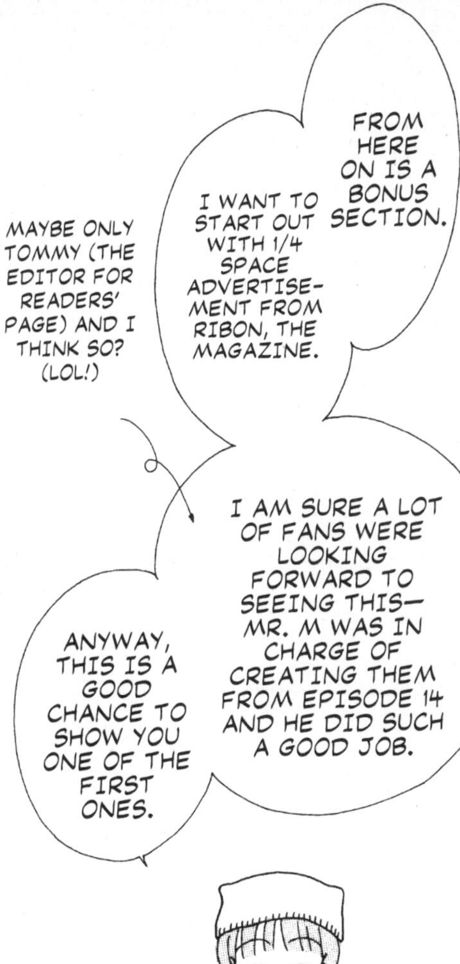
FROM HERE ON IS A BONUS SECTION.
I WANT TO START OUT WITH 1/4 SPACE ADVERTISE-MENT FROM RIBON, THE MAGAZINE.
MAYBE ONLY TOMMY (THE EDITOR FOR READERS' PAGE) AND I THINK SO? (LOL!)
I AM SURE A LOT OF FANS WERE LOOKING FORWARD TO SEEING THIS— MR. M WAS IN CHARGE OF CREATING THEM FROM EPISODE 14 AND HE DID SUCH A GOOD JOB.
ANYWAY, THIS IS A GOOD CHANCE TO SHOW YOU ONE OF THE FIRST ONES.
THIS ONE APPEARED IN THE SEPTEMBER ISSUE OF 1993.

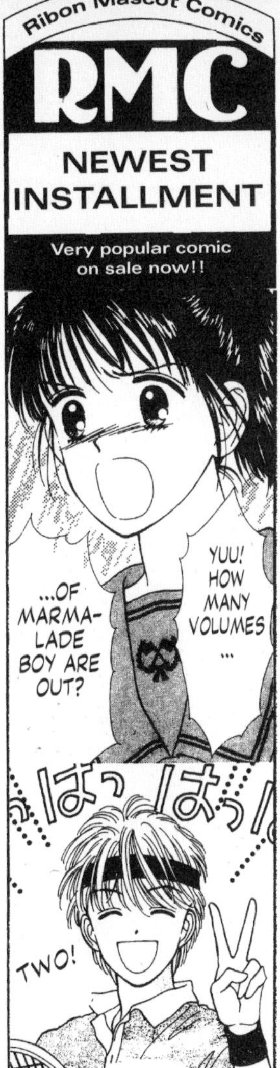
Ribon Mascot Comics
RMC
NEWEST INSTALLMENT
Very popular comic on sale now!!
YUU! HOW MANY VOLUMES ...
...OF MARMALADE BOY ARE OUT?
TWO!
MARMALADE BOY 1 & 2.
WATARU YOSHIZUMI'S SLIGHTLY ROMANTIC STORY!

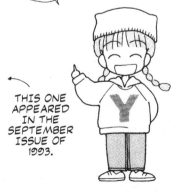

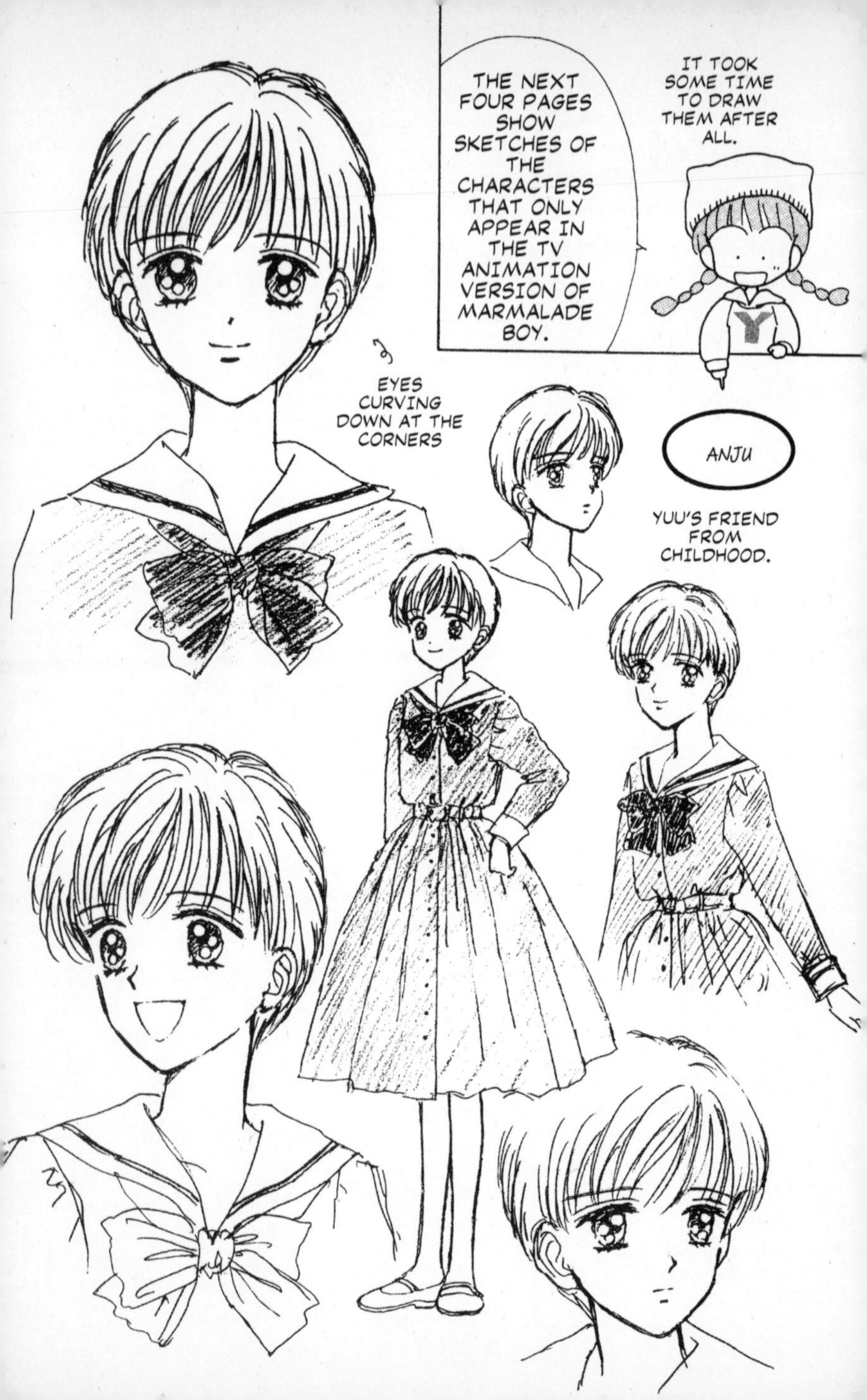
THE NEXT FOUR PAGES SHOW SKETCHES OF THE CHARACTERS THAT ONLY APPEAR IN THE TV ANIMATION VERSION OF MARMALADE BOY.
IT TOOK SOME TIME TO DRAW THEM AFTER ALL.
Y
ANJU
YUU'S FRIEND FROM CHILDHOOD.
EYES CURVING DOWN AT THE CORNERS

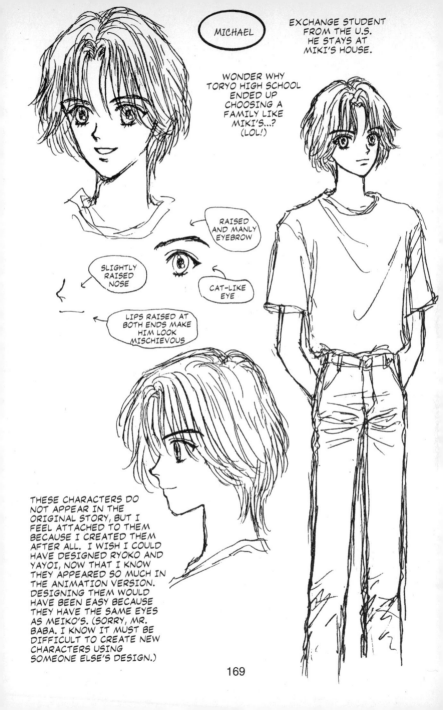

MICHAEL

EXCHANGE STUDENT FROM THE U.S. HE STAYS AT MIKI'S HOUSE.

WONDER WHY TORYO HIGH SCHOOL ENDED UP CHOOSING A FAMILY LIKE MIKI'S...? (LOL!)

RAISED AND MANLY EYEBROW

SLIGHTLY RAISED NOSE

CAT-LIKE EYE

LIPS RAISED AT BOTH ENDS MAKE HIM LOOK MISCHIEVOUS

THESE CHARACTERS DO NOT APPEAR IN THE ORIGINAL STORY, BUT I FEEL ATTACHED TO THEM BECAUSE I CREATED THEM AFTER ALL. I WISH I COULD HAVE DESIGNED RYOKO AND YAYOI, NOW THAT I KNOW THEY APPEARED SO MUCH IN THE ANIMATION VERSION. DESIGNING THEM WOULD HAVE BEEN EASY BECAUSE THEY HAVE THE SAME EYES AS MEIKO'S. (SORRY, MR. BABA. I KNOW IT MUST BE DIFFICULT TO CREATE NEW CHARACTERS USING SOMEONE ELSE'S DESIGN.)

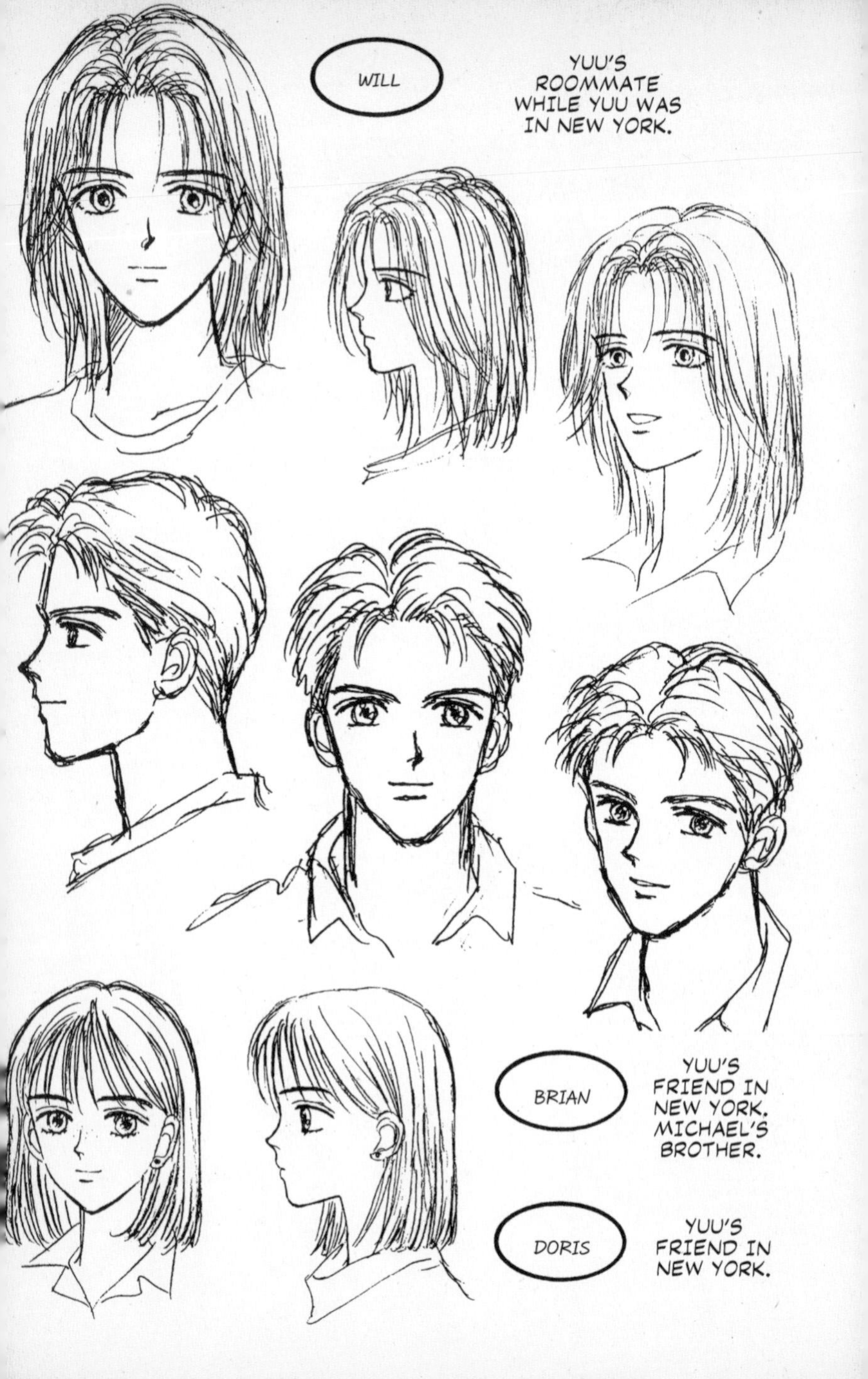
WILL
YUU'S ROOMMATE WHILE YUU WAS IN NEW YORK.
BRIAN
YUU'S FRIEND IN NEW YORK. MICHAEL'S BROTHER.
DORIS
YUU'S FRIEND IN NEW YORK.

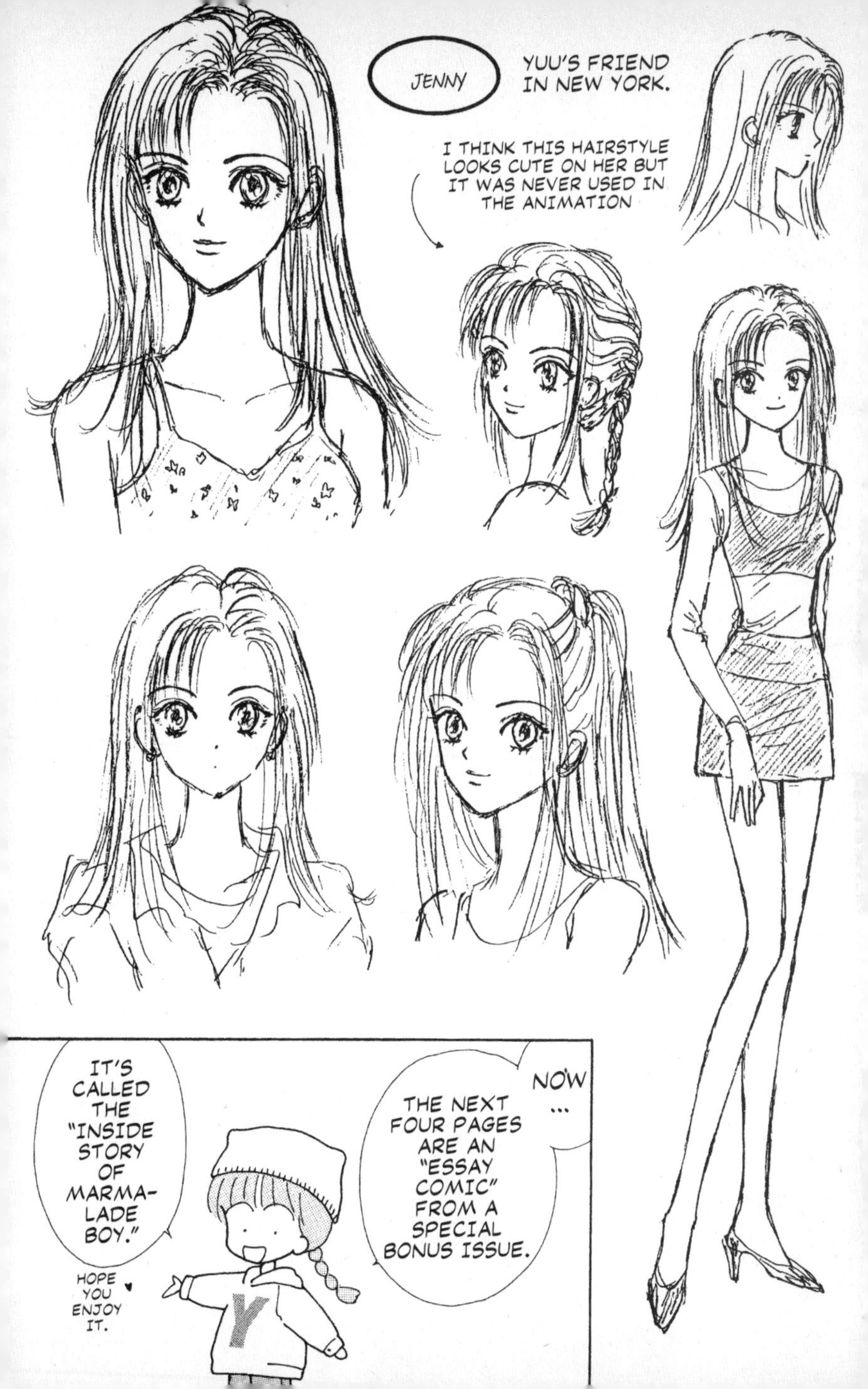
YUU'S FRIEND IN NEW YORK.
JENNY
I THINK THIS HAIRSTYLE LOOKS CUTE ON HER BUT IT WAS NEVER USED IN THE ANIMATION
NOW ...
THE NEXT FOUR PAGES ARE AN "ESSAY COMIC" FROM A SPECIAL BONUS ISSUE.
IT'S CALLED THE "INSIDE STORY OF MARMA-LADE BOY."
HOPE YOU ENJOY IT. ♥

THE INSIDE STORY OF MARMALADE BOY

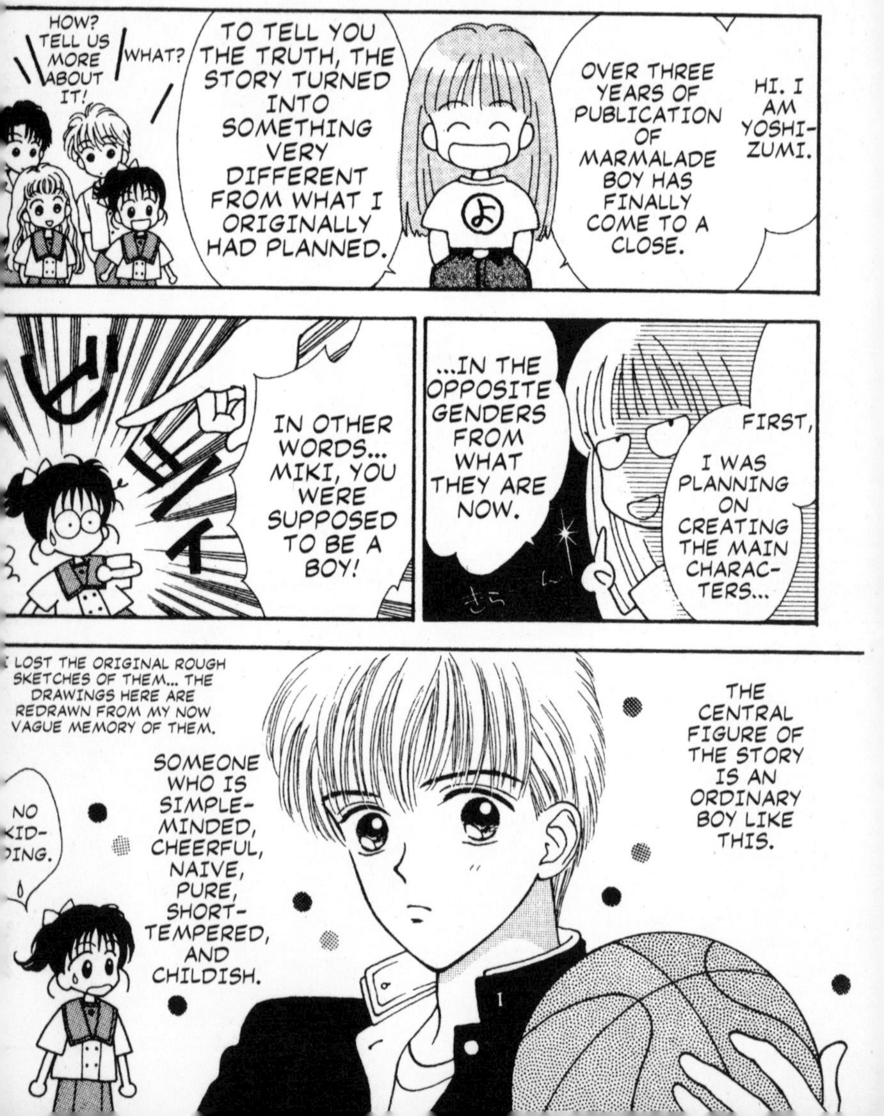

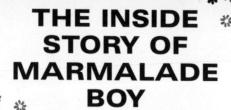

HI. I AM YOSHIZUMI.
OVER THREE YEARS OF PUBLICATION OF MARMALADE BOY HAS FINALLY COME TO A CLOSE.
TO TELL YOU THE TRUTH, THE STORY TURNED INTO SOMETHING VERY DIFFERENT FROM WHAT I ORIGINALLY HAD PLANNED.
WHAT?
HOW? TELL US MORE ABOUT IT!
FIRST,
I WAS PLANNING ON CREATING THE MAIN CHARACTERS...
...IN THE OPPOSITE GENDERS FROM WHAT THEY ARE NOW.
IN OTHER WORDS... MIKI, YOU WERE SUPPOSED TO BE A BOY!
THE CENTRAL FIGURE OF THE STORY IS AN ORDINARY BOY LIKE THIS.
SOMEONE WHO IS SIMPLE-MINDED, CHEERFUL, NAIVE, PURE, SHORT-TEMPERED, AND CHILDISH.
I LOST THE ORIGINAL ROUGH SKETCHES OF THEM... THE DRAWINGS HERE ARE REDRAWN FROM MY NOW VAGUE MEMORY OF THEM.
NO KID-DING.

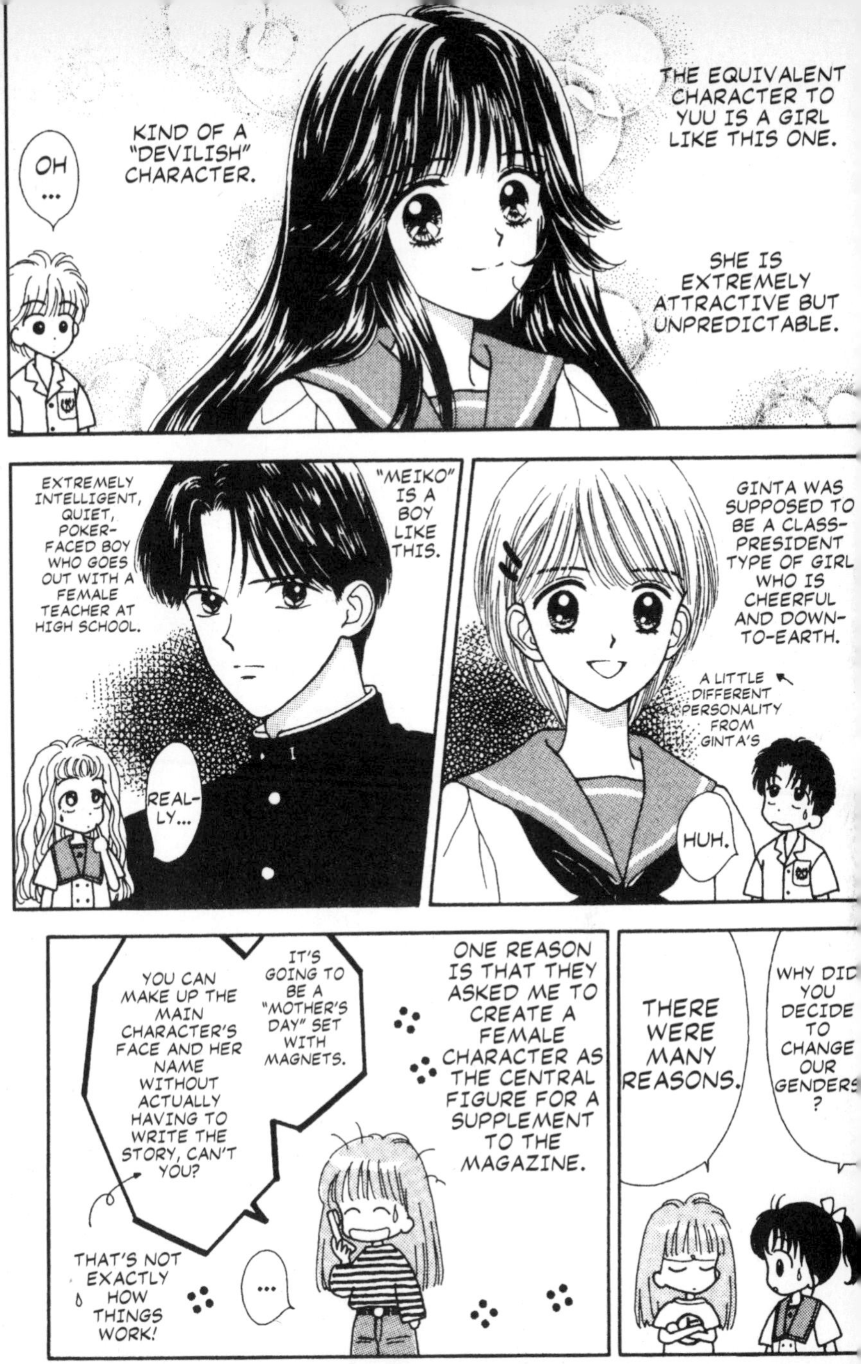
THE EQUIVALENT CHARACTER TO YUU IS A GIRL LIKE THIS ONE.
SHE IS EXTREMELY ATTRACTIVE BUT UNPREDICTABLE.
KIND OF A "DEVILISH" CHARACTER.
OH ...
GINTA WAS SUPPOSED TO BE A CLASS-PRESIDENT TYPE OF GIRL WHO IS CHEERFUL AND DOWN-TO-EARTH.
A LITTLE DIFFERENT PERSONALITY FROM GINTA'S
HUH.
"MEIKO" IS A BOY LIKE THIS.
EXTREMELY INTELLIGENT, QUIET, POKER-FACED BOY WHO GOES OUT WITH A FEMALE TEACHER AT HIGH SCHOOL.
REAL-LY...
WHY DID YOU DECIDE TO CHANGE OUR GENDERS?
THERE WERE MANY REASONS.
ONE REASON IS THAT THEY ASKED ME TO CREATE A FEMALE CHARACTER AS THE CENTRAL FIGURE FOR A SUPPLEMENT TO THE MAGAZINE.
IT'S GOING TO BE A "MOTHER'S DAY" SET WITH MAGNETS.
YOU CAN MAKE UP THE MAIN CHARACTER'S FACE AND HER NAME WITHOUT ACTUALLY HAVING TO WRITE THE STORY, CAN'T YOU?
...
THAT'S NOT EXACTLY HOW THINGS WORK!

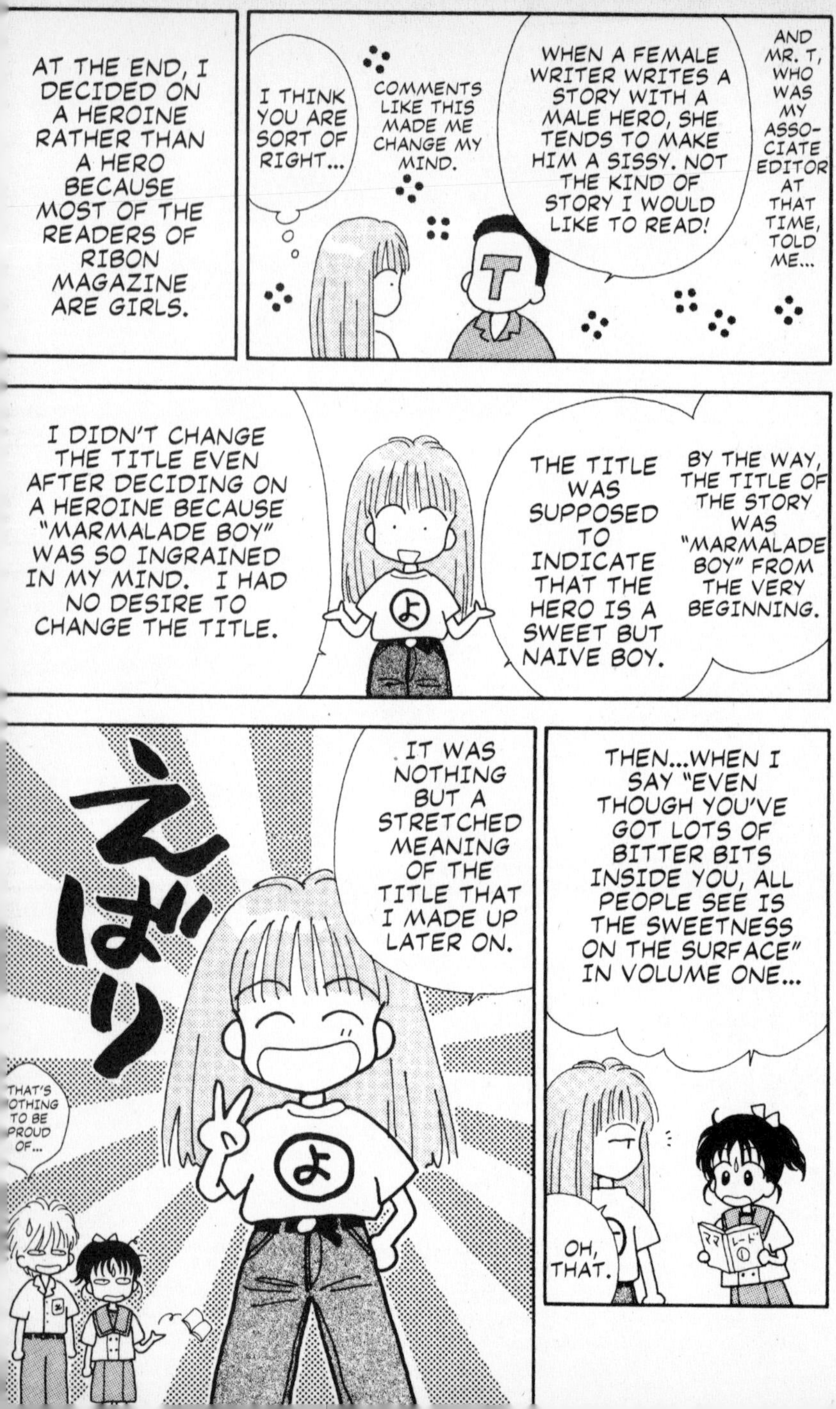
AND MR. T, WHO WAS MY ASSOCIATE EDITOR AT THAT TIME, TOLD ME...
WHEN A FEMALE WRITER WRITES A STORY WITH A MALE HERO, SHE TENDS TO MAKE HIM A SISSY. NOT THE KIND OF STORY I WOULD LIKE TO READ!
COMMENTS LIKE THIS MADE ME CHANGE MY MIND.
I THINK YOU ARE SORT OF RIGHT...
AT THE END, I DECIDED ON A HEROINE RATHER THAN A HERO BECAUSE MOST OF THE READERS OF RIBON MAGAZINE ARE GIRLS.
BY THE WAY, THE TITLE OF THE STORY WAS "MARMALADE BOY" FROM THE VERY BEGINNING.
THE TITLE WAS SUPPOSED TO INDICATE THAT THE HERO IS A SWEET BUT NAIVE BOY.
I DIDN'T CHANGE THE TITLE EVEN AFTER DECIDING ON A HEROINE BECAUSE "MARMALADE BOY" WAS SO INGRAINED IN MY MIND. I HAD NO DESIRE TO CHANGE THE TITLE.
THEN...WHEN I SAY "EVEN THOUGH YOU'VE GOT LOTS OF BITTER BITS INSIDE YOU, ALL PEOPLE SEE IS THE SWEETNESS ON THE SURFACE" IN VOLUME ONE...
OH, THAT.
IT WAS NOTHING BUT A STRETCHED MEANING OF THE TITLE THAT I MADE UP LATER ON.
えばり
THAT'S OTHING TO BE PROUD OF...

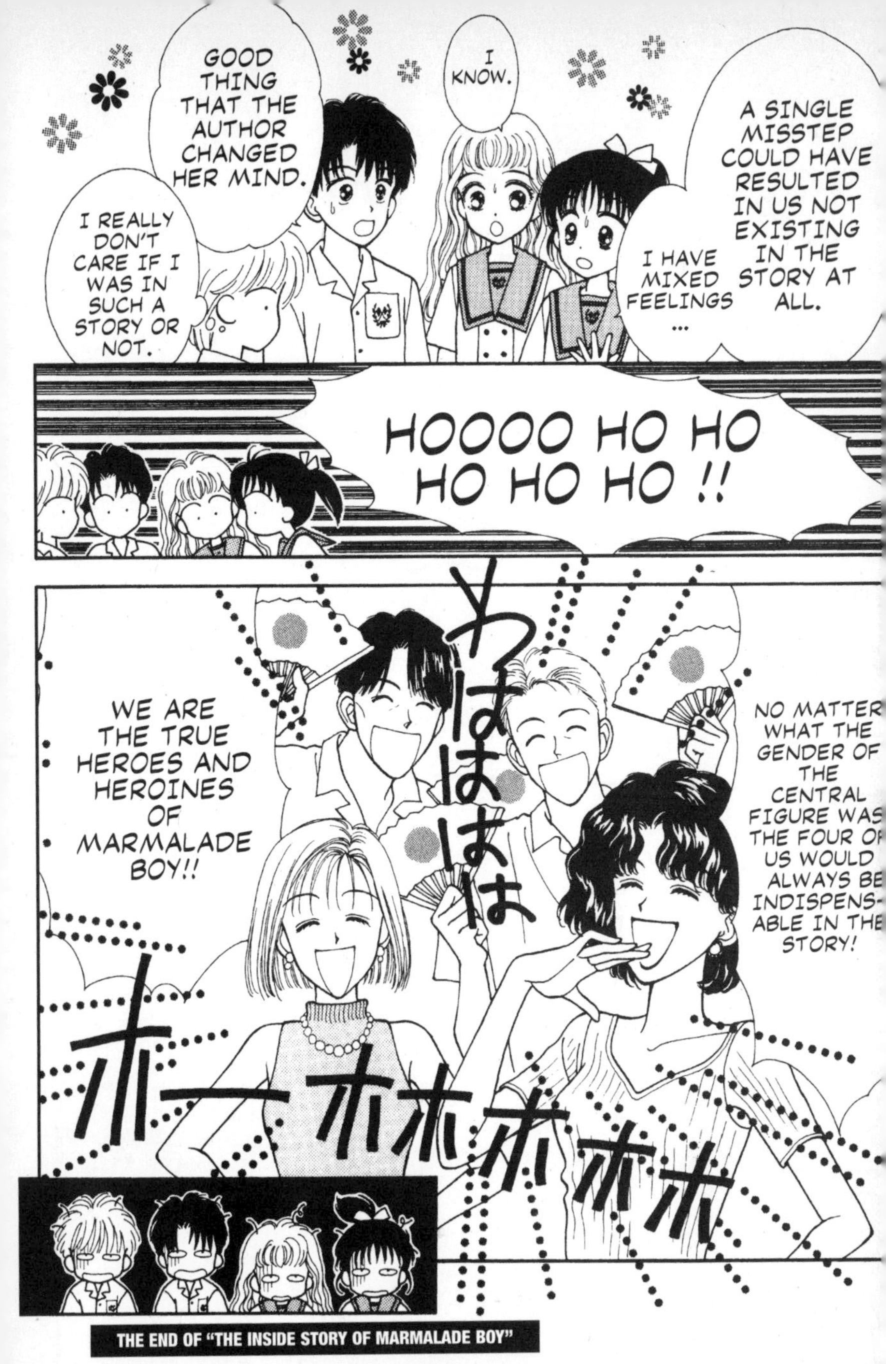
A SINGLE MISSTEP COULD HAVE RESULTED IN US NOT EXISTING IN THE STORY AT ALL.
I KNOW.
GOOD THING THAT THE AUTHOR CHANGED HER MIND.
I HAVE MIXED FEELINGS...
I REALLY DON'T CARE IF I WAS IN SUCH A STORY OR NOT.
HOOOO HO HO HO HO HO !!
NO MATTER WHAT THE GENDER OF THE CENTRAL FIGURE WAS THE FOUR OF US WOULD ALWAYS BE INDISPENS-ABLE IN THE STORY!
わははは
WE ARE THE TRUE HEROES AND HEROINES OF MARMALADE BOY!!
ホーホホホホホ

THE END OF "THE INSIDE STORY OF MARMALADE BOY"

THE INSIDE STORY OF MARMALADE BOY II

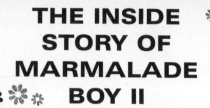

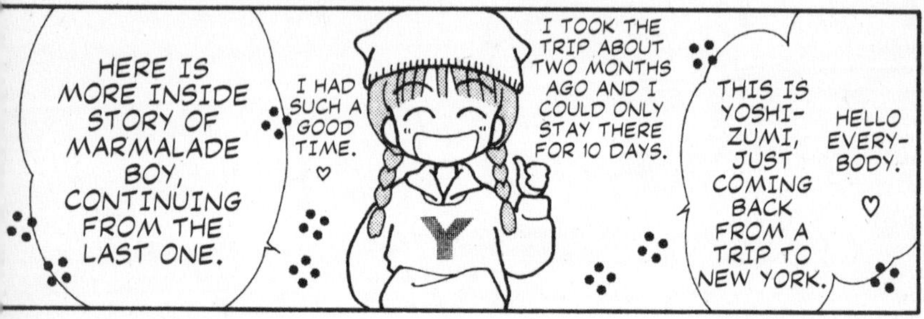
HELLO EVERY-BODY. ♡
THIS IS YOSHI-ZUMI, JUST COMING BACK FROM A TRIP TO NEW YORK.
I TOOK THE TRIP ABOUT TWO MONTHS AGO AND I COULD ONLY STAY THERE FOR 10 DAYS.
I HAD SUCH A GOOD TIME. ♡
HERE IS MORE INSIDE STORY OF MARMALADE BOY, CONTINUING FROM THE LAST ONE.

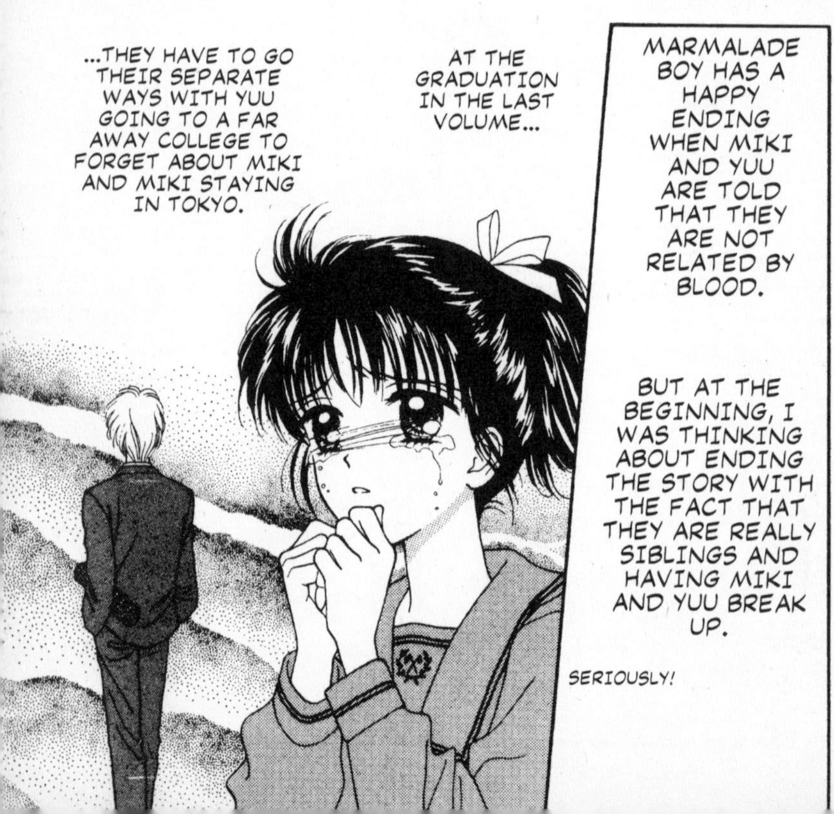
MARMALADE BOY HAS A HAPPY ENDING WHEN MIKI AND YUU ARE TOLD THAT THEY ARE NOT RELATED BY BLOOD.
AT THE GRADUATION IN THE LAST VOLUME...
...THEY HAVE TO GO THEIR SEPARATE WAYS WITH YUU GOING TO A FAR AWAY COLLEGE TO FORGET ABOUT MIKI AND MIKI STAYING IN TOKYO.
BUT AT THE BEGINNING, I WAS THINKING ABOUT ENDING THE STORY WITH THE FACT THAT THEY ARE REALLY SIBLINGS AND HAVING MIKI AND YUU BREAK UP.
SERIOUSLY!

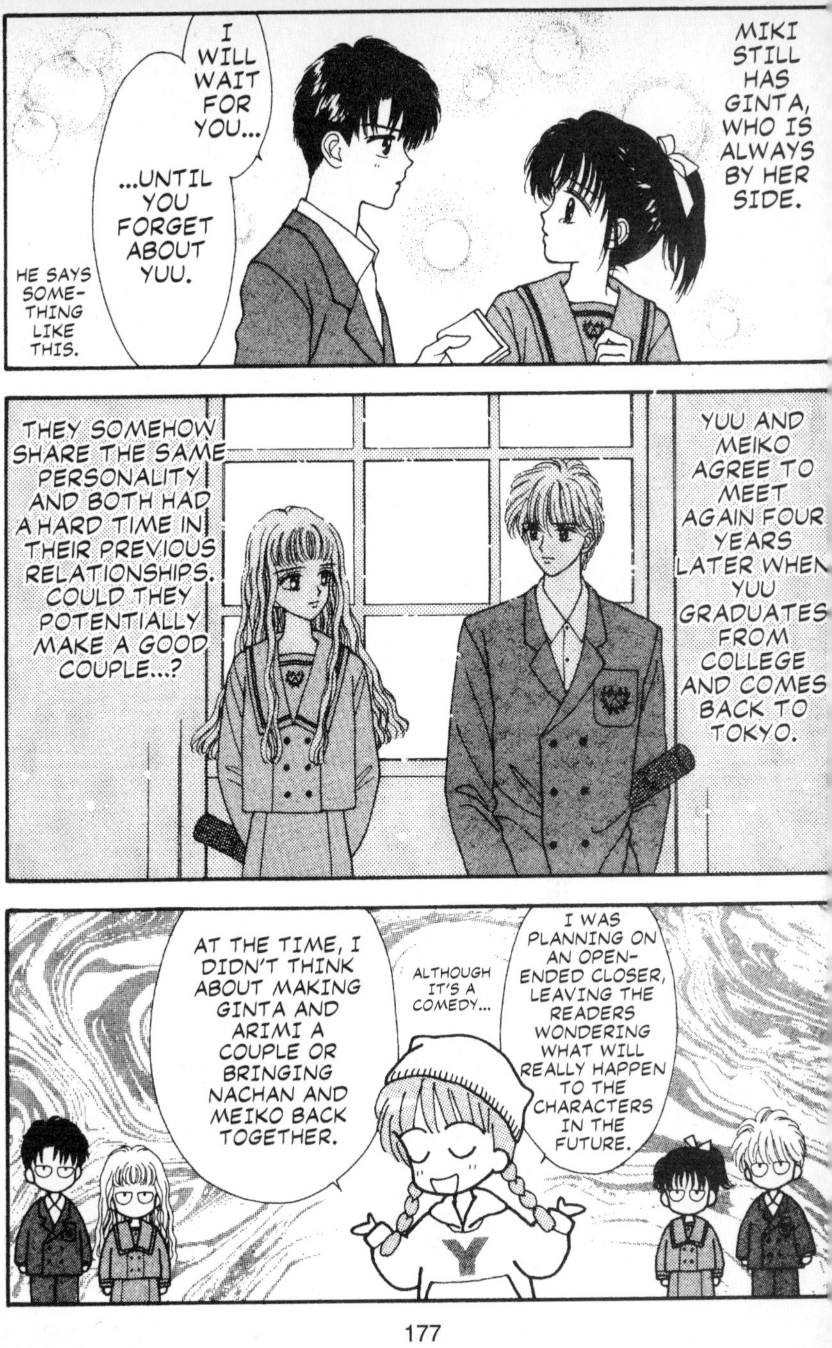
MIKI STILL HAS GINTA, WHO IS ALWAYS BY HER SIDE.
I WILL WAIT FOR YOU...
...UNTIL YOU FORGET ABOUT YUU.
HE SAYS SOME-THING LIKE THIS.
YUU AND MEIKO AGREE TO MEET AGAIN FOUR YEARS LATER WHEN YUU GRADUATES FROM COLLEGE AND COMES BACK TO TOKYO.
THEY SOMEHOW SHARE THE SAME PERSONALITY AND BOTH HAD A HARD TIME IN THEIR PREVIOUS RELATIONSHIPS. COULD THEY POTENTIALLY MAKE A GOOD COUPLE...?
I WAS PLANNING ON AN OPEN-ENDED CLOSER, LEAVING THE READERS WONDERING WHAT WILL REALLY HAPPEN TO THE CHARACTERS IN THE FUTURE.
ALTHOUGH IT'S A COMEDY...
AT THE TIME, I DIDN'T THINK ABOUT MAKING GINTA AND ARIMI A COUPLE OR BRINGING NACHAN AND MEIKO BACK TOGETHER.

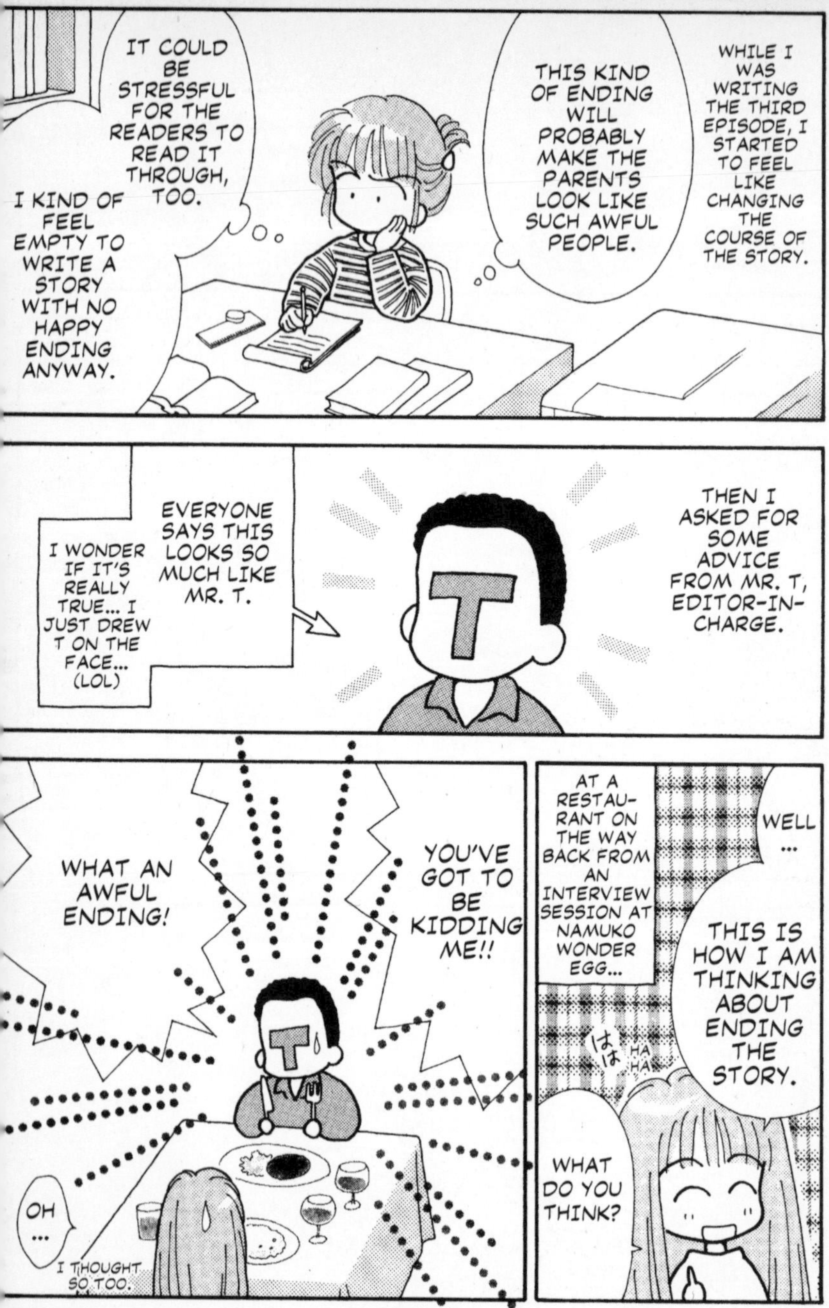
WHILE I WAS WRITING THE THIRD EPISODE, I STARTED TO FEEL LIKE CHANGING THE COURSE OF THE STORY.
THIS KIND OF ENDING WILL PROBABLY MAKE THE PARENTS LOOK LIKE SUCH AWFUL PEOPLE.
IT COULD BE STRESSFUL FOR THE READERS TO READ IT THROUGH, TOO.
I KIND OF FEEL EMPTY TO WRITE A STORY WITH NO HAPPY ENDING ANYWAY.
THEN I ASKED FOR SOME ADVICE FROM MR. T, EDITOR-IN-CHARGE.
EVERYONE SAYS THIS LOOKS SO MUCH LIKE MR. T.
I WONDER IF IT'S REALLY TRUE... I JUST DREW T ON THE FACE... (LOL)
WELL ...
AT A RESTAURANT ON THE WAY BACK FROM AN INTERVIEW SESSION AT NAMUKO WONDER EGG...
THIS IS HOW I AM THINKING ABOUT ENDING THE STORY.
はは HA HA
WHAT DO YOU THINK?
YOU'VE GOT TO BE KIDDING ME!!
WHAT AN AWFUL ENDING!
OH ...
I THOUGHT SO TOO.

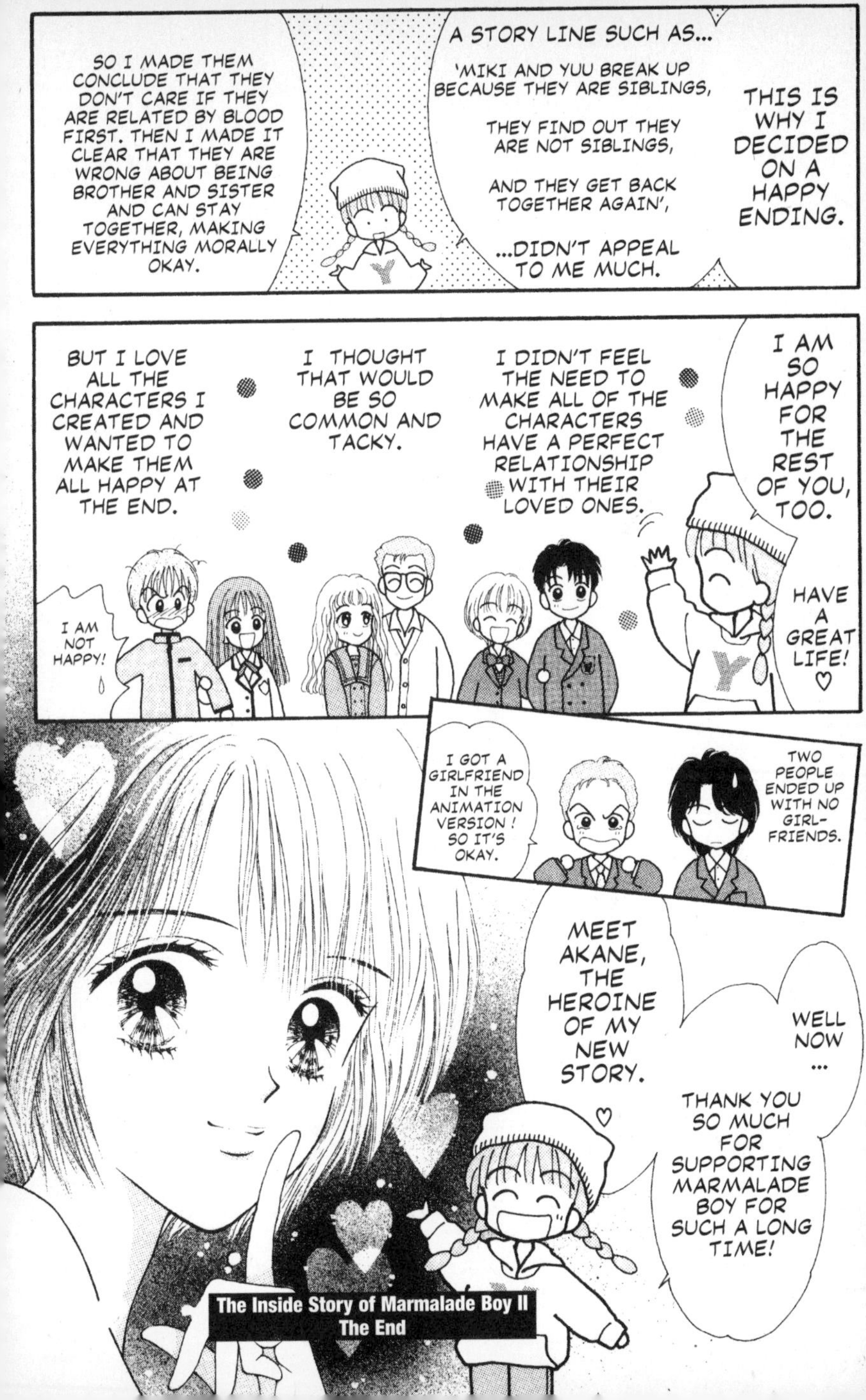
THIS IS WHY I DECIDED ON A HAPPY ENDING.
A STORY LINE SUCH AS...
'MIKI AND YUU BREAK UP BECAUSE THEY ARE SIBLINGS,
THEY FIND OUT THEY ARE NOT SIBLINGS,
AND THEY GET BACK TOGETHER AGAIN',
...DIDN'T APPEAL TO ME MUCH.
SO I MADE THEM CONCLUDE THAT THEY DON'T CARE IF THEY ARE RELATED BY BLOOD FIRST. THEN I MADE IT CLEAR THAT THEY ARE WRONG ABOUT BEING BROTHER AND SISTER AND CAN STAY TOGETHER, MAKING EVERYTHING MORALLY OKAY.
I AM SO HAPPY FOR THE REST OF YOU, TOO.
HAVE A GREAT LIFE! ♡
I DIDN'T FEEL THE NEED TO MAKE ALL OF THE CHARACTERS HAVE A PERFECT RELATIONSHIP WITH THEIR LOVED ONES.
I THOUGHT THAT WOULD BE SO COMMON AND TACKY.
BUT I LOVE ALL THE CHARACTERS I CREATED AND WANTED TO MAKE THEM ALL HAPPY AT THE END.
I AM NOT HAPPY!
TWO PEOPLE ENDED UP WITH NO GIRL-FRIENDS.
I GOT A GIRLFRIEND IN THE ANIMATION VERSION! SO IT'S OKAY.
WELL NOW...
MEET AKANE, THE HEROINE OF MY NEW STORY.
THANK YOU SO MUCH FOR SUPPORTING MARMALADE BOY FOR SUCH A LONG TIME!
♡
The Inside Story of Marmalade Boy II
The End

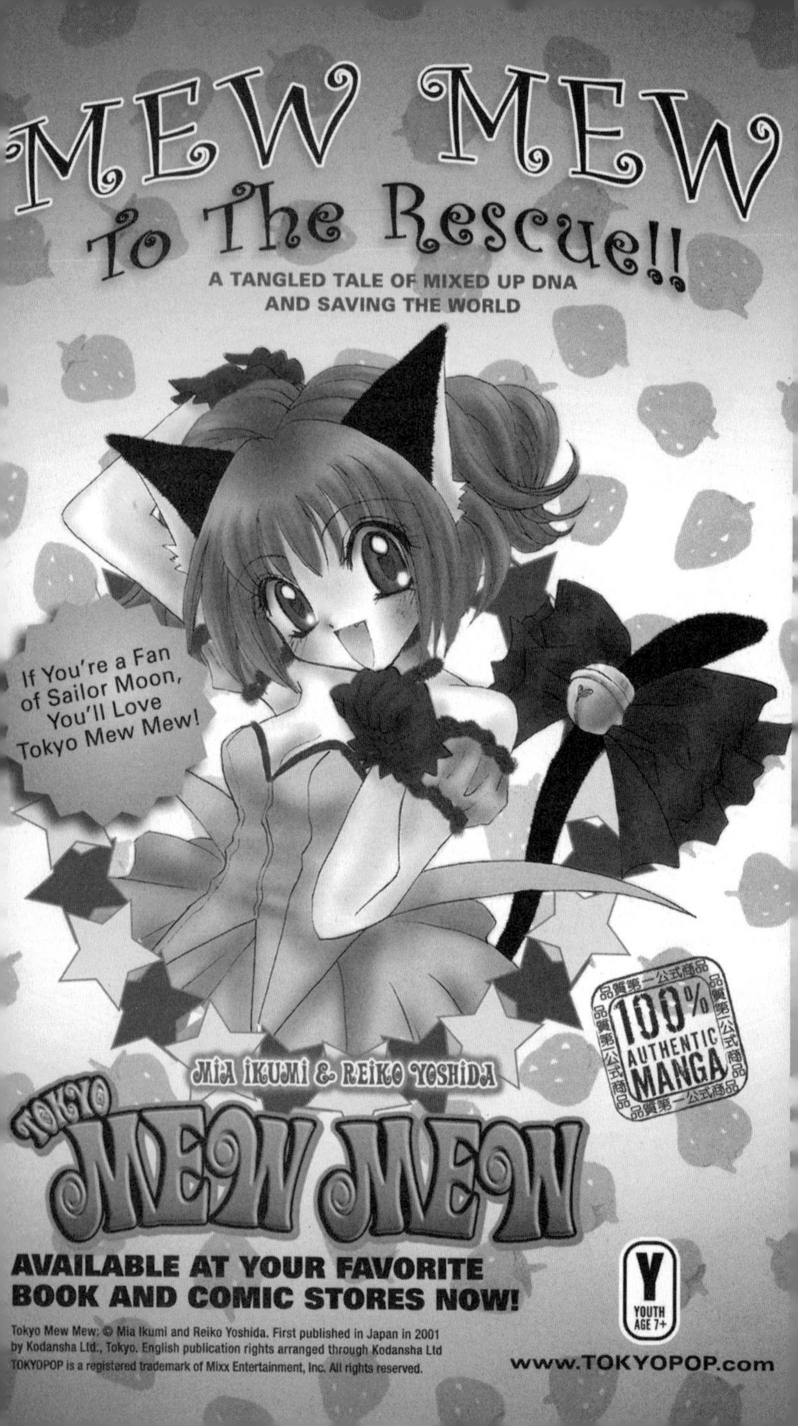
MEW MEW
To The Rescue!!
A TANGLED TALE OF MIXED UP DNA
AND SAVING THE WORLD
If You're a Fan of Sailor Moon, You'll Love Tokyo Mew Mew!
品質第一公式商品
100% AUTHENTIC MANGA
MIA IKUMI & REIKO YOSHIDA
TOKYO MEW MEW
AVAILABLE AT YOUR FAVORITE
BOOK AND COMIC STORES NOW!
Y YOUTH AGE 7+
Tokyo Mew Mew: © Mia Ikumi and Reiko Yoshida. First published in Japan in 2001 by Kodansha Ltd., Tokyo. English publication rights arranged through Kodansha Ltd
TOKYOPOP is a registered trademark of Mixx Entertainment, Inc. All rights reserved.
www.TOKYOPOP.com

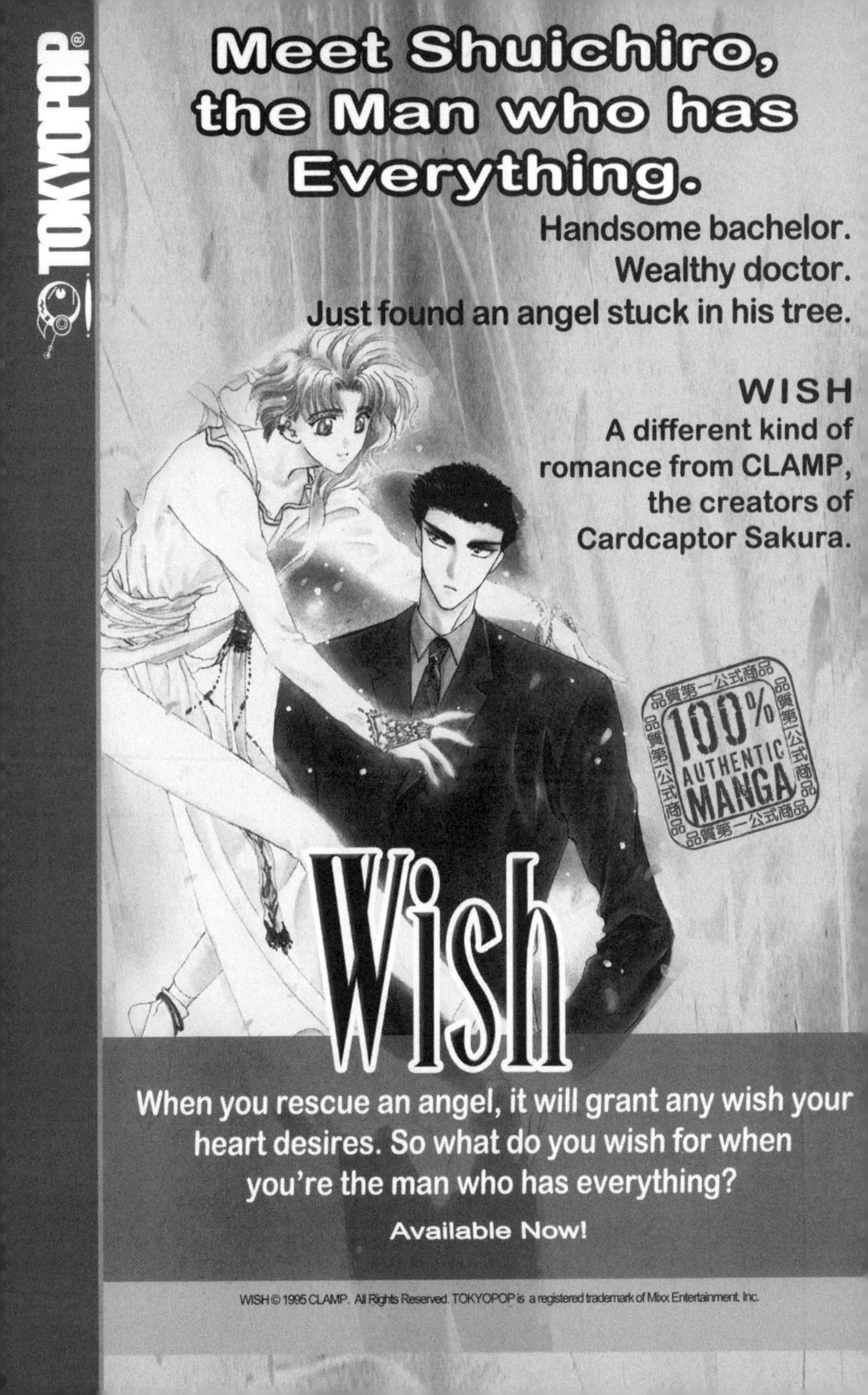
TOKYOPOP®
Meet Shuichiro, the Man who has Everything.
Handsome bachelor.
Wealthy doctor.
Just found an angel stuck in his tree.
WISH
A different kind of romance from CLAMP, the creators of Cardcaptor Sakura.
品質第一公式商品
100% AUTHENTIC MANGA
Wish
When you rescue an angel, it will grant any wish your heart desires. So what do you wish for when you're the man who has everything?
Available Now!

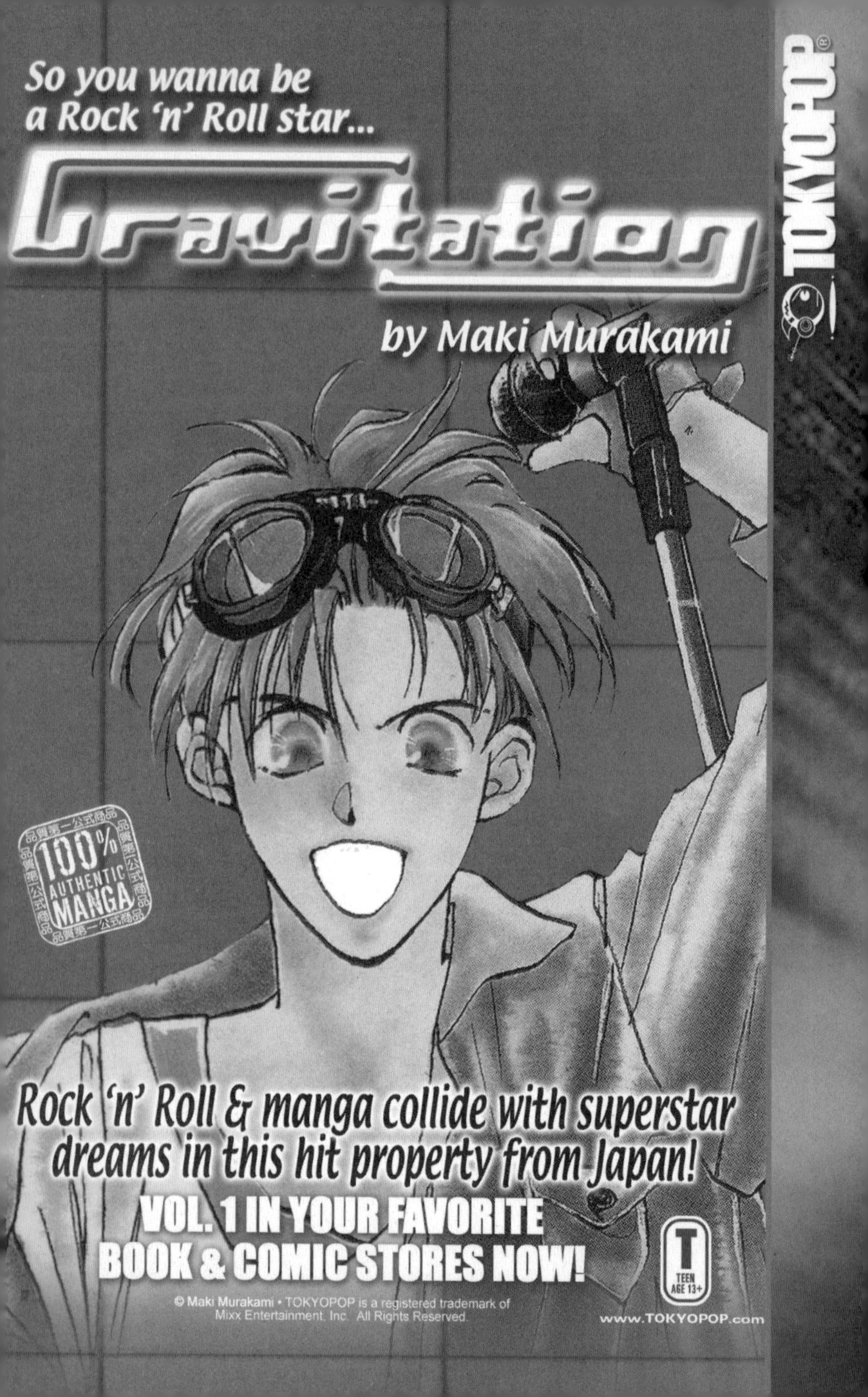
So you wanna be
a Rock 'n' Roll star...
Gravitation
by Maki Murakami
TOKYOPOP
100% AUTHENTIC MANGA
Rock 'n' Roll & manga collide with superstar
dreams in this hit property from Japan!
VOL. 1 IN YOUR FAVORITE
BOOK & COMIC STORES NOW!
T TEEN AGE 13+
© Maki Murakami • TOKYOPOP is a registered trademark of
Mixx Entertainment, Inc. All Rights Reserved.
www.TOKYOPOP.com

IT'S TIME THE WORLD RECOGNIZED YOUR GENIUS!

●FAME! ●FORTUNE! ●GET PUBLISHED!

Everything an aspiring manga-ka hopes for and dreams of. TOKYOPOP wants to make your dreams come true! Beginning June 1, 2003, and running through September 1, 2003, TOKYOPOP will conduct the second "Rising Stars of Manga" Contest, the sequel to America's original, first- ever and best manga competition.

Vol. 2 Coming Dec. 2003

Check www.TOKYOPOP.com for contest rules, and find out if you have what it takes to be included in the second volume of "The Rising Stars of Manga"!

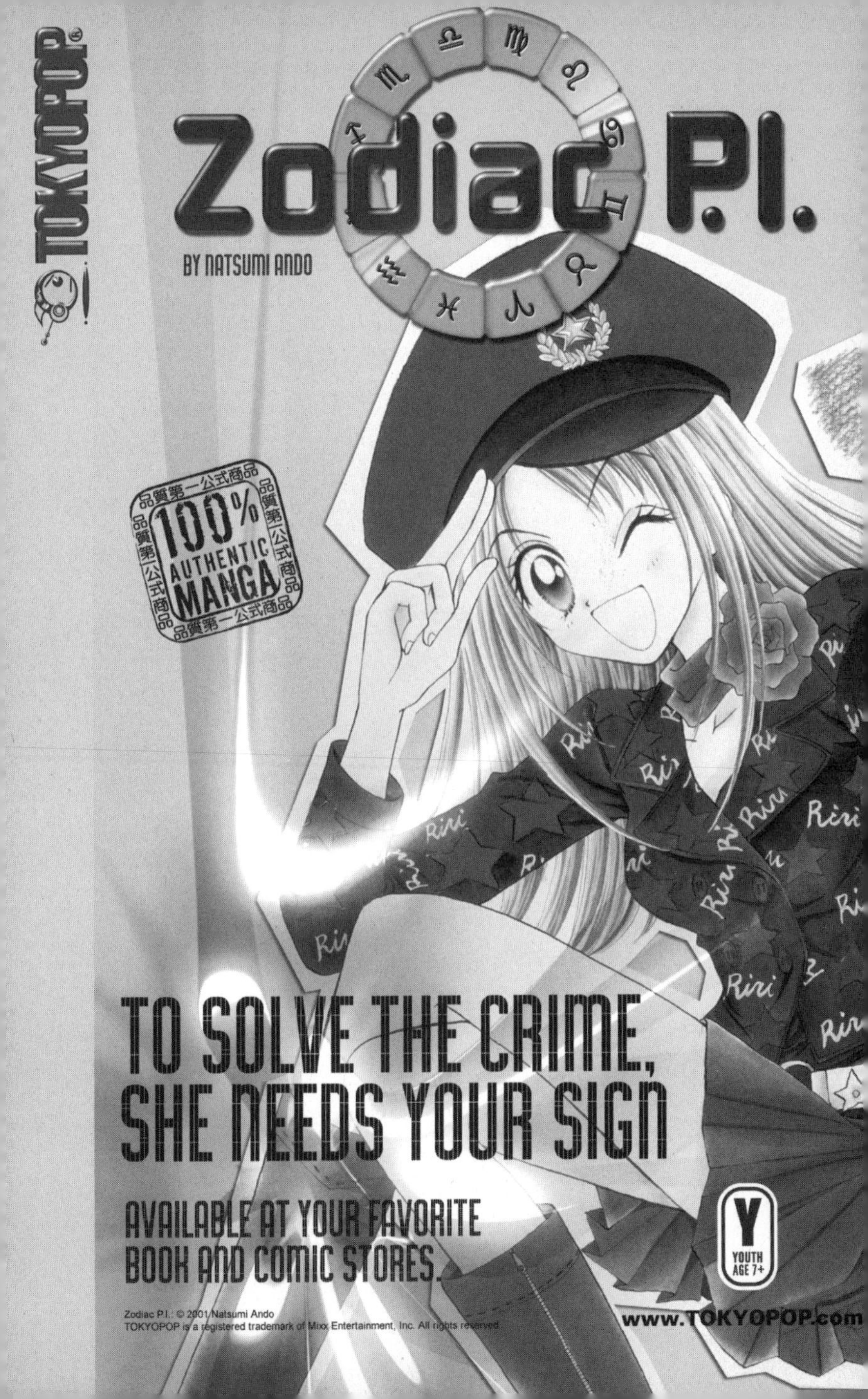
TOKYOPOP®
Zodiac P.I.
BY NATSUMI ANDO
品質第一公式商品
100% AUTHENTIC MANGA
TO SOLVE THE CRIME, SHE NEEDS YOUR SIGN
AVAILABLE AT YOUR FAVORITE BOOK AND COMIC STORES.
Y YOUTH AGE 7+
Zodiac P.I. © 2001 Natsumi Ando
TOKYOPOP is a registered trademark of Mixx Entertainment, Inc. All rights reserved.
www.TOKYOPOP.com

CLAMP SCHOOL DETECTIVES

The Hit Comedy/Adventure
Fresh Off the Heels of Magic Knight Rayearth

Limited Edition
Free Color Poster Inside
(while supplies last)

品質第一公式商品
100% AUTHENTIC MANGA
品質第一公式商品

From the creators of Angelic Layer,
Cardcaptor Sakura, Chobits,
Magic Knight Rayearth , Wish,
The Man of Many Faces,
Duklyon: CLAMP School Defenders,
Miyuki Chan in Wonderland
and Shirahime-syo: Snow Goddess Tales

AVAILABLE AT YOUR FAVORITE
BOOK AND COMIC STORES NOW!

A
ALL AGES

www.TOKYOPOP.com

TOKYOPOP®

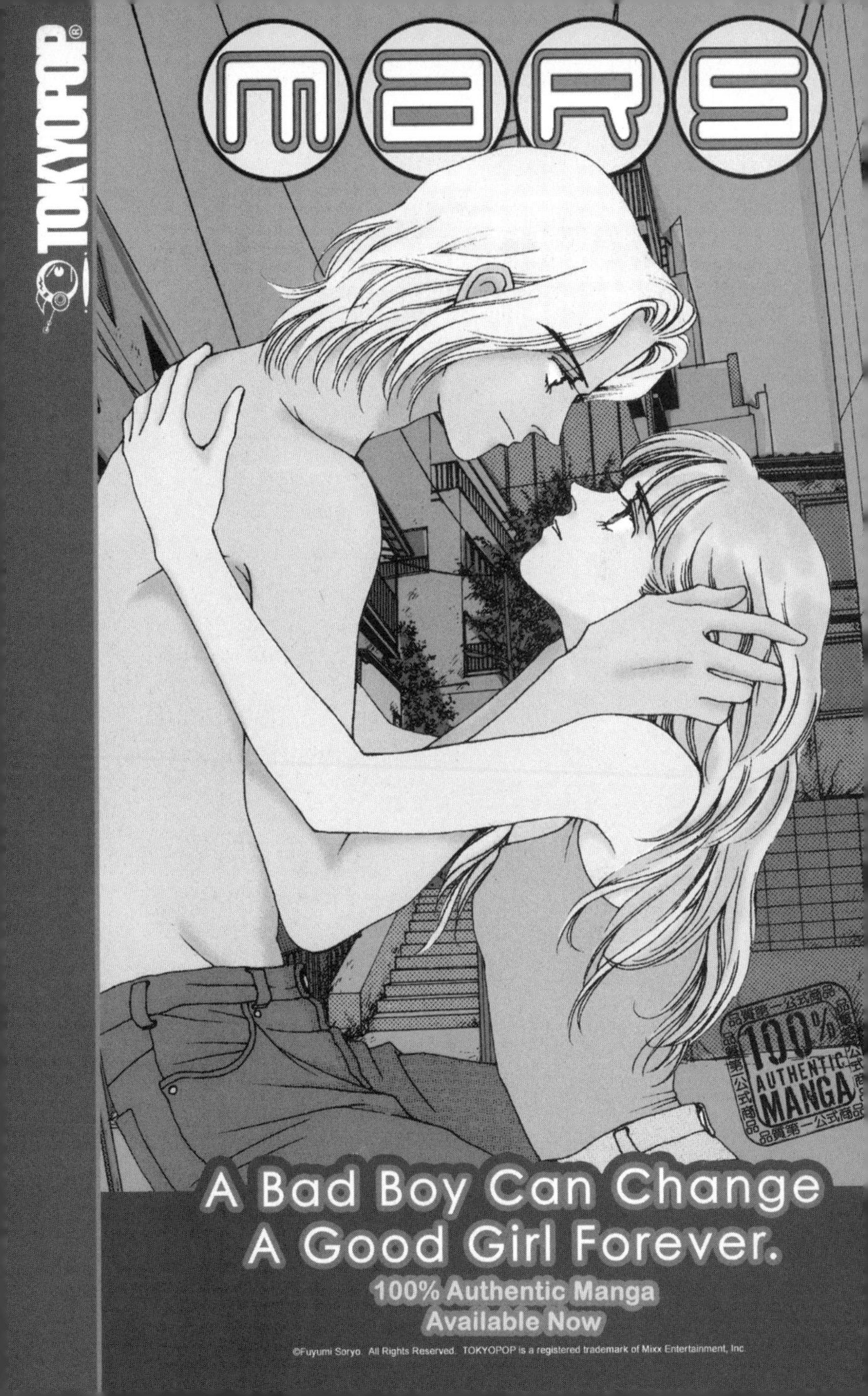
TOKYOPOP
MARS
品質第一公式商品
100% AUTHENTIC MANGA
A Bad Boy Can Change
A Good Girl Forever.
100% Authentic Manga
Available Now
©Fuyumi Soryo. All Rights Reserved. TOKYOPOP is a registered trademark of Mixx Entertainment, Inc.

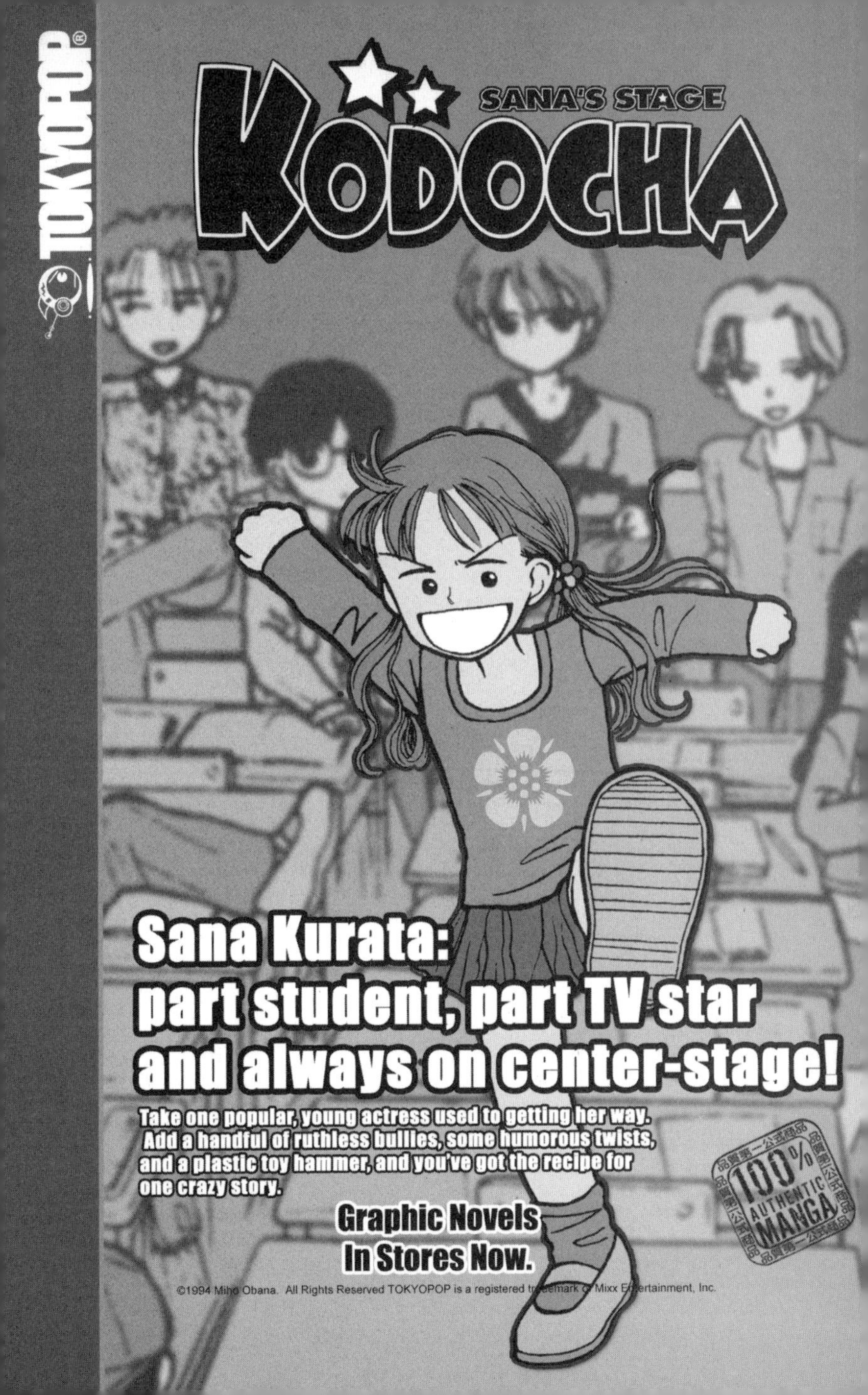
TOKYOPOP
KODOCHA
SANA'S STAGE
Sana Kurata:
part student, part TV star
and always on center-stage!
Take one popular, young actress used to getting her way.
Add a handful of ruthless bullies, some humorous twists,
and a plastic toy hammer, and you've got the recipe for
one crazy story.
Graphic Novels
In Stores Now.
100% AUTHENTIC MANGA
©1994 Miho Obana. All Rights Reserved TOKYOPOP is a registered trademark of Mixx Entertainment, Inc.